In Memoriam
Gavin Stamp
1948–2017

Contents

ROSEMARY HILL

Time's Witness
History in the Age of Romanticism

ALLEN LANE
an imprint of
PENGUIN BOOKS

ALLEN LANE

UK | USA | Canada | Ireland | Australia
India | New Zealand | South Africa

Allen Lane is part of the Penguin Random House group of companies
whose addresses can be found at global.penguinrandomhouse.com

Penguin
Random House
UK

First published 2021
001

Copyright © Rosemary Hill, 2021

The moral right of the author has been asserted

Set in 10.5/14 pt Sabon LT Std
Typeset by Jouve (UK), Milton Keynes
Printed and bound in Great Britain by Clays Ltd, Elcograf S.p.A.

The authorized representative in the EEA is Penguin Random House Ireland,
Morrison Chambers, 32 Nassau Street, Dublin D02 YH68

A CIP catalogue record for this book is available from the British Library

ISBN: 978-1-846-14312-0

www.greenpenguin.co.uk

MIX
Paper from
responsible sources
FSC® C018179

Penguin Random House is committed to a
sustainable future for our business, our readers
and our planet. This book is made from Forest
Stewardship Council® certified paper.

Contents

List of Illustrations

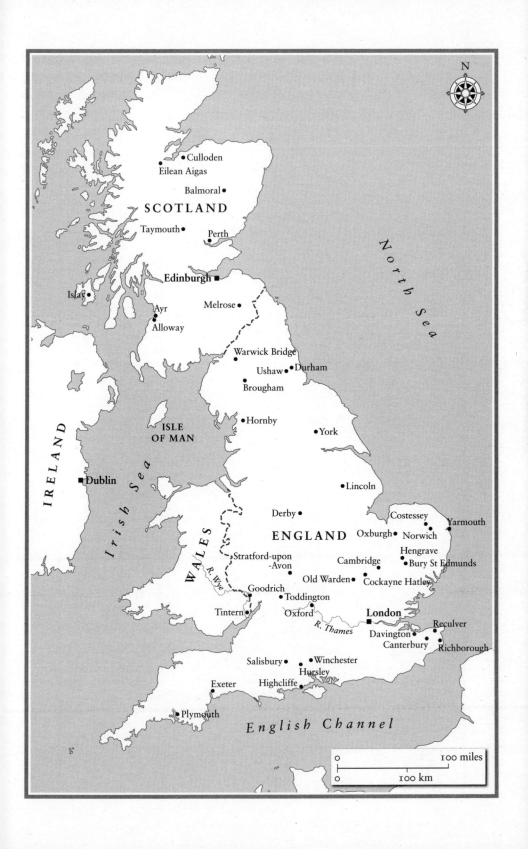

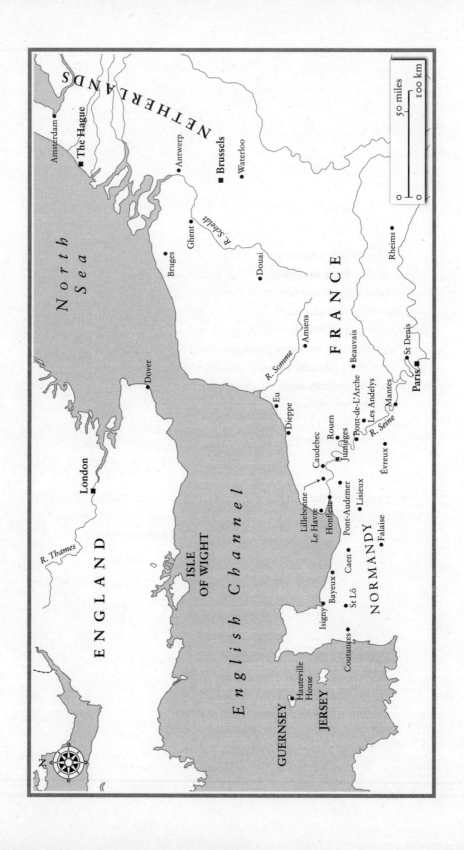

I hope I shall not appear too presumptuous in thus venturing as an author from the lowest rank of antiquaries . . . There are some who despise and scout the whole pursuit of antiquity as an impertinent inquiry into past things. Their authority I neither totally reject, nor do I much regard their judgment. I want not arguments to recommend this undertaking to honest and worthy men . . . If there are any who wish to remain strangers in their own country and city, and children in knowledge, let them enjoy their dream. I have neither written nor laboured for them.

William Camden, Introduction to the Britannia,
Richard Gough (ed.), 1789

History is indeed the witness of time, the light of truth, the life of memory, the teacher of life, the messenger of antiquity.

Walter Raleigh, History of the World, *1614*

Preface

To say that the French Revolution changed history is not to say anything very original, but what is usually meant is that it changed the history that came afterwards. My contention here is that it also changed the history that had gone before. Specifically, it changed ideas about what counted as history, what history was for, who it was for and who could be a historian. History in the eighteenth century was, like most intellectual activity, almost entirely the preserve of upper- and upper-middle-class men. It was written to instruct by example, it dealt with public events and public figures and was taught in the universities only to a very limited extent. By the time Queen Victoria was crowned it had become, as Thomas Carlyle wrote in 1838, a 'truth, which looks like a truism ... that the bygone ages of the world were actually filled by living men, not by protocols, state-papers, controversies and abstractions of men. Not abstractions were they, not diagrams and theorems; but men, in buff or other coats and breeches, with colour in their cheeks, with passions in their stomach, and the idioms, features and vitalities of very men.'[1] History had expanded, and it had at the same time become more rigorous. The broad narrative sweep had given way to documentary detail. Historians were now expected to cite their sources before they set out their theories. 'Direct inspection and embodiment: this, and this only, will be counted.' Until then, Carlyle said, philosophy 'must wait at the door'.[2]

Of course, it was more complicated than that. Great changes are never the product of a single event, even one so tremendous as the French Revolution. The process it dramatically accelerated was detectable much earlier in the century. In 1750 Dr Johnson, putting the case for biography as a form of history writing, contrasted it with the 'huge canvasses' of most histories, which depicted the 'consultation of senates, the motions of armies and the schemes of conspirators' but offered little that was 'applicable to private life'.[3] That the past might have something to offer the everyday life of ordinary people was an idea whose time was coming, and it was in the period from 1789 to about 1851 that it arrived. But Carlyle's confidence that this was a permanent transformation was misplaced. From the mid-nineteenth century onwards, as it developed into a profession and an academic discipline, history changed again. In his masterful essay *The Romantic Movement and the Study of History*, from which much of my own work takes its impetus, Hugh Trevor-Roper characterizes these years in which 'the philosophy of the eighteenth-century historians – Hume, Robertson, and Gibbon' was transformed into 'the philosophies of their nineteenth-century successors – Macaulay, Michelet, Ranke' as, by implication, a kind of hiatus, in the development of historical studies.[4] On the question of what happened in the interval he gives due weight to the influence of Walter Scott, but Scott, he observes, was 'not a scholar'; rather he was someone who, in Carlyle's words, 'knew what history meant'.[5] Scott certainly did know what history meant and he was immensely successful in deploying it. Long before he was an historical novelist, however, Scott was an antiquary, and it is antiquarianism in its various forms that carried the study of the past forward through the missing decades of Trevor-Roper's account.

Over these years many men, and some women, studied history in ways that were not new, but had been largely in abeyance since the seventeenth century. In scale their activities were unprecedented. They pushed 'history' into private life, often under the catch-all phrase 'customs and manners'. They studied the tangible remains of the past of every size and kind, from manuscripts to cathedrals. This was the period that saw either the birth or the first effective development of social and architectural history, medieval studies, costume history, oral history and the history of theatre, of literature and dialect. Among the antiquaries' achievements were the preservation of the Bayeux Tapestry, the analysis and dating of Gothic architecture, the first publication of *Beowulf* and *Sir Gawain and the Green Knight*. It was in these years that the modern idea of the museum took hold, and archaeology as we understand it today was born. Most importantly, there was a change in the way in which past and present were seen in relation to one another. By and large, in the eighteenth century history was seen as a resource, used when useful, ignored or destroyed if not. Medieval buildings were either left to fall into ruin or confidently modernized with sash windows and whitewash. Not everybody thought like this. Here too Dr Johnson was an exception, reflecting gloomily in 1773 that 'our ... cathedrals are mouldering by unregarded dilapidation. It seems to be part of the despicable philosophy of the time to despise monuments of sacred magnificence.'[6]

In the years around 1789 there was a change. The concept of what we now call 'heritage' began to dawn, the idea that the present has a responsibility to the past, and to the future, which involves respect for the remains of history, regardless of whether they are in themselves useful or attractive. Today it seems, as Carlyle has it, a truth which is all but a truism, that historic buildings and artefacts should be, wherever possible, preserved. To most Georgians it was equally axiomatic that medieval art was ugly and irrelevant. The Middle Ages were another gap in history, the interval between the fall of Rome and the rediscovery of Classical art at the Renaissance. There was no department in the British Museum for 'national', that is non-Classical, antiquities, and antiquaries were often laughed at or despised for taking an interest in them. The re-conception of history as a continuum in which generations do not simply replace one another in a forward march of improvement, but form links in a chain, was perhaps the greatest and most enduring legacy of what I have called Romantic antiquarianism, for Romanticism was both its underlying driving force and the all-embracing context in which it flourished.

But Romanticism is a slippery thing. The word is so amorphous, so diffuse, that the American philosopher Arthur Lovejoy almost gave up, arguing that it had 'come to mean so many things that, by itself, it means nothing'.[7] Such defeatism was countered by Isaiah Berlin, who had 'a certain sympathy' with Lovejoy but insisted that 'there was a romantic movement', and that since it 'did create a great revolution in consciousness' it was 'important to discover what it is'.[8] What it was not, as is sometimes said, was a wholesale rejection of the Enlightenment. It was, rather, a challenge to the Enlightenment's faith in the sovereign power of reason. Thus William Blake, writing in about 1800:

3

Mock on, mock on, Voltaire, Rousseau;
Mock on, mock on, 'tis all in vain!
You throw the sand against the wind,
And the wind blows it back again.

Blake's belief that a great force for change was blowing in the wind did not stop him from observing the rules of meter and rhyme. Romanticism did not deny reason and order, but it wanted to put them in their place. Reason, the Romantic philosophers argued, cannot comprehend the totality of everything that is, what they called the Absolute. The Absolute lies beyond the scope of reason as it is also beyond the experience of the individual. It is by deploying reason and emotion together, in what Coleridge described as the 'union of deep feeling with profound thought', that we can reach towards the Absolute, while knowing that it remains forever beyond our grasp.[9] That longing for the unattainable ideal permeates Romantic art and literature. As a theory of consciousness, Romanticism understood human experience as neither wholly objective nor wholly subjective, locating it in the combination of interior and exterior realities, the something 'far more deeply interfused' that Wordsworth found in his 'Lines Written a Few Miles above Tintern Abbey ... 13 July 1798'. This insight was central to the Romantic 'revolution in consciousness'. As it applied to the study of the past, the combination of thought and feeling dictated empiricism on the one hand, the close study of details, 'direct inspection' of primary sources and material evidence; on the other it called for sensitivity and imagination in order to understand history in human terms and make the past a recognizable place, inhabited by individuals.

Wilhelm von Humboldt (1767–1835) set out the Romantic method in a lecture of 1821 on 'The Historian's Task'. He argued that facts, like reason, are necessary but not sufficient. Humboldt was one of the founders of Berlin University, and he had a profound respect for research and the analysis of primary sources. Yet he also believed that the historian requires imagination, that it is necessary to bring oneself to one's work. Intuition, observation and personal experience of human behaviour should all be part of historic method. 'The more humane [the historian's] disposition is by nature and circumstances, and the more freely he gives rein to his humanity, the more completely will he solve the problems of his profession.'[10] History for Humboldt was the Romantic 'fusion of the inquiring intellect and the object of the inquiry'. 'Understanding is not merely an extension of the subject,' he wrote, 'nor is it merely a borrowing from the object; it is, rather, both simultaneously'.[11]

This was the sensibility that the late Georgians and early Victorians and, with local variations, their contemporaries in France and Germany brought to the study of the past. One striking consequence was a remarkably flexible attitude, by today's standards, to the concept of 'authenticity'. What an object looked like and how it made one feel might count for as much as what, materially, it was. Romanticism made it possible to take seriously what one did not take literally. Thus Scott could admire a 'medieval' well that he had built himself; Robert Southey appreciated the poems of the medieval monk 'Rowley' while knowing that they were forgeries by Thomas Chatterton, and Wordsworth apostrophized the ancient chivalric glories of Lowther Castle, built by Robert Smirke between 1806 and 1814. The age of Romanticism enjoyed what has been aptly called 'a lived relationship' with history.[12] The debate that divided opinion in the previous generation over James Macpherson's *Ossian*, as to whether it was or was not a forgery, had ceased to resonate.[13] That was no longer the question. In Scott's novel *The Antiquary*, *Ossian* is cast as an old controversy, and it was in Scott that the many currents in the torrent of ideas that make up Romanticism met. He was the embodiment of the Romantic antiquary, the most influential historical thinker of the age, whose vision pervaded the consciousness of Europe to an extent that is perhaps difficult to comprehend today.

What is an antiquary? And how, if at all, does the antiquary differ from the historian? Definitions are not easy to apply to a period before disciplinary boundaries were invented, and the terms were used inconsistently and sometimes interchangeably. There was a general sense that the two activities were distinct, but no consensus on where the distinction lay. In 1770 the *Historical Account of the Origin and Establishment of the Society of Antiquaries* defined antiquarianism as the study of 'the History and Antiquities of Nations and Societies' and 'History' as 'The arrangement and proper use of facts', a definition broad and flexible enough to cover everyone.[14] On the whole, historians were regarded as intellectually and socially superior to antiquaries, so individuals' accounts of themselves are not always to be relied on. Many a fellow of the Society of Antiquaries hotly denied that he was a 'mere antiquary'. The most significant distinction for our purposes is that while antiquaries and historians all studied the material remains of the past, historians considered only written records. The antiquary, by contrast, would extend or even confine his or her enquiries to the non-verbal. Antiquaries, unlike historians, studied architecture and stone circles, pottery, sculpture, coins, bells, armour, textiles and much more.

What unites the dozen or so individuals whom I have singled out for particular attention from the two and a half generations who span the period from 1789 to 1851 is more important than what may seem to divide them as we look back from an age of academic specialization. They differed from their Enlightenment predecessors most significantly in their commitment to the use of primary sources, textual or otherwise. They did not regard a philosophical system as an adequate method for studying the past. John Lingard (1771–1851), the Catholic priest and author of the most important *History of England* since David Hume's, never thought of himself as an antiquary. But if he wanted someone to look up a document in the House of Lords or the Tower of London, or to find out the mortality rate for the plague in the week from 25 July to 1 August 1665 in the British Museum, it was to his great friend John Gage, Director of the Society of Antiquaries, that he turned. Gage and Lingard used the same sources and sometimes researched the same subjects. In 1843, when a group of antiquaries established the British Archaeological Association, Lingard became a vice-president, although by modern definitions he was even less of an archaeologist than an antiquary. He was engaged, however, in the same kind of intellectual activity as many antiquaries and so, for our purposes, he stands under the broad umbrella of Romantic antiquarianism.

Gage and Lingard also left copious correspondence, and I have generally preferred those antiquaries whose personal papers as well as their published work survive, so that they may speak in their own words and allow us to see history, as Carlyle recommended, populated by recognizable individuals. As regards subject matter, I have concentrated chiefly on what the period referred to as 'customs and manners', which covers most of what we now call social and cultural as well as some political history, and on the 'national' as distinct from the Classical past. Geographically I have dealt chiefly with England, Scotland and France, with small excursions into Wales and Germany. This is not to discount activity elsewhere, but it is within this irregular triangle that the antiquaries were most aware of each other's activities. While some antiquaries were collectors and some collectors were antiquaries, those terms are not interchangeable. Thus William Beckford (1760–1844) and John Soane (1753–1837), two of the greatest collectors of the age, make only fleeting appearances because their acquisitions were not made primarily for the purpose of understanding the past.

On the question of what use the antiquaries made of the material they gathered, how they weighed the balance between objective evidence and subjective interpretation, thought and feeling, I have chosen my examples at points along a notional sliding scale. At one end are Lingard and the architectural historian Robert Willis (1800–1875), whose work was based on rigorous interrogation of the evidence at their disposal. At the midway point, the fulcrum is Scott, who deployed history and imagination in more less equal quantity, while at the extreme far end, where imagination so greatly outweighs evidence as to all but annihilate it, we find John (1795–1872) and Charles (c. 1802–80) Allen. These two brothers, the sons of an English naval officer, who changed their names by degrees until they became the 'Sobieski Stuarts', claimed to be the legitimate grandsons of Bonnie Prince Charlie and hence the Jacobite heirs to the throne. Their place in history was secured by their book, the *Vestiarium Scoticum*, purportedly a seventeenth-century history of tartan, which they published in 1842. It was in fact all their own work. While the Allens have been generally condemned as 'imposters' or enjoyed as an amusing case study in 'the invention of tradition', I have chosen to take them seriously, if not literally.[15] The version of Scottish history they proposed appealed to the age of Romantic nationalism, and although they were largely discredited in their lifetimes, their legacy endures. They invented the concept of clan tartans, and the idea fell on such fertile ground that it flourishes still. Thus the Allens' effect on history was greater than that of many a more scrupulous historian. John Lingard's work told less convenient truths and so has never acquired the reputation it deserves. It says much about the sensibility of the age that it was Lingard, the scholarly parish priest, who was denounced by the *Edinburgh Review* as a danger to the state, while the Sobieski Stuarts' book was bought and much enjoyed by Queen Victoria.

Antiquarianism has never been acknowledged as a profession, or even a full-time job. In an age before the separation of science and humanities into 'two cultures', an antiquary might be many things. Of those who feature here and who are included in the *Oxford Dictionary of National Biography*, the descriptions attached to them, in addition to or instead of 'antiquary', include: poet, historian, architect, publisher, herald, novelist, master potter, scholar, actor manager, commercial traveller, banker, collector, priest, civil engineer, scientific adviser and forger. So it was from many directions, bringing diverse skills, that the antiquaries came to develop the understanding of the past in these years between the fall of the Bastille and the opening of the Great Exhibition. They prepared the way for the emergence of history as an academic discipline, and this to some extent was their undoing. The new academic history did not choose to involve itself with 'manners and customs' but returned instead to politics and economics. Later generations of professional historians have not generally cared to acknowledge their debt to antiquarianism, perhaps because they see the antiquaries like embarrassing elderly relatives whom one would rather keep out of sight. It is true that antiquaries were sometimes eccentric, sometimes jealous and quarrelsome and sometimes wrong. There were those whose accumulation of ever more obscure material never resulted in any useful publication, those who were blinded to the evidence by preconceived theoretical premises; a few were plagiarists and one or two became insane. Such things, however, are not unknown among the academic historians who succeeded them.

The antiquaries' efforts have been ignored or undervalued for so long that they have fallen out of sight of an age which has largely recovered their broader view of history. In 2018 one of the most distinguished living historians, Margaret MacMillan, wrote that in 1988 'cultural history, the history of food, fashion or the body, were yet to be conceived as fields of study at all'.[16] This, as we shall see, is not the case. Writing in the *Times Literary Supplement* a year later, Jean Wilson made reference to 'new scholarship' in relation to Queen Elizabeth I's progresses.[17] This was in fact the republication of *The Progresses and Public Processions of Queen Elizabeth* by the antiquary John Nichols, first published in 1826. My hope in what follows is to rescue antiquarianism from oblivion and the condescension of posterity. To paraphrase William Camden's intentions for his *Britannia*, I wish to restore history to the antiquaries, and the antiquaries to history.

In recognizing the place of imagination and subjectivity in the study of the past, the antiquaries of the Romantic age were perhaps more realistic than some of their successors. In 'On the Historian's Task', Humboldt wrote: 'Historical truth is ... like the clouds which take shape for the eye only at a distance. For this reason, the facts of history are in their several connecting circumstances little more than the results of tradition and scholarship which one has agreed to accept as true, because they – being most highly probable in themselves – also fit best in to the context of the whole.'[18]

High probability is certainly one reason for accepting a particular historical account, but it is only one. What follows here, I suggest, demonstrates that the history we have, at any given moment, is the history we want. It is the picture we choose to see in the clouds.

I

A Lanterne Unto Late
Succeeding Age[1]

Man without learning, and the remembrance of thinges past
falls into a beastlye sottishnesse and his life is noe better to be
accounted of than to be buryed alive.[2]

William Dugdale, 1655

The story of the study of the past has no beginning. There have
always been people curious to know how their ancestors lived. In
Western culture antiquarian activity can be traced back as far as
Hellenic Greece, and perhaps the first identifiable individual antiquary is the Roman Terentius Varro.[3] Interest in the remains of
history has ebbed and flowed, but overall there has been a growing
awareness of anachronism, an understanding of the ways in which
the past is different from the present in its habits, beliefs and
assumptions. This 'evolving consciousness', as Keith Thomas calls
it, of our relationship to history has been an unsteady process, 'fitful and uneven'.[4] There was some sporadic antiquarian activity in
the Middle Ages, but the first great fit of antiquarianism arose in
Europe with the Renaissance, which came late to Britain. With
these caveats in mind, and because we must start somewhere, it is
reasonable to date the emergence of antiquarianism in England and
Scotland to the Reformation, not least because this was the point
from which the antiquaries of the Romantic period themselves
traced their intellectual descent. Like many of their contemporaries,
they saw it as the determining event in British history, and in the
late-Georgian and early Victorian decades its causes and implications were once again hotly debated.

The Dissolution of the English monasteries between 1535 and 1539 dismantled social institutions that had remained unchanged for generations. The fabric of medieval England had always seen change and sometimes decay, but with the Reformation a thousand years of history was suddenly 'shut off and largely destroyed', leaving a landscape spattered with ruins.[5] For many people it was an 'unparalleled catastrophe', and even some of those who supported the religious reforms were 'shocked . . . into a sense of loss' by the scale of the destruction.[6] 'Many do lament the pulling downe of abbayes', wrote the Lincolnshire clergyman Francis Trigge in 1589.[7] If recent scholarship has made it clear that events unfolded more gradually than has sometimes been thought, that the religious and political implications were more complex and played out over many decades, the experience was nevertheless one of unprecedented fracture in the social continuum and it heightened the awareness of historic change.[8] A generation learned that the most familiar aspects of everyday experience could alter out of recognition within a lifetime. One response was to try and gather together as many of the fragments as possible. The Perthshire physician and antiquary George Ruthven recalled that he was 'about thirteen years old' at the time of the Scottish Reformation, some twenty years after the English.[9] He lived into his nineties surrounded by his collection of 'antiquities of . . . temples, monasteries and many other singularities'[10] and never ceased to lament the ruin 'by the fury of the populace' of 'the magnificent religious houses with their stately steeples'.[11] When Ruthven died, the Perth poet Henry Adamson (1581–1637) commemorated him in two sets of verses. Ruthven used the word 'gabions' for the objects in his collection, and Adamson's 'The Inventory of the Gabions in Mr George Ruthven's Cabinet' paints an affectionately teasing picture of the old man's collection 'Of uncouth forms, and wond'rous shapes'.[12] The second poem, 'The Muses Threnodie', is stranger. Adamson writes in the person of Ruthven himself mourning their mutual friend John Gall, another antiquary whose collection of 'gabions' will be lost without him and who grieve for their dead collector:

> Now must I mourn for *Gall*, since he is gone,
> And ye my Gabions help me him to mone . . .
> Who now shall pen your praise and make you knowne,
> By whom now shall your virtues be forth showne . . .
> With dust and cobwebs cover all your heads,
> And take you to your *matins* and your *beads*[13]

It is a haunting image which to its original readers would have evoked the shrouds and urns of Jacobean funerary monuments. To Walter Scott, who made use of Adamson's verse in his own last work, it conveyed the Romantic relationship between the antiquary and his collection. Without an understanding eye and organizing mind, the antiquities are reduced to random fragments, their meaning and their relation to one another lost.

Over the next century, the men who studied and documented what remained of this lost past gave rise to the first great age of British antiquarian scholarship. This is not the place to write their history. That has been well done elsewhere.[14] Here it is enough to follow the line of succession to the late eighteenth century through the antiquaries who most influenced it, those whose works were referred to, republished and in some cases published for the first time, by the antiquaries of the Romantic age. Not all of these forebears were heroes. Some served as awful warnings, and none more so than the earliest, the poet John Leland (*c.* 1503–52). Leland was commissioned by Henry VIII, just before the Dissolution, 'to peruse and dylygentlye to searche all the lybraryes of monsteryes and collegies'.[15] The king's intention, it would seem, was to obtain a catalogue of their contents. As Leland worked on, however, through the suppression of the religious houses, his subject matter began to shift about alarmingly. In July 1536 he wrote to Thomas Cromwell asking for help to preserve books which were being not only dispersed but, as word of the Dissolution spread to the Continent, being dismantled by young scholars from Germany 'that spoileth them' before taking the choicest documents abroad.[16] Leland spent six years travelling round the country, and as he went on his interests widened from books and manuscripts to monuments, topography and local history. 'He wander'd from Place to Place where he thought there were any Footsteps of Roman, Saxon, or Danish Buildings.'[17]

By the 1540s he had 'an immense Heap of Collections', from which
'he intended to compile a complete history of the Antiquities of Britain'. Being, however, short of money, and Cromwell having fallen
from grace and met his end on Tower Hill, Leland wrote a verse
appeal to Thomas Cranmer for patronage. The appeal was successful
and 'he spent about six years in digesting his papers'.[18] But whether,
as some of his friends thought, it was the difficulty of mastering his
material, or, as others suggested, the shock of all that he had witnessed, in about 1547 Leland suffered a 'fatal stop' to his work when
he suddenly lost his reason.[19] He remained for the rest of his life
'beside his wittes' and lived out his last years in the care of his
brother.[20]

Aspects of Leland's story were still familiar in the late eighteenth
century. The battle against looting, sometimes by fellow scholars, the
search for patronage, shortage of money and the tendency to amass
material on a scale that defied assimilation were all aspects of Georgian antiquarianism. Some also travelled the dangerous path from
curiosity to obsession and thence to insanity. Leland's was a poignant
case and not without romance, but it was scarcely an encouraging
precedent. It was the next generation, born after the most turbulent
years of the Reformation had passed, who brought a fresh and vigorous approach to their enquiries and gave British antiquarianism its
founding father, William Camden (1551–1623). It was for him that
the nineteenth century named the Camden Society and the Cambridge
Camden Society. His magnum opus was a survey of national antiquities, the *Britannia*. This first appeared in 1586 and was republished,
enlarged several times, translated from Latin into English and later
published in Frankfurt. Between Edward Gibson's edition of 1695
and Richard Gough's of 1789, however, there is a long and telling
hiatus marking the period that saw the fall and rise of antiquarianism
in the eighteenth century.

While Camden made some use of Leland's notes, the *Britannia* was
a work with no obvious precedent, 'a sort of learning, that was then
but just appearing in the world'.[21] Camden brought an evidence-based
approach to national history in place of the myths and legends of the
medieval chronicles. He paid due respect to Geoffrey of Monmouth's
History of the Kings of Britain, with its tales of Arthur and the supposed

founder of Britain, the Trojan Brutus. But although, as he reported, 'I have strained my invention', Camden could find no reason to believe any of it.[22] So, setting aside the chronicles, he embarked on a series of travels through the country. He studied Welsh and Anglo-Saxon, examined inscriptions and coins and took a serious if critical interest in local and oral tradition. There were difficulties. Despite 'much labour' he could make nothing of the Scots or the Picts, remaining 'perfectly in the darke' as to their origins.[23] Gradually, however, he pieced together a picture of Britain at the time of the Roman conquest. Peopled with warlike, woad-painted tribes who later intermingled with their conquerors and assumed their own place in the Roman Empire, the Britain of Camden's account was, like the chroniclers', part of the Classical world, but as a consequence of historical process rather than via an apocryphal Trojan. Camden's ambition was 'to restore Britain to Antiquity, and Antiquity to Britain'.[24] What he meant by that was to place Britain in historical time. But by telling the story geographically, county by county, as well as chronologically, the *Britannia* spoke to a readership whose sense of the past was still 'more closely tied to location than date'.[25] The model was established for the writing of county histories, which became a staple of antiquarianism from Camden to Nikolaus Pevsner, although, once again, there is a telling pause in the sequence. After Camden's there was no comparable attempt to cover the whole country until John Britton and Edward Brayley began their series *The Beauties of England and Wales* in the 1790s, at the moment when Romanticism was rediscovering the idea of history as landscape.

Camden was a scholar of European standing, but he was only the most eminent among the half-dozen or so who, over two generations, created English antiquarianism. The other leading figures included John Stow (1524/5–1605), Henry Spelman (1563/4–1641) and John Selden (1584–1654), as well as Camden's travelling companion and former pupil, Robert Cotton (1571–1631), who was inspired by the *Britannia* to found his own incomparable library. Despite the popular image of the antiquary as an isolated scholar in his study, antiquarianism was mostly a sociable, if not always a harmonious business. Camden and his friends met, compared notes and shared their discoveries, one of which could be said to be the Middle Ages itself. It was Camden and Spelman who put the term into circulation as a way of describing the period after the fall of the Roman Empire in the West to the beginning of the Renaissance.[26] They also founded the first English Society of Antiquaries in about 1585. It had forty or so members, most of whom were scholars rather than 'men of letters' and only two were clerics.[27] Their discussions dealt exclusively with national history and documentary sources: 'historical fact seen from the standpoint of the lawyer and the herald'.[28] Though most were graduates of Oxford or Cambridge, they met in London during the legal terms, and here a pattern was set; for by the late eighteenth century, while there were many more clerics and rather fewer lawyers among the antiquaries, they continued to operate mostly outside the universities through independent societies and informal networks of collaboration.

These free-range bodies were not always popular with the authorities. All forms of historical enquiry have political implications and James I 'took a little mislike' to this first Society of Antiquaries, anxious perhaps that too much dispelling of myths might raise questions about his own metaphorical descent from the Trojan Brutus, that useful symbol of the union of the English and Scottish crowns so memorably portrayed by Rubens on the ceiling of the Banqueting House in Whitehall.[29] As Walter Raleigh discovered, under James, 'who so-ever in writing a modern Historie shall follow truth too near the heeles, it may happily strike out his teeth'.[30] So, since their activities were making the king 'alarmed for the arcana of his government', 'for fear of being prosecuted as a treasonable cabal', the first society disbanded.[31] Antiquaries continued to find themselves in political trouble in the long aftermath of the Reformation with its 'intense struggle' for the past between Catholic and Protestant narratives.[32] Few Tudor and Stuart antiquaries escaped the implications of their work. John Foxe (1516–87), author of the *Book of Protestant Martyrs*, went into exile under Mary I. Stow, author of the *Survey of London*, was questioned on a charge of sedition. Selden was forced by James I to apologize and withdraw his *Historie of Tithes*, which the king felt questioned the privilege of the monarch. Cotton's library was closed by Charles I and Cotton himself imprisoned.

Camden remained on the right side of the law. From one edition of the *Britannia* to the next, with the accession of James VI and I, Britain became a legal as well as a geographic entity and the *Britannia* reinforced the Stuarts' view of their claims to the throne of a united Britain. It was amenable to an entirely Protestant reading, carefully dissociating the British Church from the Roman and avoiding any detailed discussion of individual monastic foundations. But in such divided times there was no universally acceptable position. Camden was criticized on the one hand for including the monasteries at all, incurring the charge perennially levelled at antiquaries from the sixteenth to the nineteenth centuries of being a closet Catholic, while on the other he was too Protestant for Oxford University, with which he was in a constant state of war. He fought a long campaign to be awarded his MA and was passed over for a fellowship at All Souls. Only at the end of his life did he find a way to insert himself and his subject matter into the university, when in 1620 he established and endowed the first lectureship in civil history. Spelman made a similar attempt to set up a lectureship at Cambridge for the study of antiquities of the Anglo-Saxon Church, but this was less successful. His more enduring legacy was his patronage of the next generation in the person of William Dugdale.

Dugdale (1605–86) was one of the greatest English antiquaries, a constant point of reference for the Georgians, to whom he became a kind of patron saint 'whose name is hourly mentioned with deserved respect'.[33] William Hamper (1776–1831), who edited Dugdale's diaries and letters for publication in 1827, thought his works would be 'as lasting as the languages in which they are written'.[34] Born in the year of the Gunpowder Plot, Dugdale was the son of a Warwickshire clergyman. He married young and did not attend a university, but his enthusiasm for all kinds of historical study led him via a chain of introductions to London and to the ageing Spelman. Spelman, 'a handsome Gentleman' who 'wore always his Sword, till he was about 70 or +',[35] was still vigorous but his career was nearing its end, and in Dugdale he saw an heir. He gave him transcripts he had made of monastic charters in Norfolk and Suffolk, suggesting that he should use them to collaborate with Roger Dodsworth, 'a gent. of Yorkshire' who had researched that county and in particular 'the foundations of Monasteries there'.[36] Antiquarian collaborations often worked in this way with notes and whole projects passing down the generations, some reaching completion after many years, others inevitably falling by the wayside. Spelman also ensured an income for Dugdale by getting him a job as a herald. It was a useful adjunct to his antiquarian studies, for heraldry, though often cited along with brass-rubbing and campanology as the epitome of antiquarian dullness, is vital for the study of post-Conquest history and genealogy. The tracing of family trees was an early and important antiquarian pursuit which was also, for the clergy and gentry, of considerable practical use. The re-creation of family histories established rights to titles, heraldic arms, landed property or tithes.

Dugdale's position of Rouge Croix Pursuivant came with rooms in London at the Office of Heralds and a modest salary. Thus securely established, and with Spelman's advice in mind, he got in touch with Dodsworth and the project that became the *Monasticon Anglicanum*, one of the greatest undertakings of English antiquarianism, was born. Dugdale and Dodsworth collected and reproduced all the surviving foundation charters of the pre-Reformation religious houses, records which gave insights into the history not only of the monasteries but of transfers of land, medieval legal practice and the feudal system. This was the material that Camden had avoided for fear of entangling himself in the connections between Catholic monasticism and the Anglican settlement. Yet any history of the Church in England would be 'crippled without a study of monasticism'.[37] A generation after Camden, Dugdale, a committed Anglican and a Royalist, had the courage of his convictions – and courage was needed. Puritan elements in Parliament were set on the destruction of anything that savoured of the trappings of 'popery'. This included church monuments, statues, brasses, stained glass and psalteries, wall paintings – in short, all of the antiquaries' source material. By an historic irony of which he was acutely aware, Dugdale's attempt to recover the records of institutions destroyed at the Reformation was undertaken in the shadow of a similar threat. He worked frantically up to the eve of the Civil Wars, spending days in St Paul's Cathedral and Westminster Abbey. In the summer of 1641 he toured the country, taking with him William Sedgwick, 'a skilful Arms painter', and visiting as many places 'wherein any tombs and monuments were to be found' as he could; 'to the end that the memory of them . . . ought to be preserved for future and better times'.[38]

When war broke out, Dugdale was close to events. In October 1642 he was present, as herald, at the Battle of Edgehill and continued to work throughout the war, turning its vicissitudes to advantage. In Oxford, with Charles I's exiled court, he pursued his studies in the libraries there. Dodsworth, meanwhile, managed to transcribe the charters and grants in St Mary's Tower in York before it was blown up by the Parliamentarians in the siege of 1644. After the Royalists' defeat, Dugdale's estate was confiscated and he withdrew to France, where he carried on working in the archives of the French religious houses which had had dependencies in England. Despite the Civil Wars, the death of Dodsworth and lack of funds for printing, the first part of the *Monasticon* emerged in 1655. With illustrations by Wenceslaus Hollar and Daniel King, it laid before its readers the monastic establishments of the Middle Ages in large and evocative plates. At the Restoration Dugdale came home, and worked on. There remained, however, the difficulty (which Camden had avoided) of explaining what had happened at the Reformation in such a way as to reconcile the Catholic past with the Anglican present. At this point, despite all the years he had spent amassing documentary and other material evidence, Dugdale invoked a tradition which would have strained Camden's invention to breaking point. The first of the monasteries he discusses is Glastonbury, which he describes as the oldest. Dugdale's friend James Wright translated his account in the first English edition of the *Monasticon* in 1693:

> In the 13th year after our Saviour's Passion twelve Disciples of St Philip the Apostle, among whom Joseph of Arimathea was one, came to this place, and preacht [*sic*] Christian Religion to King Arviragus. They obtained of that King the Ground where the Monastery afterwards stood, and twelve Hides of Land, and built there the first Church of the Kingdom.[39]

Thus, the *Monasticon* explains, the so-called 'Isle of Glass', later known as Glastonbury, became 'The Tomb of Saints' and the resting place of kings, including Arthur and 'Guenevera [*sic*] his Queen'.[40]

Far from discrediting Dugdale with either his Anglican contemporaries or his Romantic successors, this unsubstantiated and unlikely account of the early English Church made him indispensable to them. It showed that Christianity in Britain dated from apostolic times, half a millennium before Pope Gregory sent Augustine to England in 597. It made the case for an English Catholic Church independent of Rome and continuous through the Reformation by apostolic succession, its roots deep 'in primitive soil'.[41] This belief – myth, tradition or history according to one's point of view – was still potent in the later eighteenth century. It gained ground in the nineteenth century with the campaign for Catholic Emancipation and ran through the agonizings of the Tractarians as the Oxford Movement interrogated the Anglican settlement. Joseph of Arimathea was not much mentioned, but the belief in an English Church, 'true, independent, apostolic', persisted and was for many Anglicans essential to their faith and identity.[42] So it was that while John Lingard's *Antiquities of the Anglo-Saxon Church* of 1806 more or less destroyed the historic argument, the *Monasticon* was re-edited and republished between 1817 and 1830. The editors were based in London and Oxford. The list of subscribers includes no names from Cambridge, which had been for Parliament in the Civil Wars: Dugdale's High Anglican argument was still well understood in Georgian England. Anglicans still profess themselves part of 'one holy, Catholic and apostolic Church', while at Glastonbury the myths of Arthur and Guinevere continue to hang in the air, celebrated by New Age pagans and followers of the earth mysteries movement.

Eventually, Dugdale completed his *History of Warwickshire*, the project he had had in mind before Spelman set him on a more ambitious course. If it was not the first one-county work, it was the most influential to date, offering a model that could be imitated by any local antiquary. Many people were inspired to embark on similar histories, including John Aubrey (1626–97), who decided to make a study of his own county, Wiltshire. Aubrey was the next in that line of intellectual descent that revived in the late eighteenth century. His was one of the most original minds of his own or any age, embodying the best and worst of the antiquarian temperament. On the one hand he was imaginative, polymathic, unconventional and relentless in his pursuit of material. His *Naturall Historie of Wiltshire* was, like Camden's *Britannia*, a new kind of learning, the first 'natural history', in which Aubrey included 'a list of the county's trees and plants with their medicinal and practical uses . . . its different stones and minerals, clays and soil types with their particular properties . . . its fauna and medicinal springs, as well as its winds, mists, and storms'.[43] On the other hand, he lived in a state of permanent chaos, personal and professional. He published little, made footnotes to his footnotes and left behind a mass of manuscript material which, 300 years later, scholars with the advantage of computers are still working to edit.

Aubrey was born 'about sun-riseing'[44] on 12 March 1626. As a child he was 'always enquiring of my grandfather of the old time, the rood loft, etc, ceremonies of the Priory'.[45] He was haunted by the Reformation and 'wished Monasterys had not been put downe . . . wt a pleasure 'twould have been to have travelled from monastery to monastery . . . Nay, the Turks have monasteries; why should our Reformers be so severe?'[46] Like Ruthven he was at an impressionable age when the stream of national life was violently disrupted: 'as a cleare skie is sometimes suddenly overstretched by a dismall black cloud and thunder, so was the serene peace by the civill war.'[47] Aubrey's writing is shot through with regret for the wanton destruction of the past, especially the loss of the monastic libraries, torn up for waste paper. 'In my grandfather's dayes,' he recalled in his *Naturall Historie of Wiltshire*, 'the manuscripts flew about like butterflies. All musick books, account books, copie books etc were covered with old manuscripts . . . and gloves were wrapped up no doubt in many good pieces of antiquity.'[48] As well as artefacts, Aubrey 'did ever love to converse with old men as Living Histories', and he can claim to be the first folklorist and oral historian.[49] He knew that he was living on the cusp of an era when 'Printing and Gunpowder' had 'frighted away Robyn-good-fellow and the Fayries', and he recorded the stories of old people, among whom their memory lingered.[50]

The only work Aubrey published in his lifetime was *Miscellanies*, a collection of folk tales and superstitions which led contemporaries and some later writers to accuse him of 'open-eared credulity'.[51] Aubrey was not credulous. If he felt a certain melancholy about the passing of 'Fayries', he belonged intellectually to the world of the new learning. As a boy he read his mother's copy of Bacon's *Essays* and grasped at once the intellectual shift it represented. 'Till about the yeare 1649,' as he summarized it, "twas held a strange presumption for a man to attempt an innovation in learning; and not to be good manners to be more knowing than his neighbours and forefathers.'[52] The new principles of empirical enquiry led Aubrey to add to Camden's invention of the Middle Ages his own most original discovery, prehistory. Camden said virtually nothing about pre-Roman monuments in the *Britannia*. The illustration of Stonehenge shows a ring of wobbly, rippling stones. Nothing suggests that Camden actually visited it. For a historian working from written sources, documents, coins and inscriptions there was no point, for, as Aubrey noted: 'These antiquities are so exceeding old that no Books doe reach them.'[53] His conclusion was that 'there is no way to retrieve them but by comparative antiquitie ... writ upon the Spott'.[54] This comparative, direct method was to be the essence of subsequent antiquarianism. Aubrey found a comparator for Stonehenge at Avebury, where he was the first person to realize that the stones were not a random outcrop but a deliberate construction. He made a plane-table survey of both sites in order to get precise measurements. Exact measuring was also an innovation. Dugdale, who found prehistoric monuments as opaque as Camden had, saw no need for it. He was content to describe Long Meg, the Neolithic stone circle in Cumbria, as being 'about' as wide as the Thames opposite the College of Heralds, a comparison made simply by looking out of his office window.

Aubrey's measurements and 'a kind of Algebraical method' enabled him to find the site of what are now known as the Aubrey Holes at Stonehenge.[55] By making broader comparisons with other stone circles and monuments further afield, he reasoned that since they were found in Ireland, beyond Roman rule and in Wales where the Danes did not penetrate, they must have been 'erected by the Britons' in a time before known history began.[56] So far was Aubrey from being a credulous recorder that his scepticism extended to Christianity. He felt no need to try to fit his calculations into the biblical chronology that limited Camden's speculations. Aubrey drew up a map of prehistoric sites, and the paper on Avebury that he read to the Royal Society in 1663 is the first known archaeological treatise on any subject. But bankruptcy, unhappy or unfortunate love affairs and a temperamental disinclination to order ensured that at his death in 1697 his heaps of manuscript and other collections languished. Their fate was not helped by the fact that Aubrey had made a powerful enemy of his former friend and fellow antiquary Anthony Wood (1632–95), who made strenuous efforts to discredit him. Once again it was the later Georgians who rose to the challenge. A rescue operation began in the 1790s with the Shakespeare scholar Edmond Malone, who looked at Aubrey's papers and concluded that he 'appears to have been a very amiable unfortunate man' to whom Malone felt 'endeared'. Seeking 'to do him that justice which he has not met with at least in the present century', he began the great relay race by which Aubrey studies continue to pass down the generations to the present.[57]

'Like fire-weed [antiquarianism] . . . grows best on ravaged land.'[58] In the aftermath of the Restoration the works of Dugdale, Wood, Aubrey and some others marked the crest of a new wave of historical enquiry that spread through 'the rectories and vicarages of England', infecting 'squires, lawyers and doctors' and reaching up 'to government itself'.[59] In due course all this activity led to the formation of another Society of Antiquaries. Ironically, for a body whose purpose was to establish a factual account of the past from primary sources, the Society's exact foundation date is obscure and still in dispute.[60] What is certain is that a small number of like-minded men began meeting, more or less regularly, in 1707 at one or more London inns. Later in the century, when the antiquaries wanted to emphasize the continuity of their own efforts with the heroic age of seventeenth-century scholarship, they seem to have fudged the question of whether these early meetings really constituted the foundation of the Society as it existed in their own day, or was simply an informal arrangement that fizzled out. Later attempts to establish the truth have been hampered by the fact that the records of the early meetings are somewhat confused. As Dai Morgan Evans has observed, 'given the convivial nature of the occasion . . . it would not be too outrageous to speculate that these minutes were produced at the time of the meeting and under the influence of alcohol'.[61] What is certain is that ten years later, in July 1717, a group met at the Mitre, 'a top class Tavern', and founded a Society whose history can be followed continuously to the present.[62]

The foundation of this Society marked the climax of the first great age of national antiquarianism, 'the best sustained and the most prolific movement of historical scholarship which this country has ever seen', and also the beginning of its decline.[63] The Society of 1707 was formed to study 'such things as may Illustrate and Relate to the History of Great Britain', but already the spirit of what came to be called the Enlightenment was driving interest towards Classical civilization.[64] At Oxford Camden's lectureship was turned over to Classical antiquities, while Spelman's at Cambridge petered out altogether. The Grand Tour became an essential element in the education of a gentleman, who was expected to return from Italy with some cosmopolitan polish, several crates of antiquities of varying degrees of authenticity and his portrait by Batoni. The Society of Antiquaries reflected the changing times. By the mid-1730s its chief interest also 'lay in classical antiquities'.[65] But at the same time, it was becoming something of a backwater. The more dashing of the Grand Tourists preferred to join the Society of Dilettanti, founded in 1734. Its members were wealthy cosmopolitan men of taste who went by less dowdy and provincial names than 'antiquary'. They were dilettanti, connoisseurs, virtuosi. An increasingly secular age felt no inhibition about admiring pre-Christian civilization and looked askance at manorial records, church monuments, brass-rubbing, heraldry and bells.

What the age of Enlightenment required of the past was that it should serve the present. 'All history', said Voltaire, 'is almost equal for those who merely wish to store their memories with facts. But whoever thinks or (what is more rare) whoever possesses taste only counts four centuries in the history of the world.'[66] His centuries were the ages of Pericles, Augustus, the Italian Renaissance and the reign of Louis XIV. Voltaire and Rousseau were the guiding lights of the age of Reason; European scholarship became 'practically a French monopoly'.[67] Edward Gibbon left Oxford, having spent 'the fourteen months the most idle and unprofitable of my whole life', for Lausanne.[68] Here it was the works of the ironist philosopher Pierre Bayle (1647–1706), 'the Arsenal of the Enlightenment' as he became known, and of Montesquieu that laid the groundwork for *The Decline and Fall of the Roman Empire*.[69] At the heart of this change in historic sensibility was Voltaire's association of thought with taste. Taste is both an aesthetic and a moral concept and it dictated that only the most worthwhile and beautiful achievements of the past were to be considered. To amass ugly objects or collect information about undistinguished or plebeian subjects seemed, to most of the intellectual elite, ridiculous. Feudal society and Gothic churches offered no models of refinement or elegant diction. David Douglas perhaps overstated the case when he wrote that 'by the middle of the eighteenth century the leaders of English taste had come to profess almost a hatred of the past,' but it was no exaggeration, on either side of the Channel, to say that 'they felt disdain for those who explored it'.[70]

The great historians of the age of Reason, Hume (1711–76) and Gibbon (1737–94), wrote in a spirit of 'humanist optimism', describing a narrative of progress and improvement.[71] Gibbon saw in the havoc wreaked over two centuries by the Crusades a turning point towards the undermining of 'the Gothic edifice of feudalism', comparing it to a forest fire that cleared the way for new and better growth.[72] It would be wrong, nevertheless, to overstate the differences between the antiquaries and the scholars of the Enlightenment. *Decline and Fall* could not have been written without the French Benedictines' antiquarian scholarship, and Gibbon's last, unrealized, project was to have been a collaboration with the Scottish antiquary John Pinkerton to republish all the early British histories, up to 1500.[73] By the same token, the antiquaries of the Romantic age were inheritors of the Enlightenment, aspiring also to 'zeal in learning, breadth of interest, freedom of inquiry and an open mind'.[74] Where they took issue with their predecessors it was often for their lack of rigour: Hume knew nothing about the Middle Ages, Voltaire contradicted himself. But the fundamental difference was philosophical. It was not a question of truth versus untruth, but of truth or the whole truth; whether the artefacts of the past were to be viewed as an end in themselves, valued only for their beauty, or as a means to an end, the study of history, for which the ugly and the plebian might be as valuable as anything. For better and worse, antiquaries collected as many facts and examples relating to a given subject as they could. While the more plodding of them stopped there, the more sophisticated could not help but notice that change, not progress, is the only constant in history. As Camden wrote, 'learning ebbed and flowed', good times gave way to bad, and vice versa.[75] The antiquaries saw successive ages not as milestones on a highway of improvement, but as 'self-sufficient totalities of human life, valid within their own terms, demanding from the historian neither praise nor blame . . . but imaginative recreation'.[76] Philosophically and intellectually the antiquaries were better equipped to bear the shock of the French Revolution when it came.

Meanwhile, the Society of Antiquaries grew in numbers, especially after 1751 when George II gave his seal to the charter of incorporation and it became a royal society, but its scholarly efforts were at best mixed. The new recruits were of relatively little distinction, and discussion dwelled on 'pedigrees and manorial history, with occasional bursts of enthusiasm for hypocausts'.[77] There were, however, among this last generation of antiquaries born under the Stuarts, two remarkable figures whose influence on their late-Georgian successors was considerable. The first was Thomas Hearne (c.1678–1735). He was a medievalist, diarist, bibliographer and collector whose chief interest, like so many of his predecessors and successors, was the Reformation. It was he who began the reclamation work on Leland's notes, which had been scattered and damaged 'so that the leaves . . . fall to pieces every day'.[78] Hearne published *The Itinerary of John Leland the Antiquary* in nine volumes from 1710 onwards. As sub-librarian at the Bodleian he also made the best surviving lists of the collection, long since dispersed, that the Bodleian shared with the Oxford Anatomy School, creating the most important record of what has been described as 'the first British Museum'.[79] The other great antiquary of this generation was William Stukeley (1687–1765), a doctor by training who later became a clergyman. Stukeley was a pioneer of field archaeology, applying the medical technique of vertical dissection to his excavations. Like Hearne he took up the legacy of the heroic age. Aubrey's notes on Stonehenge and Avebury led him to make studies of both. His *Stonehenge* of 1740 was the first published survey of the monument. It was Stukeley who coined the word 'trilithon' and his book, which launched centuries of scholarship, tourism and controversy, was not bettered for 150 years.

Unfortunately for Hearne and Stukeley, as they lived on into a less sympathetic age they provided ample ammunition for the enemies of antiquarianism. Hearne was a quarrelsome man, an outspoken Jacobite and non-juror who refused to take the oath of loyalty to William and Mary. The English Revolution of 1688 which replaced the Catholic James II with his Protestant daughter and son-in-law was not a national schism on the scale of the Reformation and the Civil Wars, but it divided loyalties and opinions for generations. A significant number of antiquaries were non-jurors, and so to the old accusations of 'popery' was added the new suspicion, often as in Hearne's case justified, of treasonable Jacobite sympathies. Hearne's refusal to conform cost him his job at the Bodleian. As a result he was poor, 'very mean to look at', often at war with the university in general and with various individuals in particular.[80] One of his publications was suppressed on the grounds of 'gratuitous slander' and his general temper has been described as having 'an air of splenetic repression'.[81] Alexander Pope, looking down from the heights of polite culture, saw in Hearne the epitome of the vulgar, ramshackle world of antiquarianism. In *The Dunciad* Hearne is cast as Wormius, written off, along with his subject matter, in a couplet:

> To future Ages may thy dulness last
> As thou preserv'st the dulness of the past![82]

Stukeley offered yet more hostages to fortune. From his surveys of prehistoric sites he developed elaborate, mystical theories about the Druids, whom he believed not only to have built Stonehenge but to have been proto-Christians. In his extrapolations he 'moved rapidly', as Stuart Piggott puts it, 'from hypothesis to fact, from fact to fantasy' and became known to later generations, somewhat unfairly, as 'the least scientific and most irresponsibly romantic writer on antiquities' whose increasingly peculiar ideas were delivered to ever-sparser audiences at the Society of Antiquaries.[83] A more nuanced judgement of Stukeley was made by his contemporary William Warburton, who saw in him 'a compound of things never meant to meet together'.[84] Stukeley, as he said, was laughed at by people 'who had neither his sense, his knowledge, nor his honesty', despite which 'it must be confessed that in him they were all strangely travestied'.[85] So it was that in the age of Reason, although interest in the national past never ceased, and provincial clergymen and squires continued to dig in barrows, dredge ponds and copy monumental inscriptions, antiquarianism drifted to the cultural margins.

As a social type the antiquary was already established by the time Camden died in 1623. John Earle's satirical *Micro-Cosmographie* of

1628 offered a definition: 'A great admirer he is of the rust of old Monuments ... He will go forty mile to see a Saint's Well, or ruin'd Abbey, and if there be but a cross, or stone footstool in the way, he will be poring on it so long till he forgett his journey.'[86] Earle's antiquary was constitutionally gullible – 'beggars cosin him with musty things that they have rakt from dung-hills' – and now he became a general laughing stock.[87] In June 1772 at the Theatre Royal, Haymarket, in London, Samuel Foote's comedy *The Nabob* put a meeting of the Society of Antiquaries on the stage, probably for the first but certainly not for the last time.[88] The Nabob of Foote's title is Sir Matthew Mite, a coarse and pompous man, newly elected to the Society. The meeting begins, as meetings still do today, with the acknowledgement of gifts. Mite's mites are all items relating to British history, marking him out as a man of limited education and poor taste. They include 'a pair of nut-crackers presented by Harry the Eighth to Anna Bullen ... the wood supposed to be walnut', from which one of the antiquaries solemnly deduces that it can now be proved that 'before the Reformation walnut-trees were planted in England'.[89] Another offering is 'a tobacco-stopper of Sir Walter Raleigh's, made of the stern of the ship in which he first compassed the globe; given to the Society by a clergyman from the North Riding of Yorkshire'.[90]

Footling subjects, vulgar objects and pointless deductions are firmly associated with class. In the clergyman from Yorkshire the audience recognized a provincial nobody. The high point of Foote's satire is the paper Sir Matthew delivers to the Society on the subject of his own researches. He confirms his limitations as he announces: 'Let others toil to illumine the dark annals of Greece or of Rome my searches are sacred only to the service of Britain!'[91] His particular topic is 'the great Dick Whittington, and his no less eminent cat'. He goes on to define his terms, including 'cat' ('a domestic, whiskered, four-footed animal') and to explain that 'cat' could also mean a kind of light cargo boat (which it does) and to suggest that Whittington had used such a boat for the coastal trade on which he built his fortune, and so the legend had arisen from a slippage in terminology.[92] The audience at the Haymarket tittered appreciatively but Horace Walpole (1717–97), a fellow of the Society of Antiquaries, was not amused. Walpole's irritation was directed not at the play but at the Society, because the satire was an accurate paraphrase of a lecture that a clergyman, Samuel Pegge, had given to the Antiquaries the year before and which they had since published. The attack piqued Walpole, for he was not only an antiquary but a pioneer of the taste for the medieval as a manifestation of sensibility, a somewhat outré and private gentleman's pursuit. To see it presented as the vulgar hobby horse of a social climber was unpleasant. He would not, as he put it, be answerable 'for any fooleries but my own'.[93] Having always had a stormy relationship with the Society, he now resigned.

For more than a century after his death Walpole was condemned to be a victim of his own ironizing and facetiousness. Well into the twentieth century his Gothic house at Strawberry Hill and his interest in the Middle Ages could be dismissed as a *jeu d'esprit*.[94] In truth, Walpole's relationship with history and its artefacts was complex and sophisticated. That slow, pervasive shift in sensibility that would bring antiquarianism back to the cultural mainstream began with the creation of Strawberry Hill. Yet the antiquaries of the Romantic age were too close to see it. For the most part they despised Walpole and thought Strawberry Hill ridiculous.[95] The row provoked by Foote's play marked a turning point, a collision of ideas at the moment when one person's cutting edge was still another's lunatic fringe. It was an early symptom of the next fit of dawning historic awareness, which would propel antiquarianism into a new phase. For the moment, however, Walpole appeared, as he wished to, a remarkable figure, typical of nothing. As the century neared its end it seemed to the antiquary Francis Grose (bap. 1731–91) that the stock of antiquarianism could hardly be lower. It had, he remarked, 'long been the fashion to laugh at the study of Antiquities, and to consider it as the idle amusement of a few humdrum plodding fellows, who, wanting genius for nobler studies, busied themselves in heaping up illegible Manuscripts, mutilated Statues, obliterated Coins, and broken pipkins!'[96] But the fashion was about to change.

2

The Romantic Antiquary

Deep in antiquity he's read,
And though at college never bred
As much of things appears to know,
As erst knew Leland, Hearne, or Stowe
'A sketch of Francis Grose Esq., FAS, by a Friend'

In the summer of 1790 Francis Grose was in Ayrshire in search of material for his work in progress, *The Antiquities of Scotland.* Now approaching sixty, he belonged to that generation which had one foot on either side of the shift from Enlightenment to Romantic sensibility. A reader of Voltaire and Rousseau, his own preference was, nevertheless, for local history. After a chequered military career, in the course of which his 'haphazard' management of his regiment's finances brought him to the brink of bankruptcy, he devoted himself almost entirely to antiquarian publications.[1] His interests were wideranging, his philosophy robust. 'Ancient coins, inscriptions, or sculptures, are only so far useful, as they tend to the illustration of history, chronology, or the state of the arts, at the time they were executed.'[2] In a short, sharp essay he attacked the 'Modern Connoisseur', whose only qualifications were his money and the fact that he had been on the Grand Tour and managed to accumulate 'rare and costly articles' for the sake of acquisition and display.[3] Satirist, journalist, artist and cartoonist, Grose was as much at home in the Grub Street of Dr Johnson as at the Society of Antiquaries, possibly more so, for his wit did not always make him popular there. Like Aubrey he wrote many short biographies, some of devastating frankness, which give glimpses of what Walter Scott later called the 'bitchiferous' side of antiquarianism:[4]

> Mr. Joseph Ames was born at or near Great Yarmouth, in Norfolk, where he had a small estate. He was a member of both the Royal and Antiquarian Societies; and secretary to the latter. He was a very little man, of mean aspect, and still meaner abilities. The history of printing, published under his name, was really written by Dr. Ward, professor of Gresham college ... Many persons of rank held Mr. Ames's antiquarian knowledge in high estimation; among them were the Duchess of Portland, and the Archbishop of Canterbury.[5]

Grose was a lexicographer. His specialty was dialect, and his *Classical Dictionary of the Vulgar Tongue*, published in 1785, and the *Provincial Glossary* two years later between them included 9,000 words or meanings not in Johnson's *Dictionary*.

One word that was in the *Dictionary* in 1755 was 'antiquary', which Johnson defined in neutral terms as 'a man studious of antiquity; a collector of ancient things'.[6] In a letter to Boswell, however, Johnson remarked that 'a mere antiquarian is a rugged being', and the *Dictionary* defined 'rugged' as 'full of unevenness and asperity ... not neat, not regular ... savage of temper; brutal ... turbulent ... sour, surly, discomposed ... shaggy'.[7] If few antiquaries exhibited all of these characteristics, it must be admitted that most of them had some. Hearne was savage of temper, Aubrey was not regular and Grose was certainly not neat. He was enormously fat. 'My circumference is nearly double my height,' he boasted with some slight exaggeration.[8] He was also a heavy drinker. On his travels in Ayrshire he was introduced to Robert Burns, with whom he formed a warm friendship marinated in port. Burns had 'never seen a man of more original observation, anecdote and remark ... His delight is to steal thro' the country almost unknown, both as most favourable to his humour and his business.'[9] Theirs was a momentous meeting, for poetry and for antiquarianism. Grose asked Burns to write an account for his *Antiquities of Scotland* of the tradition of witches' meetings at Alloway Church. Burns responded with one of his greatest poems, 'Tam O'Shanter'. The next year, when Grose died, suddenly, if not perhaps surprisingly, of an apoplectic fit, Burns commemorated him in his ode

'On the Late Captain Grose's Peregrinations thro' Scotland Collecting the Antiquities of that Kingdom'. With Burns's poem the figure of the antiquary steps out from caricature into literature. Burns offers in this 'fine, fat fodgel wight / O'stature short but genius bright' a brief but vivid portrait of a large man, light on his feet despite his corpulence, who travels the country in pursuit of his 'antiquarian trade', inspecting ruins and discreetly eavesdropping on Scots speakers, noting down words and phrases. Grose was the occasion for two of Burns's most quoted lines: 'a chield's amang you taking notes / And faith he'll print it.'[10]

Grose is hardly a figure of romance, yet his apotheosis at the hands of Burns perhaps marks the birth of Romantic antiquarianism. The antiquary was moving back from the cultural margin, along with his subject matter. National history, local history, oral tradition, everything included in the popular antiquarian catch-all of 'manners and customs' was becoming interesting. Nine years after Burns's verse, Wordsworth wrote in the Preface to the *Lyrical Ballads*: 'The principal object ... proposed in these Poems was to choose incidents and situations from common life, and to relate or describe them, throughout, as far as was possible in a selection of language really used by men.'[11] Romanticism looked to history not for models but for the truth of individual experience. Wild landscape, tumbledown cottages, ruined abbeys, Highland ballads, 'old, unhappy, far-off things, / And battles long ago' were the subjects of Romantic art and literature.[12] Thus for the next half-century and more, the antiquary's interests were shared by poets and novelists, playwrights, painters, scenery designers, actors and architects as well as readers and tourists of the polite, middling classes.

As a social type Earle's eccentric persisted, the 'lover of rust' with a house full of rubbish. Fungus the Antiquary in Thomas Rowlandson and William Combe's comic *English Dance of Death* (1814–16) is a prime specimen; sitting up in bed surrounded by a chaos of books and papers, as he finally adds 'Death's dart' to his collection. At the same time, however, a more nuanced idea of the antiquary as a contemporary figure broke the surface of public consciousness with Scott's novel of 1816, *The Antiquary*. If Burns's verse description of Grose is the first portrait of an antiquary in British literature, Scott's creation,

Jonathan Oldbuck, is the first self-portrait. Like Burns, Scott treats his subject with affectionate satire. Oldbuck the antiquary is 'rugged', in that he is tetchy, untidy and prey to 'irritated and suspicious vanity'.[13] He is also typically positioned in society: 'the country gentlemen were generally above him in fortune, and beneath him in intellect'.[14] His house, Monkbarns, has been built, like his scholarship, on the ruins of the Reformation and he spends his days in 'discussions concerning urns, vases, votive altars, Roman camps and the rules of castrameta-tion'.[15] A member of various antiquarian societies, he is currently engaged in acrimonious correspondence with a Mr Mac-Cribb about the authenticity of Ossian. Oldbuck was a composite of which Scott himself was the main ingredient, but he also owed something to Scott's friend David Herd: 'a grim old Antiquary of the real Scottish caste, all feu-parchment, snuff, and occasional deep glass of whisky toddy'.[16] This character was at once so recognizable and so popular that *The Antiquary* outsold its two predecessors in the *Waverley* series and by 1818 had been through five editions. A dramatized version was a great success at Covent Garden in 1820 and scenes from *The Antiquary* became popular with artists and illustrators on both sides of the Channel. The world of antiquarianism as Scott portrayed it thus became an established part of the reading public's mental land-scape. It remained Scott's favourite among his novels.

The Antiquary, however, is not all snuff and satire. As will become apparent, it is veined with Scott's politics and his views about the meaning of the past. The portrait of Oldbuck himself is no crude cari-cature; it is made up of light and shade, and it nods towards those aspects of Romantic antiquarianism which were darker and less cheer-ful. While the antiquaries of the late Georgian years looked to Camden and Dugdale as their intellectual ancestors, their metaphysical descent came down another line, as Oldbuck knew, from 'the most deter-mined as well as earliest bibliomaniac upon record ... none other than the renowned Don Quixote de la Mancha'.[17] Quixote, protagon-ist of what is often held to be the first novel, is also the first antiquary in fiction. To the Romantics he was a patron saint, a melancholic Everyman. 'Who is there', Hazlitt asked, 'that does not own him for a friend, a countryman and a brother?'[18] Quixote, the victim of his own obsessive interest in the lost world of medieval chivalry, spends his

days and nights absorbed in Gothic romances while his estate is neglected and his studies exhaust him until, like Leland, he loses his
reason. The division between past and present dissolves and Quixote
enters the world of his books, believing he inhabits history as a personal narrative. Richard Bonington's *Don Quixote* was painted
in about 1827, as was his *The Antiquary*, and it portrays them as kindred spirits. They share a pose and an abstracted stare, as if preoccupied
with images that pass before an inward eye. In 1850, recalling those
'first impressions' that had marked him for life, Gustave Flaubert
mentioned his former drawing master, the Rouennais antiquary
Eustache-Hyacinthe Langlois, and 'Don Quichotte' in the same
sentence.[19]

In seventeenth-century illustrations of Cervantes, Quixote is drawn
as a wild-eyed maniac, literally tilting at windmills. The Romantics
turned him inside out: the windmills, the armour and the hopeless
quests are projections of his interior life. Goya's *Quixote* is haunted
by monsters that rise from his own mind. There is a hint of all this in
William Allan's portrait *Sir Walter Scott in his Study*, which shows
Scott similarly surrounded by his collection. He looks less haunted
and better fed than Adolf Schrödter's *Don Quichotte*, painted three
years later, but his posture and the setting are the same, with the piles
of books, the pieces of armour, the pale light from an unseen window
to the left barely penetrating the gloom. This brooding melancholic,
who physically inhabits the remains of the past at the cost of his life
in the present, became firmly attached to the idea of the antiquary,
and sometimes the gloom might darken further into suggestions of
the occult and associations of alchemy and magic.

In *The Antiquary's Cell*, painted in 1835 by E. W. Cooke, who was
an antiquary in his own right, there is no figure. An empty chair in a
shadowy room, its scarlet cushion the only blaze of light, implies an
imminent presence, a necromancer whose organizing mind will draw
the apparent jumble of armour and tapestry into a pattern, as a mag-
net draws iron filings. If there is a pleasant frisson in the picture, there
is, however, nothing truly sinister. In post-Revolutionary France, by
contrast, in the hands of Victor Hugo and Stendhal, the antiquary could
become the personification of history, and a figure of evil. Across Europe
in these years of revolution, war, civil unrest and the first outbreaks of

cholera, there was a revival of interest in that ultimate expression of the relationship of the living to the dead, the medieval *danse macabre*. Burns's 'Tam O'Shanter' is a Dance of Death; Scott used it as the title for a poem on the Battle of Waterloo; Rowlandson's satire turns it to Grand Guignol. Antiquaries on both sides of the Channel, including Francis Douce and Langlois, made important studies of it.

THE ANTIQUARIES THEMSELVES

While the various popular ideas of the antiquary coincided at many points with the reality, the everyday life of individual antiquaries was inevitably more complicated in some ways and more prosaic in others. There were geographical variations. What Burns called 'the antiquarian trade' displayed important differences on either side of Hadrian's Wall. Antiquarianism in Scotland had a shorter, sparser history than in England. A Scottish Society of Antiquaries was founded in 1780 by David Steuart Erskine, Lord Buchan, who was both a galvanizing and a divisive figure – as Scott put it, a person whose 'immense vanity bordering upon insanity obscured or rather eclipsed very considerable talents'.[20] Buchan's address to potential members, however, sounds many of the same notes as the advocates of antiquarian studies in England:

> The name of Antiquary, from the frivolous researches of some of them, and the prejudices of the uninformed public, has, with other still more respectable appellations, become the butt of fashionable and humorous stricture, which, if we could embrace the more useful and interesting subjects which are connected with antiquities, might be happily avoided. The most unpopular studies, when under the auspices of philosophy and philanthropy, become interesting and useful to all, and are pleasing even to the fluttering sons and daughters of dissipation. I do not expect that we shall be able to introduce antiquities with the Morning Post at breakfast, or to make them light summer reading, but a great point would be gained, if they could be rendered interesting amusement for a long winter night.[21]

For the Scots there was always an element of nationalism in their studies, particularly rampant in Buchan's case but felt by most of his compatriots, 'a patriotic fervour bred of Scotland's post-Union identity-crisis and its need to find consolation in the past'.[22] Sometimes consolation was more important than evidence. Scott, in reviewing the case of Ossian, admitted that there was 'something in' Dr Johnson's 'severe judgement' of the Scots that 'if they do not prefer Scotland to truth they will always prefer it to enquiry.'[23] If almost all Scottish antiquaries saw their studies in some kind of relation to national identity, few were so extreme as Buchan, whose growing eccentricity did nothing to further his cause. His contemporary Elizabeth Grant recalled him appearing on one occasion 'dressed as Apollo, attended by nine young girls as the Muses and a naked small boy as Cupid'.[24] Accordingly it was not Buchan but the crowd-pleasing Walter Scott who became the determining influence on Scottish antiquarianism and the deployment of Scotland's history and antiquities for the fashioning of an acceptable post-Union identity.

After 1789 the dialogue between Scotland and England became a three-way exchange with France. For the most part this was a co-operation, although there were moments when the Auld Alliance of Scotland and France against the English seemed to revive. French antiquarianism before the Revolution, like the British before the Reformation, was largely the province of the monastic orders, notably the Benedictine scholars on whom Gibbon relied. Afterwards it became much more like its British counterpart, and an awareness of the parallels fostered warm relations between antiquaries on both sides of the Channel, even when their countries were at war. The French antiquary as he emerged, almost fully formed from the chaos of the Terror, had recognizable characteristics. The meticulous Arcisse de Caumont with his mania for data, the tetchy and pedantic Abbé de La Rue, the untidy, indigent Eustache-Hyacinthe Langlois all had their parallels in the Societies of Antiquaries of London and Scotland, while in Victor Hugo the French had their Scott, the poet and novelist putting history and its material remains to political use. The account of these men's lives and work belongs, however, to later chapters, where the deep and significant differences between French and British antiquarianism can be explored more fully.

Social class is one of the aspects of antiquarianism in post-Revolutionary France which cannot usefully be compared with

Scotland or England. In Britain, while there were aristocrats who took an interest in British antiquities beyond their own pedigrees – Lord Buchan was, in every way, a striking example – most antiquaries sat, like Oldbuck, somewhere between the artisan classes and the lower ranks of the gentry. John Britton (1771–1857), who came to dominate topographical publishing in the first half of the nineteenth century, began his working life as a tavern porter, while his friend and collaborator Edward Brayley (1773–1854) had been apprenticed to an enameller. John Carter (1748–1817), the draughtsman who recorded almost all that is now known of the medieval chapel of St Stephen's in Westminster Palace, was the son of a monumental mason. His friend William Capon (1757–1827), who made an important ground plan of the medieval palace, was a scene painter at Drury Lane, while John Lingard was the son of a builder. A letter from Sir Henry Ellis, Keeper of Printed Books at the British Museum, to the Director of the Society of Antiquaries, John Gage at his Suffolk seat, Hengrave Hall, gives a flavour of the more genteel end of antiquarian life. Gage had sent Ellis some game and a copy of his latest book. 'I am quite at a loss to thank you properly for your successive kindnesses,' Ellis wrote back.[25] 'Lady Ellis was obliged by your present of a hare and pheasants yesterday: and today I receive the *History of Thingoe Hundred*, which I have passed the evening in cutting open and perusing. The book does you great honour.'[26]

Ellis (1777–1869) was knighted for his services to the museum. Gage (1786–1842) inherited a baronetcy and became Sir John Gage Rokewode. Yet neither was so well established in the social hierarchy as their titles might suggest. Ellis was the son of a London schoolmaster who had won an assisted place at Oxford and had always worked for his living, while Gage, though his family traced its lineage to the Reformation and beyond, was a Roman Catholic and thus debarred from public office, the franchise and the universities.[27] The aura of 'popery' still hung around antiquarianism, and indeed Catholics made up a proportion of antiquaries far greater than their numbers in the population as a whole. Among those who feature prominently in what follows, Lingard was a Catholic priest, John Milner (1752–1826), author of the *Antiquities of Winchester*, a Catholic bishop. Edward Willson (1787–1854), who wrote the texts for Auguste Pugin's books of architectural details from Gothic buildings, was a cradle Catholic, while the Sobieski Stuarts' Jacobite claims required them to become Catholics. In one way or another, a remarkable number of the antiquaries were socially marginal. Even Sir Thomas Phillipps (1792–1872), wealthy, Oxford-educated and one of the most important collectors of manuscripts, was not quite all that that would imply, for he was the illegitimate son of a calico merchant and never knew his mother. Many of the antiquaries were self-educated, which was not a disadvantage at a time when no university taught or even acknowledged their subject matter. One literary antiquary, a Cambridge graduate, debating where to bequeath his collection of manuscripts, was tersely dismissive of his alma mater: 'To give them to King's College, would be to throw them into a horse-pond; and I had as lieve do one as the other; they are generally so conceited of their Latin and Greek, that all other studies are barbarism.'[28]

For Catholics there could be a positive advantage in exclusion from British universities. They were often educated on the Continent and Lingard, who went to the seminary at Douai, received an education far beyond what the son of a Protestant builder could expect. He learned from the Benedictine tradition of textual analysis, became fluent in French and was able to read Spanish. Many of the antiquaries were impressive linguists. Richard Gough (1735–1809), a Director of the Society of Antiquaries, who made the last revisions to Camden's *Britannia*, taught himself Old English 'carefully and painfully' by the comparative method.[29] Gage spoke good French. Dawson Turner (1775–1858), the Norfolk banker and antiquary, was not unusual in being able to speak and read French and German. Thus, while the antiquary might concentrate on British antiquities and local history, he was not necessarily provincial. Over time, as his subject matter became more acceptable to the institutions, an antiquary might rise through the classes, buoyed up by his expertise. Such was the case of Frederic Madden (1801–73), Ellis's younger colleague and sworn enemy at the British Museum. Madden was born in Portsmouth, the eleventh of thirteen children of a captain in the marines. His somewhat stilted early journals give an impressive account of what the determined autodidact could accomplish and of the resources available to a modestly placed family in a large town. At the age of eighteen he wrote:

I never travelled further than eighteen miles from Portsmouth, & consequently derive all my ideas, not from men or manners but from books. These last are frequently calculated to mislead & deceive you & it is only by a careful comparison of one with another & making allowances for the errors on both sides that one can ever arrive at the truth. Many concurrent circumstances have given me a decided advantage in this respect: that of being allowed access to & use of many valuable libraries. I shall only notice the principal. The Marine Library, consisting of upwards of 1500 vols – chiefly on general literature, but all the best standard authors; the Revd C. Henville's – containing about 1000 vols – among which exclusive of other valuable works, is a fine set of the variorum copies; the Revd R. Cumyns: – about 800 vols & well selected; Mr Allens –comprising 400 vols & most of them old, curious, or rare editions – united with these, are my Father's of above 1000 vols & my own of 200; together with the facility of obtaining others from the Hampshire Library . . . whether I have made the best use of them or not should be determined by others.[30]

Madden made such good use of them that he grew into 'a giant of Victorian scholarship', a brilliant palaeographer who taught himself many languages including Anglo-Saxon and took lessons in Hebrew. It was he who discovered, among the manuscripts in the British Museum, the lost Middle English masterpiece *Sir Gawain and the Green Knight*.[31] Madden was knighted in 1832, becoming a gentleman of the privy chamber to William IV. Many doors might thus be open to the industrious antiquary, at least until the middle of the nineteenth century.

Election to the Society of Antiquaries was available not only to the Catholics who so notably took advantage of it, but to Jews, Unitarians, Quakers and other non-conformists who were barred from the universities. It was not open to women, any more than the other learned societies. Yet the antiquarian world was not so entirely male as it might seem at first sight. Some papers by women were read at the Society and a close examination of the work and private correspondence of many antiquaries reveals a number of active female figures in the background.[32] Dawson Turner travelled through England, France and into Germany with his wife Mary and usually one or two of his six daughters. Mary Turner was a trained and skilful artist who, with the older girls, took notes and made drawings; as is clear from Turner's detailed journals, the family regarded their expeditions as joint enterprises.

Most women took part in antiquarianism in the contingent role of wives and daughters, but some who were financially and socially independent undertook solo projects. Anna Gurney (1795–1857) was the half-sister of Dawson Turner's friend, fellow Norfolk banker and antiquary Hudson Gurney (1775–1864). Having been paralysed by a childhood illness, she was exempt from the usual female expectations of marriage and motherhood and could apply herself to the study of languages, mastering French, German, Italian, Hebrew, ancient Greek, Old English, Old Norse, modern Icelandic, Russian, modern Greek, Dutch, Danish, Arabic and Swedish. Her *Literal Translation of the Saxon Chronicle* was published in 1819, when she was twenty-four. Old English had something of a tradition of women scholars, but Gurney's was the first published translation of the Anglo-Saxon Chronicle into modern English.[33] It was presented with the usual self-effacement as being 'by a lady in the Country' and produced in a 'very limited' edition 'intended for private circulation'.[34] Nevertheless, her translation has been admired by later Anglo-Saxonists for its 'accuracy, literalism, and clear, plain style.'[35] Despite her disability Anna Gurney travelled widely, founded a school and played an important role in introducing the Manby Life-saving Rocket to the Norfolk coast. Her achievements in antiquarianism were acknowledged in 1845, when she became the first female fellow of the newly founded British Archaeological Association.

As with the Gurneys, antiquarianism often ran in families. Anna Eliza Stothard, née Kempe (1790–1883) was the sister of one antiquary, Alfred Kempe (c.1785–1846) and married another, the artist and draughtsman Charles Stothard (1786–1821), whose principal work was a study of monumental inscriptions. He also made the first visual record of the Bayeux Tapestry for 200 years. The Stothards worked together on equal terms, collaborating on the account of their antiquarian travels. *Letters Written during a Tour through Normandy, Britanny [sic] and other Parts of France in 1818* has a text by Anna and illustrations by her husband. Anna Stothard was unusual in putting her name to her work, for this was considered ungenteel, as were those antiquarian enquiries that involved scrambling about in churches or digging in barrows. Women were encouraged, if at all, to take up subjects that could be pursued indoors, with clean hands. Ballad-collecting was popular. In Aberdeen Anna Gordon (1747–1810), later known as Mrs Brown of Falkland, wrote down the traditional Scots songs she had learned from her mother, her aunt and a housemaid. She compiled a collection which remains central to the history of ballads, if in some ways contentious, for she has been suspected of a certain amount of Macpherson-like 'improvement'.[36] The content of her work belies the modesty of its presentation, however, for the ballads are 'framed from an explicitly female, indeed even feminist, perspective' and carry 'behind their courtly and magical façade' the 'frequently brutal reality' of uncensored folklore.[37]

Autograph-collecting, in the sense of literary manuscripts, not merely signatures, was also considered a 'pleasing and innocent occupation' for a girl, as Mary-Ann Nichols's (1813–1870) father told her when he suggested she take it up.[38] Her aunt, Anne Susannah Nichols (1788–1853), had also collected manuscripts, which her own father had recommended as both suitable and valuable for historic understanding, for 'the hand-writing is often the index of the Mind'.[39] The Nicholses ate, slept and breathed antiquarianism; it was more than a shared interest, it was the family business. Three generations of John Nichols were proprietors and editors of *The Gentleman's Magazine*, the first 'magazine' in the modern sense. It featured a miscellany of news, reviews, articles, poetry, readers' letters and features reprinted from other sources. When the first John Nichols (1745–1826), the son of an Islington baker, became editor he steered the content firmly towards antiquarian subjects. Among the illustrations, 'Giant Fungi and Greek Inscriptions' rapidly began to give way to Gothic architecture, until 'by 1783 there was an article on Gothic practically every month'.[40] From the heights of the *Edinburgh Review* Francis Jeffrey looked down on *The Gentleman's Magazine*'s 'miserable erudition'.[41] With its short articles, pictures, lack of any party-political stance and overall clubbability it seemed to him irredeemably middlebrow, yet it was and remains a rich repository of information both historical and historiographic. The Nicholses were at various times printers to the

Society of Antiquaries, and like many printing houses at the time they were also publishers. John Nichols published Johnson's *Lives of the Poets* as well as his own antiquarian works, which included *Literary Anecdotes of the Eighteenth Century*, *Progresses and Public Processions of Queen Elizabeth I* and *The Progresses Processions and Magnificent Festivities of King James I*, which remain invaluable to Tudor and Stuart studies. Nichols and Richard Gough developed a close, collaborative friendship and Gough became the magazine's reviews editor.

The *Gents Mag* or *The Gentleman*, as it was known, was the hub of the antiquaries' world and its forum. Jonathan Oldbuck is typically proud of having published in it an article which 'attracted considerable notice at the time ... upon the inscription of Oelia Lelia'.[42] The sociability of the Nichols's milieu was especially welcome in the last years of the eighteenth century, when the Society of Antiquaries was languishing. At meetings, 'scarce a dozen persons' could be found to listen to someone 'droning over a dull paper ... about Roman antiquities in the North'.[43] This complaint was made by Gough. He was the director, yet even he was so bored that he 'adjourned to ... Dick's Coffee-house'.[44] Like many antiquaries over these years, he kept faith with the Society for the sake of its history and tradition, while pursuing his own researches outside it. The fellows' lack of intellectual enterprise was accompanied by depressing self-absorption. As the peppery Francis Douce (1757–1834), annotator of Shakespeare and scholar of the Dance of Death, complained: 'the election of officers at the Society of Antiquaries ... has always been regarded as a matter of more consequence & made more of among the members than any other subject of discussion for which that Society was more immediately instituted.'[45] Its preoccupation with its own affairs was compounded by the Antiquaries' testy relations with the Royal Society. In 1780 both bodies had moved, along with the Royal Academy, to Somerset House in the Strand. Membership overlapped between the three societies, but especially between the Antiquaries and the Royal Society, who shared a third of their members. Joseph Banks (1743–1820), the polymathic botanist, was simultaneously President of the Royal Society and a long-standing member of the Council of the Society of Antiquaries.

Unfortunately, intimacy did not make for harmony. There was much wrangling over the allocation of premises and the support of rival candidates for office. There was also a suspicion among the Antiquaries that the Royal Society would like to take them over and, as Gough put it, make them 'dependent upon the RS, as Holland is on France'; he saw Banks, 'a Botanist', as an interloper, the villainous mastermind behind the plot.[46] This bickering added to an atmosphere of small-mindedness and a reduction in active members. Gough's successor John Gage found a no more lively state of affairs and his friend Henry Ellis, who became secretary, confided to him:

> The truth, as you must know, is, that there is scarcely a Thursday evening upon which one or another of our members does not promise me a communication for the Society: and not one in ten redeems his promise at the time he names for the production of his Paper. The main readings for four successive evenings of our present session have been provided by myself (not as *Secretary* but) out of zeal for the Society, which must otherwise have had blank sittings, in consequence of these very disappointments.[47]

Material sent for cataloguing could disappear forever in the library, 'that tomb of the Capulets'.[48] The Society did make notable contributions to antiquarian studies in these years. Most importantly, it sponsored a series of engravings based on John Carter's drawings of the English cathedrals and it commissioned Stothard's study of the Bayeux Tapestry. It was forward-looking, too, in providing cheap publications on Anglo-Saxon. Despite which, overall 'its meetings were frequently extremely dull ... and their dullness was widely recognised'; thus the Society dozed on while a golden age of antiquarianism flourished beyond its walls.[49]

Two entries from Madden's journal in January and February 1833 reflect the marginal role of the Society in the broader and more agreeable milieu in which the metropolitan antiquary might move between learned societies, proof-reading at the offices of *The Gentleman's Magazine* in Parliament Street and visiting the homes of friends and the Athenaeum in Pall Mall. Founded in 1824 for those who enjoyed 'the life of the mind', the Athenaeum was the antiquaries' preferred club. Dawson Turner and Hudson Gurney were both members and it was overall a more middle-class institution than the older gentleman's clubs, where social standing mattered more and the life of the mind much less:[50]

> Thursday 28. Sir Thomas Phillipps surprised me this afternoon by his appearance. We went together to Nichols, 23 Parl. St. to settle the remaining sheets of the *Collecteana* & dined together at the Athenaeum. We afterwards went to the Antiqus. & Royal Societies. At the latter was exhibited an extraordinary fat boy, eleven yrs 10 months old, the son of a miller in Lincolnshire, who had something of this appearance [two ink drawings front and back]. The face was that of a man of 25.
> Saturday 16. Mr Gurney gives on Monday a large dinner party to the members of the Antiqs Society interested about Saxon literature – and on Friday Miss Gurney gives a Ball, to both of which I am invited.[51]

Amid this congenial round of shared ideas and interests there were inevitably less happy scenes of rivalry, rows and other examples of bitchiferousness. John Carter's engagement as draughtsman to the Society of Antiquaries was punctuated by frequent disputes, leading on one occasion to an actual fight in the secretary's office. Carter's friend the Catholic bishop John Milner made a serious attempt to get his fellow Catholic John Lingard's *History* put on the papal Index of forbidden books, and Thomas Phillipps did not continue on such warm terms with Madden after he wrote to Madden's son: 'will you tell your Papa I congratulate him on finishing Wicliff, which was a waste of his labour.'[52] 'Wicliff' was Madden's magnum opus, a 'definitive' edition of the first Bible in English which had taken more than twenty years to complete.[53] 'Such is his opinion', Madden fulminated to his journal, 'of the importance of publishing the earliest complete vernacular version of the Scriptures! But what is his opinion worth? Just nothing.'[54]

Among the most disputatious was Joseph Ritson (1752–1803). Ritson, who made the first and still the fullest collection of the Robin Hood stories and legends, was a perceptive Shakespearean critic and an example of a thin but vigorous strain among antiquaries in that he was both a Jacobite and a Jacobin. Unfortunately, almost nothing could persuade him to gather his thoughts for publication except an urgent desire to attack a fellow antiquary. His polemical career began in 1782 with *Observations on the Three First Volumes of the 'History of English Poetry'*, an onslaught on the work of the well-respected literary scholar and antiquary Thomas Warton, in which Ritson accused Warton of 'ignorance, plagiarism, and ... literary fraud'.[55] It was by no means an isolated instance of antiquaries' private quarrels spilling into print. Frederick Mackenzie, one of the artists trained by John Britton to illustrate his works, managed to smuggle into an illustration of the stained glass in Lichfield Cathedral a 'confused' inscription which, Britton noticed only too late, read: 'a fine drawing spoilt by John Britton'.[56] Britton retaliated with a special wrapper printed for the second part of the *History of Lichfield Cathedral* on which he set out his 'disappointments, from Draftsmen and Engravers' in furious italics, promising the subscribers, and threatening the mutinous illustrators, that in future, with a *'number of young Artists now coming forward ...* there will be more *competitors for fame and employment'*, so that 'Publishers will be *served* with greater promptitude and on more *moderate terms.'*[57]

THE ANTIQUARIAN TRADE

As Britton's difficulties with artists suggest, money was a perennial problem for the antiquaries. Publication was expensive. Some antiquaries maintained the tradition of simply amassing material. What was said of the expert on medieval brasses, Craven Ord (c.1755–1832), that 'He was a purposeful and energetic student of history whose works are mainly to be found in other men's books,' might be said of a number of his contemporaries.[58] For most antiquaries, however, publication was essential. It was the principal way in which they could gain a reputation and earn a living. Gough was comparatively wealthy, having inherited estates from both his merchant father and from a mother who was the daughter of prosperous London brewer, but he too noted that it was not 'easy to express what difficulties are in the way of publication ... in these dear times'.[59] The difficulties were compounded for an illustrated book, and illustrated books were increasingly in demand. A topographical work was expected to have a good number of plates and most antiquarian subjects, from architecture to armour, benefited from illustration. Many skills were involved. Authors, artists, engravers (on whose abilities much depended), printers and booksellers all had to make a living and so publications needed sponsors. Gough used his wealth to support other antiquaries' efforts, notably those of the indigent John Carter. More often, however, patronage had to be found piecemeal, sometimes for an individual plate which would appear suitably dedicated. Most major works were published by subscription and the patience of the subscribers, who put money up in advance, was sometimes sorely tried. While few would admit, as Johnson did, when asked to acknowledge the subscribers to his *Lives of the Poets*, that he couldn't because he had spent all the money and lost all the names, similar situations often arose. It was not uncommon for the parts or 'numbers' to appear late – four years late in the case of A. C. Pugin's *Examples of Gothic Architecture* – or for the whole work to fall short of the initial proposal. Britton made a characteristically self-serving semi-apology to the disappointed sponsors of his *History of Christian Architecture* in which he managed to turn an admission that his prospectus had been a fraud into a poignant apologia: 'At its commencement I promised more than has been, or ever could be well performed; and have consequently given umbrage to some persons whom I would gladly have secured as friends. I have, however, deceived myself much more than others.'[60]

Those who tried to go it alone were often fated to encounter the difficulties retailed by the Revd John Docwra Parry, whose *Historical and Descriptive Account of the Coast of Sussex*, after a respectful dedication to William IV, breaks out into a litany of complaint that, having worked 'under every possible discouragement and want of support', it was 'not easy in practice, however it be recommended in theory, to speak with perfect impartiality and good temper'.[61] His Preface is remarkably short on Christian charity and concludes by explaining that 'this volume has been executed in the most unshrinking style of expense, and has actually cost a considerable sum'.[62]

One problem was the number of copies that publishers were obliged to donate to the copyright libraries. Britton was energetic in campaigning to improve the position of publishers and authors, and his 1814 pamphlet *The Rights of Literature* took up the cudgels against Cambridge University, which was suing a printer for failing to provide copies of Samuel Heywood's *A Vindication of Mr Fox's History of the Early Part of the Reign of James the Second*. Britton argued that the legal requirement to provide the principal libraries with 'eleven copies, or complete sets of every new publication, gratis' was 'arbitrary, unjust, and impolitic'.[63] For an illustrated book the cost could be crippling. Britton and others took to publishing the text and plates separately, arguing that only the letterpress need be given to the libraries. Britton was also active in the campaign for improved copyright protection, which was extended in 1842 by fourteen years.

Before publication, however, there had to be research, and whatever aspersions were cast on the antiquaries' efforts, by posterity and by each other, they were all, even the Sobieski Stuarts, in their various ways assiduous. Empirical enquiry had been the antiquarian method since Aubrey's day, and comparative studies made 'on the spott' remained the essence of Romantic antiquarianism, especially in what became its principal subject in these years, the history and chronology of medieval architecture. The great range of professional and occupational backgrounds from which the antiquaries came brought many disciplines to bear on their studies. Thomas Rickman (1776–1841), the Quaker corn factor who became an architect and made the first reliable stylistic analysis of Gothic architecture, used his business experience to analyse and tabulate individual features. Dawson Turner, a friend of Joseph Banks, was one of a number of antiquaries whose first interest was botany. He arranged his autographs and architectural specimens into the groups and sub-groups of the natural historian. Gage was a keen student of burial rites and funerary urns, an interest in which Lingard, with whom he shared many of his thoughts and questions, declined to involve himself, having mixed feelings about his friend's 'resurrectionist' activities.[64] Gage applied instead to Michael Faraday (1791–1867), who, in February 1832, produced an 'account of the antique matters committed to my charge for chemical examination' by Gage and reported that

> . . . in regard to your question whether [the urn] has the appearance of having been heated, I must state, though with great deference, that I do

not think it has. All the carbonate & oxide of copper which encrusts it, may have been easily formed by the joint action of time, water, and air; and if it had been subjected to the same heat as that which the bones accompanying it have borne, I think it would have been melted, or at least oxidized so violently and suddenly upon the surface, as to have taken away from the distinctness of the impression.[65]

Concluding his observations on Gage's haul, Faraday posited a theory: 'So [is] it at all likely that any of the viscera or other parts of the body, have been introduced & the fat poured in with it, or upon it? The decay of such parts would account for the cavernous form of the fat & the black carbonaceous matter.'[66]

In this age before the 'two cultures', antiquaries saw no barrier to the pragmatic application of the latest and most useful methods of 'scientific' investigation to their own material. As Turner moved seamlessly from plants to buildings, so other antiquaries collaborated with geologists, pioneers in a newly important field of enquiry, who could identify the stone used in medieval buildings. The industrial potter Josiah Wedgwood and the engineer Thomas Telford were both fellows of the Society of Antiquaries. Even as we pass further along our notional spectrum, from fact to fiction, research and evidence remain important. Walter Scott, who regarded his novels as 'illustrations of historical truths', surrounded, indeed all but suffocated them in the final *Magnum Opus* edition with as many notes as the densest scholarly treatise.[67] The sadness of the Sobieski Stuarts' career, which eventually imploded under the strain of their pretensions and inventions, is that they were gifted and methodical when they chose to be. Their surviving archives bear poignant witness to years of solid research undertaken when it was too late for any reputable publisher to touch it.

There were considerable practical difficulties in working from primary sources 'on the spott' in the late-Georgian and early Victorian decades. The requisite comparisons for establishing dates or styles could be made only by eye or by accurate drawing. Antiquaries needed strong physical and mental constitutions and an acute visual memory. Travel, though laborious, particularly before the railway network spread, was essential and antiquarian expeditions had peculiar complications.

Craven Ord's brass-rubbings required large sheets of French paper which had to be kept damp in a case he had specially made for the purpose. He also carried 'a supply of printer's ink, some lengths of cloth, and an abundance of rags'.[68] Britton and Brayley, who in 1801 began their county-by-county study of architectural antiquities, struggled on by horse and donkey, carrying equipment for drawing and measuring into the remotest corners of England and Wales, as they worked their way alphabetically from Bedfordshire to Yorkshire. Mrs Rickman fell into a church vault but survived, unlike Charles Stothard, who was killed when his ladder collapsed as he was drawing a window in Bere Ferrers church in Devon.

A lost bag could mean disaster. The antiquarian artist and architect John Chessell Buckler (1793–1894) made a long expedition to Normandy, drawing medieval buildings, measuring ground plans and copying details, some 'at a dizzy height', only to lose his luggage on his return.[69] With it went:

> the whole of my manuscript notes with which were interspersed a hundred details of mouldings, ornaments, plans etc very useful, & more intelligible than the most laboured descriptions. The elevation of the N side of the chapel in the castle at Caen, the elegant chimney at St Lo, the chimney at Bayeux ... To these I might add many sketches of inferior value & to my mss I must add about 50 pages which I had composed with great care since my return chiefly upon the Elder architecture of Normandy.

Buckler concluded despondently: 'my loss has deprived me of all the interest I once felt in the subject'.[70]

Even so simple an act as lending someone a book could be difficult. Postage was expensive and intermediaries sometimes unreliable. In May 1835, Gage in Suffolk was still waiting for some books that Lingard had sent back from Lancashire six months earlier. 'I gave them to Mr Coulston (the bank manager),' Lingard explained, 'who was going to London, but who, as he did not go, entrusted them to the care of a very respectable man, a Mr Thornton, cabinet maker at Lancaster. He took them promising to deliver them in person. He is not at present in Lancaster, otherwise I should have enquired of him. But I shall do so the moment of his return.'[71]

Comparative studies required access to artefacts, and while many antiquaries were not collectors per se, in some cases the only way to study an object was to buy it or to obtain possession by some other more or less legitimate means. There were mixed feelings among antiquaries about the makers of collections. Frederic Madden had 'great contempt for this spirit . . . of collecting' by people who often mistreated or damaged their acquisitions, and in particular the 'private collectors of mss.' who kept their material to themselves. 'They are all genuine dogs in the manger.'[72] Yet others, like Madden's erstwhile friend Phillipps, Francis Douce and the expert on armour Samuel Rush Meyrick, were making the first collections in their own particular areas of 'national antiquities', gathering and organizing material that would not find a place in public museums until the High Victorian years. In the meantime, comparison required that rare objects be transported. Phillipps was understandably 'very nervous when *Uniques* travel by coaches'.[73] But Meyrick was more sanguine, sending some medieval ivories to Douce in London with a request to 'return them by the Gloucester mail'.[74] The railway in due course made transport faster, though not necessarily more secure. When it came within reach of Gage's Suffolk home, a friend drew a cartoon showing him driving an engine pulling carriages marked 'antiquities of Hengrave' with miscellaneous curiosities sticking out in all directions.[75]

There were human as well as practical obstacles. At Gloucester, Carter, who was making drawings of the cathedral, found that everyone was busy getting ready for the music festival and threw 'much hindrance' in his way, while the 'dignitaries' ignored him.[76] The draughtsman's lot was often to be obstructed and to find himself caught between the demands of his employer and the constraints he found on site. Working all day amid such difficulties, Carter was 'generally so exhausted in the evening' that he was glad to 'hurry to bed'.[77] Librarians were not always the antiquaries' friends. The young Nicholas Wiseman, later to become the first English cardinal since the Reformation, who was trying to penetrate the Marini Library in Rome, complained bitterly about Marini, a 'Cerberus' who would not let him in, even when he had a note from the Pope.[78] Wiseman was trying to look up various things for Gage and Lingard.

Mutual support of this kind was the lifeblood of international antiquarian efforts. Research on the Continent often depended on finding a collaborator in the right place at the right time and Lingard's connections with a network of Catholic priests served him well. He used them to penetrate the Simancas archives of the Spanish state, the first English historian to do so, getting Alexander Cameron, Rector of the Scots College at Valladolid, to work on his behalf. Research abroad had its own hazards, especially in France in the years of intermittent war and revolution. Thomas Rickman and Dawson Turner were both arrested in the course of their travels; indeed, it happened so often to Turner that he barely referred to it after a while. Lingard lost one of his more useful connections in Paris in the Revolution of 1830: 'The three days of July came, he fled & is gone to America, so that he was prevented from reading the despatches,' Lingard noted with exasperation. While at Calais Lord Aberdeen, later President of the Society of Antiquaries, had his trousers confiscated, for reasons that will become apparent.[79]

3

The Antiquarian Landscape:
Georgian

Henry the 8th: The Crimes & Cruelties of this Prince, were
too numerous to be mentioned ... & nothing can be said in
his vindication, but that his abolishing Religious Houses &
leaving them to the ruinous depredations of time has been of
infinite use to the landscape of England.

Jane Austen, The History of England from the
reign of Henry the 4th to the death of Charles
the 1st, By a partial, prejudiced,
& ignorant Historian, *1791*

In 1789 the antiquarian world was for the most part going about its
business as usual. In London the Society of Antiquaries heard from
the Revd James Douglas about some chicken bones he had found at a
Roman burial site near Canterbury. John Britton, who was working
as a porter at the Jerusalem Tavern in Clerkenwell, met Edward Brayley in a local bookshop and so laid the foundation for one of the most
productive of antiquarian partnerships. Gilbert White published *The
Natural History and Antiquities of Selborne,* never afterwards out of
print, and Francis Grose was touring Scotland, noting down dialect
words by day and drinking with Burns by night. Meanwhile, in Winchester, William Cave and his son, another William, were repainting
King Arthur's Round Table, which had hung in the Great Hall of the
castle since 1463, a job that satisfied the county judiciary if it somewhat hampered the efforts of later historians. The draughtsman John
Carter was also in Winchester, visiting his friend John Milner and
taking the opportunity to inspect the famous table at close quarters.

That summer Carter was going through one of his periodic estrangements from the Society of Antiquaries and so Richard Gough was obliged to send another draughtsman, Jacob Schnebbelie, to Salisbury to find out what was going on at the cathedral. The Bishop, Shute Barrington, had brought in James Wyatt (1746–1813), one of the most eminent architects of the day, to carry out a scheme of 'improvement'. Improvement was not the same as restoration, and from this distance in time it perhaps requires an effort of imagination to understand the Georgians' confidence in their own taste. The intention was to make the medieval cathedral a better building, more light, bright, symmetrical, smooth and generally agreeable to Georgian ideals of neo-Classical good taste. Wyatt wanted a clear view from one end of the cathedral to the other, and to create it he removed medieval screens and some of the medieval stained glass. Floors were lowered and tombs, including that of St Osmund, founder of the first cathedral in the eleventh century, were dismantled or moved to ensure internal sightlines. Externally Wyatt demolished what remained of the free-standing medieval bell tower (one of the last to survive). By the time Schnebbelie arrived on 24 August, the fifteenth-century Hungerford Chantry Chapel had gone. Hungerford's body had just been exhumed and Schnebbelie, like a good antiquary, sent Gough a detailed description: 'the head ... reclined to the left shoulder the hand [laid [a]cross his middle ... it was very dry and not the least smell the skeleton was very intire except the right foot.'[1] Bishop Barrington was present at the exhumation and assured Schnebbelie that he was 'a lover of antiquities and wish[ed] to preserve them as much as possible', adding that in this case it had not been possible.[2] Nor, it transpired, would it be possible to save the thirteenth-century ceiling paintings in the choir. It was 'intirely opposite'[3] to Wyatt's plan of making the whole interior one harmonious colour to leave these 'wretched daubings', as another supporter of the improvements called them, with their 'uncouth, disproportioned figures' on view.[4]

Wyatt himself was elusive, but when Schnebbelie caught up with him he confirmed that 'the whole ceiling of the choir would be made of one uniform colour and all the painting thereon totally destroyed'.[5] Furthermore, the cathedral would be closed in two weeks' time and would not reopen until the work was finished. Admittance would be granted only with Wyatt's permission, which he seemed unlikely to give to troublesome antiquaries. Gough wrote to Schnebbelie telling him to draw the paintings as fully as possible in the time available, which he did. It is thanks to him that anything is known of them, for within weeks they had vanished. But that was not the end of the matter. As reviews editor of *The Gentleman's Magazine*, Gough had other resources. He used its pages to launch an attack on Wyatt's improvements that raised much larger questions. It took the form of a letter to 'Sylvanus Urban', the editorial persona, and made ominous use of the past tense:

> I know no cathedral in Great Britain in which the imagination and taste of an Antiquary might have been indulged with more extent and advantage, than that of SALISBURY. The architecture was of the boldest and lightest style ... the execution equal to its situation, and the lofty spire the wonder of the kingdom ... Such was Salisbury cathedral till the middle of the present century.
>
> This year has completed the plan, which, under pretence of giving uniformity to the building, by laying the Lady Chapel into the choir, already of a length adapted to every purpose, has removed the monuments from the chapel ... I am sensible that the profession of the Antiquary is an object of the contempt and obloquy of modern connoisseurs; but I have the pleasure to inform you, Mr Urban, and you may proclaim it to the world at large, that what is doing to this fabric, and what be *done away* from it, shall live as long as printing or engraving can contribute to its immortality.[6]

Gough's letter marked the beginning of a revolution in attitudes to the material past. He had laid the groundwork for it the year before with another open letter in which he argued for the preservation of 'monuments of antiquity' in some systematic way, by establishing 'a select committee, for the express purpose of preserving from mutilation ... the remains of ancient edifices'.[7] It was the first preservationist manifesto. Gough's suggestion was so far in advance of public opinion that it was almost exactly a century before the Ancient Monuments Protection Act struggled into law in 1882. Gough argued that historic buildings were 'national objects' that should be preserved whether or not they were useful or attractive to the present, because they were of historical value, offering insights into the ways of life and the 'men and manners' of the past.[8] His proposal was not only a landmark in the changing attitudes to the past, it marked a change in the nature of antiquarianism itself. Until now the antiquaries' role was principally to record objects and buildings. However much they regretted those that were lost, they rarely saw it as their place to try to preserve them. Indeed, as Gough pointed out, sometimes they inadvertently made things worse. If a building had been recorded, it could be said to have been preserved. ' "The corporation intend to blow up the castle: but it is engraved" ... Conversations of this nature many people have heard.'[9] With his two open letters Gough challenged his fellow antiquaries to adopt a new, active role in their engagement with their material.

The forces ranged against Gough and his allies, Milner, Carter, Nichols and a few others, were daunting. Bishop Barrington was the son of a viscount and son-in-law of a duke. When a book was opened at Salisbury for subscriptions to the improvements, the gentleman described as 'from Berkshire' who gave £1,000 was George III.[10] Wyatt was Deputy Surveyor to the Office of Woods and Forests, which made him, in effect, a state architect. This union of Church, Crown and architectural establishment was a formidable triumvirate, formidable and not unrepresentative. While history has not been on their side in this case, these powerful men were not exceptional in their views, nor unsophisticated. Barrington was a man of compassion, who used his considerable wealth to support William Wilberforce's anti-slavery campaign. The king built up one of the finest libraries ever created by a single individual, while Wyatt, though vain, ambitious and arrogant, was, at his best, a gifted architect. The Salisbury improvements were a natural product of the established order of taste and of society.

It would be a mistake to make too much of the parallels between events in Wiltshire in the summer of 1789 and those taking place at the same time in France. Gough and his allies cannot be cast as antiquarian *sans-culottes*, yet the comparison is not facile. The challenge to the certainties of Enlightenment ideals and the established hierarchies of taste was bold and its ultimate success was due in part to the moral and intellectual shock that the French Revolution delivered to the British. Few people, perhaps, went so far as the Earl of Exeter, who, *The Gentleman's Magazine* reported, immediately removed from his library and destroyed the works of Voltaire, Rousseau and that 'grand arsenal of impiety' the *Encylopédie*, but many certainties were shaken.[11] Edmund Burke's *Reflections on the Revolution in France* of 1790 is only the most celebrated change of mind. The idea of history as a narrative of progress gave way to a more thoughtful and respectful view of the past and of its remains. Once France declared war on Britain in 1793, the 'modern connoisseurs' could no longer take a Continental Grand Tour. They and others of more modest means began to travel through their native landscape, among the ruins of the Dissolution and the Civil Wars. Gradually they came to see them not only as eye-catchers 'of infinite use' as scenery, but also, in Gough's terms, as national monuments redolent of 'the mode of life' of the past.[12] By studying the remains of history, as Charles Stothard wrote, 'we live in other ages than our own', and while the present was so troubling this was an attractive prospect.[13]

THE TREASURES OF TIME LIE HIGH

The deep past still lay as near the surface of the late-Georgian landscape as it had when Thomas Browne wrote *Urn-Burial*.[14] An antiquary need not look far for material, and in the summer of 1811 Charles Stothard took his sketchbook and set off from London in the general direction of Canterbury. At Richborough he inspected the remains of the fort and was 'agreeably surprised to find that I had under-rated it, the size and extent of its walls'.[15] Richborough now belongs to English Heritage and is 'perhaps the most symbolically important of all Roman sites in Britain', yet Stothard had it to himself – indeed, he complained of loneliness on his travels.[16] One warm Sunday he walked from Canterbury 'through woods and hop-grounds' to Reculver and the nearby Roman fort Regulbium, where he passed the time before dinner in exploring the beach. He found it:

> Strewed with Roman brick, tiles, broken pottery, etc etc. In one place
> two or three immense fragments of the Roman wall thrown down on

the sands; in another a part of it jutting out four or five yards over its foundation, supported entirely by the wonderful strength of its cement. In the cliffs . . . are to be seen human bones lying in strata for a considerable length. These I cannot suppose to be Roman, as we know they never buried the dead within their walls; so that we may conclude them to be the bones of some of the primitive Christians. Their proximity to the church, I think, favours this idea. I picked up on the shore two or three pieces of scored tile, and the best half of a ring of brass, – a green stone, a piece of glass yet remaining set in it, for an impression of which look to the seal of this, and see if you can make out what it originally represented. I have turned and twisted it all ways, but to no purpose.[17]

Stothard was writing to his future brother-in-law and fellow antiquary Alfred Kempe, who would have had an opinion on the meaning of the mysterious stone. Stothard came home loaded with curiosities: a Roman vessel he found on the beach, 'the greater part of the lid of a vessel of brass, buckles, coins and other things, of the use of which I am ignorant'.[18] As the landscape gave up its treasures, so history was coming, almost literally, into focus. Stothard's particular interest was sepulchral monuments, and in the church at Richborough he found one which 'At first sight . . . appeared an unintelligible mass, shewing nothing but that it was a human form.' Unless a medieval tomb chest was in the way of an eminent architect, the Georgians would rarely destroy it, but nor did they take much interest in it. 'On a closer inspection' Stothard found this one 'was buried in white-wash, in some places more than a quarter of an inch in thickness . . . I set to work with my penknife and nail-brush, to clear it from its coating. After a four hours' job, I was well recompensed in that I discovered. The figure from its armour, seemed to be of the time of Edward II.'[19] Over the decades, as Stothard and his fellow antiquaries carefully brushed and scraped away at the centuries of indifference, the past began to emerge.

While history was becoming ever more visible in the landscape, the present was also making its mark. In England the years between 1790 and 1815 saw one of the most intensive periods of enclosure. Private Acts of Parliament curtailed or abolished rights of access to common land, while here and there the first signs of industrialization, coal mines and iron foundries began to appear. Reviewing White's *The Natural History and Antiquities of Selborne*, *The Gentleman's Magazine* welcomed it as an inducement to 'so rational an employment . . . as the study of nature and antiquities' at a time when 'contemplative persons see with regret the country more deserted every day'.[20] Out of these combined forces came changes not only in the way the landscape looked, but in the way that it was seen. In Herefordshire, Richard Payne Knight (1751–1824), whose family fortune had been made by his ironmaster grandfather from the Bringewood Forge by the banks of the River Teme, began to fear for the 'wild obscurity and rude neglect' of the countryside of his youth.[21] His neighbour and fellow Whig squire Uvedale Price (1747–1829) also deplored the sweeping-away of cottages deemed 'unsightly' in the interests of 'mere extent . . . and dreary selfish pride'.[22] Knight and Price, with Humphry Repton (1752–1818), the first person to call himself a 'landscape gardener', developed between them the theory of the Picturesque, an idea first propounded by the Revd William Gilpin in his *Observations on the River Wye* of 1782. Gilpin's somewhat anodyne prescription for pleasing scenery, such as would be admired in a picture, was transformed by Knight, Price and Repton between 1794 and 1795 in three books which developed the Picturesque into a theory of perception, sometimes held to be 'England's major contribution to the culture of the eighteenth century'.[23] Nikolaus Pevsner, compelled into anachronism, could find no better word for it than 'psychoanalytical'.[24] This mature, Romantic Picturesque was conceived as both a riposte and a complement to Burke's categories of aesthetic experience, the Sublime and the Beautiful. The Picturesque was an intermediate state, one of mingled pleasure and melancholy, its season was autumn, its time of day twilight, its subject matter local and particular. 'A picturesque eye looks coldly', Price wrote, 'on what is very generally admired, and discovers a thousand interesting objects where a common eye sees nothing but ruts and rubbish.'[25]

The Picturesque was outdoor Romanticism. It delighted in the same cottages and Gothic ruins which appealed to the poets and interested the antiquaries. It despised artificiality. Most importantly, it questioned the nature of aesthetic experience. While Knight and Price took issue with Burke's argument that certain intrinsic qualities in an object could be guaranteed to produce a particular response, they argued that Hume went too far in suggesting that aesthetic experience was 'merely in the mind'.[26] Perception, Knight argued, occurred, like the Picturesque itself, as an intermediate experience, the exchange between object and subject, a product of what the eye perceives and what the mind brings to it by way of association, memory and imagination. Over time the Picturesque became clichéd. It was laughed at by everyone from Rowlandson to Thackeray, but the satire only worked because the theory was so widely understood. The sensibility of at least two generations was saturated in it. It made possible the great flowering of English watercolour painting at the turn of the century. Girtin, Cotman, Turner and many dozens of less well-known artists painted landscapes dotted with ruins, which were calculated to evoke states of mind through light and weather, the grandeur of storms and sunsets, the particularity of a lone cloud, the dozen shades of green in the leaves of a single tree. The poets of the Picturesque were Wordsworth and, above all, Keats, whose 'Ode to Autumn' is almost certainly indebted to his reading of Uvedale Price.[27] Its popularizers were, very often, the antiquaries, and none more so than John Britton.

In 1798 Britton, who had given up his job at the Jerusalem Tavern for a literary career, only to endure 'seven years of vicissitudes, privations, and hardships ... occasionally relieved by occupations which produced a bare livelihood', was casting about for a subject that might appeal to a wider audience.[28] He had had an offer from a publisher for a book about Wiltshire, his native county, and he started to plough through the standard antiquarian texts, which he found 'dull and uninviting'.[29] It was the literature of the Picturesque that awoke his enthusiasm, starting with *A Walk Through Wales, in August 1797*, by the Revd Richard Warner. This immensely successful book rapidly went through four editions and generated the unimaginatively titled sequel, *A Second Walk Through Wales in August and September 1798*. Britton saw in it a way of writing about places unencumbered by 'technical terms ... dull details of genealogy, manorial and parochial history, and useless lists of rectors and vicars'.[30] He went on to read Gilpin and the works of Knight, Price and Repton. When, as was perhaps inevitable, the latter three began to disagree in print, Britton, who was tireless and fearless in his desire to get on socially and professionally, decided to go and visit all the 'literary belligerents' in person. The 'pedestrian tour' he made in the summer of 1798 was the first of many strenuous journeys undertaken for the production of books that combined popular Picturesque topography with architectural antiquarianism.[31] It was a project that would occupy him for the rest of his life.

In time, like his audience, Britton became more demanding. Six years after this first tour he looked back on his earlier self as a mere 'moonraker' who in his ignorance 'was ... more to be pitied than despised'.[32] The details came to seem less dull, but the anecdotes were still of interest and sensibility was of the essence. In 1801 he and Brayley embarked on their first major joint effort, the twenty-five-volume *Beauties of England and Wales*. The publishers, Vernor and Hood, commissioned it as a typical cut-and-paste compilation of 'fine seats, picturesque scenery &c' gathered from secondary sources.[33] The authors, however, were more ambitious, insisting on the 'necessity of visiting places, in order to describe them'.[34] They were also set on including accounts of 'antiquities' amid the seats and scenery. The battle with their editors lasted decades, but in the long run, as Britton did not hesitate to point out, he was justified in his estimate of the developing market.

THE PURSUIT OF THE GOTHIC

William Gilpin notoriously suggested that the ruins of Tintern Abbey could be improved by 'a mallet judiciously used'.[35] The next generation saw in the architecture of the Middle Ages something more than an assortment of ornamental landscape features, but it did not begin to understand it. Price, whose own taste was Classical, could admire the effects of Gothic, the 'dim and discoloured light diffused ... through unequal varieties of space, divided but not separated', which created an atmosphere that led the eye and the mind beyond the immediately visible.[36] He thought King's College Chapel, Cambridge 'more Christian, more grand' than any other building 'ancient or modern', but like many of his contemporaries he also thought that medieval architecture had 'no rules – no proportions – and consequently no definitions'.[37]

The attempt to counter this view of Gothic was one of the most energetic antiquarian projects of the late-Georgian years. The establishment of a chronology, terminology and structural analysis of medieval architecture was not only an object of curiosity, it was essential to the preservation campaign to show that Gothic buildings were more than random heaps of detail. Aubrey had been the pioneer. 'No person', as Britton noted, had 'preceded him in attempting to distinguish the successive changes, in style and decoration', and 'by observing architectural features and details' establish a date for a building.[38] Unfortunately, by the end of another century few had succeeded him either. The antiquaries now made up for lost time. While Aubrey had relied chiefly on comparisons of window tracery, most of those who considered the subject in the later Georgian decades thought that the key feature was the pointed arch, the element in which the Gothic differs most obviously from the Classical. The quest for its origin became something of an obsession, in pursuit of which much ink was spilled, many theories were propounded and, inevitably, many quarrels carried on. This is not the place for a blow-by-blow account of the long and often tedious quest; what matters is the principal questions that were asked and how they were answered.

The first requirement was to settle the terminology, beginning with the word 'Gothic' itself, originally intended as a disparaging term, suggesting the perceived crudeness of medieval art. Carter was one of those determined to ban the word, this 'rag of prejudice, this scum of innovation'.[39] Alternatives were suggested. Britton proposed 'Christian', his friend the Lincoln architect Edward Willson more accurately, but much more contentiously, suggested 'Catholic', while many people opted for 'pointed', but in the end Gothic stuck. It lost its pejorative connotations and the implication that it originated with the Visigoths, which would give it 'too early a date by a great many centuries', as Milner noted.[40] On the question of its origins, Milner and Carter were among those who believed that Gothic was English and felt too passionate a commitment to the idea to look objectively at the evidence. Christopher Wren's suggestion that it derived from Saracenic architecture and came to Europe with returning Crusaders was offensive to many more people who thought that, if not English, the Gothic was essentially Christian. Milner was dismissive, arguing that 'throughout all Syria, Arabia, etc there is not a gothic building to be discovered, except such as were raised by the Latin Christians'.[41] The debate rumbled on and has continued to the present day, when Wren's theory is thought to have been, essentially, accurate.[42] Milner and Carter, however, subscribed to the idea that the pointed arch derived from the interlaced arcading of the earlier round arch. In his *History . . . and Survey of the Antiquities of Winchester* Milner traced its origins to his beloved home city, to the cathedral and the twelfth-century Hospital of St Cross.

Meanwhile the Society of Antiquaries embarked on the first of its great contributions to the antiquarian achievements of the late Georgian years. Gough and his friend Henry Englefield (1752–1822), a vice-president of the Society, decided to commission sets of engravings of medieval buildings. Englefield was a member of the Society of Dilettanti, which published detailed studies of Classical architecture such as James Stuart and Nicholas Revett's *Antiquities of Athens*. This was the model for the Antiquaries' series, and the intention was to show that Gothic architecture was as much worth studying as Classical, that it merited equally fine and detailed plates and the same valued position in the gentleman's library. The series began in 1790 with the Chapel of St Stephen in the Palace of Westminster.[43] Founded by Edward I and altered by Edward III, St Stephen's had been England's Sainte-Chapelle, one of the glories of medieval Christendom, but the structure and its decoration had long been obscured by Wren's arrangements to accommodate the House of Commons, which had met there since the sixteenth century. John Carter, who was the chief draughtsman for the series, was obliged to crawl with a lantern behind the seventeenth-century panelling to make his drawings.

The Society then moved on to the medieval cathedrals, beginning with Exeter. The project met with frequent objections from fellows who complained that it was a waste of time and money to document buildings they regarded as formless and, significantly, tainted with 'popery'. That Englefield was another of the Catholic antiquaries no doubt added to suspicions. He and Gough pressed on. By 1797 Carter was at work in Durham. Here fate dictated he should encounter the antiquaries' old enemies, Bishop Barrington and James Wyatt. Wyatt had by now a reputation for 'improving' cathedrals. To the horror of the antiquaries, he had worked his way through Lichfield and Hereford and added further to their alarm with a recently completed report on Ely. His friend and patron Barrington had in the meantime become Bishop of Durham, and duly invited Wyatt in to advise on alterations. One of his proposals was to ensure better access to the west entrance of the cathedral by demolishing the chapel at that end, known as the Galilee Porch. Built in 1189 and now a World Heritage Site, it is the burial place of the Venerable Bede and one of the finest examples of Norman architecture in Europe. Its survival is largely due to Carter.

While he was drawing at Durham, Carter learned from the dean about the plan to destroy the Porch. After a furious argument in which Carter failed to change the dean's mind he came south again, having tipped off local friends to keep an eye on developments. Back in London he heard reports that the deed was done. At the next meeting of the Society of Antiquaries, on 29 June, he showed his drawings of the Galilee Porch to illustrate what had been 'lately destroyed by James Wyatt esq. architect'.[44] As it happened, Wyatt had been proposed for election to the Society and this was the meeting at which his election was to be put to the vote. The ballot was supposed by Wyatt's sponsors to be a formality. They were unpleasantly surprised, though perhaps in the circumstances they should not have been, when no fewer than eleven fellows blackballed Wyatt and he was 'declared ... to be *not* duly elected'.[45] The king was annoyed, Wyatt was humiliated, his sponsors were embarrassed. Another, more carefully organized ballot was held in December and Wyatt was duly elected. It transpired that Carter was misinformed: work to demolish the Galilee Porch had been stopped. Wyatt had, however, almost entirely demolished the Chapter House, an undeniable fact which he flatly denied.

Wyatt's ultimate election was a pyrrhic victory for his supporters. He never attended another meeting, but the Society was scarred by the row. Gough resigned as director. Milner – who had written a paper outlining the reasons why Wyatt should not be elected and had had it confiscated by the Society, which refused either to let Milner read it at the meeting or give it back to him – learned that several pro-Wyatt fellows had been going into 'booksellers shops and other places' and telling people that Milner's paper had been *'kicked out of the Society'* as insufficiently scholarly.[46] Infuriated, he published it as *A Dissertation on the Modern Style of Altering Antient Cathedrals, as Exemplified in the Cathedral of Salisbury*. Nichols printed it. From now on Gough, Nichols, Carter and Milner formed the nucleus of a new, interventionist school of architectural antiquarianism, working outside the Society through journalism, books and pamphlets as well as through the first conservation campaigns of the kind familiar today. The Antiquaries' journal, *Archaeologia*, bears little trace of the great debates and scholarly advances of the next decades; those are to be found in *The Gentleman's Magazine*, where, from 1798, Carter had a regular column. Under the sobriquet 'An Architect', he wrote a total of 212 campaigning, often vitriolic articles on the need to preserve historic buildings from the efforts of the 'modern architect'.

All this time, the search for the origin of the pointed arch went on. 'A subject of as much fruitless discussion as the ... identification of the Man in the Iron Mask', it generated a high proportion of heat to light.[47] Much of the heat came from Carter and Milner in their determination to claim Gothic for England. Milner's popular essay of 1802 on the subject of the 'Rise and Progress' of Gothic benefited from readers' patriotism at the time of the uneasy lull in hostilities that followed the Peace of Amiens. Carter was even more outspoken about 'the infernal dispensers of "liberty and equality"' across the Channel and the capacity of the Gothic to remind England of its heroic victories over 'perfidious France'.[48] Like many academic disputes, the argument raged on long after the facts had been established. While the origins of the pointed arch remain contested today, the site of its first use in Europe, the first emergence of what can be called Gothic architecture, was discovered in 1802 by George Whittington (1781–1807). A well-educated and well-connected young man, Whittington made a tour of France and Italy during the Peace of Amiens in 1802–3 and wrote a treatise, *An Historical Survey of the Ecclesiastical Antiquities of France; with a view to illustrate the rise and progress of Gothic architecture in Europe*, published in 1809. Whittington having died in 1807 at the age of twenty-six, the book was seen through the press by his friend and travelling companion the Earl of Aberdeen.

Whittington had analysed, by eye and by comparison with surviving documents, half a dozen of the most important Gothic churches of Paris, Rheims and Amiens and deduced that Gothic should properly be said to derive from Abbot Suger's alterations to the chevet of St-Denis in 1140, a conclusion that has been supported by all subsequent research.

Without Whittington to defend it, however, his discovery was crushed between opposing prejudices. His friend the earl, Byron's cousin 'Athenian' Aberdeen, was not an admirer of Gothic and his Preface made no attempt to disguise the fact. 'The subject is not in itself very generally interesting,' he wrote, discouragingly.[49] And while Whittington's friends could not bring themselves to admire Gothic, those who did admire it had no time for the likes of Whittington. A combination of inverse snobbery and the commitment to Gothic as a peculiar and unique product of English history and culture led Carter to savage the book as a work of 'Gallic scientific presumption', the 'mania of travelled prejudice' and 'blind delusion'.[50] Despite some more perceptive reviews, it was to be decades before Whittington got his due.[51] In the meantime, the antiquarian quest reached its wildest extreme with the Scottish antiquary Sir James Hall's *Essay on the Origin, History and Principles of Gothic Architecture*, which argued that it had developed from wickerwork. Milner brushed off the 'learned baronet' and his 'new and favourite system' in a single sarcastic footnote.[52]

Although Milner and Carter pursued the facts (albeit selectively), their attitude to the Gothic was infused with Romantic sensibility. Carter prefaced his works with engravings of imaginary scenes in which the buildings of the Middle Ages were restored and repopulated. The frontispiece to his *Specimens of the Ancient Sculpture and Painting* (1780–94) shows Edward III in Westminster Abbey 'on a progress', while a bishop ('whose dress is copied from a brass plate in the Abbey chancel at St Albans') points out an interesting royal monument.[53] The Romantic Picturesque, with its emphasis on sequential views, Price's 'unequal varieties of space, divided but not separated', tended always towards narrative. In attacking Wyatt's work Milner pointed out that by opening up the whole interior of Salisbury the effect was spoiled, eliminating just those varieties of space which allowed the mind to experience what Burke had called the 'artificial infinite'. For Milner the aesthetic was also the spiritual; his was a sacred Picturesque. The criterion 'by which we are to judge of the construction and alterations of Churches, and particularly of Gothic Cathedrals' was, he believed, 'as they are more or less calculated to impress the mind with a religious awe'.[54]

Together, Carter and Milner put their beliefs into practice by building a church themselves. St Peter's, Winchester was consecrated on 5 December 1792, just a year after the second Catholic Relief Act made it legal to build a Catholic parish church. It was not the first new Gothic church since the Middle Ages but, as Kenneth Clark observed, it was the first to be built from 'what we might call Gothic Revival motives'.[55] Those motives can be deduced from the relationship in which Milner placed his church to its surroundings, actual, spiritual and historic. It stood on a spot where, 'except during a few stormy intervals', there had always been a Catholic chapel.[56] It was approached literally through its historic origins, via a 'Saxon portal' which Milner had reconstructed after it had been removed 'by piecemeal, from the church of St Magdalen's hospital'.[57] Milner wanted to weave his church physically into the fabric of the past, to repair the wound of the penal years and elide the lost centuries since the Reformation. In his *History of Winchester* he placed the account of St Peter's at the end of the second volume, as a continuation of the 'Survey of Antiquities'. From a chronological point of view it belonged in Volume I, which covers the newest buildings. But for Milner his church was not new. It was like the cathedral and the Hospital of St Cross, a humble member of the same community of architecture whose fabric was imbued with the sacred power of the Gothic. Milner and Carter were not alone in their beliefs, and many more people, if they did not see medieval buildings as specifically Christian, believed them to be intrinsically spiritual. The 'twilight saints and dim emblazonings' of Gothic were taking on the character of a Romantic living symbol, the physical manifestation of a metaphysical reality.

On the question of taxonomy, the great breakthrough came in 1812 with the first version of Thomas Rickman's essay *An Attempt to Discriminate the Styles of Architecture in England, from the Conquest to the Reformation*. Rickman was a Quaker living in Liverpool. One of eleven children of a surgeon-apothecary, he grew up on slender means, destined for a medical career. Having found that he disliked medicine, he went into business as a corn factor. His friend, the polymath William Whewell, described him as 'a little, round, fat man, with short, thick legs, and a large head ... perpetually running from one side of the street to the other to peep into whatever catches his attention ... very good-humoured, and very intelligent and active'.[58] To his passionate interest in Gothic architecture Rickman brought a strong organizational intelligence supported by a powerful memory. He had no particular interest in the nationalist implications of Gothic or, for the moment, in its religious connotations. Unlike Milner, Rickman had no Latin to read the records. He had to rely on his eyes. It was in many ways an advantage. He categorized and analysed, compared mouldings, tracery, capitals and other details, noting which features occurred together and which were later additions. It no doubt came as a relief to his readers to learn that his essay was not 'a lengthy disquisition' on the origins of Gothic but a division of the periods of medieval architecture by date and characteristics which he developed into the phases still recognized today: Norman, Early English, Decorated and Perpendicular, the last his own coinage.[59]

Rickman's theory was first published in a popular journal, *Smith's Panorama of Science and Art*. By 1817 he had tested it under 'rigid scrutiny' and was, he told his friend and fellow antiquary Edward Blore (1787–1879), 'every day more & more strengthened in the conviction of my division of the stiles & the principles on which I have founded that division'.[60] In 1817 he brought his essay out in book form. It set a standard. 'I hope Sir James will not be offended,' Rickman wrote to Blore, who had drawn the whimsical frontispiece for Hall's book showing a basketwork cathedral set in a forest, 'but the more I consider it the more I am convinced that no man can be taught by wicker work alone or principally to make a window still less a moulding.'[61] The general opinion was with Rickman. No more was heard of basketwork and the *Attempt* went through five editions in Rickman's lifetime. His original terms, after some modification, were universally adopted and his assertion that his system was 'the only one which will stand the test of continued research' was justified.[62]

On the question of what constituted the best of Gothic, Rickman also offered no opinion. Carter and Milner held that it was the Decorated of the age of Edward III when, as Carter wrote, England 'arrived at its meridian' in 'the glorious display of architecture', which, he implied, had somehow helped to defeat the hated French at Crécy.[63] It was not necessary to take such an extreme nationalist view to concur with what came to be known as the 'biological fallacy'. A consensus emerged around the belief that, like a living creature, Gothic had grown out of the heaviness of the Norman or, in the coinage of William Gunn, Rector of Irstead in Norfolk, in 1819, the 'Romanesque', into the purity of Early English, blossoming, over more or less the biblical human lifespan of three score years and ten, into the glories of the Decorated, with its complex vaulting patterns, ogee arches and delicately elaborated window tracery, before succumbing to the influence of the Renaissance with the more orthogonal Perpendicular. Informed taste no longer found late-Gothic buildings such as King's College Chapel and Henry VII's Chapel at Westminster Abbey, with their symmetrical tracery and fan vaults, as admirable as those like Price, who judged by the criteria of Classical architecture, had done.

The year of Rickman's essay was a watershed. It saw the death of Carter and the beginning of a new phase in the discovery not only of the Gothic, but of the whole historic landscape. In London Henry Ellis, in collaboration with Bodley's librarian, Bulkeley Bandinel, in Oxford, was beginning work on the new edition of Dugdale's *Monasticon*. Ellis also produced an Introduction and Index to Domesday Book. The text had been available since the government published it in 1783, but was only now, with Ellis's academic apparatus, made usable. The war with France had ended in 1815, and while the country was far from peaceful or prosperous, it became possible to contemplate new building. Gradually, then more rapidly, as if the tracts and dissertations of the antiquaries and the landscapes of the watercolourists were manifesting in three dimensions, the country began to be dotted with new Gothic buildings. Some, like Strawberry Hill, or Wyatt's Fonthill Abbey, built for William Beckford, were still the individual creations of wealthy men and women, but increasingly they were villas of the more middling sort and the smaller country mansions. For a person wanting to commission such a modern Gothic dwelling there was, however, a difficulty about finding an architect.

The Georgians had no formal system of architectural training. The usual route into the profession was via a clerkship in an architectural office. An aspiring architect would study Classical proportions and orders, but would learn nothing about the Gothic. Yet the time had passed when a square Classical design could be simply Gothick-ed up with a few plaster crockets. The polite public were too well informed about medieval design and they despised the ignorance of their parents' generation. The only people who understood medieval buildings, who had measured and drawn them, calculated stresses and noted construction techniques, were the antiquaries, and so a new hybrid emerged, the antiquarian-architect.

Willson, Blore, J. C. Buckler and the Pugins, father and son, were among them, but it was Rickman who succeeded best in distinguishing himself equally in both fields. From studying historic buildings he moved on to repairing them and then to building new ones. His letters to Blore, who followed the same professional route, show how the strands of his working life were interwoven. He had been on a trip to Barnsley, where the churchwardens wanted him to examine their church: 'which I have done & condemned it as very insecure – this job well paid my expences & as I was so far on my Road I wishd to visit some Friends & Relations in Lincolnshire & Yorkshire I therefore went from Barnsley to Sheffield Mansfield Nottingham Newark Fulbeck Lincoln Barton Hull Beverley York Leeds Bradford Halifax Bury Bolton – home I was out 16 days & continued personally to examine & take notes of about 70 churches.'[64] By 1822 Rickman had four pupils, or 'apprentices' as he referred to them, three clerks, 'a most able assistant in my youngest brother', and was establishing a career that included a commission from St John's College, Cambridge, where he built New Court and 'The Bridge of Sighs' over the Cam.[65]

In the countryside, commissions for Gothic buildings were mostly private and domestic. In urban areas the reverse was true. The emptying of the countryside, lamented by *The Gentleman's Magazine*, had seen working people flooding into the towns and cities, which expanded, largely without planning, leaving their new populations deracinated in the unfamiliar townscape of warehouses, mills and factories. Civil unrest was a constant threat and one way to counter it was the creation of new parishes to promote social cohesion and local attachments. In 1818 the establishment of the Church Building Commission did away with the necessity for an Act of Parliament to build a new church. Only a minority of the first Commissioners' churches were Gothic, and of those many were unimpressive. Rickman's St George's, Everton and St George's, Chorley are honourable exceptions. The age of the Gothic church as a great building type lay in the future with the Victorians, but what came to be called the Gothic Revival was under way.[66]

Edward Willson and his friend the French refugee draughtsman, Auguste Pugin (1767/8–1832), together with a team of young artists trained by Pugin, published two series of *Specimens* and *Examples of Gothic Architecture*. The plates showed selections of precisely measured details taken from real medieval buildings ready to be copied, and were thought by *Arnold's Library of the Fine Arts* to mark 'an epoch'.[67] Willson accompanied the illustrations with thoughtful essays on Gothic and its potential. He compared it to a dead language, which should be learned by working from the best 'original examples', yet, he argued, this need not be mere imitation.[68] Just as a Classical scholar might put forward an original argument in Greek, so an architect, once steeped in medieval sources, might make an original building. For Willson, a devout Catholic, this meant no diminution of sensibility; it was not the triumph of archaeology over Romanticism, but the fusion of the two. Like Milner he believed that an eternal truth, invulnerable to any Reformation, adhered to the stones. In his will he asked to be buried not in a Catholic graveyard but at St Mary's, Hainton, a medieval parish church he had restored.

'Friend Britton', as Rickman referred to him with an element of irony, was also busy, leading the popular campaign for Gothic.[69] To the *Beauties* were added, in due course, series on *The Architectural Antiquities* of England and Wales and *The Cathedral Antiquities*. By 1830 Britton's artists and draughtsmen were criss-crossing the country like bees, returning with full drawing bags. To some extent they were victims of their own success. As one of them reported from Fountains Abbey, it could be difficult now 'to get any view that is not hackneyed'. He fixed on the cloister, 'As there is nothing of the kind quite similar'.[70] The reading public was ever more discriminating, and by the time he embarked on the *Cathedral Antiquities* Britton too had matured. Salisbury Cathedral, the *beau ideal* of Gothic and symbol of antiquarian initiative, was not presented in a landscape, but as a landscape. Approached from the north-east, Britton shows it as 'A series and succession of pediments, pinnacles, buttresses, windows and bold projections, crowned with the rich tower and lofty spire . . . [that] fill the eye and mind as a homogeneous whole'.[71]

The plates included measured details and perspectives, accuracy and artistry mutually reinforcing. One of the illustrations is a view based on a watercolour by Turner, looking from the cloisters through a broken trefoil; another has the west end anatomized, shown in plan, section and elevation like an *écorché*. As Britton explained in his Introduction, both aspects mattered: 'Whether contemplated as objects of grandeur, science, art, or history, [the cathedrals] alike claim the attention and admiration of all persons of taste and learning.'[72]

FIGURES IN THE LANDSCAPE

The Romantic landscape was not uninhabited. The unknown dead who built the medieval churches, inhabited the cottages and ploughed the land, the humble departed of Gray's *Elegy* and the *Lyrical Ballads*, began to rise from their graves and to be dressed, housed and set in motion. As the 'Topographer for the Year 1789' observed, many 'who do not come within the narrower compass of Biography, are the proper subjects of Topography'.[73] While they might be lost as individuals, their way of life, their 'manners and customs' could be recovered, bringing the past closer in all its detail. History, once populated only by kings and heroes, was becoming a crowded panorama, a field of folk.

The pioneer in this branch of antiquarianism was Joseph Strutt (1749–1802). The son of a prosperous Essex miller, he trained as an engraver and was part of the circle around Richard Gough. He belonged to the older generation of late-Georgian antiquaries, and his *Horda-Angel-Cynnan: Or a Compleat View of the Manners and Customs, Arms, Habits etc. of the Inhabitants of England* appeared between 1775 and 1776. Perhaps the Anglo-Saxon title deterred readers, or maybe Strutt was too far ahead of his time; in any event the book was not a great success. Now in his fifties and much better informed, he returned to the subject. *A Complete View of the Dress and Habits of the People of England* was published between 1796 and 1799 and was the first detailed and properly referenced history of dress in English. Strutt, in his self-deprecating 'Address to the Public', warned that 'in the prosecution of this extensive work many errors will be unavoidable', going on to explain that 'in numerous instances I am necessitated to labour, as it were, in the dark'.[74] The problem with costume, as with architecture, was that written sources were of limited use. People do not write detailed descriptions of what is obvious to themselves and their contemporaries. Accounts of dress tended to be 'vague and nugatory'.[75] Strutt's method was the tried-and-tested compare and contrast. He looked for parallels between written accounts in legal reports, inventories, chronicles, poems and illustrative material. His great innovation – what indeed made his work possible – was his decision to give visual sources equal weight with the written ones. Assessing them against textual references, he 'exerted the utmost' of his ability 'to unite the two sources of information'.[76] He realized that representations of dress and accoutrements in illuminated manuscripts, tomb effigies or wall paintings were, for the most part, reliable. If writers do not describe contemporary dress in detail because their readers already know about it, by the same logic artists are unlikely to make mistakes or introduce anachronisms which would be obvious to themselves and others.

After a long Introduction covering ancient civilizations up to the end of the seventh century, Strutt's main study began with the Anglo-Saxons, and despite the promise in the title of continuing up to the 'present day', the greater and most valuable part of the book deals with the period before the Reformation. Strutt was interested not only in what people wore but what their clothes were made from, and where and how. Like the antiquaries studying Gothic architecture, Strutt identified a golden age in the reign of Edward III, the commencement of the 'English' era, when distinctions between Anglo-Saxon and Norman lost any meaning. It was Edward who realized that if, instead of exporting wool to Flanders, the English wove it themselves and sold the cloth, the trade would be more profitable. He imported weavers from the Low Countries, who attracted local hostility; and through the disputes and regulations that ensued Strutt drew information both about clothes and also about those individuals beyond the compass of biography, such as the weavers of Kidderminster, who petitioned Henry VIII to regulate the freelance manufacturers who were spoiling their trade. Strutt's text was peppered with evocative medieval terms for which he provided glosses: 'kersies', 'samite', 'pelisson' and 'camelot' (a kind of camel hair derived from Asia). In the plates, scenes from books of hours were arranged 'as pleasingly as the nature of the subject would allow' among illuminated letters and religious monuments.[77] Strutt hoped that history painters would make use of his work, and they did; but increasingly, to the lay reader, it was history itself that appealed, as it emerged in its everyday clothes.

Two years later, Strutt followed *Dress and Habits* with one of the most engaging of all antiquarian studies, for which he again indulged his fondness for complicated Anglo-Saxon titles. *Glig-Gamena Angel Deod, or the Sports and Pastimes of the People of England* relies principally on visual sources and concentrates on the Middle Ages. It was an expensive book, reflecting the growing market, and the plates, all coloured, present a pageant of the past at play: hunters, mummers, chess players, acrobats, adults and children, men and women, of all classes enjoying themselves. Strutt explained as best he could the rules of obscure games such as kayles, a kind of ten-pin bowling, and loggats, a version of kayles 'played chiefly by boys and rustics'.[78] His justification for his subject was that 'the character of any particular people' is revealed in its leisure pursuits.[79] The great events of history, wars and political crises, create atypical situations and enforced behaviour. The occupations that a society chooses freely for its leisure time reveal more fully its 'natural dispositions'.[80] In due course, individual characters began to emerge from the crowd of common folk.

One of the first to appear was Robin Hood, the subject of a compact two-volume study by the splenetic but industrious lawyer Joseph Ritson. Ritson, that relative rarity among antiquaries, a Jacobin, went to Paris in 1791 and reported with some triumph that 'There are three magnificent libraries; two of which at least, are infinitely beyond either Bodleys or the Museum, both for printed books and manuscripts . . . All three are open to every one.'[81] At home he worked under the gaze of portraits of Voltaire, Rousseau and Thomas Paine.

Robin Hood: a collection of all the ancient poems, songs, and ballads, now extant, relative to that celebrated English outlaw: to which are prefixed historical anecdotes of his life appeared in 1795 and reflected the contradictions in Ritson's character by combining research so thorough that it has never been substantially superseded, with violent political polemic. Ritson's Robin Hood was, like Ritson, a revolutionary, 'a man who, in a barbarous age, and under a complicated tyranny, displayed a spirit of freedom and independence, which has endeared him to the common people, whose cause he maintained, (for all opposition to tyranny is the cause of the people)'.[82] Yet Ritson was not so partisan as Carter and Milner in his scholarship. He knew he was dealing largely with a myth and weighed his sources accordingly, warning his readers: 'The materials for the life are not in every instance, so important, so ancient, or, perhaps, so authentic, as the subject seems to demand; although the compiler may be permitted to say, in humble second-hand imitation of the poet Martial: Some there are good, some middling, and some bad; / But yet they were the best that could be had.'[83] Ritson enjoyed working at that point where folkloric tradition met historical biography. His next subject was King Arthur, and he has some claim to be the first modern Arthurian scholar. [84]

While the Middle Ages received ever more antiquarian and popular attention, the period before the Conquest remained on the whole obscure. The first significant attempt to illuminate it was made by a young attorney, Sharon Turner (1768–1847). Turner came from a middling family. His education at Dr James Davis's academy in Clerkenwell finished when he was fifteen, but it had given him a good grounding in the Classics and a method by which to undertake his own studies of Anglo-Saxon. With an office in Red Lion Square, convenient for the British Museum, Turner worked on manuscripts that had been neglected for centuries. As he wrote in his Preface to a third edition of his book, the Anglo-Saxon age had been 'nearly forgotten by the British public'.[85] His *History of the Anglo-Saxons, from the Earliest Period to the Norman Conquest* was published between 1799 and 1805 to instant acclaim. The first volume was enough to gain him election to the Society of Antiquaries. He took a strongly nationalist view of 'Our Great Ancestors', especially 'Our Alfred', and a correspondingly hostile view of the Normans, which he modified in later editions. His critics complained that he was too credulous on some points and he rashly allowed himself to be drawn into a controversy about Bards and Druids, the graveyard of many an antiquarian career. He was, however, the first scholar to trace the diffusion of the Arthurian legends from Britain to northern France and it was he who brought to public notice the long-forgotten epic *Beowulf*, which was printed, as a result of Turner's work, for the first time in 1815.

Ritson, Strutt and Turner were all making use of fiction to establish facts: poetry, paintings and ballads were among their most valuable sources. It was perhaps inevitable, in an age so preoccupied with individual subjectivity, so fascinated by narrative, that facts and fiction should become ever more closely interfused.[86] Like Carter, with his imaginary medieval scenes, Strutt, having looked for so long at the Middle Ages at work and at play, began setting it in motion. He wrote a novel, 'Emma Darcy or the manners of old times exemplified under the form of a legendary Romance', in which he could deploy all the evocative medieval terms and details he had discovered, leading his readers through 'The Stately Edifices of the Nobility the sumptuous furniture, belonging to them, together with the pompous entertainments frequently made by their owners . . . nor are the modes of living among the middling class of People, forgotten, descending even to the Rustic in his cottage . . . the exhibitions of the wandring [sic] Minstrels, Jugglers, and the Narrators of Tales.'[87]

When Strutt died in 1802 he left 'Emma Darcy' incomplete, but the mature historical novel, a story in which the life of the past – the food, the clothes, the sports – give texture and detail to the plot, was imminent. The Gothic novels of the eighteenth century were set in an atmosphere of darkness and mystery at a time when the Middle Ages were, to most people, dark and mysterious. Now the lights had gone up on the medieval world and it might be the setting for any kind of narrative, love stories, adventures, battles or comedy. The presiding genius of this process, nothing less than the invention of the modern novel, was of course Walter Scott. But Scott was not yet the figure who bestrode European literature. As a poet he was only beginning to be known. Apart from his legal work, his chief occupation at this date was antiquarianism. He was in correspondence with Francis Douce and Ritson over his *Minstrelsy of the Scottish Border*, an attempt to record oral traditions, and to 'contribute somewhat' to the history of Scotland.[88] Ritson, though naturally he had criticisms, was uncharacteristically enthusiastic about the project, a 'most curious and valuable literary treasure'.[89] One ballad, *Sir Tristrem*, a 'metrical Romance of the thirteenth century', was too long for the anthology. Scott was attempting, as best he could against a background of building work in his new house and a new baby, 'whose pipe, being of the shrillest, is heard amid the storm, like a boatswain's whistle in a gale of wind', to edit it with Douce and Ritson's help.[90]

Douce had two manuscript fragments of a French poem on the subject and Ritson was consulted on Tristrem (or Tristan) and the Arthurian tradition. Scott was very much the junior of the trio, treating both the others with the deference due to his own status as 'an inferior antiquary'.[91] He visited Douce in London to look at the manuscripts, while Ritson overcame his dislike of Scotland for long enough to visit Scott, whose great good nature brought out the best in two of the most notoriously bad-tempered men in the antiquarian world. Douce was generous with information and Ritson offered 'the readiest, kindest, & most liberal assistance in the objects of our joint pursuit'.[92] In 1803, however, Ritson's volatility, combined with a series of strokes and financial failure, triggered an episode of mania. He burned many of his manuscripts before his final collapse and death in September. He had made many enemies, and his obituarists were not always kind. Four years later Scott was still 'indignant' at the insults to Ritson's memory.[93]

Yet while Scott admired 'Ritsonian strictness' on the question of authenticity, he completed the fragmentary 'Sir Tristrem' in a manner that would have horrified Ritson, with fifteen stanzas of his own.[94] It was a 'considerable addition', which, his bibliographers point out, was introduced to the main text somewhat vaguely as 'abridged from the French metrical romance, in the stile of Tomas of Erceldoune'.[95] Ritson would have regarded this as fraudulent, as have many people since. Yet forgery was not fakery. The new stanzas were, to Scott, no more dishonest than Rickman's churches built in the style of the thirteenth century. To the Romantic antiquary the medieval tradition was not dead, but, as Willson argued, only dormant. It could be reawakened and continued with authenticity. By 1807 Scott was at work on 'a legendary poem, to be entitled, "Marmion, or a Tale of Flodden-Field" in six Cantos'.⁹⁶ Scott's antiquarianism fed all his later work. His son-in-law and biographer John Lockhart saw in *Minstrelsy of the Scottish Border* 'the primary incident, or broad outline of almost every romance ... which [he] built in after life on the history or traditions of his country'.⁹⁷ In 1808 the publisher James Ballantyne asked him to complete Strutt's 'Emma Darcy'. It appeared as *Queenhoo Hall,* and so took Scott one step further in what he called his 'advance towards romantic composition' and the novel.⁹⁸

Fact and fiction became ever more intermingled. Another protégé of Douce was Samuel Rush Meyrick (1783–1848), a collector and expert on historic armour. Meyrick was working on his first publication and, like Rickman, he had been influenced by the typology of the natural sciences in devising a system to categorize and date individual elements of his subject. Douce, Nichols and Ellis supported Meyrick's candidacy for the Society of Antiquaries in 1810, despite the fact that, in Douce's opinion, the Society was 'fast going to D—',⁹⁹ and Douce gave him the run of his own magnificent library which became Meyrick's 'private British Museum'.¹⁰⁰ With Charles Hamilton Smith, whose subject was historic dress, Meyrick wrote *The Costume of the Original Inhabitants of the British Islands, and Adjacent Coasts of the Baltic ... from the Earliest Periods to the Sixth Century,* published in 1815. Smith made a vast number of drawings for this joint effort, while Meyrick had compiled 'three large quarto manuscript volumes [of] whatever relates to the inhabitants of the Britannic Isles, from their first arrival'.¹⁰¹ The book was essentially scholarly, but, unlike Strutt, who copied visual sources as accurately as he could, adding nothing, Smith and Meyrick's colourful plates filled in the blanks. They set their figures in landscapes and gave them character. Boadicea appears as 'a full-grown handsome woman, but of a stern countenance with long yellow hair flowing over her shoulders'.¹⁰² With her spear and bracelets she stands on a small mound, her warriors behind her with a horse-drawn chariot. By the time Smith and Meyrick got to the Druids and 'The Grand Conventional Festival of the Britons' at Stonehenge, caution had been thrown to the winds. The panorama of the 'Guaith Emreis ... in its original splendour decked out for the celebration of the Helio-arkete ceremonies', in so far as it had a source, relied on the unreliable theories of William Stukeley.[103] The plate shows a priest leading a procession complete with drummers into the stone circle, where the trilithons are draped in banners depicting the mystic serpent. Like Strutt, Smith and Meyrick intended their work to be useful to artists. Not surprisingly, it also found a following among theatre designers.

The same year saw the publication of Scott's latest antiquarian effort, *The Border Antiquities of England and Scotland* and his first novel, *Waverley*, set during the Jacobite rising of 1745. He had decided against a medieval subject. The 'indifferent reception' of *Queenhoo Hall* had persuaded him that 'the manners of the middle ages did not possess the interest which I had conceived'.[104] Not until 1819, in *Ivanhoe*, did he set a story entirely in medieval England, by which time both author and subject matter were of considerable interest to the reading public. *Ivanhoe* was Scott's greatest success to date, opening up 'the freedom of the Rules', as he put it, to 'exercise his powers' on English history.[105] Set in the reign of Richard the Lionheart, it was, like Strutt's 'Emma Darcy', designed 'to illustrate the domestic antiquities of England', and it drew on the work of antiquaries, notably Sharon Turner, Strutt and, for the Robin Hood plot, Ritson.[106] Scott was anxious to present *Ivanhoe* as a new departure. He ensured that details of the plot were 'communicated to no person whatsoever' outside the publisher's office and he further distanced it from his earlier work by assuming the persona of an antiquary-narrator, Laurence Templeton, a friend of Jonathan Oldbuck and of his friend, Arthur Wardour, supposedly the owner of the manuscript of *Ivanhoe*.[107]

This kind of playful masquerading was central to Scott's modus operandi. It enabled him simultaneously to say and not say a great deal about his work. The Preface to *Ivanhoe* is the key to his theory of historical fiction. Scott, or 'Templeton', explains the principle, comparing himself to a landscape painter, rearranging the past into a composition whose truth is aesthetic rather than literal. Scott's ability to calibrate the level of authenticity acceptable to his contemporaries and to set out the landscape of history in the best Picturesque manner made him the most successful and widely read author Europe had yet known. His characters now roamed the countryside. In 1818 Keats,

on a walking tour to the Lake District and Scotland with his friend
Charles Brown, considered himself an 'old-stager' in the Picturesque,
finding that at Ambleside 'the tone, the coloring, the slate, the stone,
the moss, the rock-weed; or if I may so say, the intellect, the countenance' of the place overwhelmed him, an experience such as 'must
surpass every imagination and defy any remembrance'.[108] As they
went along Brown told Keats the story of Scott's *Guy Mannering* and
when they came to Kirkcudbrightshire, where the novel is set, Keats
saw it as 'Meg Merrilies's country'. Meg, the Gipsy nurse who resolves
the cases of mistaken identity in the story, seemed to grow out of a
landscape 'exactly suited to her'.[109] As Keats wrote in his ballad on
the theme, 'Her Brothers were the craggy hills / Her Sisters larchen
trees'.[110]

So it was that the process whereby the landscape had become readable, its ruins comprehensible and its past imaginable, had reached
the point where the process was reversible. Grand Tourists had often
sought out landmarks associated with Horace and Virgil, but it was
only now that domestic travellers began to visit places made famous
in modern novels or poems, as they still do today, sites where no historic event occurred but where the power of the place is sufficient,
combined with the power of art, to create an experience that is felt to
be authentic. All the while, the medieval world continued to manifest
in architecture. Scott's readers, like Thomas Peacock's Mr Mac Quedy,
looked up from the page and saw that 'The land was covered with
castles.' Robert Smirke designed Eastnor in Herefordshire in 1810.
Thomas Hopper's hefty Norman fortress, Penrhyn in Gwynedd, was
begun in 1822 and in Westmorland, Lowther Castle, another of
Smirke's efforts of 1806, embodied the chivalric past successfully
enough to inspire Wordsworth:

> Lowther! In thy majestic pile are seen
> Cathedral pomp and grace . . .
> And charters won and guarded by the sword
> Of ancient honour[111]

Wordsworth, like Edward Willson, believed that although the castle
was not old, neither was it fake. It stood for an 'authentic story', the
proud tradition that was 'England's glory!'

A NATIONAL IMPROVEMENT
IN FEELING

As the Georgian age passed through the Regency and drew towards its close, the antiquaries knew that they 'no longer stood alone'.[112] The handful of cranks who had taken on the established order of taste in 1789 now had history and sensibility on their side. The Prince Regent was turned into George IV by way of a hugely extravagant coronation intended as an approximation of medieval precedent. In architecture the Gothic Revival was increasingly dominant, albeit in the somewhat stilted form of elements assembled from A. C. Pugin's books of measured details. Reviewing Britton's *Cathedral Antiquities*, Robert Southey, now Poet Laureate, marked the change, anathematizing Wyatt's 'improvements' at Salisbury. Enlightenment confidence in the better judgement of succeeding generations was giving way to respect for the integrity of historic artefacts, whether material or literary. There were, of course, many battles still to be fought, and many were lost.[113] The worst defeat was at Westminster, where the aftershocks of Wyatt's rejection by the Antiquaries culminated in one of the most malignant acts of destruction ever perpetrated by an architect.

Wyatt's ambition and his capacity for pulling strings had landed him a plum commission to design a new House of Lords at the Palace of Westminster. He and the antiquaries had continued in a state of open war, with Carter attacking Wyatt regularly in *The Gentleman's Magazine*. When, in August 1800, it fell to Wyatt to adapt the Commons Chamber, the former St Stephen's Chapel, for the accession of Irish MPs following the Act of Union, he saw a chance for revenge. The removal of Wren's panelling revealed the fourteenth-century wall paintings behind it almost pristine. Under the pretence of creating more room for seating, Wyatt had them pick-axed. Carter begged to be allowed at least to record them. As he told Gough: 'I said here is a public building of the first consequence in the kingdom, losing some of the most exquisite beauties of ancient art therefore I thought it a laudable act in me to endeavour to preserve them by my pencil', but it was to no avail.[114] Wyatt had him barred and the paintings were destroyed. The work of another antiquary, J. T. Smith, who got on site while Wyatt was away, and Carter's own earlier drawings, made from behind the panelling, are the only records we now have of one of the most important cycles of English medieval art. When, in 1813, Wyatt was thrown from his carriage and killed instantly, he was not much lamented among antiquaries. In December 1825, just before Southey's article appeared, the tower of Fonthill collapsed, taking with it not only what was left of Wyatt's reputation but the taste of the age he represented.

It was an incident Southey did not forbear to mention. The growing appreciation of the architecture of the Middle Ages was, he wrote, 'proof of national improvement in feeling as well as in taste and knowledge'.[115] Feeling was important. The belief in the associative, metaphysical power of the Gothic was not confined to antiquaries or Catholics. 'Chatterton', Southey wrote, 'would have been a poet, wherever he might have been born and bred, but it was Redcliff Church that made him call up the ghost of Rowley.'[116] That the great medieval church of Bristol should have the power to bring a fictional poet into existence was perhaps an extreme of Romantic sentiment, but the medieval undoubtedly brought poetry into existence, from Keats's 'The Eve of St Agnes', which borrows the hammer-beam roof of Westminster Hall with its 'carved angels, ever eager-eyed ... with hair blown back' to Tennyson's 'many-towered Camelot'. Salisbury Cathedral, so much in need of improvement by the standards of the 1780s, was now a symbol of national identity and a reproach to the modern age. If some of its appeal was due to Wyatt's rearrangement of the Close and a harmony in the interior created by his interventions, that was not much mentioned. Cobbett, on his *Rural Rides* in 1826, paused and reflected: 'For my part, I could not look up at the spire and the whole of the church at Salisbury without feeling that I lived in degenerate times. Such a thing never could be made *now*. We *feel* that, as we look at the building.'[117]

4

Revolution, War and Peace

In three days were destroyed the work of twelve centuries.
Dom Germaine Poirier, 1793

In Paris on 2 October 1789, while Wyatt was closing Salisbury Cathedral to keep the antiquaries out, the newly created French National Constituent Assembly annexed all the property of the Church in France. Soon afterwards it added the property of the émigrés and of the Crown. Overnight France had done what it took Henry VIII eight years to achieve, and then gone further. The state now owned virtually everything, and the state was in uproar. That month, thousands of impoverished women marched to Versailles and the royal family returned to Paris and an uncertain future. Equally uncertain was the fate of the vast numbers of buildings, furnishings, land, works of art and valuables which now belonged in theory to everyone, and so, in practice, often, to no one. In histories of the Revolution the effect of this upheaval, the earthquake, as Dawson Turner (and Byron) called it, that rearranged the physical as well as the social landscape, has not been enough considered. The great dispersals and destructions of the Revolution and the wars that followed gave rise to new collections and new constructions in which the material past was permanently reconfigured. The role of the antiquary, on both sides of the Channel, was transformed as events in Paris mirrored those in Wiltshire on a vastly magnified scale. French antiquarianism, like British, was propelled into a new phase, from passive documentation to active and, in time, desperate and dangerous attempts at preservation.

There were, however, significant differences. In France before the

Revolution, as in England before the Reformation, most historians were in monastic orders. The Benedictine communities, especially that of St-Maur, made important collections and transcriptions of historic documents. The Bollandists, a Jesuit society until the suppression of the order in France in 1764, whose principal interest was the lives of the saints, classified historic material, weighed evidence of primary and secondary sources and printed what they regarded as the most reliable version. Their work was for the most part purely textual. There were exceptions. Jean-François Pommeraye, a Benedictine of St-Maur, published an illustrated history of the Abbey of St-Ouen at Rouen in 1662, and in 1706 his fellow Benedictine, Michel Félibien, made a similar study of St-Denis. On the whole, however, the Middle Ages received little attention. Roger de Gagnières, born in 1642, who made a great collection of images illustrating medieval manners and customs, and two early-eighteenth-century antiquaries, Jean Mabillon and Antoine Lancelot, are more or less isolated figures. A turning point came with the Abbé Bernard de Montfaucon's five volumes of Les Monumens de la monarchie françoise, published between 1729 and 1733, which illustrated works of French art from the reign of Theodosius to the fifteenth century. As Francis Haskell observed, the subtitle was significant: 'qui comprennent l'histoire de France', which comprise the history of France.[1] The concept of works of art as historic evidence, comparable in value to texts, was thus introduced to the French tradition.

Yet, as Haskell also points out, Montfaucon did not in practice give visual sources equal weight, nor did he complete his project. In France, even more than in Britain, the age of Voltaire viewed the Middle Ages with disdain as a period of crude art and coarse manners. Montfaucon did not disagree, suggesting only that in these 'centuries of barbarism', when people had 'no conception of the beauty of painting, of the elegance of statuary, or of the proportions of architecture', there was nevertheless some historic interest.[2] The Middle Ages had after all produced 'several of the inventions that are most necessary to life ... water mills, windmills, glasses, the compass, windowpanes, stirrups, printing and other things, all useful and several absolutely necessary.'[3] Not enough readers agreed, however, and the Monumens remained unfinished.

French antiquaries, sometimes known as *antiquaires* or *savants* but more often and increasingly as *érudits*, had a public presence in the Académie des inscriptions et belles-lettres. One of the five academies of the Institut de France, it was founded in 1663 and expanded and reorganized in 1701 under the auspices of Louis XIV. It met regularly at the Louvre. The French society was therefore older than its English and Scottish counterparts and considerably more dignified than the early London gatherings with their port-stained minutes. The London Society began to publish its findings in the journal *Archaeologia* only in 1770, while the *érudits* published regularly and promptly from the beginning. (The young Gibbon invested £20 in a complete set of the académie's proceedings.) Despite this, the Classical preferences of the Enlightenment meant that the *érudits* were despised by the *philosophes* of the yet more venerable Académie française, founded by Richelieu in 1635.

French antiquaries in the age of the *encyclopédistes* were highly methodical, achieving a level of detail and order in their researches far superior to the British. What they lacked was breadth, that interest in local history, oral history, biography and topography which had been the backbone of British antiquarianism since the days of Dugdale and Aubrey. As a contemporary French historian writes, while the British fell far short of the 'analytical precision' of the *érudits*, they had accumulated a body of material that was 'incomparable in both scope and coherence'.[4] By the 1780s, however, the Romantic interest in domestic and national antiquities was beginning to make itself felt in France. Pierre Jean-Baptiste Le Grand d'Aussy, who introduced the terms 'dolmen' and 'menhir' from the Breton to describe megalithic structures, published his *Histoire de la vie privée des français* in 1782. It dealt not with kings and wars, but with the middling people. Intended as 'the portrait of our fathers', it was an attempt to repopulate the past, to recover 'the Bourgeois in his town, the peasant in his cottage, the gentleman in his chateau'.[5]

Thus, in summary, matters stood in 1789.

LUCIFER'S OWN METROPOLIS

On 13 October the newly established Commission des monuments historiques was charged with making an inventory of each category of recently acquired state property. The thirty-year-old antiquary and naturalist Aubin-Louis Millin de Grandmaison was instructed to document the antiquities. He set to work at once, and on 11 December 1790, 'l'an second de la liberté', presented the first volume of his *Antiquités nationales ou receuil de monumens* to the National Assembly, who approved it. Prudently, Millin chose as his first subject the Bastille, the most important monument of and to Revolutionary France, 'for the terror which its existence inspired and for the joy that was caused by its fall'.[6] By then the Bastille had been largely demolished, but Millin gave a detailed and unexceptionable account of the building, its statuary and the various documentary sources for its history. Millin, who had already begun his own study of historic churches, was an admirer of the English tradition and he worked in the same way by comparison of material evidence and written sources. His bibliography was in itself a significant piece of scholarship. The illustrations in his *Antiquités*, however, lacked detail and the selection of subjects, understandably, suggests contingency. They included costumes, monastic robes and clocks as well as buildings and sculpture, interleaved with anecdotes and remarks on such topics as the splendid echo in the hall of the Palais de Justice in Rouen.

Millin drew parallels between post-Revolutionary France and post-Reformation England. These were indeed striking. In November 1792 the Commission des monuments ordained that there should be a full inventory of 'toutes les richesses que possède la République'.[7] Absolutely everything in all eighty-three *départments* was to be recorded with a view to a redistribution which would bring the greatest works of art to Paris, while spreading the rest more evenly in museums to be set up across the regions. It was a project on an immense scale for which the various librarians, booksellers, artists and *érudits* who found themselves charged with it were hopelessly ill-equipped. There was not enough money even to frame pictures or, if already framed, to buy a ladder to hang them.[8] François Moysant, the librarian of the University of Caen, who found himself suddenly responsible for Normandy, embarked on a tour of monastic libraries, as Leland had once done. Moysant himself made the comparison, and called his account the *Monasticon Neustriacum* (Neustria being the Roman name for Normandy), in reference to Dugdale's *Monasticon Anglicanum*.

Moysant did not, like Leland, go mad, but the experience transformed him. Increasingly disillusioned with the Revolution, he decided to go to England to pursue his studies in a more congenial setting, whereupon he was put on the list of émigrés and forbidden to return.[9]

The Louvre, meanwhile, was itself declared a monument in 1791 and rapidly acquired a magnificent array of works from the royal collections and from churches and monasteries. By 1793 it was 'a museum the like of which had never before been seen', reflecting the Jacobin taste for the purest Classicism.[10] This was an ideological as much as an aesthetic preference. The great republics of Sparta and Rome were the models for the post-Revolutionary French state. The Committee of Public Instruction promoted 'an unbendingly severe taste' in the new 'muséum républicain'.[11] Medieval art and architecture were regarded now not only as crude but as tarnished by association with monarchy and the Church and, as Revolutionary enthusiasm swept the country, medieval monuments were under increasing threat, as were its defenders. In Rouen the citizens held a meeting and voted to destroy the fourteenth-century episcopal throne in the cathedral because 'this gothic monument is equally offensive to good taste and to the principles of equality'.[12] There was only one dissenting voice, a M. Roger, who was immediately arrested and eight days later sent to the guillotine. At this terrifying moment the only effective defender of medieval works of art was Alexandre Lenoir (1761–1839), a painter working in the studio of Gabriel François Doyen. Doyen had been appointed to help organize the new museum of the Louvre, but, seeing the way the wind was blowing, took advantage of an invitation to go to St Petersburg. Lenoir was left in his place. He got permission to use the now vacant monastery of the Petits Augustins, on the Left Bank of the Seine opposite the Louvre, as a warehouse for displaced monuments not wanted elsewhere. Lenoir was and remains a controversial figure. To some a hero and to others an opportunist, in truth he was something of both. Perhaps only a combination of passion, nerve and commercial sense could have enabled him, eventually, to create the museum which in its short life helped to shape the historical consciousness of two generations on both sides of the Channel.

Lenoir's greatest test came in August 1793. To mark the first anniversary of the abolition of the monarchy it was announced that the royal tombs in the ancient Abbey of St-Denis, burial place of kings and queens of France since the tenth century, were to be destroyed. St-Denis was promptly invaded by iconoclasts. One eyewitness was the abbey's archivist, the Benedictine Dom Germain Poirier, who recorded the loss of fifty-one monuments between 6 and 8 August.[13] As the devastation went on, destroying not only sculpture and metalwork but disinterring and disposing of bodies, Lenoir's was almost the only voice raised in opposition. There was nothing to be done about the metalwork. Bronze and lead were stripped for salvage. But in the name of the Commission des arts, he demanded to be allowed to remove the statuary to the depot at the Petits Augustins. When argument was not enough, he was prepared to defend the monuments physically. At the tomb of Cardinal Richelieu it came to a straight fight which Lenoir won, but not before he had lost a finger and the cardinal had lost his nose. In other churches and monasteries where monuments were being destroyed, Lenoir intervened more subtly, painting lead to look like plaster to protect it. Gradually the Petits Augustins began to fill up with works of medieval and Baroque art, fragments of stained glass and statuary.

The Terror reached into every part of France and every level of society. Among the antiquaries with whom we are concerned, Moysant was already in England. Millin was in prison, though he emerged unscathed after the fall of Robespierre. Anti-clericalism became increasingly violent. About 3,000 clergy who would not conform to the new regime were killed and roughly a quarter of the rest emigrated. Among them was the Abbé de La Rue, who was to play a leading role in collaborative Anglo-French antiquarianism. He sailed from Le Havre with 100 others in the autumn of 1792. Some months later the twenty-two-year-old John Lingard, a seminarist at the English College at Douai, climbed the town walls along with three of his friends. Letting themselves down with ropes on the other side, they too headed for the coast, a day's ride ahead of the Revolutionary commissaires. But not everyone was alarmed: indeed, for some people this disordered state of affairs was highly congenial. William Beckford, 'in his lonely compulsion the most interesting collector in England', took full advantage of the pandemonium in Paris, 'Lucifer's own metropolis'.[14] 'Happy, aye thrice happy', he wrote, 'are those who in this good Capital and at this period have plenty of money. Their kingdom is come, their will is done on earth, if not in heaven.'[15] Beckford, who spoke French well enough to pass as a native, witnessed the fall of the Bastille and remained almost constantly in Paris until May 1793, shopping. 'To the admiration and desolation of penniless Dukes, Counts and half-pay ambassadors', he rented large houses for almost nothing and took over the Prince de Condé's box at the opera.[16] He witnessed the execution of Louis XVI, and although he retreated for a time in 1793, he remained in Paris intermittently until 1814, acquiring lacquer ware that had belonged to Madame de Pompadour, furniture, carpets and paintings, including Gerrit Dou's *The Poulterer's Shop*, one of more than a dozen of Beckford's purchases now in the National Gallery in London.

After 1792 France was at war, first with Prussia and Austria and, from 1793, with Britain, fighting to preserve the physical integrity of the Republic. Alongside the military conflict, another struggle for the post-Revolutionary state raged with equal bitterness: the fight to safeguard its cultural heritage from dealers and collectors who, if they lacked Beckford's funds, shared his ambition. The 'patrimoine de la République' was constantly under threat from the rapacity of foreigners. *Les Observations de quelques patriotes sur la nécessité de conserver les monuments des arts*, published in 1794, roundly blamed the 'ferocious and wily' Pitt and the insatiable Empress Catherine of Russia for sending envoys to France specifically to acquire 'the most precious' works of art.[17] Indeed, art and antique dealers, some working to commission, operated in Paris throughout the Revolution and the war; nor would the peace of 1815 bring an end to this particular conflict. At the same time, national monuments not at risk from foreigners were in danger from the French themselves. The survival of the Bayeux Tapestry was a near-miracle. Having endured a long period of obscurity after the fifteenth century it was rediscovered in the eighteenth, when it became known, though not in detail, to antiquaries on both sides of the Channel. Montfaucon illustrated it, as 'The Trajan's column of barbarian history', in his *Monumens*, although it seems unlikely that he saw it himself.[18] Had he done so he would have known that it was not a tapestry but an embroidery. In

1792, when all citizens were under instructions to destroy any work of art reflecting the vanity of monarchy, the people of Bayeux decided to cut it up to cover the wagons of soldiers on their way to war. M. Lambert Léonard-Leforestier, the quick-thinking commissary of police, hastily provided some canvas that could be used instead. He then moved the tapestry to his own office. Two years later, for the Festival of the Goddess of Reason it was suggested that the tapestry should be cut up to make ribbons for a float. Later that year, not a moment too soon, the Commission des arts took charge of it. After August 1794, when the events of Thermidor led to the fall of Robespierre and the end of the Terror, those 'patriotes intelligentes' who were horrified by the destruction felt able to speak. The Abbé Grégoire, Bishop of Blois, reported to the Convention of le 14 fructidor an III (31 August 1794) on the need to bring a halt to the devastation or, as he called it, 'ce *vandalisme*'.[19] The word went immediately into the French language, and soon afterwards into English.

By this time Lenoir had accumulated a vast amount of material in the Petits Augustins, much of it bearing the forbidden iconography of Christianity and monarchy, and he was wondering what to do with it. His first thought was the apparent oxymoron of a closed museum. This would bring together 'objects which by their very nature cannot at present be shown to the public', but 'where artists could study them for their own benefit'.[20] Gradually, however, as the political climate eased, it seemed the Petits Augustins could be opened to the public, if its contents were carefully presented to avoid giving offence. Lenoir decided to arrange it not as an art gallery but as a history of France told through its monuments. However pragmatic the basis for the decision, however commonplace it is today to find a collection arranged chronologically in this way, Lenoir's presentation of artefacts as historic evidence was at the time revolutionary. He opened the doors of the Musée des monumens historiques in 1796. The following year, as Bonaparte contemplated an invasion of Britain, the Bayeux Tapestry was brought to Paris, under the auspices of the artist and archaeologist Vivant Denon (1747–1825), and displayed at the Louvre, now Le Musée national, to remind the French of the most successful precedent for such an expedition. Like the objects in the Petits Augustins, it had been saved by being set in a new context. No longer a symbol of monarchy but an emblem of national pride and a weapon of propaganda, it was acceptable to a patriotic audience and so was safe.

There was no invasion, but the war continued. France was now on the offensive as Napoleon 'exported the vortex' of the Revolution across Europe.[21] News percolated to Britain of the fascinating museums, the splendour of the Louvre and the Bibliothèque nationale, to which French conquests in due course brought a great influx of looted treasures, and of the curious display at the Petits Augustins, but closer inspection was for the moment all but impossible.

MEANWHILE IN ENGLAND

If the political climate in Britain in the 1790s was less dangerous than that in France, it was nonetheless oppressive. Pitt's government introduced draconian measures to root out Revolutionary sympathizers and spies, sedition was liable to the death penalty and *habeas corpus* was suspended. Among the antiquaries Ritson, having made his bold expedition to Paris in 1791, remained defiant. Dating his letters by the Revolutionary calendar, he wrote to his 'citizen nephew', Joseph Frank, that he was impatient for a revolution in England, adding that since hanging a portrait of the 'enlightened' Tom Paine opposite his study door, 'scarce anybody has entered it'.[22] In June 1796, as invasion threatened, he ended a letter which dealt mostly with the inadequacy of a newly published and 'totally incompetent' parochial history of Stockton: 'They say the French are coming! Health and fraternity!'[23] At the other extreme were Carter and Milner, who raged against 'perfidious' France as they claimed the Gothic for England. There was a wide middle ground. A significant number of the British, even at the height of hostilities, were fascinated by Napoleon and had mixed feelings about the war. In 1797 Douce, who had also been to Paris since 1789, remarked that 'The French revolution if it had been left to itself and undisturbed would in time have recovered from the disorder that its excesses had occasioned. England stepped in as a doctor, and by its violent & coercive measures prevented, as many other physicians do, the simple and easy operation of nature.'[24]

British antiquaries were aware of their French counterparts. Ritson read and admired Le Grand's 'elegant' *Histoire de la vie privée des Français*, adding that with such an example, 'it becomes a matter not of lamentation only, but of surprise that no person has attempted a work of this nature for England'.[25] Strutt may well have had Le Grand in mind in planning his *Complete View of the Dress and Habits of the People of England*. The war, however, did not entirely prevent cross-Channel collaboration; indeed, in certain ways it enhanced it. In 1792 the Benedictine François Philippe Gourdin wrote to the London Society of Antiquaries from Rouen, warning them that he would soon have to leave France. It is possible that he arrived on the same boat as La Rue. In any event, the Society was well prepared to welcome émigrés. La Rue seems to have made straight for London, and soon after his arrival was elected a fellow. The most fruitful and enduring friendship he formed in exile was with Douce.[26] In many ways they were ill-matched. Douce sympathized with the Revolution, admired Napoleon, was sceptical about religion in general and deeply hostile to the Catholic Church. Antiquarianism, however, conquered all. Both men were interested in 'manners and customs', particularly the history of fools and minstrels; and their correspondence, which lasted until a few months before Douce's death, ranged over La Rue's work on the Anglo-Norman poet Marie, his study of the early troubadours, the works of Walter Scott, Gothic architecture, the history of the Dance of Death and the Bayeux Tapestry. La Rue stayed with Douce in his home in Upper Gower Street, within easy reach of the British Museum, on and off until 1796 while he seized the opportunities offered by adversity to pursue his studies. Working between London and Oxford, he assembled the Beaumont Charters, a sequence of documents relating to Norman abbeys, now in the John Rylands Library at Manchester University. He got to know Isaac D'Israeli, Joseph Banks and the great bibliophile John Ker, 3rd Duke of Roxburghe, though La Rue found, as did others, that 'his grace is somewhat ill-tempered'.[27]

It is not clear in what language Douce and La Rue talked to each other, but in their correspondence each wrote in his own. The abbé's paper 'On Anglo-Norman Poets' was probably written in French and translated by Douce, who read it to the Society of Antiquaries on 29 March 1798. It was eventually published in the Society's journal,

Archaeologia, by which time La Rue was sufficiently naturalized to give vent to the general exasperation at the Society's haphazard proceedings: 'What is the point of drawing from obscurity these men who did credit to England, only for the Society of Antiquaries to submerge them again by failing to publish my work.'[28] Despite such occasional testiness, the most striking fact about the friendship between Douce and La Rue is the consistency with which the antiquarian endeavour was prosecuted. They agreed on methods. 'Cover the ground, make comparisons, build systems', as La Rue put it.[29]

In 1798 La Rue felt it safe to return to France. In Paris he found himself in an antiquarian gold mine and reported back to Douce on the embarrassment of riches. In the wake of France's victories, the tides of war that had swept works of art, antiquities and refugees across Europe for nearly a decade were bringing quantities of manuscripts into the French archives from the Vatican and elsewhere in the conquered territories. La Rue found examples of the songs of Marie unrepresented in the manuscript collections he had seen in England, and as events propelled him from Normandy to London, Oxford and back to Paris he realized that his involuntary study tour had made him an unrivalled authority. While he was willing to share his researches with Douce he kept his cards close to his chest with Le Grand, who was now librarian at the Bibliothèque nationale and was always trying to draw him out about his research. 'I keep it corked,' he told Douce.[30] Despite which, by July 1799, with 50,000 manuscripts in front of him and 'no catalogue', even La Rue was feeling overwhelmed.[31]

Overall, the fortuitous collaboration of the war years fostered peaceful relations. The fact that La Rue's papers were read and respectfully received at the Society of Antiquaries over a period of eighteen years, despite being submitted latterly from a country with which Britain was at war, speaks of the limited extent to which national hostilities were reflected in the antiquarian enterprise and how, indirectly, the Revolution and the war positively benefited English and Scottish antiquaries. Not only were the British now confined to their native islands, where they began to look more kindly and patriotically on the remains of their past, but the vandalism of the Terror handed Wyatt's opponents a powerful weapon. Wyatt and

Barrington's destruction of tombs and the removal of bodies, including St Osmund's, in the name of good taste began to seem like very bad taste indeed. In his dissertation on the work at Salisbury, Milner compared their activities with the Revolutionaries' desecration of churches and graveyards, and specifically with the violation of the tomb of an English king, James II. James died in France in 1701 and was buried with some of his family in the Benedictine church of the Faubourg St-Jacques. Their monuments had been broken up, the corpses 'carried round the streets so that people could pay to see them', after which the king's body was thrown away.[32] The general revulsion at these atrocities was grist to Milner and Carter's mill.

The other beneficial consequence of the vandalism was of interest to many more than antiquaries. As Carter recalled:

> At the beginning of the French Revolution an almost total dispersion of church ornaments took place (the most sacred of which, being first destroyed as shrines, crucifixes, crosses, chalices etc.) and made their way into different countries; with us, many most invaluable Paintings, illumined m.s. found their safe deposite ... the most inestimable performance that has yet come under my inspection, was a painting for an altar by Mabuse, of a bishop and a saint in converse and a monastery in the distance: it was perfect and so highly and elaborately finished that the art of man seemed expended thereon. It was sold at a sale in Charles St Berkely Squ. 17 for 10 guineas to me as purchaser for Mr Barret who, in his collection of pictures at Lee esteemed it one of the greatest jewels among them.[33]

Carter was bidding on behalf of Thomas Barrett, whose Gothic house, Lee Priory in Kent, was canonized by Horace Walpole as 'a child of Strawberry'. Walpole also admired the painting by Mabuse (who is now more generally known as Jan Gossaert, c.1478–1532), and in 1794 was urging Barrett to hang it over his library chimneypiece, but Barrett's architect objected. The architect was the ubiquitous Wyatt. It may be imagined that during Carter's many and various commissions from Barrett his path crossed Wyatt's from time to time, and that this did not improve relations.

There was, of course, nothing new about the spoils of war: what was new was the world of auction houses and art dealers who put on show the work they hoped to sell. The great names, Sotheby's and Christie's as well Colnaghi, the first commercial art gallery, were established in London by the mid-eighteenth century. Now they came of age and were joined by others. Bonham's was founded in 1793, Phillips's in 1796 and by 1802 the number of auctioneers in the Post Office Annual Directory had nearly tripled.[34] Whether, like Carter, they went to bid for a client or simply out of interest, a great many people visited salerooms for a sight of antiquities, paintings and sculptures such as they could never previously have expected to see. William Hazlitt, born in 1778, felt like many of his contemporaries that he 'set out in life with the French Revolution', and it was not only the ideals of republican liberty that inspired him.[35] He was twenty when he saw the most famous and important collection to go on show in London, that of the Duc d'Orléans, Philippe Égalité, who had sold his paintings in 1791 to pay off his debts and to finance the political career which ended in 1793 at the guillotine. His collection was rich in works by Poussin and Claude. It included Titian's *Diana and Callisto* and its pair, *Diana and Actaeon*, now jointly owned by the National Galleries in London and Edinburgh, as well as *Venus Rising from the Sea*, which is in Edinburgh. Hazlitt was not alone in finding the exhibition a life-changing experience. It became a great social and educational event. At a time when there was no such thing as a public art gallery in Britain and when a certain level of initiative and status was required to penetrate the private galleries of country houses, the sale viewings were almost always free, as were the catalogues. Suddenly a world of masterpieces opened up to the general public. The papers began to talk of 'Orleans mania'.

UNEASY PEACE

On 25 March 1802 Britain and France signed the Peace of Amiens. La Rue was delighted and immediately wrote to Douce about the papers he was planning for the Society of Antiquaries. He also asked Douce to look after his friend the Abbé Lavoisine, who was taking advantage of the peace to come to England and start a new life. Moysant, having found that however clement the intellectual climate in England, the actual climate was too cold and wet for him, returned to France and these two joined a great flood of cross-Channel traffic. After nine years of war, friends and families were reunited, antiquaries went to look at French architecture, frustrated Grand Tourists struck out for Italy and people of many tastes and none flocked to satisfy their curiosity. The great actor-manager and theatrical antiquary John Philip Kemble (1757–1823) embarked on a tour which marked the beginning of his friendship with the greatest French actor of the day, François-Joseph Talma. Talma and Kemble discussed historical costume in Shakespeare's Roman plays, and on Kemble's return audiences at Covent Garden were treated to a more authentic style of toga. Ritson was characteristically an exception amid all this busy enthusiasm. His revolutionary principles had not prevented him from investing heavily on the Stock Exchange in companies involved in military provisions and arms. On a visit to his nephew in Stockton he got a letter telling him that he was 'utterly ruined'. As he wrote sadly to his cousin Mary, his was a far from uncommon case: 'the sudden peace' meant that 'many in my situation suffered much greater losses'.[36] Ritson had hoped to make another trip to France, but this shock seems to have triggered the calamitous physical and mental breakdown that led to his death the next year.

It was now that the young George Whittington set off on the journey that would enable him to answer one of the most pressing questions about the origin of Gothic architecture with his *Historical Survey of the Ecclesiastical Antiquities of France*. He went with two friends, his Cambridge contemporary George Gordon, 4th Earl of Aberdeen (1784–1860), whose tepid presentation of Whittington's posthumous book did so little to make it better known, and the Norfolk banker and antiquary Hudson Gurney. Aberdeen, who would one day become one of 'the least remembered of nineteenth-century prime ministers' and a President of the Society of Antiquaries, was eighteen, Gurney nine years older.[37] Their friendship was based on shared literary ambitions. They exchanged poems and other 'mildly scurrilous' writings.[38] Otherwise they had little in common. Gurney came from Quaker stock and was the half-brother of the Anglo-Saxonist Anna. He had a particular interest in the history of the Iceni and much less interest in running the family business, which he nevertheless did efficiently. The trip through France to Rome and Naples strained his relations with Aberdeen, whose patrician manners and extensive luggage Gurney found irritating. As a result his journal is fuller and funnier than it might have been had more of his thoughts found expression in conversation. It offers a textbook example of the clash of Classical and Gothic tastes. The party set off on 19 November 1802, and after a wretched Channel crossing during which they were all 'sick to death', reached Calais.[39] The earl had already annoyed Gurney by bringing his dog, which he was 'constantly kissing & suffering to lick his face', so it was with a certain relish that Gurney recorded the instant confiscation of all Aberdeen's possessions, including '8 pairs of leather breeches, 24 pr of shoes & 16 of boots' as 'the citizens thought in a sans culottes country such a magazine of unmentionables was rather too bad'. The furious earl who, surprisingly, seems to have had no French, demanded that Gurney intervene, but Gurney had forgotten his dictionary so simply 'roard [sic] . . . & after many bows & much stammering it was agreed that a petition & remonstrance shd. be sent to the minister of the finances of the republic of France one & indivisible . . . on this iniquitous affair'.[40]

The trio pressed on towards Paris. One of Gurney's chief objects was to learn more about the history of medieval architecture, of which he was as yet 'profoundly ignorant'.[41] Aberdeen was no help, merely 'descanting on the charms of virtuosity' in between yawns, but the energetic Whittington 'skipp'd all day from church to church' and 'mark'd down their forms & ages'.[42] At Amiens Gurney admired the cathedral, but worried that his lack of experience made him overrate it. He 'shd much like to know the date of those French buildings which resemble our saxon & gothic'.[43] His journal shows him not merely learning about dates but falling under the Romantic spell of the Middle Ages. At Avignon the beauty of the town's setting and its 'noble ruins' evoked 'that period, when taste and learning first began to mingle with chivalrous manners & gothic magnificence', and by the time he reached Milan and entered the cathedral he was convinced of 'the incalculable superiority of the Gothic architecture for religious edifices', bemoaning the recent loss of the stained glass ('broken by the cannon of a civil festival') but which when *in situ* 'must have made a darkness visible mournful yet pleasant to the soul

& ... accordant to ... devotional feelings'.[44] Whittington could by now have answered many of Gurney's questions and no doubt did so, but his voice is absent from the journal, drowned out by Aberdeen's confident opinions. Whittington's judgements survive only in his *Survey*. About one object of the trip, Lenoir's museum, now the Musée impérial des monumens français, he had mixed feelings.

The museum's chronological arrangement illustrated, among other things, Lenoir's preferred theory of the origins of the pointed arch, which was Wren's: that it derived from the architecture of the Middle East as seen by the Crusaders. Whittington thought this was wrong, and it was certainly debatable, but many of his other complaints were less reasonable and evinced a remarkable disregard for the circumstances in which the collection had been assembled. He thought the museum was too small and that the thirteenth century was underrepresented, although he admitted that the contents 'considered by themselves, [were] of inestimable value'.[45] But the importance of the museum derived precisely from the objects not being seen 'by themselves' but as an historical sequence. Beginning in the former Chapel, the visitor was led through the centuries. The decoration and the light, often filtered through salvaged stained glass, encouraged an emotional response, but the effect was not simply Picturesque. Lenoir intended his visitors to experience the passage of the centuries, to 'live' history.[46] This 'sensibility', as Whittington dismissively referred to it, lay at the heart of the museum's astonishing influence, but to the somewhat literal-minded Whittington it was evidence only of Lenoir's 'vanity and affectation which perpetually expose him to ridicule'.[47] A fuller and more evocative account will have to wait for the arrival of a more sympathetic English visitor.

Gurney, who was more realistic about recent history, noted with dismay the determined destruction of the Revolutionaries, who had removed 'with infinite labour' the heads of all the figures on the front of the church at Abbeville. The vandalism was still going on, albeit now for pragmatic rather than ideological reasons. At Avignon in the Convent of the Cordeliers, which contained the tomb of Petrarch's Laura, 'the axle of a water wheel [was] driven into the side' and the 'cursed' workmen were 'shovelling up the ashes of the dead & chipping tombstones to make staircases'.[48] Gurney's journal reflects the mixed feelings that many of the British experienced in relation to the Revolution, the war and the French themselves. At Versailles he was nauseated by the 'tawdry' taste of the ancien regime.[49] Marie Antoinette's toy village, the Hameau, evoked a 'supernal . . . contempt for the old rulers' and led him to the uneasy conclusion that 'the French character never has nor perhaps ever will change wch perhaps may be as well, as situation obliging us to hate it is a comfort to be able to despise'.[50] Gurney and Whittington left Aberdeen in Naples, from where he proceeded with more enthusiasm to Greece while they returned over the Alps in early April 1803. At Auxerre, when Gurney went to the prefecture to get his 'passport', the necessary local permit, he noted its far from friendly wording. Leaving Paris, he wrote that '[it] makes me think we shall have war, whch I believe on the whole may be better for us than this hollow & insincere peace'.[51] He was right. The war resumed the following month, just when, as La Rue wrote sadly to Douce, they were beginning to enjoy 'les douceurs de la paix'.[52]

WAR AGAIN, PEACE AGAIN

The antiquaries had had a tantalizing glimpse of pastures new. To all but the most chauvinist it was now evident that the search for the origins of Gothic must be undertaken on both sides of the Channel. The Louvre had made a great impression and Lenoir's museum a still greater one. The level of interest the latter aroused among British travellers is reflected in the fact that, remarkably, the catalogue had been translated into English, but another twelve years of war and frustration lay ahead, abroad and at home. The Society of Antiquaries, which had done so much to foster scholarly relations with the French, was less irenic with its compatriots and still quivered with the aftershocks of the row over Wyatt. In 1811, on the death of the Society's president, the Earl of Leicester, Sir Henry Englefield was elected by the Council to replace him. Englefield, the friend of Gough, supporter of Carter's cathedral series and a Roman Catholic, was also an outspoken critic of Wyatt. Any one of these facts would have counted against him with many of the fellows, but the combination made him unacceptable. After an energetic campaign by Englefield's enemies the Society rejected the Council's decision and chose instead as its new President Gurney's travelling companion, the Earl of Aberdeen. Aberdeen had returned from his tour to Greece more interested than ever in Classical antiquities, and even more inclined to yawn at the Middle Ages.

There was, however, one national or rather international antiquity that received serious attention at the Society's meetings in these years: the Bayeux Tapestry. After centuries in which it had been little more than a poorly documented rumour, many of the British visitors to Paris during the peace had now seen it in the Louvre. The *Gentleman's Magazine* published an account of it in which 'Antiquariolus' rashly asserted that it was made in France and was acknowledged 'by all connoisseurs, as contemporary with the Conquest'.[53] This triggered a predictable flurry of querulous letters disputing the date and origin of the tapestry, questions which were then far from settled and are not entirely resolved today. In November 1812 Douce read his translation of La Rue's paper on the tapestry to the Society. La Rue argued that it was made in England some considerable time after the events it depicted. The ensuing controversy demonstrated contrasting French and British antiquarian methods. La Rue was essentially a palaeographer and he assessed the tapestry in the context of written sources. Since it was not mentioned in the will of Queen Matilda he took absence of evidence as evidence of absence. The borders of the tapestry include scenes from Aesop's fables which, La Rue believed, were not known in Western Europe at the time of the Conquest. His British counterparts were more concerned to inspect the tapestry itself for information. Here, however, the debate stalled, for the tapestry, which had been returned to Bayeux, was out of reach while the war continued.

Peace was proclaimed on 30 May 1814 with the Treaty of Paris. Gurney set off promptly for Bayeux and found the tapestry in the prefecture. It was 'coiled round a machine, like that which lets down the buckets to a Well' and he had the opportunity of unwinding it and studying it at leisure over a table.[54] He looked to the embroidery to tell its own history. The thread was still 'bright and distinct' and the superscriptions legible. Gurney applied his antiquarian knowledge, noting that in the architecture there was 'no trace of a pointed arch . . . but there *is* the square Norman buttress'.[55] The armour too was suggestive. It was 'ring armour' or chain mail, and there were no armorial bearings, which were a post-Conquest innovation.[56] The story the tapestry told, he suggested, was not that of the Conquest of England, as the French thought, but of the justice of William's claims to the English throne and the fall of the imposter Harold. Passing through Caen, Gurney just missed La Rue, who was sorry not to have seen him but was confident their conclusions would agree. With great respect, however, Gurney decided that La Rue was wrong. The tapestry was of the date of the events it depicted and of Norman work. All agreed, however, that further analysis would require an accurate, coloured copy of the tapestry and the Society of Antiquaries turned its mind to commissioning one.

Meanwhile, on the very morning the peace treaty was signed, Gurney's friend Dawson Turner set out for France with his wife, two of his daughters and two friends, arriving in Paris on 10 June.[57] Until now Turner's chief intellectual pursuit had been botany. No doubt his conversations with Gurney played a part in turning his interest towards Gothic architecture and they must certainly have accounted for his equipping himself with a copy of Whittington's book. Turner's travels in France marked the beginning of a new and lifelong interest in antiquarian subjects. 'Nous voici donc a Paris,' he wrote in his journal, 'in the midst of the wonders of the world, full of expectations & hope & anxiety & bent upon acquiring information.'[58] The Turners were an adventurous and talented family. They seem to have spoken French, Italian and German. Mary, Turner's artist wife, encouraged her daughters and together they made a visual record of the people and places they saw. They took a lively interest in every aspect of French life, history and art and Turner's journal includes comments on theatre scenery, table manners and farm implements. With Whittington's *Survey* in hand he inspected St-Denis and the Ste-Chapelle, but the party's main objectives were the Louvre and the Musée des monumens français. They were not alone. On their first visit, the Louvre was too crowded to see much. All of London, as the popular song had it, was in Paris.[59]

The Turners managed several more successful visits to the Louvre during their stay and pondered the questions, ethical and aesthetic, posed by the museum. A large proportion of the contents was in effect loot, yet the chance for the general public freely to enjoy famous works of art was surely to be welcomed, while the implications for Britain, where there was still no such opportunity, gave pause for thought. On one occasion they fell into conversation in the gallery with a French army officer, who found it difficult to believe that in Britain most works of art were still in private hands. 'This it is in its various ramifications,' Turner noted perceptively, 'that seems to constitute one of the leading points of difference between France and England.'[60]

> In the former country everything is the property of the nation & the Government is the principal, if not the only, spring that puts in motion the energies of artists & men of letters, & gives birth to public institutions. In the latter it is quite the contrary; the Government is exclusively confined to its own affairs; in the arts, the sciences, even in hospitals & often in roads, individuals do all, have all, & are all. Thus more splendor [sic] is in France, more enjoyment in England.[61]

In 1803 Gurney had thought the Louvre so badly organized as to represent the worst of both worlds. 'These stupid thieves', he wrote, had no idea how to display their booty. Some pictures were in the dark and others obscured by 'a glare of light'. Sculptures were shoved back against the walls and the Capitoline Venus which Gurney had seen in Rome in a room 'where you walked round her pedestal . . . as you repeated the circle of her beauties' was now 'stuck up at the end of a room rubbing her perfectly formed posterior against the wainscot'.[62] By 1814 matters were better ordered; Turner thought the 'light brown colour of the walls (which at the upper end are hung with silk, in other parts covered with stucco & painted)' made a background which 'harmonizes agreeably with the pictures'.[63] Like Gurney, however, Turner's orderly mind and botanist's respect for taxonomy found the arrangement lacking in consistency. The 'Salle des hommes illustres', for example, included statues of Minerva and Mercury, while the Venus de Medici, who had joined her Capitoline rival in 1803, was dwarfed.[64]

Yet whatever they thought of the Louvre's arrangement and its legitimacy, neither Gurney, the Turners nor any other tourists were in doubt about what kind of objects they were discussing. These were works of art, created, displayed and discussed as such. At the Musée des monumens français the case was less clear. Here what was on offer was something closer to narrative, that lived relationship with history that was the essence of Romantic antiquarianism. While some like Whittington found the arrangement distasteful and its theatrical aspect trite, for many more the experience was revelatory. It left an indelible impression on the generation who were to shape the historical sensibility of post-Revolutionary France, including the young Jules Michelet and Victor Hugo, while among British visitors, it was noted, the Petits Augustins was generally more popular than the Louvre.[65] Lenoir's ever-expanding catalogue was explicit about the effects he intended and about the nature of the exhibits. Some were complete and original, some, such as the figure of Blanche of Castile, were entirely 'ficitif' and created to fill a gap in the chronology, while others were composites. These latter included the tomb of Diane de Poitiers and the most famous and popular of all the exhibits, the tomb of Abélard and Héloïse, which stood in the former Convent grounds, now transformed by Lenoir into a funerary 'Jardin Élysée'. The monument was made up of the effigy of Abélard and that of a female figure of the same date whose face had been replaced by Lenoir with a copy by a living artist of an image believed to be of Héloïse. Over the recumbent figures was a canopy built from Gothic tracery, salvaged from St-Denis.

However questionable it may seem today, for the Turners and many of their contemporaries, Lenoir's museum was less problematic than the Louvre, and, with its chronological arrangement, more coherent. Turner's journal gives a picture of the impression it made on the *homme moyen sensual*:

> The entrance is by a spacious hall containing a general outline of French art, from some rude Gallic altars whose dates go back to the earliest periods of the Roman Empire, thro' a variety of gradations to the very summit of perfection in sculpture, the beautiful mausoleum of Diane de Poitiers; (this tomb was actually broken to pieces by the Democrats but M Lenoir has with great skill and judgement caused it to be

restored) ... the whole of this room is calculated to produce effect &
to impress a stranger with a feeling of awe, which the consciousness
that all around is sacred to the dead & the general solemnity of the
building are equally fitted to encrease [sic].[66]

The funerary monuments were accompanied by other architectural
fragments, reliquaries, busts, plaster casts and pieces of armour to
which Lenoir's catalogue provided an accompaniment, fleshed out
with biographical anecdotes and colourful historic episodes.

Turner was not uncritical. He thought some of Lenoir's wall decorations unsuitable for the funereal atmosphere, but in the Jardin
Élysée he was once again captivated. Lenoir had assembled the tombs
of Descartes, Molière, the antiquary Montfaucon, La Fontaine and
others. The 'leading feature of the garden', the tomb of Abélard and
Héloïse, was a scene from Rousseau retouched in the colours of the
Romantic Picturesque, a Gothic fane 'embosomed in a thicket of large
cypresses'.[67] The catalogue encouraged visitors to imagine while
standing beside the lovers' grave that they heard 'Sighs of tenderness
and love; the air resounds to their gentle tones, and the plaintive echo
repeats on all sides: Héloïse! Abélard.'[68] Turner and his party, well
aware that this combination of objects dated back little more than a
decade, nevertheless cut sprigs of greenery 'for presents to our friends
at home'.[69] Association was everything. Their experience was therefore slightly spoiled by the presence beside the tomb of 'a young
French officer' who was 'humming a tune & cutting capers'.[70] This
was not the right figure for a landscape which required a Werther to
complete it. As Turner wrote: 'Had we been but a week or two sooner,
we might have seen some sentimental German sighing or even weeping on the spot.'[71] The tomb was built on the border between the
sublime and the ridiculous and in the end sublimity prevailed. It
entered history on its own terms and is now in the cemetery of Père
Lachaise where, carefully restored, it remains one of the most visited
monuments, usually strewn with roses left by hopeful or sorrowing
lovers.

Before leaving Paris, Turner bought some missals 'of great beauty
& at a low price' but was otherwise disappointed that there were not
more bargains to be had.[72] William Beckford, who had more nerve

than Turner and much more money, was also in Paris and was not to be thwarted. In 1802 he had walked in the procession on the occasion of Napoleon's elevation to First Consul, and now he was ready to pick off the emperor's treasures. Pursuing shady dealers through backstreets by a 'cut-throat quarter god knows where', he came away with Aubusson carpets and furniture from Josephine's château at Malmaison.[73] In time a whole tide of antiquities would be loosed, but not yet. Dealers were aware that the situation was still uncertain. The Abbé de La Rue was also worried as he carried on his long-standing argument with Douce about Napoleon. La Rue was furious that Britain had dealt so leniently with him. Elba, he warned, was not far enough; 'he will come back, it would take Milton to describe his diabolic genius'.[74] On 1 March 1815 the abbé had the melancholy satisfaction of being proved right. He wrote furiously to Douce, as if he were personally to blame for the fact that the English had let the 'ogre' escape, 'now see, poor France and all of Europe set as a scene for devastation and carnage, what is to become of us?'.[75] So began the Hundred Days of Bonaparte's last campaign.

5

The Field of Waterloo

Stop! – for thy tread is on Empire's dust!
An Earthquake's spoil is sepulchred below!
Is the spot mark'd with no colossal bust?
Nor column trophied for triumphal show?
None; but the moral's truth tells simpler so
                Byron, Childe Harold's Pilgrimage, *Canto 3, stanza 17*

In so far as that shift in sensibility which brought the past into a new relationship with the present began with the Revolution, it was completed on the plains of Waterloo. The Allies' victory ended the closest thing to a world war there had yet been and it was seen, immediately, as marking an epoch. The anonymous poet who wrote that 'chronologers hence forth' would date Britain's glory (remarkably little was said about the critical role of the Prussians) from that year expressed a widespread feeling that this was the dawn of a new age, an event comparable perhaps in its import to the dawning of 'the Christian acra' itself.[1] Hence it followed that if all that came after Waterloo belonged to the future, all that went before it was history. Waterloo became the *terminus ante quem* for the past. The site itself and any object connected with it was instantly historic. Thousands flocked to see the battlefield, while thousands more bought relics or paid to see them in museums in Britain, where Napoleon's defeat was to have 'a strong and lengthy impact on the exhibition business'.[2] Scott and Byron, Southey, John Soane and David Wilkie were among the early visitors and they were part of a vast and varied crowd. The aftermath of Waterloo has been described as marking, not least, the 'opening of a new, more democratic chapter in the history of tourism'.[3]

It may seem at first surprising that in a period when architects excelled at triumphal arches, columns and heroic busts, there was no British Waterloo monument either at home or on the battlefield. There were many proposals. Soane, James Elmes and the painter John Martin were among those who proposed designs. Yet nothing was built. Various explanations have been offered including government parsimony, which should never be underestimated, but the true answer was Byron's. The battlefield was its own memorial. The visitors who flocked from Britain after nearly a quarter of a century of war were the children of the Picturesque. The power of association, the spirit of place, the effect of natural landscape marked by human experience had shaped the sensibility of a generation. Wilkie described Waterloo as a scene of 'Salvator like ruins'.[4] The crowds came in order to stand where Napoleon had stood and 'beheld his hopes crushed and his power destroyed', and to see the Wellington Tree, where the duke had positioned himself while 'an empire ... withered under its shade'.[5] It was a scene of suffering and triumph, the fall of a tragic hero and a famous victory. Visitors carried away anything they could get their hands on as souvenirs, including most of the Wellington Tree. The British, it has been pointed out, 'seemed unable to resist viewing the landscape ... through the eyes of museumgoers', and indeed Waterloo exercised something of the same fascination as the Musée des monumens historiques.[6] In a sense it was Lenoir's museum writ large, history told through its material remains.

To that extent all the tourists might be said to be antiquaries, but there were also among the crowds that flooded to Paris and Waterloo four of those self-proclaimed antiquaries already familiar to us: John Gage, Walter Scott, Eliza Stothard and Dawson Turner. The first three went to the battlefield. Gage was there immediately after the battle, Scott came some weeks later and Eliza Stothard visited it in 1820. Turner went to Paris to watch the dismantling of the Louvre. If the battlefield was a museum, the museum in the aftermath of Waterloo was a kind of battlefield, one where questions of ownership and the rights and rules of war were fought out between the French and their late enemies who came to repossess their treasures.

'THE GROUND LOOKED AS IF EVERY MOTE HAD BEEN CONTENDED FOR'

Thackeray has been accused of exaggerating when he writes in *Vanity Fair* that in the weeks before Waterloo 'men of fashion and ladies of note' set off in droves for France, 'not so much to a war as to a fashionable tour'; yet that was more or less what John Gage did.[7] If not a man of fashion, he was a member of the gentry, from an old Catholic family, and he was twenty-eight in the summer of 1815. Born three years before the French Revolution, he belonged to the generation who had known only war and for whom a Grand Tour was impossible. 'I am young in my travels', he wrote at the beginning of his 'Journal of a visit ... to Holland, Belgium 1815'.[8] Precisely why he decided to set out in early June 1815 is not clear. It would seem that as it became apparent the war was reaching a decisive point, Gage was simply one of those Britons tired of being cooped up on his island. Many of his acquaintance were already there. He arrived at the Hague on the 12th and called on 'some English families' before making his way via Amsterdam to Utrecht.[9] He admired various sights, including the pictures in the palace at Amsterdam, and deplored the bribery necessary to get his *laissez-passer* from the police. He thought the botanical gardens rather good, 'but inferior to the Gardens at Liverpool'.[10] He was cautiously observant of historic architecture, aware, like Gurney, that he had seen too little to make comparative judgements. Like all English Catholics, he found the sight of Mass held openly in the great churches and cathedrals poignant and could not help feeling that at home 'a portion of his liberty' was taken from him, although he was also typical of English Catholics in finding the accoutrements of Continental worship, the statues dressed in tinselly robes and other 'childish ornaments', offensive.[11]

The Battle of Waterloo was fought on 18 June. Gage was then at Utrecht, where conflicting rumours of the fortunes of the British and the Prussians abounded until on the 20th the arrival of some wounded officers brought 'more certain & brilliant accts.' of victory.[12] By the time he set out for Gouda, flags were flying on every boat on the Canal '& in every village garlands of flowers & coloured paper & many flags are hanging from the houses'.[13] On the road from Rotterdam to Antwerp he met a man who lived near the inn of La Belle Alliance, where Wellington and the Prussian general Prince Blücher met at the end of the battle. From him Gage had his first eyewitness account. He continued to jot down his mixed impressions of people and houses and landscape until he reached Brussels, where the realities of war become apparent.

'It was Sunday all the shops were shut, it rained, and nothing was to be seen but sick & wounded in carts or litters or at the windows . . . I felt a cloud hanging over the place difficult to explain.'[14] Every house had wounded men in it. Gage's now rather wan attempt to continue sightseeing led him to visit 'Donoots the banker', who had a celebrated collection of pictures, including works by Rubens and a Rembrandt self-portrait, all hung in the best room of his house.[15] Also in that room when Gage visited was a badly wounded Hanoverian officer who lay asleep on 'a handsome couch' while Gage tiptoed around him, whispering his admiration of the paintings.[16] The scene evokes in miniature Byron's account of the Duchess of Richmond's ball the night before the battle in its pungent mix of high culture and naked violence. The town was so full that Gage was forced to take rooms at the expensive Hôtel de Bellevue, where he found that the fighting had made 'sad havoc' among his friends.[17] He ran into the parents of one of them, Sir James and Lady Crawfurd, who told Gage that their son Thomas had been killed. Most of the rest of Gage's journal is devoted to his visit to the battlefield with Sir James. The road out from Brussels was strewn with dead horses and abandoned carts, the field itself covered in 'hats, capes & the remains of every species of army accoutrement'.[18] Some of the dead lay barely covered with earth, other bodies were being brought from the cornfields and burned, the fires still smoking. At the spot where twenty-one-year-old Thomas Crawfurd, a captain in the 3rd Regiment of Guards, had fallen his father found his stock.

They went to Hougoumont, the farmhouse where the British had held the French back against heavy odds. The fighting had been terrible, but the garden remained curiously untouched and there, in a shallow grave, they found Crawfurd's body and had it exhumed. Gage returned to Brussels after four hours, filled with a sense of horror, and agreed to escort the corpse back to England while the Crawfurds remained in Brussels. It was a nightmarish journey. The roads were crowded, transport was difficult and at Ostend there was no place to stay except 'a hideous pot house' where Gage slept on chairs, his friend's decomposing body beside him under a sail.[19] It was with huge relief that he reached port at Wivenhoe and the safety of the Suffolk fireside which he had been, only weeks before, so excited to leave. Crawfurd's remains were taken to the Gages' seat, Hengrave Hall, and buried in the churchyard. Gage had brought back the most awful possible relic of Waterloo. He was older now in his travels and the experience left its mark. His journal concludes that 'you have only to visit foreign climes to return home more satisfied [to] yr fire side. valete'. In time he recovered from the horror of the journey and travelled again in France, but in all his later dealings, both as Director of the Society of Antiquaries and in the often bitter campaign for Catholic Emancipation, his considerable influence was always deployed on the side of peace and reconciliation.

Five years later, a visit to the battlefield was still disturbing. 'I know not if I ought to say that [it] gave me pleasure,' Eliza Stothard wrote to her mother in October 1820, 'I could not get to sleep, thinking upon the horrors I had heard ... described.'[20] There was remarkably little triumphalism among the antiquaries about this 'day ... memorable to English glory' which was, to Stothard, also 'a day replete with horror, bloodshed, and misery, the glory of Human carnage. And for what?'[21] It was not only those who visited Waterloo who had mixed feelings about the victory and its cost. Douce wrote savagely in his notebook:

> A great and most sanguinary battle has been fought in Flanders in which more than 40,000 men have perished and the French Emperor been worsted. The real effects are not yet appeared, but the ministers & silly people at home are indulging in their horrible & insane exultations & a publick illumination is ordered for the deaths of 10,000 English soldiers who might have been better employed than in this cowardly crusade of kings with their hired murderers against the liberties of mankind.[22]

WALTER SCOTT AND
'THE DANCE OF DEATH'

While Gage was in retreat in the ancestral peace of Hengrave Hall, Scott was advancing towards Waterloo, setting sail in August. He was now one of the most famous British poets and, by some distance, the most famous novelist. This, however, was his first trip abroad. He, too, was young in his travels, if older in years and less sensitive in some regards than Gage or Eliza Stothard. He was rapacious, as a writer and as an antiquary, snatching up details and souvenirs at every opportunity. His account of his visit, published the following year as *Paul's Letters to his Kinsfolk*, dwells heavily, indeed shockingly, on the quest for material relics. Among Scott's own souvenirs was the skull of a Life Guardsman. The sight that met him on the field was less horrifying than that which greeted Gage. The ground had been tidied, the dead and the dismembered limbs had been disposed of, while enterprising local people had collected and preserved anything they thought they might be able to sell. Scott's guide was General Adam's aide-de-camp, Captain Campbell, who took him to the spot where Napoleon had stood to watch the battle. Here Scott experienced 'a deep and inexpressible feeling of awe'.[23] There was not long, however, for quiet contemplation. Almost at once:

> Men, women, and children rushed out upon us, holding up swords, pistols, carabines, and holsters . . . the great object of ambition was to possess the armour of a cuirassier . . . A relique of greater moral interest was given me by a lady, whose father had found it upon the field of battle. It is a manuscript collection of French songs, bearing stains of clay and blood, which probably indicate the fate of the proprietor.[24]

In *Paul's Letters to his Kinsfolk* Scott reproduced the blood-stained ballads in his own translation. They were not, he noted, particularly ancient or distinguished, their value was associational: 'I cannot divide them from the interest which they have acquired by the place and manner in which they were obtained.'[25] 'The Troubadour' and the 'Romance of Dunois', though recent, dealt with medieval themes and were written, by the time Scott had finished with them, in a medieval style. They connected Waterloo to Agincourt and Crécy. Dunois was a

1. William Camden (1551–1623), founding father of British antiquarianism.

2. Title page of Camden's *Britannia*, 1610.

3. William Dugdale (1605–86), author of the *Monasticon Anglicanum*.

4. John Aubrey (1626–97), one of the most original minds of his or any age.

5. Alloway Kirk from Francis Grose's *The Antiquities of Scotland* (1789–91), for which Robert Burns wrote 'Tam O'Shanter', based on the tradition of witches' meetings at Alloway.

6. Francis Grose (bap.1731–91), Burns's friend and an inspiration for his poetry.

7. John Philip Kemble (1757–1823) as Coriolanus. Kemble pioneered correct historical costume in productions of Shakespeare.

8. Francis Douce (1757–1834), expert on Shakespeare and the history of the Dance of Death.

9. Dawson Turner (1775–1858), a botanist who became an expert on the antiquities of Normandy, a friend of and sometime collaborator with Hudson Gurney.

10. Joseph Ritson (1752–1803), Jacobin, vegetarian and specialist on the Robin Hood legends.

11. Anna Gurney (1795–1857). Though paralysed from childhood, she published the first English translation of the Anglo-Saxon Chronicle and was the first woman admitted to the British Archaeological Association.

12. Hudson Gurney (1775–1864), Anna's half-brother, banker and authority on the Bayeux Tapestry.

13. *The Antiquary's Last Will and Testament*, Thomas Rowlandson, from *The English Dance of Death* (1814). The Romantic age saw a revival of interest in the Danse Macabre.

14. Stonehenge, as imagined in Smith and Meyrick's *Costume of the Original Inhabitants o the British Islands* (1815). History, fiction and drama were becoming ever more entwined.

15. John Britton (1771–1857) dominated topographical and architectural publishing in the late Georgian decades. His *Beauties of England and Wales* was the last full county survey until Pevsner's.

16. Edward Willson (1787–1854). Willson's essays on medieval architecture inspired his young friend A. W. N. Pugin to see the Gothic as uniquely Catholic.

17. Frederic Madden (1801–73), librarian and palaeographer who discovered the manuscript of *Gawain and the Green Knight*.

18. John Lingard (1771–1851), Catholic priest, author of *The History of England* (1819–30).

19. Alexandre Lenoir (1761–1839) defending the royal tombs in St-Denis from the revolutionaries, c.1793.

20. Violation of the royal vaults at St-Denis, 1793. 'In three days were destroyed the work of twelve centuries.'

21. The Salle d'introduction, the former convent chapel, at the Musée des Monumens Français, where the tombs from St-Denis were displayed. Jean-Lubin Vauzelle, c.1804–7.

22. Thomas Rickman (1776–1841), the first person to establish the dates and periods of Gothic architecture in Britain, c.1819.

23. Eugene-Hyacinthe Langlois (1777–1837), Norman antiquary, Bohemian and tutor to Flaubert. Self-portrait engraved by Mary Dawson, c.1820.

24. Temporary burials after Waterloo at Hougoumont Farm, where John Gage found the body of his friend Thomas Crawfurd.

25. Waterloo cuirasses and a sword among Walter Scott's battlefield souvenirs. The battle was seen to mark an era, and the battlefield became an instantly historic landscape, with British sightseers collecting every fragment of material remains they could get their hands on. Scott's visit was the impetus for his novel *The Antiquary*, published the following year.

crusader, the Troubadour a gallant wandering minstrel whose refrain rang variants on the lines:

> 'My arm it is my country's right,
> My heart is in my true love's bower;
> Gaily for love and fame to fight
> Befits the gallant Troubadour'.[26]

The verses were to poetry what the new face of Héloïse was to the tomb in Lenoir's Jardin Élysée, a grafting of the present on to history for emotional effect. Scott wrote two Waterloo poems of his own. One, published to raise money for the widows and orphans of the battle, was a critical failure that lumbered from the clod-hopping opening line 'Fair Brussels thou art far behind' and teetered on the ridiculous. Scott lacked Byron's reach. The other was better and more revealing, not least in its title, 'The Dance of Death'. It makes no attempt to venture into the arena of European politics; instead, like the ballads, it fuses past and present, filters the great events of history though personal sensibility and transforms Waterloo into a melancholy Scottish romance. In its form the poem, with its gesture towards Burns's 'Tam O'Shanter', already has one foot in Caledonia. It opens just before dawn on the battlefield, where, in an echo of Richard III's dream before Bosworth, the Highlander 'grey Allan', who lies between sleeping and waking waiting for the day to break, is visited by spirits, 'ghastly forms' that gleam 'through mist and shower'.

> But there are sounds in Allan's ear,
> Patrol nor sentinel may hear,
> And sights before his eye aghast
> Invisible to them have pass'd,
> When down the destined plain
> 'Twixt Britain and the bands of France,
> Wild as marsh-born meteors glance,
> Strange phantoms wheel'd a revel dance,
> And doom'd the future slain.
> Such forms were seen, such sounds were heard,
> When Scotland's James his march prepared
> For Flodden's fatal plain[27]

Allan is killed and buried at Waterloo, 'far from his Highland heath'.[28] In truth, however, he carries the Highland heath within him and it is now implanted on the battlefield. Scott had captured the narrative ground. Twenty-five years later, when Scott was dead and his novels had long since taken the French reading public by storm, Thackeray looked round the Paris Salon of 1840 with its many *Waverley*-inspired paintings and reflected that 'Walter Scott from his Castle of Abbotsford, sent out a troop of gallant young Scotch adventurers, merry outlaws, valiant knights, and savage Highlanders who ... did challenge, combat and overcome the heroes and demigods of Greece and Rome.'[29] It was in 1815 at Waterloo that Scott's invasion of Europe began.

In Paris, Scott visited Lenoir's museum, which inspired mixed feelings. His reservations were not Whittington's: he was perfectly satisfied that Lenoir had arranged his collection in 'the best and fittest order' of chronology.[30] It was the subjective experience that left him dissatisfied. For the novelist the story was too fragmentary, he was distracted by awareness of the context from which the exhibits had been so roughly taken, comparing them to prints cut from a book to make up a scrap album. It was the whole book that he wanted, and he later wrote it in *Ivanhoe* and *Quentin Durward*, filling in the gaps in history, rebuilding the ruins and colouring in the background detail. For the moment, however, he returned to Scotland, where like Gage he felt on his return 'The contrast between this quiet birds' nest of a place with the late scenes of confusion and military splendour which I have witnessed'.[31] The effect was 'something of a stunning nature' and he found the writing-up of his travels tedious.[32] He was distracted, too, by his publisher's demands for the novel he had promised by June and which he had yet to begin. In December he settled down and wrote with remarkable speed, even by his standards. The novel, completed in mid-March 1816, was *The Antiquary*.

Waterloo marked the consciousness of Europe. It is a determining episode in some of the greatest novels of the nineteenth century. *War and Peace*, *Vanity Fair*, *La Chartreuse de Parme* and *Les Misérables* retell it in Russian, English and French. But these were all works of the next generation. Stendhal's *La Chartreuse de Parme*, the first of them, appeared twenty-four years later, *War and Peace*, the last, in 1869. The novel that could truly be said to have been born on the field of Waterloo was *The Antiquary*, in which the idea of a lived relationship between past and present, enacted through artefacts, emerges for the first time as a theme in literature. It is not, in the usual sense, an historical novel. Its theme is the experience of the past in the present. The action is precisely dated. It unfolds over less than four weeks between 15 July and about 12 August 1794, spanning the fall of Robespierre. It was not unequivocally praised. John Wilson Croker, reviewing it in the *Quarterly Review*, was puzzled by the figure of Jonathan Oldbuck, for 'though ... [he] gives his name to the work, ... [he] can hardly be called its hero; and, indeed, though the peculiarity of his character induces the author to produce him very frequently and forwardly in the scene, he has not any great share in the plot, and is evidently recommended to the high situation which he occupies by his humour rather than his use'. Croker had a point.[33] Oldbuck is not there to move the story on, he is there to anchor it. In him the streams of past and present meet.

The experience of Waterloo and the image of the Dance of Death linger in the *Waverley* novels. In the Dedicatory Epistle to *Ivanhoe* the author is described as wandering like 'Lucan's witch' over the battlefield of the past, 'to select for the subject of resuscitation by his sorceries, a body whose limbs had recently quivered with existence, and whose throat had but just uttered the last note of agony'.[34] As Waterloo passed further into history and history became ever more vividly realized in Romantic painting, theatre and fiction, the heroes of the battle itself, far from diminishing in number, multiplied. In *La Chartreuse de Parme* the young Italian Fabrice del Dongo is accidentally caught up in the action. He is not sure at the time if he is in the battle or not and later wonders if he was even there, but at the end of his life he is acknowledged as one of Napoleon's bravest men.

By the time Stendhal was writing there were many similar cases, most notably George IV, who came to believe that he had led his army into battle and been principally responsible for Napoleon's defeat. The portrait of the 3rd Lord Grantley in military uniform that hangs in his ancestral home at Markenfield in Yorkshire is not the only instance in which the Waterloo medal has been revealed in the course of conservation work to have been painted on later. For the future course of antiquarianism, however, the most consequential of the shadowy figures who emerged from the fog of war were the brothers John and Charles Allen. Among the many claims the future Sobieski Stuarts made was that they had fought in the battle on the French side. Or as they put it:

> Their polished points red dripping as they passed,
> Dashed two young horsemen through the parting smoke [35]

'REFLEXIONS UPON THE MUTABILITY OF HUMAN FORTUNE'

Dawson Turner's first visit to France the year before had whetted his appetite and he longed to return. In September 1815, however, before he had made any firm plans, word reached Yarmouth that the Allies were dismantling the collection in the Louvre. It was now or never if he wanted to see it again. With the painter Thomas Phillips, who happened to be in Yarmouth at the time, Turner set off post-haste to see what remained: 'no time was to be lost ... every day brought accounts of fresh pictures being taken away'.[36] Turner, as usual, kept a journal of the visit. It is a chronicle of the collapse of empire, told through the traffic in art and memorabilia.

On the road they met the painter William Beechey, 'just arrived from France', who told them that the Louvre was now closed to all but the military in case the removal of the works of art caused riots.[37] From Brighton Turner and Phillips set sail aboard the topically named *Duke of Wellington*. Their fellow passengers included many people they knew and everyone was telling stories of the goings-on in Paris. One account had it that a British officer, 'very fond of antiquarian researches', had been admiring a rare book in the Bibliothèque royale when Blücher came in and told him he could have it. By the time they reached Dieppe the antiquaries' blood was up. There they ran into Mr Palmer, a cutler who was now proprietor of the recently opened Waterloo Museum at 97 Pall Mall. Palmer was carrying back in triumph twenty boxes of Napoleon's possessions as well as 'the carriage & wardrobe of the king of Rome, the colors [sic] made for the national guard of Elba ... a number of medals, a print of Napoleon going on board the *Bellerophon* and a variety of other articles'.[38] His haul, he assured them, contained 'everything belonging to Napoleon', things that, like Scott's ballads, were 'in themselves neither rich nor rare, but curious as having appertained to the great man'.[39] Hurrying on towards Paris they ran into the sculptor Francis Chantrey, coming the other way, who also urged them to be quick if they wanted to see the galleries before they were 'totally stripped'.[40] When they arrived the city was full. Among the English were the great society portraitist Thomas Lawrence and the poet Samuel Rogers. The hotels were overflowing with soldiers and tourists, Prussians, Russians and Austrians having great difficulty in making the waiters understand their requirements for breakfast, while 32,000 British troops were camped in the Bois de Boulogne.

With difficulty, but by dint of dogged persistence and aided by Turner's fluent French, they talked their way into the Louvre. There they found a remarkable contrast to the visits of 1814. They were almost alone in a scene of eerie desolation. The 'solitude and deathlike silence' of the galleries that Turner had last seen packed with art lovers was broken only by the heavy tread of the Austrian guard, who marched in 'à pas de charge' and stood with drawn swords, one in front of each of the paintings.[41] Most of the sculptures were still *in situ* but many pictures had gone. Empty frames were propped against blank walls and Raphaels lay, unframed, on the floor. Amidst it all sat one young woman, calmly copying Domenichino's *Institution of the Rosary*. As the day wore on more visitors arrived, nearly all English or Prussian. Turner and Phillips found the Medici Venus in a crate 'ready to be nailed down' and quite inadequately packed, Turner feared, for the long journey across the Alps.[42] In successive visits over the next days they watched the Apollo Belvedere, brought to Paris in triumph sixteen years before, go down the stairs on a sledge, followed by the Laocoön. They saw Raphael's *Transfiguration*, 'the great glory of this Palace, the boast of France, the wonder of the world', carried out past a small but indifferent crowd in the courtyard who were 'fully occupied with ... a couple of conjurers and a mountebank with a monkey'.[43] If that were not a telling enough allegory, then in the Emperor of Austria's stables they found the Triumphal Quadriga of St Mark's. These four bronze horses, the pride in turn of 'Corinth ... Athens ... Rome ... Constantinople ... Venice ... and Paris', were lying now on straw in open carts. 'Napoleon himself at St Helena',

Turner reflected, 'would hardly be more fit to call up reflexions [*sic*] upon the mutability of human fortune.'[44]

It was the fortunes of art, however, that interested him more. Who, he asked himself, had the title and the moral right to these things? His sympathies swung to and fro between the Allies and the French. On the one hand the French had behaved badly, the treaties by which they claimed legal title to the works of art being much like those made 'between a man who has a watch & another who has none, & nothing but a pistol to buy one with'.[45] Turner, who had a copy of Millin's *Antiquités nationales* with him, met its author at the Bibliothèque nationale, where he was now a curator in the department of antiquities. Turner heard that Millin was 'all things to all men', and he initially formed a poor opinion of him having seen him bullying Mr Costa, the young emissary of the King of Sardinia, who was trying to get some of the Sardinians' books returned.[46] Millin told him to come back with an army if he wanted them.[47] Yet as Turner watched the Allied soldiers' cavalier treatment of paintings and sculpture and noted the pictures being crated up as personal gifts to the Prince Regent and Lord Holland, he began to think that the English and the Prussians were as bad as anyone. He was horrified at the thought of the Titians going back to Spain, where they had been so poorly treated. '[A]ny person ... however fond of justice & averse from revolutions' must wonder, he concluded, 'what satisfaction can there be in returning them to the possession of those who know so ill how to appreciate them'.[48]

He got a chance to discuss some of these questions with the great Italian sculptor Antonio Canova, who was at the Louvre to reclaim works on behalf of the Pope. Canova was an attraction in himself. Turner made notes on him much as he would have done on any other curiosity, for, 'having lost the sight of so much, it was no small satisfaction to have an opportunity of seeing a man of such deserved eminence'.[49] Canova, 'a thin man about 55 years of age & about 5.5 high narrow shoulders & flat-breasted, pale, dark with a long nose & eyes deeply seated in his head; his expression mild and pleasing', was preoccupied in trying to locate 360 cases of the Borghese Marbles, of which the French were denying all knowledge.[50] He admitted to Turner that whatever he did recover would go to Rome. The little towns of the Papal States would be unlikely to get their Madonnas back; they were destined instead for a public gallery, which, Turner pointed out, was exactly what the French were being castigated for doing. He concluded that the Allies should have declared the Paris collections public property by right of conquest and kept them together. As the age of the modern museum dawned, these questions, matters of debate again today, were born with it.

Turner had another, more agreeable encounter with Millin and a chance to talk, antiquary to antiquary. Millin showed him his drawings of Italian antiquities and confirmed Turner's earlier impression by explaining that in France nothing could be published without government support as there was not enough interest from private people to raise subscriptions. He conceded that these matters were better ordered in England, and they agreed in their disgust at collectors whose wealth was unaccompanied by expertise, who 'by mere dint of money' were taking things 'from places where they might be useful to moulder unknown'.[51] A visit to Millin's home further improved relations and gave more points for comparison. Looking at his collection of prints and drawings, assembled for a work on French topography, Turner was unimpressed. There was 'a great mass certainly', but it only served to reinforce his view that 'nothing has been done towards this object in France compared with what there has in England, where some of our antiquaries could produce four times as much in illustration of a single county as M Millin had got for any French Department'.[52] Summing up 'this extraordinary man', Turner concluded:

> ... the variety of his attainments & his ingenuity in turning them to account were greater than his depth in any particular subject. He is always at work, (his *Magazin encyclopédique* is proof enough, it covers all the arts and sciences as well as the theatre – original memoirs – ie papers – and transactions of the Institute and other literary societies and others across Europe, obits and book reviews) & yet, with all this mass of interesting matter, conducted by such a man & with the local advantage it has derived from Paris having been so long the seat of the Arts and capital of continental Europe, the number of copies printed has been only 300. No wonder then that M Millin says he never made a shilling from any of his publications, but continued them for his amusement and fame.[53]

Turner and Phillips went on exploring, spotting famous people of various nationalities. They visited the great Prussian naturalist and explorer Alexander von Humboldt, who introduced them to Vivant Denon. Denon had accompanied Napoleon on the Egyptian expedition and his *Travels in Upper and Lower Egypt*, published in 1802, was the impetus for a wave of fashions in architecture and furniture, and the basis of a new field of archaeological study. Napoleon had made him Director of the Louvre. Turner found him 'a man of the most polished manners (short and about 65) bald on the top of his head over which his grey hair is combed' who welcomed them to his home 'most civilly'.[54] It was an antiquary's paradise, 'most beautifully furnished [and] ... stuffed with art and natural curiosities', with a lion skin in every room.[55] Mementoes of Napoleon, including Canova's bust and a collection of medals, the rarest commemorating the return from Elba – and, Turner noted, 'the prices for these are going up all the time as it is expected that they will soon be made illegal' – were placed among Denon's Egyptian collection: hieroglyphics, 'figures from the Sepulchres at Thebes, fragments of the Pyramids & sphinxes'.[56] Napoleon was now as much a part of history as the Pharaohs.

After this trip, botany was permanently relegated to second place in Turner's busy life behind the study of historic art and, especially, architecture. For, unhappy as the fate of many individual works of art had been during and after the Revolution, the plight of historic buildings was, as Gurney had seen, even worse. In Paris the medieval chapel at the Hôtel de Cluny was in use as an anatomy school. Turner managed to see the interior only by sitting through a stomach-turning lecture on obstetrics, illustrated with a 'most disgusting apparatus'.[57] All along the road to and from the coast he saw secularized churches and monasteries used as grain stores, cotton mills, prisons and sometimes, as in the case of the Romanesque Abbey of Jumièges, merely as quarries for local builders. The journey, which had begun in the hope of a last sight of the collection in the Louvre, became the beginning of a new antiquarian pursuit. For the next seven years Turner and his family devoted their considerable energies to visiting and documenting France, becoming part of the great cross-Channel antiquarian project that was the rediscovery of Normandy.

6

Anglo-Norman attitudes

Where am I? Where is England?
                    Eliza Stothard, A Tour in Normandy

After 1815 the cross-Channel collaboration of the war years blossomed naturally into a sense of shared antiquarian endeavour, concentrated initially on the 'rediscovery' of Normandy. The reason Normandy needed to be rediscovered was that, like all the French provinces, it had been dissolved in 1790. It was replaced by five *départments* as part of the Revolutionary regime's policy of subordinating local habits, dress, customs and all *particularisme* to a sense of shared national identity. The Normans had never taken kindly to this. Normandy was one of the wealthiest regions of France, well situated on the route between Paris and England, economically prosperous with a rich history and a vigorous intellectual life. It did not want to be absorbed into the 'one family of France' and after 1815 it rapidly set about constructing 'une identité retrospective' out of the ruins of war and revolution.[1] It was a project for which the English were felt, and felt themselves, to be essential. As Dawson Turner's son-in-law Francis Cohen Palgrave put it in the *Quarterly Review*:

> [Normandy is] the most important of *our* transmarine provinces. The French King must not be offended ... My Lord Coke has given an opinion, in his fourth Institute, that the King of England has not lost his legal right of entry on the Duchy of Normandy ... this, perhaps, is a state-affair, and ... we do not choose to meddle ... but it is quite

certain that in Normandy an Englishman feels himself as much within the pale of English history as if he were in Yorkshire.[2]

Nobody seriously argued that Normandy belonged to the British, any more than that it needed to be rediscovered in a literal sense.[3] The shared territory was the past, and that required a better map. As the English had learned more about their own architecture, early literature and folk traditions, it became ever clearer that part of their history lay across the Channel. By 1815 British antiquaries were itching to get to France, not least because they were running out of subject matter at home. As Palgrave observed:

> Every nook in our island has now been completely ransacked . . . If we call over the Counties one by one, their historians will be seen marshalling their ranks in quarto and in folio. The humbler antiquary of the Ancient Borough ekes out his octavo with chronicles of Shreeves and Mayors, and transcripts of the wills of the founders of the Green-coat school and the Almshouse: and every hamlet, raised by the opulence of the state into the rank of a watering-place, possesses some diligent 'Guide'; in whose slender duodecimo, the card of the Master of the Ceremonies, and the description of the assembly-rooms, are introduced by an historical dissertation upon the Silures or the Trinobantes . . . It would be difficult to name any structure of the 'olden time' which has not been transmitted into the portfolio and the library.[4]

It was just this kind of detailed, comprehensive topographical history which, as Turner had remarked when visiting Millin, the French lacked. They were well aware of the deficiency. Charles Duhérissier de Gerville, a Norman aristocrat and antiquary who had spent his eight years of exile teaching Latin in Colchester, remarked that 'Neither the Romanesque nor what is generally called Gothic have attracted the attention of French antiquaries . . . it is to England that we must look for authors to guide us in the study of our ecclesiastical architecture.'[5] It was still the case in 1839, as André Pottier, head of the public library at Rouen, acknowledged: 'we know how far ahead of us the English are in understanding medieval antiquities'.[6] If there was something grudging in Stendhal's remark that 'Our archaeology came to us from England, like the diligence, the railways and the steam ship', it was no more than the truth. [7] As the French set about recording their historic architecture, the manners and customs, 'les moeurs, les habitudes', and all the once-threatened *particularisme* of regional life, they modelled themselves on the British. The Society of Antiquaries was the pattern for the Académie celtique, a connection emphasized in 1814 when the name was changed to the Societé royale des antiquaires de France. The Societé des antiquaires de Normandie was founded in Caen in 1823 and rapidly acquired a number of English corresponding members including Auguste Pugin, John Britton and Francis Douce.

STITCHES IN TIME

The first great Anglo-Norman project was the investigation of the Bayeux Tapestry. Hudson Gurney's paper was read to the Society of Antiquaries on 4 July 1816 and within days the Society had sent Charles Stothard to Bayeux to make drawings for engraving and circulation in order to further the discussion. The tapestry was still in the Hôtel de Ville at Bayeux, still on its roller and, Dawson Turner noted on his visit, 'rubbed at the beginning, torn towards the end'. [8] It seemed doubtful that it would survive much longer. The Society's study of the tapestry was to be its greatest contribution to the antiquarianism of the early nineteenth century, and, in ways unimaginable at the time, one of the most enduring. Nevertheless, the project got off to an uneven start. Such was the speed with which Stothard was dispatched that nobody thought to tell La Rue, who was now living once more in his native Caen. The abbé petulantly assured Douce that, misconceived as the entire project was, he would in no way interfere with it; he certainly would not be giving Stothard any introductions, which might prove a difficulty since the mayor of Bayeux was unlikely to give permission to draw to anyone arriving 'with no qualifications or locus standi'. [9] Douce hastily wrote a letter of introduction for Stothard to take to the abbé, who then graciously arranged everything and got Stothard a convenient room to work in. La Rue was determined to defend his position on the date of the tapestry 'to and against everybody', especially the 'ignorant' Gurney, though he was somewhat mollified by a letter from Gurney so 'frank and extremely kind' that he could not but reply to reassure him 'that if we do not go by the same route, we are nevertheless tending towards the same end, which is the truth'.[10]

Stothard worked steadily, taking wax impressions to improve the accuracy of his drawings, over three visits until March 1819. By February 1818 some of his 'striking and elegant delineations', half actual size, were on display in London at the Society of Antiquaries.[11] The principal questions at issue were whether this was a Norman or an English work, when made and by whom. Then there were matters of interpretation: what story did the tapestry tell? It was clearly a narrative and the Romantic generation were predisposed to read it as a Romantic narrative, assuming that it dealt with events in terms of the motives and experience of individuals. It was generally also assumed that embroidery was women's work and that the 'tapestry', which nobody seems to have considered renaming, although the records in Bayeux describe it clearly as 'broderie', must therefore have been made by a woman or women. The traditional candidate was the Conqueror's queen, Matilda. La Rue attributed it to her granddaughter, the Empress Matilda, making it almost a century later. On this point he found ranged against him, alongside Hudson Gurney, Thomas Amyot (1775–1850). Amyot was a lawyer of Huguenot descent, the son of a Norwich watchmaker and a fellow of the Royal Society and the Society of Antiquaries. Like Gurney, Amyot placed the tapestry within living memory of the Conquest. The ensuing debate was a test of methods. La Rue's approach was that of the historian, taking notice only of the written sources. The antiquaries, by contrast, were using their knowledge of costume, heraldry, armour and architecture, and making comparisons with the evidence of the tapestry itself. The comparative method produced a reciprocal benefit, for the tapestry, with its 'delineations . . . of our ancient costume', amplified what was already known.[12] It was, as Amyot noted, a source as well as a subject.

On 25 February 1819 Stothard read a paper on his own findings to the Society of Antiquaries. It was, and arguably remains, the most important single contribution to the understanding of the Bayeux Tapestry. Based on internal evidence such as the absence of heraldry, the style of the armour and of the architecture, he inferred that it was made soon after 1066 and was 'a true picture of the time when it was executed'.[13] He made the point that pre-Renaissance art does not represent past events historically, it depicts people and places at they looked at the time the work was made, as if in a continuous present. It would take another 'fit' in that dawning sense of anachronism before artists felt any need to show history in its own clothes. Now, as the late Georgians went through their own such fit, the growth of historical consciousness as a process was itself becoming visible. On the question of the maker or sponsor, Stothard made no reference to Queen Matilda or the empress. Indeed, there is no evidence for either. He pointed out that there are other prominent figures in the tapestry as well as the principal actors in the Conquest:

> The words, '*Here is Wadard*,' are simply written without more explan-
> ation. Who Wadard might have been, history does not record; we must
> therefore conclude he was a character too well known to those persons
> acquainted with what was passing in the army of William to need any
> amplification to point out his rank, but not of sufficient importance to
> be recorded in history.[14]

Amyot agreed with Stothard and added to his argument by pointing out that Wadard, along with Turold and Vital, who also appear in the tapestry, are mentioned in Domesday as tenants of Odo, Bishop of Bayeux and brother of the Conqueror. Over the next decade Odo came to be widely accepted, and still is today, as the most likely sponsor for a work so closely linked to Bayeux and its more prominent citizens.[15]

Stothard devoted the latter part of his paper to explaining his methods in making the drawings, particularly in dealing with damaged areas of the canvas, where the threads were missing and the only clue was the surviving needle holes:

> On attentively examining the traces thus left, I found that in many
> places minute particles of the different coloured threads were still
> retained; a circumstance which suggested to me the possibility of mak-
> ing extensive restorations. I accordingly commenced on a small portion,
> and found it attended with so much practicability as well as *certainty*,
> that I believed I should be fully justified in attempting to restore the
> whole . . . I have succeeded in restoring nearly all of what was defaced.
> Such parts as I have left as traced by the needle, either afforded no

vestiges of what the colours were, or such as were too vague in their situation to be depended on.[16]

It was on these notional restorations in Stothard's drawings that the discussion of the tapestry's narrative was based. Not everyone accepted them. Thomas Dibden found them 'a little too artist-like'.[17] Amyot, however, supported Stothard and nearly everyone was now against La Rue, who stuck to his version of the tapestry's date ever more stubbornly as the evidence against it mounted.

Stothard and his wife, Eliza, his companion and collaborator at Bayeux in 1818, used textual sources as well as the tapestry. For their interpretation of the narrative they turned to the chronicles, where the accounts of the Battle of Hastings are sparse and sometimes contradictory, while for the death of Harold there is no reliable evidence. William of Malmesbury's *Gesta Regum Anglorum* of *c.*1125 and Henry of Huntingdon's *Historia Anglorum* of 1130–40 recount that he was killed by an arrow in the eye. This was good enough for Lingard, the first volume of whose *History of England* appeared in 1819.[18] Other chroniclers tell other stories, however, and among antiquaries there had always been scepticism. A correspondent to *Archaeologia* noted that Giraldus Cambrensis, in his *Itinerarium Cambriae* of *c.* 1196–1223, refers to Harold being wounded in the eye at the battle but surviving.[19] The story struck Amyot as having all the hallmarks of a familiar myth: 'A similar fable has since been related, and partially believed, of the escape of James the 4th of Scotland from Flodden Field. King Arthur, Charles of Burgundy, and Don Sebastian of Portugal, have also been made heroes of popular tales of this description.'[20]

Harold's death, as it occurs at the end of the tapestry, is somewhat anticlimactic, both aesthetically and as a narrative. The evidence of the fabric suggests that some last scene or scenes may be missing. Eliza, who read the tapestry's story as a vindication of Harold, found in Lingard and the chronicles support for a more satisfactory conclusion:

> Harold, who united the enthusiasm of determined valour with the necessary skill and judgment of command, received a fatal arrow in his eye, before the victory was decided; he fell with many a brave adherent. When Harold was slain and fallen to the ground, some base hand plunged a spear into his thigh. History relates that William afterwards

disgraced the man who did it, for having been guilty of so cowardly an act ... The tapestry agrees entirely with these historical relations; ... Harold is represented receiving the arrow in his eye, he falls to the ground; a soldier pierces him in the thigh, with a sword.[21]

This was the dramatic finale the Stothards were looking for and they found it, or at least they found the image of Harold being wounded in the leg under the words 'Haroldus Rex interfectus est'. To the left of that figure is another, who wears different-coloured hose. He has his back to the fallen king and his right hand raised as if holding something. Whatever that object was had disappeared by 1818. This was one of the places where, according to Montfaucon's plates, the stitching was missing. Stothard drew a line between the holes by the soldier's head and added feathers at the far end, making it into an arrow going into the man's eye. Yet the holes Stothard interpreted as an arrow moving towards the figure, visible in Montfaucon's illustrations, which he was using as a guide, might as easily be seen to suggest a spear being thrown by a soldier. Despite this and the difference in their dress the Stothards concluded that both figures were meant for Harold:

> A single character in some parts of the Tapestry is so often repeated, almost in the same place, and within so small a space, that the subject becomes confused ... [as] in the death of Harold, who appears first fighting by his standard-bearer, afterwards where he is struck by the arrow in his eye, and lastly where he has fallen, and the soldier is represented wounding him in the thigh.[22]

Until Stothard's 'restored' copy gained currency, the antiquarian discussion of the tapestry had made no reference to an arrow in Harold's eye. The Huguenot Andrew Ducarel's Anglo-Norman Antiquities Considered of 1767 reproduces Montfaucon's plate, and the discussion in The Gentleman's Magazine debate of 1803 took it for granted that Harold's death is represented only once, and that the figure to which the text 'Haroldus Rex interfectus est' refers shows him prone: 'He dies with his arms in his hand ... extended on the ground. A horseman, without dismounting, pierces Harold's thigh.'[23] Frank W. Wilkin, who painted his monumental The Battle of Hastings, now at Battle Abbey, in 1820, when the antiquarian argument was in full swing, shows Harold thus prone and dying in his soldiers' arms. Stothard's interpretation was highly questionable. It had the advantage, however, of drama, personal detail and suffering as well as being more dignified than a thigh wound received on the ground. It filled a physical gap in the fabric and an imaginative one in the story.

Stothard had made no physical alterations to the tapestry. It was only when, long after his death, the city of Bayeux came to create a museum for it in 1842 that the fabric was restored, using Stothard's drawings as a guide. Thus the arrow went into Harold's eye and hence into history. E. A. Freeman, in his *History of the Norman Conquest* of 1870–76, notes: 'This scene, the turning point of all English history' is 'vividly shown in the Tapestry.'[24] Freeman had 'that confidence in the Tapestry as I look on it as a primary authority . . . in fact the highest authority on the Norman side'. Staunch in defence of the empirical antiquarian method, he explained that 'stitchwork' is unambiguous, 'it must tell its tale simply', it cannot indulge in 'rhetoric' or 'invective'.[25] Thus by a circular process the tapestry came to be cited as the earliest account of Harold's death, when in reality it was the most recent.

A LITTLE TOUR FOR THE FIRESIDE

Eliza Stothard, as a freelance writer with a living to earn, made full use of the trip with Charles. Her *Letters Written during a Tour through Normandy, Britanny [sic] and other Parts of France in 1818* appeared in 1820 under the name of Mrs Charles Stothard. The book was presented with the properly genteel, feminine distaste for publication and the modest assurance that it had been written purely for her family as a 'little illustrated tour for the fireside', an 'unaffected picture' of a lady's travels.[26] Happily, this was not true. Like her brother Alfred Kempe, now a staff writer on *The Gentleman's Magazine*, Eliza was a well-informed and intrepid antiquary, more than willing to climb ladders, explore suggestive ruins and form her own opinions. Hers was one of three books based on English antiquaries' travels in that year. Dawson Turner's *Account of a Tour in Normandy* also appeared in

1820, while Thomas Frognall Dibdin's more lavish and extensive *Bibliographical, Antiquarian and Picturesque Tour in France and Germany* came out in 1821. They were among the first and best of dozens of similar works published over the following decade. Each addressed a slightly different audience and each author took a different route, but the cardinal points of the Norman tour were established. Sailing usually to Dieppe, the antiquarian traveller would visit Rouen, Caen and Bayeux, the indispensable Norman cities. The great cathedrals of Lisieux and Évreux, the ruined abbey at Jumièges, Falaise, the Conqueror's birthplace and Mantes which he besieged in 1087, were also of interest. The Stothards continued to Brittany, Dibdin went on as far as Vienna while Turner confined himself to Normandy, but between them they offer a fair representation of what might be called Anglo-Normandy as a post-Napoleonic antiquarian construct. They covered customs and manners, architecture (especially the much-discussed and disputed early Gothic), artefacts, including coins, inscriptions, tombs and manuscripts, all the meat and drink of antiquarianism. Books were Dibdin's special passion; he may have coined and certainly popularized the term 'bibliomania', a condition from which he suffered acutely. Eliza Stothard had a particular interest in the theatre, while beyond their individual enthusiasms British antiquaries also reported in detail on the present state of France, French antiquarianism and the effects, good and bad, of the Revolution.

All travellers have preconceptions. The British had long since absorbed the Romantic Picturesque and went in search of evocative scenery, the spirit of place, and the effects of association. These views, in both senses of the word, overlay their experiences like the tissue paper over the plates in the books they bought. Normandy, 'the land of castles churches and ancient chivalry', offered plenty to enjoy.[27] The approach to Rouen was generally admired for its 'steep hills covered by hanging woods, valleys, and chateaux', while in the flatter country around Le Havre 'monotony even of excellence' was displeasing.[28] The Seine Valley was the perfect Romantic route, comparable with the Wye, replete with ruins, and Dibdin was one of many visitors to find at Jumièges Normandy's own Tintern. He stopped there to enjoy a picnic by the place where the heart of Charles VII's mistress, Agnès Sorel, *la dame de beauté*, was buried after her death in 1450:

The situation of the abbey is delightful. It lies at the bottom of some gently undulating hills, within two or three hundred yards of the Seine. The river here runs gently, in a serpentine direction, at the foot of wood-covered hills – and all seemed, from our elevated station, indicative of fruitfulness, of gaiety, and of prosperity, – all – save the mournful and magnificent remains of the venerable abbey whereon we gazed![29]

But the ruins of Jumièges told a story of more raw and recent iconoclasm than Tintern, and the destruction was still going on. The Picturesque outline of the abbey's remains was at this date largely the creation of M. Lefort, a timber merchant, who had bought it in 1802 and blown up much of the building for the stone. The rest was being dismantled for materials and souvenirs even while Dibdin was enjoying his lunch. At Bernay Dawson Turner saw the gravestones from the abbey stacked up by the church door. Headstones had been forbidden under the Revolution, but these were waiting now 'not for preservation, but for sale!'.[30] As an antiquary aware of the historic value of monuments he was dismayed, and as a Romantic antiquary given to quoting Gray's *Elegy* the razed churchyard presented to him a 'comfortless sight'. The dead were deprived of historic afterlife, as if 'the memory of man should terminate' with death and take from the living the pleasures and comforts of recollection.[31] Everywhere, Eliza Stothard wrote, 'The unfeeling ravages of the revolution' impressed themselves on the travellers, who were shocked by the apparent indifference of the French.[32] France, as they already knew, 'did not abound in topographical writers', and the British antiquary's usual method of seeking out the oldest inhabitants and cross-questioning them about local history also met with mixed success.[33] Eliza Stothard, though she spoke French, was frustrated. 'Every where abounds with the most beautiful gothic structures, and interesting remains of antiquity, that must excite the admiration of all persons who have least taste for the productions of art . . . yet upon the French such works are entirely lost.'[34] Enquiries usually elicited a reply along the lines of: 'It's ugly, it's crude, it's old, it's nothing.'[35] Exhausted and impoverished, the French had not yet sufficient historic distance to lend enchantment to the ruins of their past.

Yet there was an advantage for the Anglo-Norman antiquary in arriving at sites where neither conservation nor improvement had tidied away the evidence of history, distant or recent. In Notre-Dame at Eu the Stothards climbed down into the crypt after Sunday Mass to explore the burial place of the Counts of Eu, and found themselves transported to the height of the Terror. Eliza wrote:

> Every monument had been torn down and dreadfully shattered, fragments of broken Gothic arches, and columns, were piled amidst dirt and rubbish ... The fury of the revolutionists [seems] yet to speak in these stones, they lie tossed confusedly about as if scattered by the wild ferocity of madness. Day-light broke into this vaulted and subterraneous apartment, through some iron gratings towards the east, and cast a pale gleam on the surrounding objects, which ... gave a feeling of horror to the place.[36]

In a corner the fifteenth-century marble effigy of Jeanne, wife of Charles d'Artois, who died in 1449, lay where it been thrown against a wall, its head half buried.

Caen, where La Rue, 'the great archaeological oracle of Normandy' as Dibdin called him, was now a professor at the university, was a popular resort for the British.[37] When Dawson Turner arrived, there were about thirty family parties in residence and he enjoyed the city greatly, despite being arrested on arrival for a missing signature on his passport. He was by now an old hand in dealing with the French authorities. Dibdin noted that Caen was known as 'the dépôt of the English' and an 'amazing number of our countrymen' were there, not all for antiquarian reasons.[38] 'One family comes to reside from motives of economy; another from those of education; a third from those of retirement; and a fourth from pure love of sitting down, in a strange place, with the chance of making some pleasant connection, or of being engaged in seeking some strange adventure.'[39] As Palgrave said, the British felt at home in Normandy. The other Norman tourist centre was Rouen, which formed a striking contrast. Dibdin called Caen 'still-life' in comparison with Rouen's raucous conversation piece.[40] Rouen had some of the most remarkable late Gothic architecture in France set amid a bustling industrial city. Factories and bleaching grounds lined the roads into the centre, where the jutting upper storeys of medieval, timber-framed houses hung over narrow streets, crowded with people and rubbish, some of the houses so decayed, Eliza Stothard thought, 'that they appear ready to fall upon their inhabitants'.[41] Poverty, as Turner observed, was 'the inseparable companion of a manufacturing population', while La Rue, prejudiced in favour of his native Caen, put it more bluntly to Douce that Rouen was known as 'the chamber pot of France'.[42]

This did not deter the British, especially not the artists and the antiquaries. Rouen Cathedral, despite the loss of the bishop's throne, was still an encyclopaedia of every age of Gothic culminating in the Tour de Beurre, built in the early sixteenth century, its lacy stonework seeming to float 'interwoven like a slender web' against the sky.[43] The interior was 'so imposingly beautiful' that it struck even the trenchantly anti-Catholic Eliza Stothard into 'involuntary awe': the Palais de Justice, the Hôtel de Bourgtheroulde, with its bas-reliefs of François I and Henry VIII at the Field of the Cloth of Gold, the site of Joan of Arc's martyrdom and the Church of St-Ouen were among the other attractions.[44] There was also the medieval cemetery at the Church of St-Maclou, with the remains of a Dance of Death around the walls and the Abbeys of St-Wandrille and St-George (sic) de Bocherville close by. It was in its very roughness and variety that Rouen appealed. It had every Picturesque requirement. Turner described it in terms of foreground, middle distance and background as if in one of the hundreds of watercolour views which the city inspired for the rest of that century and beyond:

> ... verdant walks ... spacious manufactories ... strange and picturesque buildings, and the numerous spires and towers of ... churches, many of them in ruins, but not the less interesting on account of their decay, presents a foreground diversified with endless variety of form and color ... the middle distance is composed of a plain, chiefly consisting of the richest meadows, interspersed copiously with country seats and villages embosomed in wood; and the horizon melts into an undulating line of remote hills.[45]

To capture it Turner commissioned John Sell Cotman (1782–1842), one of the greatest of a brilliant generation of British watercolourists. Cotman, who taught the Turner daughters drawing and sometimes travelled with the family, loved Normandy, especially the south, which he called 'the Wales of France'.[46] His work for Turner became a celebrated book, *Architectural Antiquities of Normandy*, with letterpress by Turner himself. Cotman set off from Norfolk armed with an introduction to La Rue, but their meeting only confirmed the element of mutual incomprehension between the French and British at this date on the subject of Picturesque landscape. La Rue wrote in bafflement to Douce: 'Mr Coteman [*sic*] is travelling through the province to draw Norman antiquities ... [he] goes too fast to produce anything good ... Mr Coteman speaks no French ... [he] appears to me to know nothing, he has an artist's skill but none of the mentality of an antiquary.'[47]

Not all the French were so conservative. The tendrils of Romanticism were beginning to soften the severe Classical taste of the Revolutionary age, and as cross-Channel antiquarianism blossomed the process accelerated. Gerville admired Cotman, as did his fellow Rouennais, Auguste Le Prevost. Le Prevost, who was on the brink of a distinguished career as the author of works on Norman dialect, place names and local history, was a friend of Douce and after a visit to London in 1817 his English correspondents included John Gage and Henry Ellis. British and French antiquaries alike felt the urgent need for 'immediate and concerted efforts' to 'snatch from destruction and oblivion ... all that is left to us of the monuments and the memories rooted in our soil', while La Rue, as the pivot of the Anglo-Norman axis, was now in correspondence not only with Douce but with Dawson Turner, Gurney, the Stothards and various other 'distinguished Englishmen'.[48] A close and effective network had come rapidly into being.

THE ANTIQUARY IN FRANCE

French antiquarianism was transformed by the Revolution and its aftermath. Antiquaries were to be found across a wider social and professional spectrum. No longer were most of them in holy orders. Their subject matter was becoming ever broader, with national antiquities and the Middle Ages now a focus of interest. Research was no longer primarily palaeographic but extended to any and all material remains. After 1815 the transformation was increasingly apparent in the contrast between two generations. The older, their experience marked and in some cases perversely enhanced by revolution, war and exile, were sometimes impatient with the optimistic fresh-faced youngsters born after 1789, who looked on antiquarianism as an exciting new venture. La Rue's history of Caen was published in 1820, but he was still struggling with his magnum opus on troubadours, unable, as he told Douce, to get through the chapter on the origins of the French language. This perhaps added to his irritation with the 'young normans' snapping at his heels with an enthusiasm he considered out of all proportion to their knowledge.[49]

The contrast between Caen and Rouen, the one so respectable the other so ramshackle, was reflected in their most prominent antiquaries. The Rouennais counterpart of the proper, somewhat pedantic La Rue was Eustache-Hyacinthe Langlois (1777–1837), who became something of a tourist attraction in his own right. Artist, antiquary and co-founder of the Rouen Musée d'antiquités, he was the author of a pioneering study, *Receuil de quelques vues, sites et monumens de France, et specialement de la Normandie et des divers costumes de ses habitans* (*A Collection of Several Views, Sites and Monuments of France, Especially of Normandy and its Various Costumes and Inhabitants*), published in 1817. His *Essai historique et descriptif sur l'Abbaye de Fontenelle ou de Saint-Wandrille* appeared in 1827, but his chief interest was the history of the Dance of Death, a study inspired in part by the vestiges in the cemetery at St-Maclou and in part by his own savagely satirical temperament. Langlois, whose strange life and miserable death embodied much of the drama and trauma of recent French history, exerted a powerful fascination over many of his fellow antiquaries, while in others he provoked equally strong revulsion. Born in 1777 at Pont-de-l'Arche, twenty kilometres south of Rouen, he was the son of an official in the Royal Department of Woods and Waters. His father lost his job when waterways and forests were nationalized, and Langlois, abruptly liberated from his father's expectations for him, decided to become an artist. He made his way to Paris in the perilous months of 1793 to the studio of Jacques-Louis David. In the political tumult David had little time for students, but he used the handsome young Langlois as a model. The figure of Romulus, which occupies the central position in David's masterpiece *The*

Intervention of the Sabine Women, frozen forever in a moment of crisis between action and suffering, was based on Langlois. Those who knew him saw it as an apt depiction, for there were in him 'two quite different temperaments', described by contemporaries in terms of the Classical and Romantic strains that met or, as some thought, fought in him.[50] A later age might reach for other terms, such as depressive or bipolar. In his writing Langlois was certainly Janus-faced, at times scrupulously factual, evincing contempt for the superstitions of the past, caustic about the Church and 'our ancestors' extreme credulousness', at others weaving fiction and narrative into his antiquarian studies with fantastical abandon.[51]

By 1806 he was a married man with seven children and life as an unsuccessful artist in Paris was untenable. He retreated first to Pont-de-l'Arche and thence to Rouen. Virtually destitute, he took his family to live in the abandoned Convent of the Visitation, where he stayed for the rest of his life in abject poverty with his alcoholic wife while the children ran wild. It was in the cloisters of the convent that Langlois first assembled the fragments of stained glass, carving and other salvaged curiosities that would become Rouen's Musée d'antiquités. Upstairs he worked by day at the commercial art which gave him his meagre living, designing letter heads, jam-pot labels and anything else that was needed locally in a hurry. By night, and very slowly, he worked on his own books in the style of antiquarian authorship known and satirized since the Renaissance. Beginning with a drawing of some object, a piece of manuscript or a fragment of stained glass, he would engrave it, add a short caption, and send it to the printer. Then another engraving of another, related subject would come to him and he would amend the first caption. Once that was typeset he would edit it again, cutting up the proofs and reassembling them as he went on before sending them back to have the deletions, insertions and other alterations made. This 'demonic rearrangement' would go on, 'to the utter despair of the printer', until the text had grown gradually, like coral, into a book.[52]

Langlois liked to be interrupted in his bread-and-butter work by anyone willing to brave the chill and chaos of the convent. With his caustic humour and profound knowledge, he acquired many friends and correspondents in Britain and France. The Turners were among his regular visitors: Mary Turner engraved his self-portrait. Gage was particularly fond of him, dealing gently with Langlois's letters in which he poured out his feelings of desperation. Auguste Pugin, who with John Britton took advantage of the vogue for all things Norman to compile a book of *Architectural Antiquities of Normandy*, found Langlois helpful for getting plans and tracings of buildings. But not everyone was charmed. Among Pugin's pupils travelling with him in 1824 to make drawings for the book was the young Benjamin Ferrey. Ferrey, later a competent if uninspired architect, noted primly that Langlois 'was the type of a class of men who rank high in French estimation'.[53] He combined 'genius ... taste and a cultivated mind' with a home that was 'meanly furnished ... all [its] arrangements characterized by economy'.[54] 'In this country', Ferrey continued, meaning in England, 'things are rather different; it must be admitted that, in general, a man of talent unfortunately placed in M. Langlois' circumstances could not mix in society on equal terms.'[55] Yet while Ferrey was half admiring and half scandalized by the high-minded French disregard for anything but a man's 'mind and accomplishments', Langlois's friend and biographer, Charles Richard, took an exactly opposite point of view.[56] He lamented the French neglect of Langlois, which left the English to make his reputation:

> Langlois's work, which was unknown among his fellow citizens, achieved a high reputation in England; his archaeological opinions carried great weight there ... eminent foreigners, especially English scholars, travelling in Normandy made it their first duty to come and visit Langlois ... can we think, without blushing, of the state in which his admirers found him when they came to see him in his adopted town![57]

There is some truth in both views. Langlois was admired by the English, the more conventional among them making allowances for him as a kind of exotic, while at home he was not bereft of friends. He made an impression on the boys to whom, in another attempt to eke out a living, he taught drawing. One of them was Gustave Flaubert, whose portrait Langlois drew; Flaubert remembered him with fondness. He used a plate from Langlois's study of the stained glass of Rouen in his *Trois contes* to show the irrelevance of historic sources to fictional narrative. It was a perverse point that Langlois would have enjoyed. Now, by chance, the two men lie in adjacent graves.

In the more sedate ambiance of Caen the most prominent representative of the rising generation was Arcisse de Caumont (1801–73). Caumont was largely instrumental in founding the Society of Antiquaries of Normandy, of which La Rue was tactfully invited to be president, and had come to antiquarianism, like Turner, from the natural sciences. He was a geologist who based his argument for the integrity of Normandy on the continuity of its rock formations which constituted, he argued, a primordial identity impervious to any shifting political divisions on the surface. A great and methodical organizer of information, his chief contribution to antiquarianism was not so much in original scholarship as his immense energy as a synthesizer. His *Cours d'antiquités monumentales*, which began appearing in 1830, took some of its inspiration from Britton and Bayley's *The Beauties of England and Wales*, embracing history and topography. By the time the series was concluded in 1841, Caumont had covered the whole of north-west France, and his *Cours* remained the principal source on the subject into the twentieth century. This did not prevent him from being criticized by his elders. Gerville complained to Gage of Caumont's narrowness, adding unkindly that Caumont 'calls himself a Professor when he is really only a copyist'.[58] This was unfair. Antiquarianism on both sides of the Channel was always in need of systematic, organizing minds to give usable form to the accumulation of material. For every Aubrey there had to be a Camden.

In Paris, too, the effects of recent history were being worked out. Lenoir's museum was abruptly closed. His success in adapting the presentation to every succeeding regime had ultimately made it unpopular with all of them. A silent witness to the excesses of the Revolution and to 'twenty-five years of looting', it was now a painful sight, especially repellent to the restored Bourbon monarchy.[59] Lenoir was heartbroken. Though willing to restore objects to their original settings where these survived, he pleaded to be allowed to keep those monuments now 'orphaned', of which there were many.[60] But despite a direct appeal, Louis XVIII signed the order for its closure on 18 December 1816. The Petits Augustins was handed over to the École des beaux-arts, while some of the more massive pieces were left in what remained of the bedraggled Jardin Élysée to rot for years in wind and weather.

In truth, its moment had passed. After seeing the real aftermath of the Revolution, Eliza Stothard found the tomb of Abélard and Héloïse unconvincing: 'one of those combinations which Monsieur Le Noir is so fond of displaying, at the expense of truth'.[61] Arguably the museum was more influential because it disappeared in reality and so lived on as an unspoilt memory for the future historians on whom, as children, it had made the greatest impression. Not only Jules Michelet, but François Guizot and Augustin Thierry imbibed something of their sense of history from it. Michelet recalled the effect on his generation in his *Histoire de la Révolution française*: 'How many souls were quickened with the spark of history, the fascination of magnificent memorials, the intangible longing to travel back through the ages.'[62] For one adolescent, however, it was not the museum but its dismantling that was to make a lasting impression. In 1816, as an impoverished divorcee, Sophie Hugo moved into an apartment in the rue des Petits-Augustins which opened into the courtyard of the former museum. Her sons, Victor and Eugène, watched from their study as the tombs and monuments were dismantled and removed. To the fourteen-year-old Victor it seemed like a second violation, as terrible as the sacking of St-Denis, and confirmed what he later called his 'antiquarian instinct', his preoccupation with the Gothic and the Middle Ages, with architectural conservation, 'with death and history'.[63]

The British were in touch with a number of Parisian antiquaries, including Millin and another pioneer in the study of medieval art, Nicolas Xavier Willemin (1763–1839). A native of Nancy, Willemin had published an influential study of Classical dress and furniture in 1798, which had an immediate influence on costume in the French theatre and was used as a source book by David. Since 1806, however, he had been at work on his next great project, the *Monuments français inédits* (*Unpublished French Monuments*), which was to do the same for the Middle Ages. The main title was, in full, *Monuments français inédits pour servir à l'histoire des arts: depuis le VIe siècle jusqu'au commencement du XVIIe*, an attempt to replicate Lenoir's museum, using objects as the basis of an historical account. After 1823, when Seroux d'Agincourt's *L'Histoire de l'art par les monuments, depuis sa décadence au quatrième siècle jusqu'à son renouvellement au seizième* (*The History of Art through its Monuments from its Decline in the Fourth Century to its Revival in the Sixteenth*) was published, Willemin's work also became a manifesto and an apologia. Whereas d'Agincourt, as his title suggests, saw in the art of the Middle Ages a period of decline, Willemin wanted to celebrate it. Sadly, as Dibdin discovered when he visited him in 1818, Willemin had not only the essential qualities of the antiquary – tenacity, industry and a capacious memory – but the common faults as well, accumulating material without attempting to order it. What interested him was collecting examples, drawing and then engraving them. In this way he had worked on through the personal and political vicissitudes of thirty years; obliged to sell off his own spectacular collection of antiquities, he lost by stages his money, his eyesight and ultimately his mind. Dibdin's *Bibliographical, Antiquarian and Picturesque Tour in France and Germany* includes a touching picture of 'the unassuming and assiduous author' in his rooms on the third floor 'towards the eastern end of the Rue St. Honoré', where 'several young females ... in the ante-room' were 'colouring the plates of that work; which are chiefly in outline and in aqua-tint'.[64] The Stothards also visited the 'ingenious M Willemin' and Eliza felt the same pity for him. His work attracted 'so little encouragement, that ... he had sometimes scarcely sufficient even to live'.[65] His beloved wife was dead, as was his son, killed in the war. Circumstances and temperament combined to thwart his progress. Only after his death in 1839 did his daughter, with André Pottier, manage to get his work published in two magnificent folio volumes.

After 1815 the ranks of the London Society of Antiquaries were swollen by French fellows. Gage was director. The president was now Aberdeen, who, despite his lack of interest in the Middle Ages or national history, was anxious to boost membership, telling Gurney that he entirely approved of 'filling up' the Society with 'De Caumont & the other Normans & getting up a *good* list of foreign members'.[66] Le Prevost assured Gurney, who in turn told Gage that Caumont was 'un gentleman extrêmement recommandable' for election.[67] He was joined by others including Gerville and Langlois, who was not at all 'un gentleman' but whose 'high esteem and affection' for Gage were fully reciprocated.[68]

UNWHITEWASHED AND UNDESCRIBED

At the heart of the Anglo-Norman project was the question that had puzzled and divided British antiquaries since the 1780s, the origins of Gothic. Even for those like Turner, who had read and accepted Whittington's study, the details of the precise connections between English and Norman architecture, and later between English and French Gothic, remained obscure. What was the chronology? When did the Saxon style end? Rickman's terminology was, by the later 1820s, almost universally adopted in Britain, supplemented by William Gunn's 'Romanesque', while in France *flamboyant* or flaming was in use for late French Gothic, a coinage attributed to various antiquaries including Langlois. The categories were still fluid, however. Turner, faced with the remains of the castle at Arques-la-Bataille, reached wildly for 'florid Norman Gothic', adding pre-emptively, 'I forbid all cavils respecting the employment of this term.'[69] It did not catch on. Turner's interest in architecture being relatively recent, he was often at a loss to know what he was seeing. In Dieppe he decided that the Church of St-Rémy was seventeenth-century, which left him puzzling over the massive columns, resembling 'our earliest Norman or Saxon churches'.[70] Eliza Stothard's better-trained eye recognized a building of several phases, an 'intermixture of all styles of architecture from the twelfth down to the middle of the sixteenth century'.[71] 'Norman or Saxon' was increasingly the question. Over time it was becoming clear that in England the answer was almost always Norman, and that very little of the Saxon period survived, but more comparisons were needed.

On the French side Gerville and Le Prevost worked on chronology and terminology, making long tours in the Cherbourg peninsula and Upper Normandy respectively. Gerville's was the first French attempt at a division of styles, and here the influence of the English was not helpful. He tried, unsuccessfully, to make the distinction between Norman and Saxon but confided to Caumont that he thought it false, moving instead towards the idea of '*architecture Romane*' thereby arriving independently at the same point as Gunn. Le Prevost, drawing on Gunn and Rickman, divided the architecture of the Middle Ages into periods, settling on the round arch or '*plein cintre*' for everything between the ninth and eleventh centuries, then the lancet style for the thirteenth, the *'rayonnant'* for the fourteenth, *'flamboyant'* for the fifteenth and choosing to extend the Gothic up to the death of François I in 1547, in a concluding phase he called *'fleuri'*. La Rue thought this took Gothic on far too late. He also protested that the Romanesque had nothing directly to do with the Romans, something which Gunn and Gerville knew perfectly well. La Rue had never been sympathetic to the attempt to establish a history of architecture, which he thought a comparatively trivial subject. In so far as he took an interest, he characteristically preferred to use documentary evidence rather than the buildings themselves. However, the 'young people' disagreed.[72] In 1824 Caumont published what had become the consensus view in his *Essai sur l'architecture religieuse du Moyen Âge, particulièrement en Normandie* (*Essay on the Religious Architecture of the Middle Ages, particularly in Normandy*), which was addressed 'not so much to scholars as to the public', and there was now in France such a public, interested in the Middle Ages, Gothic architecture and the 'national landscape'.[73]

In 1832 Rickman himself made a French tour. Despite the destruction and neglect of recent decades he relished the prospect of *terra incognita* and so many buildings still 'unwhitewashed and undescribed'.[74] His travelling companion was William Whewell (1794–1866), the historian, philosopher of science and originator of many of the terms that gave expression to the expanding nature of empirical enquiry in his lifetime. Among these were 'archaeology' in its modern sense of excavation and 'scientist'. They had met when Rickman was working at St John's College, Cambridge and the young don took an instant liking to the methodical Quaker. Two years earlier Whewell had published his *Architectural Notes on German Churches*, the first significant study of the Gothic in Germany.[75] The plan for this tour was to test Rickman's classifications against French buildings to see by comparison the connections and variations. Both men published accounts of their trip, undertaken on similar comparative principles. Rickman cast his in the usual form of letters, addressed in this case to Gage, describing his methods for ascribing dates, which 'I am aware I can not prove by documentary evidence'.[76] Documents, he added, perhaps with an eye to La Rue, though he had 'the highest respect for them', had their limitations. 'It very often happens that the most important point, viz. whether the building now existing is the one really referred to in the document, must, after all, rather be collected from inference or analogy, than be considered directly proved.'[77]

On the Norman or Saxon question Rickman thought that the re-classifying of the Saxon had perhaps now gone too far and under-estimated its extent in England, but his conclusion was that the Norman style was to all intents and purposes one and indivisible on both sides of the Channel: 'About the year 1000 there appears to have begun that style which may, I think, justly be called Norman; for under William the Conqueror and William Rufus, we have both in France and England a series of magnificent works in a style so much the same, that to an ordinary observer they would appear identical.'[78]

Rickman and Whewell went to the usual places. From Boulogne to Abbeville, Amiens, Beauvais, Rouen, Jumièges, Évreux, Lisieux, Caen, Bayeux, St-Lô, Coutances, Carentan, Isigny, Honfleur, Pont-Audemer, Caudebec, Lillebonne, Harfleur, then home via Le Havre. They met Le Prevost, who showed them round what was left of Jumièges, and Caumont, who was delighted to entertain 'M Wewhel and M Riekmann'.[79] They were arrested, as was de rigueur by now, and held for some hours by the National Guard. According to Whewell, however, they had better luck than Eliza Stothard in obtaining local information. Rickman was in Quaker dress, which attracted attention, as did his 'good-humoured and very intelligent' enquiries.[80] Whewell appreciated how much more he was learning than if he had travelled alone. While it is possible that Rickman had a more engaging manner than Eliza Stothard, his relative success was largely a reflection of the difference effected by the fourteen years between their visits. The Revolution and the war were passing into history. Certain wounds had healed and public taste had changed. By 1824 it had shifted sufficiently for some of Lenoir's surviving collection to be shown at the Louvre.

The advance of Romanticism in France was undoubtedly accelerated by the exchange of ideas with Britain. French painters, and the French public, were being wooed away from neo-Classical landscape painting towards the Picturesque, 'la *view* à l'anglaise'.[81] In 1820 antiquarianism and Romanticism combined to produce one of the great

French publishing projects of the nineteenth century, the *Voyages pittoresques et romantiques dans l'ancienne France*, the work of Charles Nodier and Isidore, later Baron, Taylor. Nodier (1780–1844) was a poet who had spent time in England and, even more profitably, in Scotland, entranced by what he insisted on calling 'Caledoniam' with its sublime mountains and black Ossianic lakes.[82] Taylor, (1789–1879) who was English on his father's side, was an author and translator of plays. A committed Romantic, born in the year of the Revolution, he was among those children on whose imagination Lenoir's museum had made a profound impression. Nodier and Taylor's series of large and lavish volumes appeared at a stately pace over more than half a century. They were illustrated with lithographs, still a relatively new technique which Nodier thought might have been especially invented 'to fix the free, original and rapid inspirations of the traveller who gives an account of his sensations'.[83] The *Voyages pittoresques* covered all the provinces of France. Like Caumont, the authors were almost certainly influenced by Britton and Brayley's *Beauties of England and Wales*, but theirs was an enterprise conceived on a scale far beyond anything ever attempted in Britain. It was a 'romantic manifesto', a journey across the landscape and through time, to a past now irrecoverable except by means of art and the power of association.[84] *Ancienne* means not merely old but 'former', or 'one-time'. These were monuments to a lost world; 'they reveal in their ruins other ruins, vaster and more terrifying to contemplate, those of the institutions which for so long supported the monarchy, and whose fall was the ineluctable omen of its collapse'.[85] If any English antiquarian work bore comparison with the *Voyages pittoresques*, it was not so much the *Beauties* as the *Monasticon Anglicanum*, England's own survey of a lost social order; and, like the new edition of the *Monasticon* appearing simultaneously in Britain, Nodier and Taylor's work attracted a particular class of subscriber, including several European monarchs.

The first volume of the *Voyages pittoresques* was naturally devoted to Normandy, 'la province gothique par excellence'.[86] In it Nodier made the case that Carter and the Society of Antiquaries had made thirty years before with their series of engravings of medieval cathedrals presented in the same format as the Dilettantis' Classical subjects. Normandy,

Nodier wrote, was as worthy of study as any Classical site, Rouen the equal of Palmyra or Thebes. Yet neither Nodier nor Taylor was an antiquary. They relied heavily on those who were and were open about their debts. No words could do justice, Nodier wrote at the end of Volume II, to their gratitude to Le Prevost, whose 'brilliant erudition' had been an inspiration and a model. Le Prevost himself was not flattered to be implicated in a work he despised, remarking to Gerville that Nodier would have done better to call his book 'novel, fantasy, lies about the monuments of Normandy'. Caumont agreed.[87] Despite Nodier's 'brilliant and poetic style' it was, he thought, a shame that the Picturesque was emphasized at the expense of accuracy and that points of fact which could have been checked quite easily were omitted.[88] Whether the antiquaries liked it or not, Romanticism was blurring the frontiers between history and fiction. Factual detail had to contend with truth of feeling.

The Normandy volume appeared in 1820, the same year as the French edition of *Ivanhoe*. Scott's earlier works had been translated, and as far as Nodier and his fellow Romantics were concerned he was established as 'Le brillant Ossian ... moderne'.[89] *Ivanhoe*, however, marked a new phase. The first of the *Waverley* novels set in the Middle Ages, it took Scott's fame in France to a different level. A tale of love and war in the reign of Richard the Lionheart, it is an Anglo-Norman romance in which the Saxon hero, Wilfred of Ivanhoe, joins forces with the Plantagenet king to defeat the wicked Prince John. There is a tournament, a siege, in which the Saxons are joined by the king and 'Locksley', who is eventually revealed to be Robin Hood. The lovely Rebecca is kidnapped by the vile knight Front-de-Boeuf and rescued, though her love for Ivanhoe is doomed, as he will marry Rowena. It was Anglo-Normandy brought to life, to colour and romance. It was, according to Victor Hugo, 'the true epic of the age'.[90]

While Scott had drawn on the work of his fellow antiquaries, Sharon Turner, Ritson and Strutt, *Ivanhoe* in its turn became the inspiration for Thierry's *L'Histoire de la conquête de l'Angleterre par les Normands* (*History of the Conquest of England by the Normans*) of 1825. Written with the narrative *élan* of *Waverley*, Thierry's *Histoire* opens with the mournful drama of the Conqueror's funeral and proceeds by way of a consideration of the legend of Robin Hood to tell the story of the rough but noble Anglo-Saxons preserving their liberty in the face of the invader. The reciprocity of narrative history and fiction was complete. Also complete was that literary invasion that Scott had launched on the field of Waterloo. In 1823 *Quentin Durward*, a novel set in France concerning the fortunes of the eponymous Scottish archer during the reign of Louis XI, made his position unassailable and by 1830 a third of all the novels published in France were by Scott. The fashion for everything *à l'Écosse* boomed until, as one journalist remarked, out of 3,000 women promenading in the Tuileries Garden, it would be hard to find ten who were not wearing tartan ribbons.[91]

Scott's influence encouraged the Romantics in their assault on the canons of Classical taste still rigorously enforced in French theatre and at the annual Salons at the Louvre. In drama the Aristotelian unities, in painting Classical subject matter, represented standards held much closer to the heart of national identity than any comparable conventions in Britain. As Balzac wrote in *Lost Illusions* at that time: 'there were then only two parties, Royalists and Liberals, Romanticists and Classicists: an identical hatred in different guise, a hatred great enough to explain why guillotines had been set up under the National Convention'.[92] In February 1830 Victor Hugo's *Hernani*, a drama set in sixteenth-century Spain, famously provoked a riot on the opening night with the Romantics, including Hugo, Hector Berlioz and Théophile Gautier, taking on the Classicists in the audience. By the same token the annual Salons of 1824 and 1827 were crises in which subjects from Classical history and mythology were challenged by others from national history and from fiction, especially Scott's. Between 1827 and 1833 an average of twenty-five pictures a year were of scenes from the *Waverley* novels.[93] French artists researched their antiquarian detail in British collections. The visitors' book from the home of Douce's friend Samuel Rush Meyrick reveals that Géricault came to look at his collection in 1820, when he was interested in depicting horse armour.[94] Paul Delaroche, Hippolyte Bellangé and Eugène Lami all came in 1822, and Delacroix was there in 1825 to inspect and sketch the collection. As Meyrick wrote in *The Gentleman's Magazine* in April 1826: 'There now exists a feeling for correctness of costume and accessaries [*sic*], both here and on the Continent, in painting ... that cannot retrograde.'[95] The admiration was mutual. Delacroix's *Massacre de l'évêque de Liège*, a scene from *Quentin Durward*, was a particular success at the Royal Academy in 1830.

There is, however, a caveat to be borne in mind when considering Scott's torrential impact on French art, literature and narrative history writing and that is the role of his translator. Among those who crossed the Channel from France to England in the aftermath of Waterloo, the lawyer Auguste-Jean-Baptiste Defauconpret (1767–1843) is not now much remembered, yet no French visitor had more influence on popular literature. On arrival at Dover in September 1815 Defauconpret had a furious argument with customs officials in the course of which they confiscated his drinking chocolate. He was livid and the visit never recovered. As recorded in his caustically comic memoir *Quinze jours à Londres*, he disliked everything: the architecture, 'des briques, des briques', the food, the weather, the dreariness of an English Sunday and the prices.[96] Despite which he returned the following year, possibly to escape creditors, and settled to earning a living from translation. In due course he became the principal translator of the *Waverley* novels, which, particularly in his earlier efforts, he adapted to his own ideas of Classical good taste by omitting what he considered to be British vulgarities. These included characters he deemed superfluous, non-chronological narrative, anything savouring of *couleur locale* or marriages that transgressed social rank. His interventions and rearrangements in *Ivanhoe* were less drastic than in some of the earlier stories, but the most important of them, as one French critic has written, are 'unfortunately in the very heart of the novel'.[97] Defauconpret ironed out the clash of civilizations at the core of the drama by making the Saxons more sophisticated, going so far as to improve their table manners. This was not due to any lack of understanding. Defauconpret knew what Scott had written and thought it tasteless. He introduced epithets and similes in the Classical style where Scott used vividly particular imagery and he cut down the antiquarian detail. Perhaps it was just as well. For, taking his cue from Sharon Turner's view of the Conquest, Scott's portrayal of rough but virtuous Saxons pitched against a brutal Norman aristocracy is less flattering to the idea of Anglo-Norman identity than Defauconpret's translation rendered it.

BAL COSTUMÉ

Louis XVIII died in 1824 and was succeeded by his brother, Charles X. Unlike the plump and prosaic Louis, Charles was a Romantic bent on reviving the historic dignity of the house of Bourbon. His coronation in June 1825 was an antiquarian pageant and a royalist manifesto. It took place at Rheims, where Kings of France were crowned in the Middle Ages, and attracted visitors from across the Continent in such numbers that they became the subject of satirical sketches and a comic opera by Rossini, *Il viaggio a Reims*. By May, word of the preparations had reached England and Charles Kemble, now actor-manager at Covent Garden, sent James Robinson Planché, an antiquary, herald and playwright, bilingual in English and French, to document the occasion. In Paris, Planché was accorded 'every facility ... of inspecting the regalia, the royal robes, the state dresses of the great officers, the magnificent uniforms of the "Cent Suisses" etc.' before going on to Rheims for the ceremony itself, then hurrying back to London with his notes and drawings.[98] On 19 July, Covent Garden staged *The Pageant of the Coronation of Charles X* with almost as much splendour as the original. This was the epitome of Romantic antiquarianism, a consciously antiquarian event, based on historic precedent, represented as a modern drama based on recent history. If at this point there was a dividing line between fact and fiction, theatre, art and history it was of no interest to the late-Georgian audience, who could also amuse themselves with a virtual visit to Normandy by way of the Diorama in Regent's Park, where the light shows in 1828 included evocative views of the cloister of St-Wandrille.

The new king's antiquarian enthusiasms were shared with his sister-in-law, the Duchesse de Berry. Marie-Caroline de Bourbon-Sicile (1798–1869) was the mother of the heir to the French throne, the Comte de Chambord, known as *l'enfant du miracle* because his birth, after the assassination of his father the Duc de Berry in 1820, had assured the male succession in the Bourbon line. She was thus a figure of both social and political significance. A cultivated woman, a collector, patron of the arts and a leader of fashion, her château at Rosny, romantically sited on the Seine, was painted by Bonington. In 1824 her visit to the ruins of Jumièges established its status as the essential Romantic tourist site. She also went to Rouen, where she was escorted around points of historic interest by Langlois, whose friends hastily clubbed together to get him some respectable clothes. In her own appearance the duchesse led the mania for Scott and Scotland, favouring 'le gothique corsage à la Marie Stuart', a preference given full rein in an elaborate costume ball held at the Tuileries on 2 March 1829.[99] The 'Quadrille de Marie Stuart' was a re-enactment of the visit of the Queen of Scots' mother, Marie of Lorraine, to her daughter in France. Costumes were researched in the Bibliothèque royale and the whole affair recorded in a book of lithographs by Eugène Lami, whose visit to Meyrick ensured that he could draw the historic armour accurately. The tragic Queen of Scots was 'played', there is no other word for it, by the duchesse herself with Lady Stuart de Rothesay, wife of the British ambassador, as Marie.

The event attracted a great deal of notice, not all of it favourable. In the increasingly misty hinterland between history and fiction it was still possible to see the political implications of nostalgia for the *ancien régime*. It was, to say the least, tactless. But the Bourbons took famously little account of recent history or public opinion. Within eighteen months the July Revolution had overthrown them forever. The duchesse's fate was elided with that of her alter ego as she set sail for exile in Scotland. A portrait, now in the Bordeaux Museum of Fine Arts, depicts her aboard ship wearing a Highland bonnet and sixteenth-century dress in Legitimist white as she looks her last on France. On a stool beside her are papers dated 1561, the year of Mary's return to Scotland after the death of her husband, François II. Fancy dress had become iconography, the costume party, party propaganda.

The weight of historic association that the Bourbons invoked had, in the end, helped to crush them. Romantics, including Hugo, who had at first supported them, were disillusioned by concessions made to the Church, the attempt to reverse the reforms of the 1789 Revolution and, not least, by the fact that the Bourbons' interest in restoration was confined to themselves. The destruction of historic monuments continued apace. The general discontent in Paris, 'now grossly overcrowded and . . . in the throes of a recession', erupted in 1830.[100] The 'three glorious days' of the July Revolution, a brief, relatively blood-less and highly theatrical uprising, saw the Romantics press on to victory. While Delacroix's painting of the murder of the Bishop of Liège was being admired in London he produced in Paris a work that achieved far greater fame, *Liberty Leading the People*. At the moment the Revolution broke out the Paris Opéra was rehearsing Rossini's *Guillaume Tell*, a celebration of popular revolt, and it was said that on the line 'liberty or death' the chorus left the stage, still in costume, to join the revolutionaries. Victor Hugo stopped work on *Notre-Dame de Paris* for the duration. A constitutional monarchy was established under a member of the Orléans branch of the family, Louis Philippe, known as the Citizen King. Two historians, François Guizot (1787–1874) and Adolphe Thiers (1797–1877) were prominent in the new administration. Guizot was a professor at the Sorbonne, Thiers the author of the popular, *Waverley*-inspired *Histoire de la Révolution française* of 1823–7. They were implacable rivals. Conflicting versions of history and of the kind of future to be predicated on it were from the outset a feature of what became known as the July Monarchy.

After the July Revolution the Romantics' campaign to get official recognition and protection for historic monuments began to make headway. In 1832 Hugo published a rousing article in the *Revue des Deux Mondes*: 'Guerre aux démolisseurs'. In 1833 Louis Vitet was appointed as the first official Inspector of Monuments. A year later the post was taken over by Prosper Mérimée (1803–70), author of the *Chronique du règne de Charles IX*, 'an "ideal" ... imitation of Scott' and his young assistant, Eugène Viollet-le-Duc.[101] In 1837 Mérimée and Viollet took charge of the new Commission des monuments historiques. The concept of the *patrimoine* came of age. As well as a victory for the antiquaries and the Romantics it marked the beginning of a gradual but permanent shift in relations between Britain and France. From now on it was increasingly the British who looked across the Channel with envy; their own attempts to secure state pro-tection for historic monuments continued to be vigorously opposed. While medieval artefacts were soon on display in the Louvre, it was to be two decades before 'national antiquities' were admitted to the British Museum. In October 1833 Meyrick, who had just come back from Paris after his first visit since 1817, commented on the difference the intervening years had made. The city was much improved and so were the museums, as he reported to Douce. 'I wish most heartily our national collection of coins instead of being locked up in boxes in the Brit. Mus. was displayed in show-glasses arranged according to countries, with tickets to tell how long each King reigned.'[102]

French literature, meanwhile, was moving beyond the shadow of Scott. Two months after the July Revolution had interrupted it, Hugo returned to *Notre-Dame de Paris*, completing it on 15 January 1831. The novel is both a homage to Scott and a critique. Set, like *Quentin Durward*, in the reign of Louis XI, it tells the story of Quasimodo, the hunchback who inhabits Notre-Dame and his doomed love for the beautiful Gipsy, Esmeralda. The overarching drama, however, is the dying world of the late Middle Ages. *Notre-Dame*, which has been called 'a potted dialectical history of the architecture of past and present', is an attempt to wrench the Gothic back from the Bourbons, to portray it as a democratic art, arising from the people, its story to be read in its very fabric.[103] 'When you know how to look you may find the spirit of an age and the likeness of a king in a door knocker.'[104]

Hugo had written in a review of *Quentin Durward* that he thought Scott's view of the past somewhat pallid and prosaic.[105] His own was much less comfortable. The cosy glow of the Olden Times is replaced in *Notre-Dame* by the lurid light and heavy shadows cast by France's recent history. While *Notre-Dame* takes its *point d'appui* from *Quentin Durward* and shows the influence of *Ivanhoe* in the character of Esmeralda, the differences are telling. Like Rebecca the Jewess, Esmeralda is a member of a despised and outcast race who falls victim to the frustrated lust of a powerful man. In Scott's novel Rebecca is rescued by Ivanhoe, who acts as her champion in the lists. Esmeralda, championed only by the deformed Quasimodo, is publicly hanged in front of the cathedral, an end that is more violent and more plausible. The final discovery of Quasimodo's body in Esmerelda's grave, their skeletons entwined, is a grotesque version of the tomb of Abélard and Héloïse in Lenoir's abandoned garden, at which Hugo, as an adolescent, had gazed from his study window.

The figure of the antiquary himself emerged in French literature in another great novel completed in the aftermath of the July Revolution.

Balzac's *La Peau de chagrin* (*Wild Ass's Skin*) of 1831 is the Faustian tale of Raphael de Valentin, who obtains from a dealer of antiquities a wild ass's skin that is both magic and fatal. Balzac's antiquary is to Jonathan Oldbuck what Esmerelda is to Rebecca – a darker figure, sinister and malignant in his indifference. His appearance so closely resembles Bonington's painting it seems likely that Balzac had it in mind. 'A little old man, thin and dry, dressed in a black velvet gown, a broad silk sash gathered round his hips. On his head a velvet cap, also black, let fall from either side of his face long strands of white hair.'[106] His curiosity shop is a version of Lenoir's museum, an assemblage of deracinated fragments telling a story of ruin and revolution, human folly and the fate of princes. 'A writing desk that cost a hundred thousand francs and was sold for a hundred sous, lay near a secret lock whose price was once enough to ransom a king.'[107]

The mournful notes of the *danse macabre* play through French reflections on history, fictional and antiquarian, to which Langlois contributed his own curious effort, the prose poem *Hymne à la cloche* (*Hymn of the Bell*). Bells were popular subjects for antiquaries because they are easy to date and hard to destroy, yet one of the most comprehensive areas of the Revolutionaries' vandalism was the plundering of church bells to be melted down for cannon. This adds to their poignancy in *Notre-Dame*. In his own account of the Abbey of St-Wandrille Langlois described the breaking of the abbey bells. The biggest of them took the best part of a day to destroy, resisting 'with appalling groans the great blows of the iron weights with which the strongest men, working in relays, assailed it'.[108] This awful, resonating image of determined destruction, a perversion of the bell's true purpose, so that it howls like an animal and tolls for its own death, is developed in the *Hymne à la cloche*, which was finished, according to Langlois's colophon, set in the shape of a bell, on New Year's Day 1831, exactly a fortnight before Hugo finished *Notre-Dame*.

L'ELGINISM

At the same time as the initiative in antiquarian activity was passing from Britain to France there was a noticeable cooling in the spirit of collaboration. As the French began to undertake the systematic conservation of their historic monuments they became increasingly outraged at the behaviour of the British, whose mania for the olden times was stripping the country under the nose of the Commission. By the 1830s a flood of antiquities, many of them 'salvaged' from French and Flemish churches and religious houses, was pouring out of France. Carved wood, stained glass, architectural fragments of every kind went in huge consignments. English dealers sometimes chartered whole ships and Hugo, in 'Guerre aux démolisseurs', justifiably accused them of encouraging vandalism by offering to buy antiquities that were still *in situ*. Langlois, trying to find the stained glass removed from the Charterhouse in Rouen, wrote to Lenoir to ask if he had ever seen it. Lenoir confirmed that the windows had passed through his hands and he had tried to buy them: 'To my great regret I failed; I believe they have disappeared into the gulf called *England* where all our works of art now disappear.'[109] While the majority of the purchasers were not antiquaries, the antiquaries were no better. Dawson Turner, arriving in 1815 at the Church of Molineaux, remarked that although the building was derelict the stained-glass windows were intact:

> Either the antiquaries in France are more honest than in England, or they want taste, or objects of this kind do not find a ready market. We know too well how many an English church, albeit well guarded by the churchwardens and the parson, has seen its windows despoiled of every shield, and saint, and motto; and we also know full well, by whom, and for whom, such ravages are committed.[110]

As Turner implied, it was antiquaries, who should have known better, who often behaved worst. At Jumièges the statues were sold off to Englishmen who, as Langlois put it, 'took the plundering so far that unless it had eventually been put a stop to there would not now be at Jumièges a single crocket of a capital left'.[111] He presumably did not know that his acquaintance Auguste Pugin and his pupils were responsible for sawing off and removing an entire capital.[112] Meanwhile, at Caen the ducal palace had been virtually stripped of its encaustic tile floor by the time Dawson Turner saw it. In 1824 the twelve-year-old Welby Pugin, who been travelling with his father and the drawing school, noted excitedly in his journal that he had brought back 'some tiles from the Ducal Palace, Caen'.[113] One can only hope that the tiles, now in the Victoria and Albert Museum, had already been removed from the floor, but that seems far from certain. In their first volume on Picardy published in 1833, Nodier and Taylor recorded the demolition of the château at Les Andelys. Taylor's protest was heartfelt and reasonable: 'We would not feel such bitter resentment if all these works of art had been taken to England to make a museum where we could go to admire and study our national antiquities ... but these works of art have gone to decorate a few country houses or aristocratic parks where they play at the Middle Ages à la Walter Scott.'[114]

The great oriel window from Les Andelys, along with some panelling from Jumièges, was indeed destined for Highcliffe Castle, home of Stuart de Rothsay, the British ambassador whose wife played so prominent a role in the Duchesse de Berry's costume ball. The couple had already Gothicized themselves by adding the 'de' to their name and proceeded to Gothic-up their house. The oriel is still there and is now the property of Christchurch Council.

7

The Romantic Interior

At the bottom of the stairs is a statue of a monk, in a niche.
John Britton, Historical and Descriptive Accounts
of Toddington, Gloucestershire The Seat
of Lord Sudeley, *1840*

Wemmick's house was a little wooden cottage ... and the top
of it was cut out and painted like a battery mounted with
guns.
Charles Dickens, Great Expectations, *1861*

Whatever the changing scenes of life that passed by the antiquary's
window, his home was his own, and for many it was there that the
lived relationship with the material past, which was the essence of
Romantic antiquarianism, found its fullest expression. In some cases,
like Meyrick's Goodrich Court, the antiquary's home was literally his
castle, but it was also possible in more modest establishments to collapse the imaginative space between past and present and thus to
inhabit history. On that spectrum of antiquarian attitudes that extends
from the objectivity of a Lingard at one end to the subjectivity bordering on delusion of the Sobieski Stuarts at the other, and where Walter
Scott occupies the broad middle ground, the Romantic or antiquarian
interior begins somewhere between Lingard and Scott. Its importance
in establishing or reinforcing its creator's identity grows proportion-
ately towards the extreme. The Highland home of the Sobieski Stuarts,
which we shall visit in the next chapter, a farrago of tartan, antlers
and dubious Jacobite relics, was so integral to their pretended place in

history that without it they were fatally diminished, snails without shells.

The Romantic interior had ancestors. They include the strange, symbolic buildings William Stukeley created around his Lincolnshire vicarage between 1730 and 1747, some variations on the theme of the hermitage and the folly and, its *fons et origo*, Horace Walpole's spectacular mind palace at Strawberry Hill.[1] It was essentially different, however, from the Cabinet of Curiosities with which it is sometimes bracketed. A cabinet was to be looked at, visited and displayed. An antiquarian interior was to be lived in, occasionally, if the occupant so chose, in complete privacy, in communion with the past. Sir John Soane's house in Lincoln's Inn Fields, which survives as a museum, is sometimes described as a Romantic interior, and so it is, inasmuch as it is the outward expression of an individual sensibility; but its purpose was to dramatize Soane's life and his architectural ideas, not his relationship to history. Soane was not an antiquary. Antiquarian interiors of the sort that concern us here began to multiply from about 1780, until by the middle of the nineteenth century they had spread so far beyond antiquarian circles that they had become 'a major strand of taste in interior decoration'.[2] They were to be found in France as well as Britain. Not all were in private houses and not all were secular. Some contained important artefacts, many did not. Wemmick's battlemented cottage in Walworth was as true to the spirit of the antiquarian interior as Meyrick's Goodrich. What they shared was that fluid Romantic attitude towards authenticity whereby the appearance of things and the emotions and associations they evoked counted for at least as much as what, physically, they were. In the Romantic interior, time was not so much suspended as rearranged to suit the inhabitant.

The most influential example was Walter Scott's home, Abbotsford, created as an expression of the man and his work all in one. In William Allan's painting *Sir Walter Scott in his Study*, Scott appears seated in the throne-like carved oak chair that was an essential ingredient of the antiquarian home. On his lap is a parchment, Mary Queen of Scots' proclamation of her marriage to Darnley, while around him stretches an array of armour and objects resonant with historical and personal significance – the sporran of Rob Roy, the keys of the old

Tolbooth and Napoleonica from Waterloo. All of these things belonged to Scott and all had featured in his work; they represented his imagination in three-dimensional form. Abbotsford itself was one of Scott's most carefully crafted fictions. In October 1812 he noted that he had just finished building a well. 'Constructed out of a few of the broken stones taken up in clearing the rubbish from Melrose Abbey . . . It makes a tolerable deception and looks at least 300 years old.'[3] When he bought it, the house had the unromantic name of Cartley Hole Farm, rendered still more unappealing by the local nickname, 'Clarty' (dirty) Hole. In renaming it Scott at a stroke connected Abbotsford to the Middle Ages, implying that his home had been built, like antiquarianism itself, out of the ruins of the Reformation. In *The Antiquary*, Jonathan Oldbuck's study is a slightly caricatured version of Scott's as it appears in Allan's picture. 'A lofty room of middling size, obscurely lighted by high narrow lattice windows', one end 'entirely occupied by book-shelves, greatly too limited in space for the number of volumes placed upon them', the floor covered with 'a chaos of maps, engravings, scraps of parchment, bundles of papers, pieces of old armour, swords, dirks, helmets and Highland targets'. Against the panelling hang 'two or three portraits in armour, being characters in Scottish history, favourites of Mr Oldbuck, and as many in tie-wigs and laced coats, staring representatives of his own ancestors'.[4] In Oldbuck's insertion of his family among those historic characters with whom he feels the greatest affinity, Scott puts his finger on the mainspring of the antiquarian interior, its capacity to weave the individual into the grand narrative of history.

Among the antiquaries with whom we are concerned, several had homes of this sort. As well as Scott, Meyrick and the Sobieski Stuarts, Britton had his own suburban version while Gage, who had a truly historic home at Hengrave, nevertheless installed stained glass and it was probably he who acquired the suits of armour that were the star attraction when the contents were dispersed in 1897.[5] Willson, who appears in his portrait as a neat, conventional Justice of the Peace, is revealed by his post-mortem sale in November 1854 as the owner of a perfect catalogue of antiquarian accessories. Three hundred and ninety-five lots of books were followed by prints, paintings, 'ancient and mediaeval remains', 'antique porcelain' and 'miscellaneous', which included the following:

449 An Oak Panel, with the Crucifixion carved in high relief, and three ditto, Heraldic badges

451 Various fragments of Stained Glass . . .

452 Carved Oak Arm chair

453 A Panel containing rich pieces of ditto, of the fourteenth and fifteenth centuries . . .

455 A Demi-suit of Armour . . .

456 A Helmet and Breast Plate, and the Head of a Pole-axe . . .

461 An old Sheep Bell . . .

462 A very large Roman Urn, with narrow mouth, *faulty* . . .

464 A quantity of old Tapestry

468 A Large Number of Fragments of ancient Manuscripts . . .

469 A large Whip, known as a '*Caistor Gad*'

470 Bronze Head of an Indian Staff of Honour, and an embroidered Chinese Slipper

471 Cast of the Bust of Shakespeare at Stratford on Avon . . .

474 Sundry Vertebrae of the Ichthyosaurus with other Organic Remains[6]

It isn't possible to know how Willson arranged these things around himself, but a letter from his exuberant young friend Welby Pugin suggests they shared a taste for complete immersion. Having just furnished his own rented house in Ramsgate, Pugin invited Willson to stay: 'Glad I shall be when I can Lodge you in an ancien [*sic*] [room] with tapestry hangings round the walls . . . and every thing en suite. You will then be able to fancy yourself transported back to the fifteenth Cent. and not discover your mistake till you Leave the roof of your sincere friend A Welby Pugin.'[7]

The language used to describe the antiquarian interior was often similarly antiqued. Furnishings were 'leathern' and 'oaken'. Sometimes there was a nod towards the darker side of the antiquary's pedigree, as in E. W. Cooke's *The Antiquary's Cell*. Cooke, an antiquary himself, used his own collection as props, including the 'fine carved chair', various rolls of parchment, armour and a large piece of scarlet silk to create his Hogarthian 'scene of furniture'.[8] This version of their persona as magus appealed to a number of antiquaries. Thomas Frognall Dibdin's breathless account of Francis Douce's home teetered on the edge of parody:

> It will delight you, I am sure, to hear that Prospero is yet in the full exercise of his 'enchanter's wand' ... His maple-wood bookcases rejoice the eye by the peculiar harmony of their tint, – with the rich furniture they enclose. Here a bit of old bright stained glass – exhibiting the true long-lost ruby tint: – there, an inkstand, adorned in high cameo-relief, by the skill of John of Bologna ... the rarest China cups ... chess-men ... used by Charles V and Francis I on their dining together ... the very staff with which Regiomontanus used to walk on his house-top by moonlight ... Magic lore, and choice Madrigals ... and the parchment roll which Handel wielded in beating time on the first representation of the Messiah.[9]

Other antiquaries had no time for this sort of thing, including, as it happened, Douce. 'All absolute Bedlam' was his response to Dibdin's effusions. 'Not one of these articles do I possess or know anything about them.'[10] Douce's huffish reluctance to be associated with such a *galère* should not, however, obscure the fact that among the antiquities he did possess were an 'ancient rolling pin', fragments of a rood screen from Southwold, 'parts of a mummied Ibis' and a plaster cast of an hermaphrodite. He also owned that *sine qua non* of the alchemist's sanctum, a 'Gnostic crocodile', which he may or may not have suspended from his study ceiling.[11] As with so many aspects of Romantic antiquarianism, there was a degree of ambivalence among some of its practitioners and they are not necessarily to be relied on when describing their relationship to it.

If it was, in conception, the most personal of creations, in practice the Romantic interior partook of the full spectrum of antiquarian activity, from scholarship and research to the burgeoning trade in 'salvaged' goods which was putting such a strain on the *entente cordiale*. The flow of antiquities into England, the richest and most stable market in Europe, gave rise not only to the expansion of the auction houses but also to an increase in the number of brokers in whose premises the origins of the modern antique shop are recognizable.

Some dealers were also antiquaries and nearly all antiquaries were de facto dealers. Prices soared after Waterloo, reaching a peak between 1820 and the 1840s, when the number of curiosity and antique shops rose from fewer than ten to at least 155 as enthusiasm for antiquarian interiors grew.[12] In 1842 *The Gentleman's Magazine* reported:

> The prevalence ... of a taste for Antique Furniture is most decidedly manifested, not only by the examples which every one may happen to know of either ancient mansions, or modern houses ... filled with collections of this description, but by the multitude of ware houses which now display their attractive stores ... in almost every quarter of the metropolis ... large importations have in consequence been made from the Continent ... not only entire pieces of furniture ... but great quantities of detached and fragmentary portions, and ... architectural carvings.[13]

The government naturally turned its mind to raising revenue from the boom and introduced hefty importation duties. Manuscripts were taxed by weight at one shilling a pound, to the dismay of Thomas Phillipps, who bought 650 items at the sale of the Meerman Library in the Hague and wrote plaintively to the Exchequer complaining that the duty was 'so enormous', particularly for manuscripts bound in wooden covers.[14] The trade in imported antiquities always had its shady side, and now to the dubious matter of provenance was added a lively sideline in smuggling. Pugin, for one, being an able sailor, took his own boat to the Continent and brought his purchases back to Ramsgate, where he landed them under the cliffs well down the coast from the Customs office.

Not all the trade was international. There was heavy demand for domestic antiquities. In April 1821 Meyrick went to a sale at Christie's to bid on Scott's behalf as well as his own. He reported that he had no success, having been outbid on every lot Scott had asked him to try for. 'Two or three gentlemen were determined to have the things they wish for at any price', Meyrick explained. They were willing to go to 100 guineas for a sword 'bearing the inscription "Prosperity to Scotland"'.[15] It was perhaps poetic justice that Scott, having created the mania for all things Caledonian, was now priced out of the market.

The centre of the London trade was Soho. It is no coincidence that Jonathan Oldbuck's neighbour, friend and rival, whose taste in antiquities is 'neither very deep nor very correct', should be called Sir Arthur Wardour, for Wardour Street was home to the greatest concentration of dealers.[16] Those whose names have come down to us include Edward Hull, John Swaby, John Webb, John Colman Isaac and Samuel Pratt. Among the china, armour, manuscripts and tapestry in their shops were objects that were not old, but pieces, especially furniture, composed, like Scott's well at Abbotsford, from a mixture of old and new elements in a process known as 'sophisticating'. The disparate elements were washed over with a layer of dark stain, recipes for which were to be found in most brokers' back rooms, to create a homogenously 'oaken' effect. Although oak darkens naturally with time the sooty blackness of most old oak today, of any age, is due to its having been stained in the nineteenth century.[17] As the term 'sophisticating' suggests, this was not usually an attempt to deceive but another aspect of a relaxed view of 'authenticity'. J. C. Loudon in his *Encyclopaedia of Cottage Farm and Villa Architecture and Furniture* of 1839 was advising his readers rather than warning them when he explained that in antique shops, 'there are abundant remains of every kind of Elizabeth [sic] furniture to be purchased ... These when in fragments are put together and made up into every article of furniture now in use.'[18] Brokers offered pattern books, from which customers who wanted, for example, a Gothic piano stool could chose designs to be made to order.

The trade in 'sophisticating' and the antiquarian study of furniture history progressed in tandem. Meyrick collaborated with another antiquary, Henry Shaw (1800–1873), who was one of Britton's best artists, on *Specimens of Ancient Furniture Drawn from Existing Authorities*. It appeared in 1836 and made a great advance towards establishing a chronology for furnishings including tables and chairs, sideboards, beds and mirrors. Working by analogy with Gothic architecture, for which the dating was now more or less secure, Meyrick assessed individual pieces by eye, by the style of carving or other ornament and also by the documentary evidence of illuminated manuscripts, inventory rolls, wills and royal records, including the wardrobe accounts of Edward I and the Privy Purse expenses of Henry VIII, sources in which a wealth of information lay still largely untapped. Meyrick built on the work of others, notably Willemin, Montfaucon, Strutt and Planché, whom he acknowledged, but his was the first significant attempt to establish a chronology for decorative arts and interior furnishings. He was anxious to demonstrate what the general reading public is often still reluctant to believe, that the medieval world was not monochrome or darkly 'oaken' but vividly, even gaudily, colourful:

> Instead of fancying ... the stately knights and dames of old sitting within bare walls, and resting their feet on rushes ... we must now do them the justice to allow, that while their tables glittered with plate and jewels, their beds dazzled with the richness of their hangings, and their seats were decorated with refulgent draperies, the Gothic carving of their furniture became brilliant by scarlet, blue and gold, and the walls of their apartments had the most interesting, as well as most effective appearance from the grand paintings or the rich tapestry which were placed upon them.[19]

Historic studies of the applied arts fed the taste for historic decoration which antiquaries and dealers in turn collaborated to serve. Meyrick meant the illustrations in his book to be used as designs for new pieces and Pugin, while he waited to embark on his mission to re-Gothicize Britain, turned out three pot-boiling pattern books for Rudolph Ackerman: *Gothic Furniture in the Style of the 15th Century* in 1835, and *Designs for Gold and Silversmiths* and *Designs for Iron and Brass Work in the Style of the XV and XVI Centuries* in 1836.

ROMANCES IN STONE

Few antiquarian interiors survived the buffeting of successive waves of taste and fashion. Those that have been preserved, such as Abbotsford, are greatly diminished by outliving their creators. Like the 'gabions' in Ruthven's elegy on Henry Adamson, without their animating spirit the parts seem to shrink back and to become less than the whole. Meyrick's Goodrich Court is long gone and its contents dispersed. Some are now in the Wallace Collection, others in the

Bodleian Library, the Victoria and Albert Museum and at Warwick Castle, but Goodrich is well recorded and to visit it in the mind's eye, where arguably it enjoyed its fullest existence, is perhaps as good a way as any to experience the late-Georgian Romantic interior.

Meyrick was a lawyer and a graduate of Oxford from a family that was less than rich but more than comfortable. In person he was a 'slight active figure' with a 'dry, yet polished voice', and 'there hung a well-bred irresistible charm about the knight, when he wished to please'.[20] As that last caveat suggests, while he was capable of the long, collaborative friendships he enjoyed with Douce, Scott and others, Meyrick was volatile. 'By turns snobbish, impulsive, liberal, pompous, kind, tight-fisted and romantic', his biographer concludes that he was 'not an easy person to know or . . . to like at all times'. His personal life was 'a similar roller-coaster of disaster and triumph'.[21] The first disaster was Meyrick's father's objection to his son's marriage. Samuel was abruptly disinherited and the Meyrick fortune passed in due course to his son Llewelyn, who, luckily, grew up to share his father's enthusiasms and was touchingly keen to fund his purchases. Meyrick's first interest had been the history of dress, which culminated in his co-authorship of *The Costume of the Original Inhabitants of the British Islands*, after which he began to concentrate on armour. As he researched his magnum opus, *A Critical Inquiry into Antient Armour . . . from the Norman Conquest to the Reign of King Charles II*, he acquired more and more examples and the Meyricks' London house gradually filled up with greaves, breastplates, helmets, swords and miscellaneous weaponry. The collection took over 'the garrets, the staircase and the back drawing room', after which it began to advance on the bedrooms.[22] By 1824, the year the *Critical Inquiry* was published, even Meyrick thought this was becoming 'quite a nuisance' and he began looking for a more suitable setting.[23]

Meyrick's interest in armour was equalled only by his passionate enthusiasm for his Welshness. On this point his usually rigorous interrogation of the evidence relaxed. He was determined to be descended from the Meyricks of Anglesey who included such compelling figures as Rowland, the sixteenth-century Bishop of Bangor and his son Sir Gelly Meyrick, who was beheaded for taking part in the Earl of

Essex's rebellion, although, as one fellow antiquary disobligingly observed, by what possible route he could trace this lineage 'it would be difficult for him to show'.[24] In his search for a new home Meyrick's eye lit on the twelfth- and thirteenth-century Goodrich Castle in Herefordshire, a stupendous, ruinous border fort in rosy-pink stone overlooking the Wye at the epicentre of the Picturesque. Goodrich was admired by Wordsworth and painted by innumerable watercolourists. Meyrick told Scott that 'the former possessors ... were so identified with the history of the times as to confer on it an éclat ... coupled with the traditionary [sic] anecdotes and pleasing romantic scenery' that he simply had to have it.[25] He entered into negotiations, keeping his friend Edward Blore on standby to 'show his judgement in rendering it habitable with scrupulous attention to preserve its present character'.[26] But although Goodrich was ruinous it was also famous, and the owners wanted more than the Meyricks could afford. So, with that characteristic Romantic indifference towards what another age might regard as glaring anachronism, Meyrick bought a piece of land on the river next to the castle where, as he told Douce, he proposed 'to build instantly a dwelling in the style of Edward 2nd under the superintendence of the first gothic architect of the age my friend Edward Blore'.[27] This in no way compromised his 'perfectly antiquarian motives' which were to insert himself in that landscape so essential to his version of his own history.[28]

Blore accordingly made designs for what became Goodrich Court. Blore and Meyrick had both advised Scott on aspects of the design of Abbotsford and Goodrich was in some ways its sibling. Scott chose Scots Baronial for his Perthshire home, and on the same principles of propriety Blore and Meyrick modelled Goodrich on the Edwardian castles of the Welsh Marches. Sited on 'a commanding eminence' above the Wye, it was built 'of the very best masonry' in the style of the 'architecture of Edward II', complete with drawbridge, portcullis, battlements, turrets and machicolations, despite which ferocious appearance it was, from the beginning, open to the public.[29] This was, as Thomas Roscoe's guidebook put it in 1837, 'a romance in stone' of which the first actual stone was laid by Llewelyn on St George's Day, 1828.[30]

As the castle rose out of the ground it absorbed many Wardour

Street purchases, such as folding doors 'from Louvain' and, most dramatically, the seventeenth-century ceiling from 'the Breda Government House in Holland' which was installed in the library, where a friend recalled that Meyrick liked showing visitors his treasures, 'opening those curious miniatures by Holbein' in between 'rapid and frequent production from the book-shelves, of a print or authority'.[31] Blore 'sophisticated' a sideboard 'of the time of Edward II' and had it carved with the armorial bearings of William de Valence, the owner of Goodrich Castle in the reign of Edward I. Thomas Willement (1786–1871), a fellow antiquary, herald and artist in stained glass, was engaged to design wallpapers and, for the entrance hall, a spectacular window incorporating the Meyrick arms and a portrait of their earliest bearer, Meuric ab Llewelyn, 'esquire of the body to Henry VII'. If the pedigree was faulty, the armour at least was entirely correct. The hall was adorned with weaponry. As at Abbotsford there were arms retrieved from Waterloo, and Meyrick also collected and displayed weapons from the Chartist riots at Newport of 1839. Goodrich, like most antiquarian interiors, was thus not intended simply to recreate the past, but to bring it seamlessly into the present, albeit from a very particular angle. It was also typical in being up to date in standards of comfort and convenience. Meyrick, like Scott and Pugin, used plate glass rather than leaded lights in most of his windows, and although Goodrich was later than Abbotsford to have gaslight, which Scott installed in the 1820s, Meyrick saw no reason not to have a billiard room as well as a portcullis.

There was a grand banqueting hall, off which led the Hastlitude Chamber. 'Hastlitude', meaning 'spear play', is a sixteenth-century term for jousting. Here visitors encountered a life-size tableau of a tournament 'complete with list, a royal box, figures dressed as heralds and all manner of jousting armour and lances from the period of Henry VI to Queen Elizabeth'.[32] Beyond the chamber lay the main armoury, *the raison d'être* of Goodrich, a gallery eighty-six and a half feet long by twenty-five wide, lit by skylights and hung with heraldic banners painted by Willement. It was arranged in strict chronological order, although the grandeur of the effect was somewhat spoiled, according to one visitor, by multiple notices saying: 'Don't touch anything'.[33] Suits of armour were shown on figures and horse armour on wooden horses sporting real manes which Meyrick obtained, with some difficulty, from knackers' yards.

Meyrick's armoury marked the turning point from the private realm of the antiquarian interior towards the coming age of the public museum, a moment in which Romantic engagement and scholarly investigation were precisely balanced. Meyrick was unperturbed by the fact that his 'Edwardian castle' was new, but factual inaccuracy infuriated him. He repeatedly petitioned the Duke of Wellington to be allowed to reorganize the Royal Armouries in the Tower of London. None of the armour on show there as 'medieval' in fact predated Henry VII, and the item shown as Elizabeth I's 'stomacher' was in reality a *garde-de-reine* of Henry VIII's time designed to protect his 'sitting part'.[34] Anyone wearing it on the abdomen would be unable to bend at the waist. The *Critical Inquiry* pursued this campaign and attracted an admiring review from the Whig wit and politician Sydney Smith. Smith remarked that as he read Meyrick's book, the Tower Armouries were made to 'vanish like the palace of Aladdin, before the spell which our author seems to possess of *historic truth*'.[35] Smith concluded with the logical extension of the *Critical Inquiry*'s argument that the state should take responsibility for what after all was 'a national collection' of unique historic importance. Why, he asked, should it not be moved to the British Museum? The British Museum still did not collect national antiquities and so the Armoury was not moved, but in 1826 Meyrick got his way and was allowed to reorder it, albeit on such a small budget that he was obliged to build a lot of the displays himself. His work there and his writings, especially for the *Critical Inquiry*, remain the basis for all subsequent studies and for displays of arms and armour across Europe.[36]

In 1834 Meyrick's old friend Douce died. Apart from a major bequest to the Bodleian, he left everything to Meyrick, his 'carvings in ivory or other materials, together with my miscellaneous curiosities'. He had, his will stated, 'the fullest confidence' that Meyrick would find 'some small apartment in his noble mansion at Goodrich' to display them.[37] Meyrick, who had had no warning of his friend's intentions, rapidly created three rooms, which he named the Doucean Museum. This, in addition to Meyrick's own acquisitions, meant that Goodrich, while it lasted, was home to 'the most important collection of mediaeval and Renaissance objects in Britain' and one of the most significant in Europe.[38] Meyrick died in 1848, Llewellyn having, to his father's great grief, predeceased him. Goodrich Court clung on through a century of rising and mostly falling fortunes until in 1950 it was demolished.

Few antiquaries could attempt anything on such a scale. Goodrich was the epitome of the Romantic interior created *de novo*. Many, perhaps most others were developed like Abbotsford, out of existing buildings. For this it was not necessary to have Meyrick's resources; the countryside was littered with tumbledown houses. The drift towards the towns lamented by *The Gentleman's Magazine* in 1789 continued. Disused medieval buildings, if they were not famous like Goodrich Castle, could be bought for almost nothing. The expert on brasses, Craven Ord, wrote teasingly to Douce urging him to buy a house that was for sale near Bury in Suffolk, built in the aisle of a disused church, 'the finest situation for an antiquary possible', where at every touch and turn the eye lit on 'a spiral groove, a zig-zag moulding, an embattled fret or a sculptured saint'.[39] Douce would never have contemplated anything so outré, but Thomas Willement, Meyrick's heraldic painter and decorator, did.

In his long career Willement worked in many of the most important country houses and historic buildings in Britain. One of his, possibly self-coined, honorifics was 'artist in stained glass to Queen Victoria'. Having begun in his father's house- and coach-painting business in London and married Katherine Griffith, the daughter of a master saddler, Willement's antiquarianism eventually transformed him into the patron of his own medieval manor and private chapel, complete with a coat of arms and motto: 'Thinke and Thanke'. His creation, Davington Priory in Kent, survives in private hands and has retained to a remarkable degree the character and ethos of the Romantic interior. Originally a Benedictine convent founded in 1153, by 1527 Davington's community had dwindled to two and the priory passed, without being suppressed, into the possession of the Crown in 1535. Later in the sixteenth century the parish church, which was attached to it, fell (or was pulled) down, after which the nuns' church was used for services. By the later eighteenth century that too was falling into disuse. Two explosions at the nearby gunpowder mills caused more damage, until by the 1840s it was a rookery, 'almost every room . . . inhabited by a different family' and in a state of such 'extreme dirt and decay' that when it came up for sale in 1845 nobody but an antiquary would have wanted it.[40] Willement took his chance and, having 'dislodged' the various inmates, he set about inhabiting the debris, embarking simultaneously on archival research and close examination of the fabric.[41] Having worked on the restoration of St George's Chapel, Windsor and the Church of the Holy Sepulchre in Cambridge (the Round Church), he brought his experience to bear, feeling his way back through the centuries. He calculated the original dimensions of the great hall, before the ceiling was lowered. It had also been shortened to make the prioress's parlour into a dining room where 'within a closet on the east side' he found that 'there yet remains the jambs of the ancient fire-place'.[42] He noted where doors had been made, windows blocked and a staircase inserted.

Willement repaired, decorated and furnished the church. He built a sacristy. He supplied a pulpit 'sophisticated' out of sixteenth-century Continental carving and a stone font, worked by John Thomas, the carver who was, at the same time, supervising work at the new Palace of Westminster, and he designed glass and wall paintings. If local people thought Willement eccentric, they nevertheless appreciated his efforts. Public worship resumed and the parish clubbed together to buy an altar. Much of Willement's contribution to the church has now been erased, being 'only Victorian', but the house itself, which is reached through a door in the nave, speaks of him as eloquently as the antiquary's empty chair in Cooke's painting. In his *Historical Sketch of the Parish of Davington, in the County of Kent, and of the Priory There Dedicated to S Mary Magdalene*, Willement inserted himself, as Milner had in his *History of Winchester*, into what he believed to be his true, if not his actual place in history. He listed the previous proprietors in a direct line from Fulco de Newenham, Davington's twelfth-century founder, all the way down to himself. It was important to Willement that Davington was never suppressed; he was not in possession of stolen Church property. His belief that he was the real and natural inheritor of the house he had in fact bought is made explicit in the interiors at every opportunity in painted texts on the chimney pieces, cornices and doorways. At the entrance to the dining room Newenham's arms appear on one side, Willement's on the other, with between them the seal that Willement, using his heraldic scholarship, himself designed for the priory.

The Willements' home was gradually enriched with medieval stained glass, including some from Rouen Cathedral and the Château d'Écouen, there was sixteenth-century ebony panelling in a bedroom where the oak bed, hung with seventeenth-century green Genoese silk, had come from Warwick Castle. Thomas and Katherine had only one child, Arthur Thomas, named for England's mythic king, and for his father. He was about twelve when they moved in and his parents must have hoped that they were founding a dynasty that would make Davington its ancestral home. When Katherine died seven years later she was buried in the vault of the priory church and it would have been a solace to Willement that his son was thriving. Arthur entered Christ Church, Oxford as a commoner, but a year later he was killed by a fall from a horse on the Woodstock Road. He too was buried at Davington, where Willement lived on alone until 1871, when he in his turn was laid to rest in the building he had helped to save and made his own.

Goodrich and Davington between them take us from the Georgians to the High Victorians. Over these decades, as the tide of taste for the olden times rose, the antiquarian interior reached its third generation and its feelings about its grandparents were mixed. In 1842, when the contents of Strawberry Hill were auctioned off, the sale was a sensation. There were traffic jams on the Twickenham road as more than a thousand visitors a day, including the queen and Prince Albert, went to the viewing. The wildly hyperbolic catalogue by the famous auctioneer George Robins was a best-seller and a parody of it, *Gooseberry Hall*, was soon going the rounds. For many people in this new Victorian age, with its ever-growing understanding of the architecture of the Middle Ages, Walpole's house and contents were risible. John Britton, from the heights of his own residence at 27 Burton Street, St Pancras, complete with Octagonal Cabinet Room, looked down on Walpole's 'paste-board house' as a mere 'Gothic toy-castle'. It was just the sort of place, he said, that an estate agent would talk up as the 'most-to-be-admired example of modern domestic monastic architecture in Europe'.[43] Disregarding Britton's misplaced condescension, it is worth pausing to note that by 1842 'modern domestic monastic' was a term in the estate agent's vocabulary. *The Times* wrote off Walpole's collection as 'gewgaws, gimcracks, trinkets, and trumpery trifles'. Many of these objects are now in national museums on both sides of the Atlantic, but like Britton *The Times* was blinded to their quality by a distaste for Georgian sensibility. Wit and irony looked now like whimsy and triviality, and there was also an intangible aura of decadence about the place which added to both the attraction and the revulsion. Pugin's visit elicited a one-word diary entry: 'disgusted'.[44]

Some antiquaries, like the Irish folklorist Thomas Crofton Croker (1798–1854) and his friend and neighbour Thomas Baylis (d. 1875), who bought from the sale, were more perceptive, though they were sanguine about the mutable nature of the Romantic interior.

> Strawberry Hill has passed away
> Every house must have its day[45]

Baylis's home, The Pryor's Bank at Fulham, had devoured its predecessor, the once-famous Vine Cottage. The creation of Walsh Porter, who died in 1809, its spectacular entrance hall was designed as a cavern hewn from living rock, while the dining room, in which Porter occasionally entertained the Prince Regent, was a scale replica of the ruins of Tintern Abbey. Baylis had it all knocked down, built himself a smart new Gothic villa, adorned with battlements, fitted it up with a superior selection of the usual 'fine old oak ... rare tapestry ... Genuine Suits of Ancient Armour ... and an assemblage of highly interesting objects of vertu ... of those brilliant periods for Art and Chivalry' and renamed it Pryor's Bank to imply a monastic history, as Scott had done at Abbotsford.[46] 'The whole edifice,' according to Croker, 'from the kitchen to the bedrooms, is a museum, arranged with a view to pictorial effect.'[47] Croker, described by Scott as 'keen-eyed as a hawk and of easy prepossessing manners' and 'little as a dwarf', had his own version nearby.[48] A substantial Regency cottage once called Brunswick Lodge, it became under his ownership Rosamond's Bower in honour of a very vague tradition that Henry II's mistress, Fair Rosamond, had lived nearby. The contents included a chair 'probably' made for Oliver Cromwell's son Henry, a ring 'considered to be Shakespeare's "Betrothal" ring', faience ware and a miniature ship's cannon.[49]

Croker and Baylis were members of the Noviomagians, a dining club of fellows of the Society of Antiquaries which enjoyed parodying the Society's official meetings, and there were frequent jolly, Pickwickian gatherings at Pryor's Bank and Rosamond's Bower, including masques, dinners and amateur theatricals in which the female roles were taken by '*real Females!*' including Mrs Baylis.[50] In December 1839 they held a Christmas 'Tournament'. The Fulham revelries acquired in due course a certain fame and were admired by the *Britannia* newspaper for reviving the true spirit of old England. Pryor's Bank was, it thought, 'among the most splendid and elegant dwellings in the kingdom . . . it would be impossible to find . . . a finer example of the mingling of splendour with purity' in the tremendous display of 'ancient carvings, old pictures, armour of all classes'.[51] In their contents and display Croker and Baylis's houses represented the best of their kind, but they had ever more imitators whose enthusiasm outran their knowledge, means and taste. In 1850 an exasperated Thackeray described the unhappy result in *Pendennis*:

> They admired the dining room with fitting compliments, and pronounced it 'very chaste', that being the proper phrase. There were, indeed, high-backed Dutch chairs of the seventeenth century; there was a sculptured carved buffet of the sixteenth; there was a sideboard robbed out of the carved work of a church in the Low Countries, and a large brass cathedral lamp over the round oak table; there were old family portraits from Wardour Street and tapestry from France, bits of armour, double-handed swords and battle-axes made of carton-pierre, looking-glasses, statuettes of saints, and Dresden china – nothing, in a word, could be chaster.[52]

A decade later Dickens was more forgiving of the antiquarian interior in its humblest form in the backstreets of Walworth. Samuel Wemmick, clerk to the all-seeing lawyer Jaggers in *Great Expectations*, lives with his father, the Aged P., in a miniature castle with its own working cannon. Yet despite the element of *reductio ad absurdum*, Dickens allows it to serve the same mental and spiritual purpose as Goodrich and Davington, as a manifestation of its creator's true self, a private place of psychological safety. 'When I go to the office,' Wemmick tells Pip, 'I leave the Castle behind me, and when I come into the Castle, I leave the office behind me.'[53]

LA VIE DE BOHÈME

In post-Revolutionary France the decision to live in a ruined monastic building was more often born of necessity than antiquarian passion. It was Sophie Hugo's poverty that caused Victor to spend his adolescence in the former museum at the Petits Augustins, and it was extreme poverty that drove Langlois and his family into the convent in Rouen. The inhabiting of the material past was thus, like other aspects of French antiquarianism, an altogether more serious and at times desperate business than its cross-Channel counterpart. Langlois's home was a version of the Romantic interior, but by no stretch of the imagination could it be called a style of interior decoration. His friend Charles Richard left an account of what it was like to visit him which makes a striking Gallic pendant to Scott's description of Oldbuck's study:

> It was to the great Convent of the Visitation of St Mary, so deserted, so icy, so melancholy, that the wretched artist had come for shelter, with his seven children and his wife! To find him it was necessary to enter by the cloister door. The visitor crossed a damp and ruined gallery ... at the end of this gallery a wooden stair case, in the open air ... led to a dusty and decrepit attic. This vast antechamber was inhabited by an extensive family of pet birds which hardly moved to let the visitor through to the door of a study, the only more or less habitable corner in this vast space where the four winds met. The Heart contracted horribly on entering the room. Valuable works of art, rich and curious manuscripts, were cast hugger-mugger on the table, on the mantelpiece, on the chairs, on the ground. In winter when, frozen by the north wind, you put your hand on the stove, the iron froze your hand, for there was no fire. No fire in the grate either: the window frame quivered, covered with strips of paper to conceal the wretchedness of this desolate home; the heaps of torn papers strewn everywhere gave off strange noises, plaintive shiverings, stifled cries. It was his poor little children who ran to hide themselves in this sanctum at the approach of a stranger, like mice in their hole, for they were stark naked! ... and, in the midst of this affecting scene, you beheld a man full of dignity, of stoicism and serenity.[54]

There are parallels with the British equivalent, the profusion of objects and the mingling of the precious with the worthless, but overall the impression is very different from the home life of the English or Scottish antiquary. There is nothing deliberate about the way Langlois lives, and certainly nothing funny. The poverty is real. The cold is real, as is the nakedness of the children and, as Richard explains later in his account, the desperate alcoholism of Langlois's wife. The objects he has around him have not been bought from Wardour Street but scraped up in the aftermath of social collapse. As *Notre-Dame* is to the world of *Waverley*, more lurid, more realistic, less polite, so is Langlois's home to Abbotsford.

Yet, however raw and distressing Langlois's circumstances, Richard's description is not without conscious literary effect. The gloom, the contractions of the heart, the emphasis on the contrast between the squalor of the room and the nobility of its occupant, rising above his sufferings, are also conventions, the conventions of the newborn world of 'Bohemia'. Langlois is, after all, an artist, starving in an attic. His misfortune, which would as Ferrey pointed out be seen as a social disadvantage in England, is to Richard the dark background that sets his character off to advantage and marks him out as high-minded and a free spirit. 'His learning was so deep, so various, so certain, his imagination so lively so colourful, his speech so animated, so perceptive, that he soon made you forget the cold and the poverty, as he forgot them himself.'[55] Art and the life of the mind could flourish amid the ruins of history. This was the credo of the young French Romantics who, like Lucien and David in Balzac's *Lost Illusions*, were 'poor but fired with the love of art and science'.[56] Poverty was becoming a badge of integrity in France, a critique of bourgeois and Academic values as the Bohemians emerged from the ruins of the Revolution, literally in Langlois's case, in the 1820s. In August 1831 *Le Figaro* ran the first of a number of articles on the activities of the young men who supported Hugo in his attack on Classical drama, the set known as *les Jeunes-France*. By the middle of 1832 they were established in the minds of the newspaper-reading public as a 'bohemian group'.[57]

In the same month that *Le Figaro* gave birth to the *vie de bohème*, Baron Dupont-Delporte, recently appointed head of the Départment de la Seine-Inférieure, wrote to the Mayor of Rouen suggesting the

establishment of a museum in the city to display the antiquities rescued or excavated in the region.[58] The agreed location was the
Convent of the Visitation, where Langlois was living in such spectacular squalor and giving drawing lessons to children, including Flaubert.
A local authority in Britain would almost certainly have regarded this
as a problem. In Rouen, however, Langlois's presence on site was seen
as a positive advantage. Achille Deville (1789–?1848), a local tax
inspector and enthusiastic antiquary who was appointed first director
of the museum, immediately requested and was granted permission to
employ Langlois 'to help him with the organization and administration'.[59] The museum duly opened in 1834 with the Langlois family *in
situ*. The creation of the museum around Langlois was another per-
mutation on the theme of the Romantic interior for he became, if not
exactly an exhibit, then a living part of the display, ordering it from
within. His own collection was absorbed into the galleries during his
lifetime, and not only the antiquities. Deville, who was, like many
people, devoted to Langlois, incorporated his sword, left over from
his military service, in the collection. Wandering through the museum,
Langlois passed through his own history. After his death the museum
remained for some time both chronicle and monument of his strange
life; the cloister was renamed the Galerie Langlois.

Victor Hugo's interpretation of the Romantic interior was more
deliberate than that of Langlois. Hugo belonged to the next gener-
ation and became famous and successful enough to live as he chose. In
his apartment in the Place des Voges and later, in exile on Guernsey,
he created rooms that took the Romantic interior to operatic heights.
Dickens, who visited Hugo in Paris in 1847, was familiar with the
British version through his friend and illustrator George Cattermole.
Cattermole, who had spent time in Rouen working as an assistant to
Langlois, an experience he may have drawn on when he illustrated
'Little Nell's Home' in *The Old Curiosity Shop*,[60] had his own fine
collection of 'picturesque armour, tapestry [and] carved furniture'.[61]
Hugo's apartment was different. The rooms Dickens saw have not
survived intact, but the interiors of Hauteville House, where Hugo
spent his exile between 1856 and 1870 do, and they give a fair idea of
what Dickens was describing. They are fantastic spaces filled, or
clotted, with bituminously dark wood in every form. Carvings seem to

drip from the ceilings and to crawl up the walls. The blackness is relieved with dramatic splashes of gold and scarlet in draperies and carpets. Fragments of medieval woodwork are interspersed with bits of bricolage, the candle holders are made out of cotton reels. Delft, tapestry and damask occupy what little space remains. '*Exilium Vita Est*' is written over the dining room door. Dickens could not take Hugo's Paris apartment entirely seriously, yet while he was amused, he was also mildly scandalized. There is a nervous undertow to the jokiness:

> A most extraordinary place, looking like an old curiosity shop, or the Property Room of some gloomy vast old Theatre. I was much struck by Hugo himself, who looks a Genius, as he certainly is, and is very interesting from head to foot. His wife is a handsome woman with flashing black eyes, who looks as if she might poison his breakfast any morning when the humour seized her. There is also a ditto daughter of fifteen or sixteen, with ditto eyes, and hardly any drapery above the waist, whom I should suspect of carrying a sharp poignard in her stays, but for her not appearing to wear any. Sitting among old armour, and old tapestry, and old coffers, and grim old chairs and tables, and old Canopies of state from old palaces, and old golden lions going to play at skittles with ponderous old golden balls, they made a most Romantic show, and looked like a chapter out of one of his own books.[62]

As a character from one of his own books Hugo is 'interesting', but if, as the allusion to the *Old Curiosity Shop* suggests, he were to be accidentally propelled into one of Dickens's, the effect would be ridiculous. The drama Dickens reads into the scene with its undercurrent of sex and violence is different from the world of his own fiction or Scott's. In the *Waverley* novels, as Balzac complained, 'woman is duty incarnate' and the heroines are all the same.[63] Dickens also had trouble making young women into more than plaster saints. He was ill at ease with the overt sexuality of the Hugo women.

There were other French antiquarian interiors, like Hugo's if on a less dramatic scale, that were conceived in similar terms to the British, but they were rare. Just as the Romantic passion for the Middle Ages, while it grew to be 'almost a new religion' in France was not translated into French architecture, so interiors comparable with Willement's or

Meyrick's were scarce.[64] One, however, was of immense consequence. This was the home of a Parisian magistrate, Alexandre du Sommerard (1779–1842) in the rue Ménars. He was among the first French collectors to show a serious and informed interest in medieval art, and a portrait of him in his study in 1825 depicts a familiar scene of carved oak, armour, the inevitable 'beaufet' or sideboard and two flintlock rifles, suggesting that, like Meyrick and Scott, he saw recent history as part of a living continuum. By 1832, however, Sommerard was facing the antiquary's perennial problem: his house was not big enough. Friends urged him to move and he took rooms in the only surviving medieval house in Paris, the Hôtel de Cluny, on the Left Bank, not far from the Petits Augustins, the site of Alexandre Lenoir's museum, now the École des beaux-arts.

The hôtel was built in the fifteenth century over and among the ruins of a Roman palace, of which the baths, the Thermes, survived. It belonged to the Cluniac order until it was seized at the Revolution, when the exquisite Gothic chapel was used first as a meeting room and then as the anatomy theatre where Dawson Turner sat queasily through a lecture on obstetrics in order to see its interior. After that it became a print works, by which time it had lost much of its sculpture and most of its glass. Cluny lapsed into a run-down rooming house. Balzac's Lucien, writing home to Angoulême to describe the vastness of Paris and the exorbitant cost of living, explains: 'I am now at the Hôtel de Cluny in ... one of the poorest and dingiest back-streets in Paris, squeezed between three churches and the ancient buildings of the Sorbonne. I have taken a furnished room on the fourth floor, a very bare and dirty one.'[65]

Sommerard moved into an upper floor, taking the chapel and some adjoining rooms. The public were invited to view his collection, which he arranged to imply an historic narrative. Two suits of armour sat opposite one another across a chess board, in the chapel a model of a priest in stole and chasuble presided. As at Goodrich, reactions to the figures were mixed. Some visitors thought them 'burlesque', but many more were impressed.[66] Cluny became a meeting place for antiquaries, dealers, Romantics and Bohemians, 'one of the acknowledged centres' of the cult of the Middle Ages.[67] The year that Sommerard arrived, Albert Lenoir, son of Alexandre, put forward a proposal at the annual Salon. His idea was to turn the hôtel and adjacent Roman baths into a single, historic museum, telling, through art and artefacts, 'in strict chronological order' the history of France from the Romans in a 'museum of national antiquities'.[68] The idea was his father's: Lenoir still mourned his lost museum. Although the proposal was too elaborate to be realized straight away, it aroused interest, which was boosted from 1838 onwards when Sommerard published the first of five great folio volumes of *Les Arts au Moyen Age*, based on his own collection. By the time Alexandre Lenoir died in 1839 he had seen the groundwork laid. Cluny was bought by the city of Paris and Albert Lenoir was appointed architect for the creation of the museum. When Sommerard died in 1842, the French state bought the unified site and the collections.

Two years later the museum opened under the auspices of the Commission supérieure des monuments historiques as the Musée des thermes et de l'hôtel de Cluny, with Sommerard's son Edmond as its first curator. To begin with the collections looked disappointingly sparse, but Edmond was his father's son, and thanks to his 'extraordinary vigilance ... flair ... and a level of knowledge remarkable at the time' he steadily acquired important pieces.[69] He also compiled a catalogue, grouping the museum's 3,770 objects by types and by materials. Painting, stone carving, alabasters, enamels, armour and the other 'differentes branches d'art et d'industrie' were listed in separate sections and arranged within them in chronological order.[70] This was to be the modern, scientific way, as the antiquarian interior turned into the museum. July 1882 saw the apotheosis of Cluny when, after decades of tense negotiations and hair-raising reports of neglect and damage by the municipality of Boussac in Creuse, Edmond secured the sequence of tapestries known as *La Dame à la licorne*, gathering them into the safety of the museum, where they remain, one of the glories of Paris.

SACRED SPACES

Although most of the woodwork and stained glass imported to Britain had come from churches and other religious institutions, only a small proportion was reused in ecclesiastical settings. That proportion

26. South Transept of Notre-Dame, Rouen, John Sell Cotman, published in Dawson Turner's *Architectural Antiquities of Normandy* (1822). Turner sponsored Cotman's drawing tours to make illustrations for the book.

27. La Grande Maison aux Andelys, Normandy, being dismantled. The most attractive fragments were sold to British collectors. Illustrated in Nodier and Taylor, *Voyages pittoresques et romantiques*, vol. 2 (1824).

28. *Massacre de l'évêque de Liège* (detail), Eugène Delacroix, 1828/9 – a scene from Walter Scott's *Quentin Durward*. One of many French Romantic paintings inspired by the *Waverley* novels, it was shown to great acclaim in London.

29–31. (*left*) The figure beside the dying Harold as shown in Bernard de Montfaucon's *Monumens* (1729–33), reproduced in Andrew Ducarel's *Anglo-Norman Antiquities* (1767), with holes showing missing stitchwork. (*centre*) The same figure shown in engravings from Charles Stothard's drawings for the Society of Antiquaries of London, with the suggestion of an arrow, 1823. (*right*) The figure as it now appears in the Bayeux Tapestry.

32 & 33. Charles Stothard (1786–1821) made the most important single contribution to the understanding of the Bayeux Tapestry. He worked in collaboration with his wife, Anna, later Anna Eliza Bray (1790–1883), an author and antiquary who continued her antiquarian studies after her husband's death.

34. The discovery of the Scottish regalia, 4 February 1818. The event was elaborately staged by Walter Scott.

35. James Robinson Planché (1796–1880), playwright, herald and theatre historian who extended the use of period costume to Shakespeare's history plays.

36. George IV (1762–1830) in Highland dress. The king's visit to Scotland in 1822 launched the kilt as a form of national costume.

7. Playbill for Planché's landmark production of *King John* in 'the habit of the period', 1823. It was a sensational success.

38. *The Antiquary* shows the student of history as an abstracted dreamer lost in the past. Richard Parkes Bonington, *c.*1827.

39. *Don Quixote*, the first antiquary in literature, was to the Romantics 'a friend, a countryman and a brother'. Richard Parkes Bonington, *c*.1827.

40. Walter Scott (1771–1832). The most famous author in the world, he sits like Quixote among historic fragments representing his imagination in material form.

41. *The Antiquary's Cell* by E. W. Cooke, 1835, plays on the theme of the antiquary as mystic or alchemist, an invisible presence drawing towards him the remains of history.

42. Salisbury Cathedral from John Britton's *History and Antiquities of the Cathedral Church of Salisbury*, 1815. The cathedral came to symbolize the antiquaries' battle to save Gothic architecture. Here it is shown in receding planes, a Picturesque landscape in itself.

grew, however, through the nineteenth century against the background of impassioned debates about the status of the Anglican settlement aroused by the Tractarians. Among the antiquaries a significant number, including Pugin, Willement and Meyrick, either built, or incorporated, a church or chapel in their homes. There was, however, no direct correlation between religious belief and antiquarian practice. At one extreme Langlois, who lived in a monastery surrounded by sacred art, was a sceptic who regarded religion as mostly superstition. At the other, John Lingard, a Catholic priest, had no time for dressing up, as he saw it, in the art and liturgy of the Middle Ages. Asked to contribute to funds for the chapel at the seminary at Ushaw, County Durham, designed by Pugin on the model of the Oxford college chapels, Lingard wrote back irritably that he hoped Ushaw would not 'suffer yourselves to be bamboozled with Pugin's whims, or build a church fit for monks of the 14th century instead of ecclesiastical students of the present'.[71]

For Roman Catholics of an antiquarian cast of mind, however, it was important to build churches which in style and substance were the equal of those from which they felt they had been evicted at the Reformation. Long before Emancipation in 1829, Catholics of means, if they were discreet and lived in places as relatively remote as East Anglia, were able to proclaim their Catholicism with considerable freedom. The Gages managed in effect to ignore the Reformation altogether, having adopted the medieval parish church at Hengrave in Suffolk and made it into a private Catholic chapel and family mausoleum. (It was here that John Gage had brought the body of his friend Thomas Crawfurd to be buried after the terrible journey from Waterloo.) Not far from Hengrave was Costessey (pronounced and sometimes spelled Cossy) in Norfolk, home of Sir William and Lady Jerningham. The Jerninghams had been given the estate by Mary Tudor in gratitude for their support of her claim to the throne. By the turn of the nineteenth century they had two obsessions: the campaign for Emancipation and their claim to the barony of Stafford. They were forever 'busy about the peerage', researching their pedigree and dining with the Duke of Norfolk to discuss the best way to proceed.[72] Edward Jerningham, the heir to the estate, was a leading figure on the Catholic Board. Set up in 1807 to advance the cause of Emancipation, the board was permanently hampered by in-fighting. The principal division was between the Cisalpinists, who believed that England had its own, native form of Catholicism, and the Ultramontanes, who took their authority on all points from Rome.

Edward was a Cisalpinist, as was his friend John Milner, one of the most pugnacious members of the board. Together they designed a chapel for Costessey, which was also a manifesto. Its meaning was the same as the little Church of St Peter that Milner and Carter built in Winchester, but writ very much larger. The Costessey chapel was ninety feet long, thirty-five feet wide and forty feet high; it was modelled in part on King's College, Cambridge and dedicated to St Augustine. Its decoration proclaimed the Jerninghams' twin faiths in God and themselves. The walls of the nave were decorated with their arms, 'impaled with those of the various alliances of this illustrious family', and the windows over the family pew were filled with armorial stained glass, trumpeting the family's noble pretensions.[73] It was the glazing scheme of the twenty-two nave windows, however, which was remarkable. Under Milner's guiding hand and, at the time, uniquely, it set out a complete theological programme. Edward's father, Sir William, had a good eye and was fortunately placed near Norwich, where John Christopher Hampp and Seth Stevenson, a printer and fellow of the Society of Antiquaries, had established themselves as the biggest dealers in imported stained glass. Since 1804, 'case after case' had passed through their hands en route to private buyers, Soho dealers and Christie's.[74] Sir William selected about eighty panels of highest-quality Flemish and German glass, choosing subjects that could be arranged, by Milner, as a coherent scheme; Old Testament scenes on the north side balanced with scenes of Christ's infancy on the south. The windows thus followed the medieval system of types and ante-types, with the Old Testament prefiguring the New. Solomon and the Queen of Sheba were paired with the Adoration of the Magi, Christ's Presentation in the Temple matched with the Circumcision of Samuel, and so on.

At Costessey Milner set out in the arrangement of the windows a continuous history of the Catholic faith, expressed in the interfusion of new and old material and lived out through the successive generations of a loyally recusant family. The result was much admired by such bellwethers of polite taste as J. P. Neal, whose *Views of the Seats, Mansions, Castles etc. of Noblemen and Gentlemen in England* of 1829 praised the chapel's 'appropriate decorations ... derived from pure models'.[75] *Excursions in the County of Norfolk* also noted 'the noble windows ... filled with very fine old stained glass ... after designs of the German and Flemish schools'.[76] Inevitably, perhaps, the admiration outlasted the chapel. When in 1913 the Jerninghams abandoned Costessey, the glass was demounted and sold. It fetched £16,000 and is now distributed among museums and churches from Ohio to York Minster. Whirled together by the forces of one war, dispersed on the eve of another, the windows of Costessey stood for more than a century as witnesses of the age of Romantic Catholicism.

After Emancipation in 1829, the demand for Catholic architecture grew dramatically. Another Norfolk family, the Bedingfelds, commissioned a chapel from J. C. Buckler, and fitted it up with old glass, though not according to any discernible scheme. Meanwhile in the Church of England, and among Episcopalians in Scotland, as the 1830s went on and the Tractarian debate and the strictures of the Cambridge Camden Society struck home, ecclesiastical antiquarianism gathered momentum. No one embodied it more fully than John Keble (1792–1866), in whom Anglicanism, Romanticism and antiquarianism met. Keble, who gave his name, posthumously, to one of the greatest works of Romantic Christian architecture, William Butterfield's Keble College, Oxford, preached a sermon in 1833 on 'National Apostasy' which seemed, in hindsight, to have marked the beginning of the Oxford Movement. At the time, however, he was more famous as a poet. In 1827 he published *The Christian Year*, which became the widest-selling book of poetry in the nineteenth century, and in 1831 he was elected Oxford Professor of Poetry.[77] Like his hero Wordsworth, Keble believed the natural world to be 'the repository of types and symbols of the unseen and the spiritual', but unlike Wordsworth he interpreted that belief in purely Christian terms.[78] This sense of the immanence of the divine in the material world, natural or man-made, was manifest in Keble's decision to use profits from the sales of *The Christian Year* to rebuild the parish church at Hursley in Hampshire, where he was incumbent from 1836 until his death.

The local squire, Sir William Heathcote, who was patron of the living, had been a pupil of Keble at Oxford and was a Tractarian sympathizer. They undertook the work together. Heathcote's daughter, Charlotte, later well known as the novelist Charlotte M. Yonge (1823–1901), recalled the improvements. For her, looking back from the closing years of the nineteenth century, they appeared to mark another stage in the progressive march of taste. Amused by the Strawberry Hill antiquarianism of her grandparents' generation, she writes condescendingly about the naïvety of the previous squire, Thomas Dummer, who 'transported several fragments from Netley Abbey ... and set them up in his park as an object from the windows'.[79] Keble and her father were better informed. They went to Soho, and 'in Wardour Street ... succeeded in obtaining five panels representing the Blessed Virgin and the four Latin Fathers, which are worked into the pulpit', thus marking 'a new era' in antiquarianism.[80] More than a century later this does not seem such an obvious leap forward. Objections at the time, however, were doctrinal rather than aesthetic. Interventions of this sort were intended to reinforce the belief in a continuous independent English Church by reversing the material effects of the Reformation. This persistent tradition, which so exasperated Lingard, resonated profoundly with John Henry Newman (1801–90), who himself had tried to believe it and to remain within the pale of the Anglican settlement. He failed and in 1845 became a Roman Catholic, remarking that Keble by 'his happy magic made the Anglican church seem what Catholicism is'.[81] Newman was talking about theology, but the same could be said of the church at Hursley.

There was a great deal of such happy magic in the air at Oxford. Keble's fellow High Church Tractarian John Rouse Bloxam transformed his rooms at Magdalen into a private chapel in all but name:

> From the ceiling there hung an elaborate corona designed by A. W. Pugin, under which, in the very centre of the room, there stood a richly decorated model of the tomb of the founder of the College. On one side of the room there was a triptych which, when opened, disclosed a set of figures all richly gilt, representing the Adoration of the Magi. Round the walls of the room were several pictures, some of huge proportions ... There was also a Russian icon ... which glittered and shone in its silver setting[82]

Beyond this room, part oratory, part shrine to his alma mater,

Bloxam's antiquarian efforts extended to the college's broader ethos. He revived the now famous May Day celebration, in which the choir sings a Latin hymn at dawn from the top of the Tower. The practice had never died out, but standards had slipped. There was no longer any music, the choir kept their coats and hats on and despite the best efforts of Mr Mundy, the Head Porter, who frisked the choristers as they went up the Tower, boys had on more than one occasion brought in raw eggs and amused themselves by throwing them at passers-by. Bloxam restored dignity. He reintroduced music, put the choir in surplices and clamped down on the egg-throwing. Today the Magdalen May Day ritual is a prime example of a tradition sometimes said to have been invented by the Victorians, which wasn't, but which, like many of the medieval buildings they are accused of spoiling, would not, in all likelihood, have survived without them.

As the nineteenth century went on, ecclesiastical antiquarian interiors, like their secular counterparts, became more widespread. Mindful of the Cambridge Camden Society's ever more frequent and dogmatic lectures on the importance of maintaining and respecting historic fabric, congregations began to consider making their churches look more medieval, while in Scotland the Episcopalians wanted to distinguish their buildings as much as their theology from the austerity of the Kirk. So, by another twist of history, the iconoclasm of the French Revolution helped to make good the vandalism of the English Reformation and the Civil Wars. Churches left bare since the time of Edward VI and further despoiled under Cromwell began to blossom with medieval choir stalls and panelling, handsome brass lecterns and richly coloured stained-glass windows, some of extraordinary quality and provenance. Earl Howe, who received gifts of antique glass from George IV and William IV, donated it to the Church of St James at Twycross in Leicestershire, where Willement installed it in 1841. The panels include The Presentation in the Temple from St-Denis and four pieces of thirteenth-century glass from the Ste-Chapelle, now among the oldest stained glass in England.

At Brougham Hall in Cumbria, Willement's friend the antiquarian architect Lewis Cottingham was commissioned by Lord Brougham, the former Lord Chancellor, to fit up his chapel with an array of panelling, screens, stalls and an elaborately carved Flemish altarpiece of about 1520. Now in Carlisle Cathedral, where it is known as 'The Brougham Triptych', it may have come from Cologne, but how it got to Brougham is unclear. Brougham's was a private chapel, so he had no difficulty in getting such a 'popish' object past the authorities of the established Church. In a parish much depended on the patron of the living. The local squire had more or less equal authority with the vicar or rector and was apt to regard the church as a part of his own domain. At the medieval St Leonard's, Old Warden, in Bedfordshire, the patron was Robert Henley, Lord Ongley, whose extreme enthusiasm for all things antiquarian was not matched by his taste. He filled the interior of the small church to bursting point in a display of Wardour Street sophistication at its most florid. Old pieces were joined together with insertions of new work, compiled with a view to general effect. The interior came with its own similarly made-up history, which Ongley seems to have trustingly copied down at the dealer's dictation. To an educated eye the result is a cacophony. Nikolaus Pevsner could hardly hear himself think over the racket of anachronism:

> There is nothing in ... [the] exterior to prepare for the shock in store upon entering. One can only just register the high unmoulded Norman tower arch ... before going under in the mass of woodwork. It oppresses you from all sides; it is utterly disjointed, and can only here and there be read consecutively ... one is all the time up against the Early Victorian connecting pieces ... The many panels with the letters AC are said to come from the House of Anne of Cleves at Bruges. (What has Anne of Cleves to do with Bruges?)[83]

Clearly the brokers of Soho had seen Lord Ongley coming and made him very welcome. Nearby at St John the Baptist, Cockayne Hatley, the wealthy incumbent, Henry Cust, took up the living when the church was 'ruinous' and left it, with the help of the ubiquitous Willement, 'an object of admiration to all, who appreciate Church decorations'.[84] This was a family effort, with various members paying for stained glass and woodwork. They produced a commemorative book, published in 1851, which gives details of the pieces they acquired. These include carved woodwork from the Abbey d'Alne, destroyed at the Revolution, and the pulpit from St Andrew's, Antwerp, of which the sounding board, as it was 'not required for that purpose', was made into a front for the reading desk.[85] In his summing-up Robert Needham Cust notes, with an air of pride, that 'the woodwork has been contributed by five celebrated Flemish towns'.[86] The fact that the contributions were not voluntary did not detract from Cust's satisfaction. As the empire expanded, wider still and wider, it seemed, perhaps, only natural that the wealth of nations should flow into the parish churches of Britain.

8

Tartan, Treason and Plot

Nothing but a Popish Cabal.
George III on the Society of Antiquaries, c.1797

His loyalty is founded on would-be treason: he props the
actual throne by the shadow of rebellion.
William Hazlitt on Walter Scott, 1825

One huge libel on the whole nation.
Charles Kingsley on Lingard's History of England, *1856*

Antiquarianism, like all historical enquiry, has political implications.
Whether it was the Secretary of the Society of Antiquaries trying to
punch John Carter or Lenoir losing a finger in defence of the tombs at
St-Denis, the study and interpretation of the remains of history has
never been an entirely safe business. In France, as we have seen, for
much of this period history simply was politics. In Britain matters
were for the most part less fraught. On two subjects, however, the
antiquaries found themselves directly and unavoidably involved in
controversy. Roman Catholicism and the Jacobite cause were central
to the study of national history and antiquities; they were also subjects of present debate, dispute and fascination. The two were intimately
connected, but it might be more accurate to say that at this period
they were entangled, for they provoked curiously contrasting responses.

Catholicism, 'popery' to its enemies, was still deeply mistrusted in
Britain three centuries after the Reformation. Popular anti-Catholicism

was largely prejudice. The penal laws ensured that until Emancipation in 1829, Catholics could play no part in civic life or worship
openly. Most British people therefore knew little about them and
some felt free to imagine the worst. Bigotry was reinforced by the fact
that while Britain was fighting its way to dominance across the battle-
fields of Europe, it was waging a constant rearguard action against
rebellions in Catholic Ireland. This reinforced the idea that Catholics
were treacherous, their only loyalty being to Rome. It was Ireland
that ultimately made the Catholic question urgent, but it made it no
less difficult, for it was felt to touch on the very identity of the nation.
There were implications for 'the royal prerogative, the nature of civil
rights, the place of religion in the constitution of the state'.[1] George
III was obsessively anti-Catholic. He told William Pitt in 1801 that he
regarded Emancipation as an 'improper subject' of which there would
be no further discussion during his reign. By the time it was finally
introduced Pitt had resigned over the question, the Duke of Wellington had fought a duel and the country had been furiously and loudly
divided. Nor was 1829 the end of anti-popery. In 1840 John Henry
Newman's brother-in-law warned readers of the *British Critic* that
'Rome wishes still to govern England', and as late as 1850, when the
Catholic hierarchy was restored, the prime minister, Lord John Russell, roused the country to riot on Guy Fawkes night with talk of
'Papal Aggression'.[2]

The Glorious Revolution of 1688 was seen by its supporters to
complete the Reformation. It had removed the Catholic James II and
replaced him with the Protestant William and Mary. Since then the
Catholic Church in England had not, in reality, presented any threat
to the state. The Pope, however, had supported those who remained
loyal to the Stuart line, the so-called Jacobites, and the same could not
be said of them. In 1745 James II's grandson, the Young Pretender,
Charles Edward Stuart, had got an army as far south as Derby before
being defeated the following year at Culloden. This, the last battle
fought on British soil, was well within living memory in the last decades of the eighteenth century. It was followed by stringent government
measures to counteract 'the serious fear and sense of political threat'
posed by the adherents of the Stuart cause.[3] This was the beginning of

the Highland clearances and the prohibition of Highland dress. The early nineteenth century still saw outbreaks of agitation among the Scots. In 1820 'a brief and bloody skirmish along a dyke on the Stirling Plain' ushered in 'a year of squabble and despair, mobbing and moonlit marching', which ended in the brutal public execution of three weavers in Stirling.[4] Yet by that time Jacobitism had become a Romantic ideal on both sides of the border. Two years later George IV was squeezing himself into one of the most expensive (and extensive) kilts ever made in preparation for the first visit by a reigning British monarch to Scotland since Charles I in 1633. Highland dress became not merely legal but fashionable. This remarkable and apparently paradoxical view of history was largely due to sleight of hand by the greatest antiquary of the age, Walter Scott.

The decline of Scott's literary reputation and his own capacity for self-mockery have both led to an underestimation of the skill with which he manipulated historical traditions and artefacts to political ends. Trevor-Roper's portrait of a novelist 'carried away by his own romantic Celtic fantasies', creating out of them a 'bizarre travesty of Scottish history', summed up a certain patronizing mid-century view.[5] Since then more careful readings have shown that judgement to be factually incorrect. Scott, despite his son-in-law's reference to his 'celtification', was no admirer of Celtic antiquity. More importantly, it does scant justice to the sophistication of his historical sense. Scott was a Tory, but one with deep intellectual roots in the Whig tradition of the Scottish Enlightenment. He saw the Union as Scotland's best hope. In *Waverley*, his first solo novel, published in 1814 and set in the Jacobite Rising of 1745, he describes an England advanced in culture and commerce opposed to the feudal 'stagnation' of the Scottish Lowlands and the 'tribal' society of the Highlands.[6] It was a technique Scott was to perfect, making his argument run in one direction while a colourful plot, dense historical detail and strong characters let his readers' imaginations run in another, opposite one.

Waverley criticizes the Jacobites for encouraging the warring tendencies of the clans, while describing events in fascinating and vivid terms. The key was the subtitle, ''Tis Sixty Years Since'.[7] Scott based his story on that staple of antiquarian research, oral tradition, specifically the stories his father's friend Alexander Steuart of Invernahyle in Argyllshire had told him. Invernahyle had been 'out', as aficionados say, in both the '15 and the '45, and his tales, Scott recalled, 'were the absolute delight of my childhood'.[8] The same would have been true for many of his readers. There had always been what Boswell called 'a *liking* for Jacobitism' among people such as himself and Johnson, who would never have thought of doing 'anything violent in support of the cause'. That, Boswell thought, would be merely to indulge a 'warm whim'.[9] Two generations later the danger had receded and the whim was warmer. Anyone alive in 1814 who had had grand-parents to tell them tales would have heard, from one side or another, about the Jacobite risings. Waverley's adventures were thus thrillingly immediate, but at the same time safely shut away in a past softened by fond associations of childhood. It was possible, indeed it was tempt-ing, to be simultaneously an intellectual unionist and a sentimental Jacobite.

'HISTORY OF A MOST DANGEROUS DESCRIPTION'

In 1798 the national mood was febrile. The war with France was not going well. The ill-equipped British navy had mutinied at Spithead and the Nore, leading to Pitt's suspension of *habeas corpus* and a ban on unlicensed public gatherings. There was an uprising in Ireland. Amid this atmosphere of alarm and rumour a new fear emerged, the possibility that the nation was threatened not only by Republicans in France and Catholics in Ireland, but also, in a combination of the two, from within, by the French refugees, many of whom were religious, who like La Rue, had been forced to flee for their lives. There was much self-congratulation about the way the émigrés had been received: 'if there is any thing that eminently distinguishes the British charac-ter', Sir Henry Mildmay, MP for Winchester, declared in the Commons, it was 'the humane protection' extended to the exiled French clergy.[10] Yet, he continued, there was a need for caution for, while Sir Henry was the last person to wish to inhibit this 'spirit of toleration', he felt that the 'enormous inundation of Popish priests' was a risk to 'the safety of the church and state'.[11] In order that it should be 'checked in the bud' he introduced, in 1800, the Monastic Institutions Bill, a measure to police schools set up by Catholics and to ban monastic communities from accepting novices. Mildmay painted a lurid vision of at least 5,000 'missionaries' across the country poised to inveigle the Protestant youth of Britain into the toils of Rome.

Among Mildmay's opponents in Parliament was Richard Brinsley Sheridan. Sheridan produced a full list of émigré communities which amounted, at most, to 360 nuns and thirty-six monks. He laughed down the spectre of children being indoctrinated in Catholic schools and argued that these measures would only stir up trouble, which, on the eve of the Act of Union with Ireland, would be particularly dangerous. Furthermore, Sheridan pointed out, Mildmay's proposal was not based on evidence of a Catholic conspiracy but was the result of difficulties in his own constituency of Winchester, where a 'controversial spirit' had 'lately shewn itself' in a pamphlet war raging 'between Dr Sturges and Mr Milner'.[12] Mildmay's Bill was indeed the hysterical consequence of a row about John Milner's recently published *The History, Civil and Ecclesiastical, and Survey of the Antiquities of Winchester*. Milner, knowing that as a Catholic bishop he had to be careful, had done his best to forestall objections. The *History*'s dedication to a local notable, Countess Chandos Temple, is cast in conventionally fulsome terms, but it is also a considered self-portrait of the author as loyal, local citizen. Milner recalls making a tour of Winchester's 'sacred and invaluable monuments' with the countess and how, in the course of it, they saw the great tomb chests in the cathedral containing the remains of the Saxon kings Kinegils and Egbert and visited Hyde Abbey, the burial place of King Alfred.[13] Between these three princes, Milner suggests, Winchester could claim to have been the source of 'our Christianity our Monarchy and our Constitution', Church and State joined together under the banner of civic pride.[14]

In the text, however, he was less careful; indeed, he was severely and sarcastically critical of an earlier Bishop of Winchester, Benjamin Hoadly (1676–1761). This annoyed Sturges, who was a prebendary of the cathedral and who responded with a pamphlet. The two men were now going at it hammer and tongs. It says much about the mood of the time that such an arcane antiquarian dispute could escalate to the point where its echoes were heard in Parliament. This was because Milner's views on Hoadly touched on the tender subject of relations between State and Church. Hoadly was a latitudinarian, 'of what is called the *low church*' – in other words, he saw the established Church as a branch of the State and had conceded, in Milner's view, too much to secular authority. Milner was not arguing as a Catholic but as an 'anti-erastian', that is from his opposition to secular authority over religious institutions, whether Anglican or Catholic. 'If [the clergy] will not be good Catholics,' Milner told Sturges, with a coolness that only served to infuriate him further, 'I am desirous that they should remain good Church of England men ... I wish to prevent them from frittering away their religion.'[15] Sturges struck back on behalf of the Low Church party, triggering an exchange which even Milner conceded went to 'considerable length' and grew into a national controversy.[16]

Reviews of Milner's *History* almost invariably covered the pamphlets as well. It must have further depressed Dr Sturges that none of Milner's critics bothered to defend Hoadly, who, *The Gentleman's Magazine* noted, 'was never highly thought of'.[17] The reaction was instead a microcosm of educated public opinion on the Catholic question. There were legitimate criticisms. Milner was often slapdash with his references and sometimes whimsical in his judgement about the reliability of sources. If he had a prejudice, it was his insistence on the English origins of Gothic. Opinions on these points varied but no reviewer ignored his Catholicism, to which responses ranged from the cautiously reasonable in the *British Critic*, which found that Milner, 'Though too dignified in mind to suppress his religion, or to conceal his prejudices', was 'often acting ingenuously under both', to the hysterical *Monthly Review*, which accused him of 'a deliberated design and laboured effort to vindicate [Roman Catholicism] ... and to degrade the most distinguished advocates of the Reformation from popery, to which our country is principally indebted of the civil and religious liberty by which it has been blessed.'[18]

In the *Quarterly Review*, the antiquary and topographer the Revd Thomas Dunham Whitaker (1759–1821) was ambivalent. Milner's account of the *Antiquities* he thought 'masterly', but the *History* gave cause for concern.[19] Whitaker's unease was shared by many antiquaries. He cared about the subject matter, he admired the writer, but he could not accept history written by a papist. When the chapter of Milner's *Winchester* which dealt with 'The Rise and Progress of the Pointed Arch' was reprinted separately by the Architectural Library in a volume of essays by James Bentham, Francis Grose and others, Whitaker was audibly relieved to be able to praise it. He informed readers of the *Quarterly Review* that not only was it 'important and timely', but that Milner was 'a man of genius' and, moreover, his Catholicism gave him an advantage: he was 'struck ... with a ray of inspiration' from a source unknown to the other writers, namely 'the peculiar spirit of the religion, for the ordinances of which these edifices were constructed'.[20] Milner the Catholic understood Gothic churches as no Protestant could. Here was the rub. To admire medieval architecture was to admire the works of the Catholic Church, to regret its destruction was to regret the Reformation, that determining event in national history.

In *The Antiquary*, Scott dramatizes the dilemma familiar to many antiquaries as Oldbuck rhapsodizes amid the ruins of the Priory of St Ruth:

> There was the retreat of learning in the days of darkness, Mr Lovel ... there reposed the sages who were aweary of the world, and devoted either to that which was to come, or to the service of the generations who should follow them in this. I will show you presently the library ... And here I might take up the lamentation of the learned Leland, who ... exclaims ... like Rachel weeping for her children ... to put our ancient chronicles, our noble histories, our learned commentaries, and national muniments, to such offices of contempt and subjection, has greatly degraded our nation.[21]

Oldbuck, who is proud of his Protestant descent, is challenged by his neighbour and rival Sir Arthur Wardour, who is equally proud of his own family's role in the Jacobite risings, accusing Oldbuck of taking a popish view of the Dissolution. The antiquary finds himself trapped 'like a woodcock caught in his own springe'.[22]

As Mildmay pressed on with his Bill, Milner (on whom it would have had no effect whatever), continued to come under heavy fire in the press. Even in the usually friendly pages of *The Gentleman's Magazine* the reviewer of his collected anti-Hoadly polemics, *Letters to a Prebendary*, regretted to see 'a local history made a vehicle of religious controversy',[23] while a show of support for the prebendary came in a letter in August 1799, accusing Milner of being an inveterate troublemaker, 'so is his mind constituted'.[24] Most Catholics, the writer argued, would sympathize with Sturges and feel 'not very different' from him about Milner.[25] The significance of this particular letter was that it came from Milner's fellow Catholic bishop, Joseph Berington. Mildmay's Bill had now been drafted. Berington was horrified by its implications and furious with Milner for stirring up trouble. Far from there being any 'cabal' of British Catholics, the small community was deeply divided. As well as the doctrinal split between the Ultramontanes and the Cisalpinists, there were disagreements about tactics. Milner's uncompromising, often inflammatory style was deplored by a number of those who agreed with him in principle. Berington had reason to be worried, for despite Sheridan's evidence, the Monastic Institutions Bill passed the Commons. Fortunately it was lost in the Lords, though not for want of spirited advocacy from the Bishop of Winchester.

Among the antiquaries with whom we are concerned five of the British Catholics, Milner, Carter, Willson, Lingard and Gage, span the generations who lived through the French Revolution. Between them they give a fair impression of the range of English Catholic opinion. Milner and Carter were the oldest, born in 1752 and 1748 respectively. Carter never admitted to being a Catholic, at times indeed he explicitly denied it; but his close friendship with Milner, his collaboration in the building of St Peter's, Winchester and his published view of the Reformation as 'impiety and devastation ... ignorance and mistaken zeal' had placed him since 1786 in the Catholic camp.[26] Lingard belonged to the next generation. He had grown up in Winchester, and had known and disliked Milner from childhood. He thought his militancy counterproductive and his history slapdash, complaining that he 'seldom referred to a passage or even quoted it, without committing a blunder or an infidelity'.[27] Milner for his part thought Lingard too temporizing and too cool. Lingard never attacked Milner in public, but it was not in Milner's nature to be so restrained. Almost the only thing they had in common was the enmity of the Revd Thomas Whitaker.

Lingard published his first book, *The Antiquities of the Anglo-Saxon Church*, in 1806. It opens with a statement of method which is an implicit criticism of the prevailing style of narrative history as exemplified by Hume. Lingard worked from primary sources, 'the original historians', for 'who would draw from the troubled stream, when he may drink at the fountain-head';[28] and he could read Anglo-Saxon, which, as he modestly put it, 'though an easy, is not a common acquirement'.[29] His immediate predecessor in the field was the attorney Sharon Turner's *The History of the Anglo-Saxons*, which in its first edition described a vigorous, independent Anglo-Saxon society, crushed by the Norman invaders. Despite Turner's modifications in later editions, it remained squarely set in a nationalist reading, intended to gratify 'patriotic curiosity' about the origins of England's greatness.[30] Implicit in Turner's account is the existence of an independent English Church. He describes King Alfred telling the Pope that he would honour the rubrics of his ancestors regardless of 'whatever writings' might issue from 'the apostolic seat as you choose to call it'.[31] This 'favourite hypothesis' of the English, as Lingard called it, the belief in 'the independence of the Anglo Saxon church' that underpinned Anglican apologetics from Dugdale to the Oxford Movement of the 1830s, was not borne out by the evidence and Lingard 'did not chuse to assert that, of which no solid proof can be adduced'.[32] Whitaker opened fire in his review in the *Quarterly Review* with the bald statement: 'This is the work of a Catholic priest.'[33] Unfortunately for his own rhetorical purposes, Whitaker was too well informed to argue for an independent Anglo-Saxon Church. He was reduced to protesting that it didn't matter what the Saxons believed: 'Who were they? A set of pirates just emerging from barbarism, and scarcely capable of comprehending their own wretched systems.'[34] He could not deny Lingard's 'intelligence and research', but nor could he overcome his belief that Lingard must be 'bold and crafty' and set on undermining the Church of England.[35] In the end he had to base much of his criticism on a footnote which makes disrespectful reference to the principal architect of Elizabeth I's religious settlement, Archbishop Parker.

The Antiquities of the Anglo-Saxon Church was launched on stormy waters, for in 1807 the Emancipation debate came to another crisis. A

Bill was proposed to admit Catholics to the army and navy. It was a pragmatic as much as a liberal suggestion, as manpower was badly needed. The king forced its withdrawal, as a result of which the government resigned. The subsequent election was fought largely on this single issue. The prime minister, Spencer Percival, campaigned on an anti-Catholic manifesto of 'Support the King and the British Constitution'. The British Catholic Board was formed in response as an attempt to unite Ultramontane and Cisalpine factions in the cause of Emancipation.[36] It happened that one of the most energetic opponents of Emancipation was the antiquaries' old foe Shute Barrington, Bishop of Durham, who, when he was not fighting Carter for Wyatt's right to pull down the Galilee Porch, was occupied in keeping alive 'almost single-handedly' the spirit of 'No-popery' in his diocese.[37] Lingard was one of the Catholics in Barrington's diocese. He took the bishop on in an essay which accused him of 'combating a phantom of (his) own creation' and the exchange made Lingard, in a small way, a national figure.[38] It also persuaded him that polemic was pointless. In order to sway public opinion he needed to write something that would be read by non-Catholics, and so he settled down to write a history of England from the Roman invasion to the Glorious Revolution. In 1811 he resigned his post at the seminary at Ushaw and took a living as a priest in the small parish of Hornby, where he had 'a house well furnished with a garden and croft and a good salary' and peace and quiet to work.[39]

Meanwhile, Milner had no intention of giving up controversy. With the recurrence of George III's incapacitating illness and the regency of his Whiggish son, the Board of British Catholics saw a chance for compromise on Emancipation. A Bill brought in in 1813 was defeated in the Commons, but not before Milner had campaigned against it, because it allowed the government the right of veto over episcopal appointments. His most vocal supporters were the Irish bishops and this, along with Milner's personal closeness to Daniel O'Connell, rendered his efforts entirely counterproductive. The exasperated Catholic Board expelled him. Nothing daunted, Milner set out for Rome. Pius VII, who had been imprisoned for four years by Napoleon and was anxious to make an ally of the British government, told Milner to 'refrain from the use of irritating language towards his adversaries'.[40] The Pontiff no doubt found Milner quite irritating on his own account.

It made no difference. In 1821 when, following George III's death, yet another Bill to relieve Catholic disabilities was introduced, Milner once more fought it. Sending Gage a drawing of a carved pillar he had discovered 'nearly opposite the western porch of Wolverhampton parish church', he wrote: 'I suppose that many of yr acquaintance are railing against me at a fine rate, while infinitely the greater part of Catholics are extolling me far beyond my deserts. But what then? Was it to be expected that I would surrender my crozier into the hands of a knot of lawyers & fox hunters? . . . Believe me, Dr Sir, a different mode of proceeding must be followed if Emancipation is ever to be gained.'[41] Gage's reply expressed interest in the pillar but discreetly ignored the politics, and Milner wrote back reproaching him for preferring to correspond about 'trifling subjects of antiquity' rather than the 'all-important & everlasting concerns of Religion'.[42]

It was in this climate of fraught disunity on the question of Emancipation that the first three volumes of Lingard's *History* appeared in 1819. They covered the period up to the accession of Henry VIII and were published only after the printer, Mawman of Ludgate Street, had been reassured by Lord Holland, his secretary John Allen and his friend Henry Brougham, who had all read the first 300 pages, that it was a sound work of scholarship and not papist propaganda. It was the Whigs of the so-called Holland House set who offered the most consistent support for Lingard and the Catholic Board. Holland had been the first peer to move a Bill for Emancipation in the Lords, arguing that restrictions on Catholics were unjust in principle as 'a retrospective penal statute against a large class'.[43] Such high-level support was necessary in the face of the attacks that followed publication, and worse was to follow with the next two volumes. These covered the Reformation and were published in 1820 and 1823, on either side of the 1821 Emancipation Bill. Thomas Kipling, Dean of Peterborough, 'famed' according to Lingard 'for his Latin solecisms', threatened to have him tried in Westminster Hall for treason unless he withdrew the phrases 'the new church of England' and 'the modern church of England'. 'The church by law established in this country', Kipling wrote, is so 'inseparably interwoven with the British constitution that whatever is calumny upon the former, must be calumny upon the latter.'[44] Lingard's view of the Anglican settlement was too much even for his former guarantor, John Allen, who in a lengthy essay in the *Edinburgh Review* declared that this was history 'of a most dangerous description'.[45] The first edition ran to 500 copies and sold out in eight days.

The most contentious points were predictable: Henry VIII's relationship with Anne Boleyn, his motives for the break with Rome and the character of Cranmer. Lingard brought to these subjects an unprecedented quantity of primary evidence. His international connections among fellow priests enabled him to send researchers into the archives of the Vatican and, still more significantly, to the Simancas Archives. These were the papers deposited by Philip II in 1566 in the small Castilian village of Simancas, and they included his own correspondence. No previous English historian had made use of them. At first Lingard's emissaries were not allowed to take notes, but over time, with that combination of stubbornness and courtesy which often has a mollifying effect on archivists, they were able to see more. The archives provided the Spanish side of many of the principal events: the marriages of Catherine of Aragon first to Prince Arthur and then to his brother Henry, the Marian persecutions, the excommunication of Elizabeth I and events leading to the Armada.

With this material Lingard cast new and often unwelcome light on events which had long since taken on a set and semi-mythical form in the English national consciousness. Philip II, he suggested, was not Sharon Turner's 'vindictive arm of the papacy' but cautious, strong-minded and opposed to the Marian persecutions.[46] The delay in the marriage of Henry to Catherine of Aragon was not, according to the archives, due to those scruples about marrying his deceased brother's wife, which Henry later cited when he wanted a divorce, but to his father Henry VII's fondness for a bargain and much haggling over the dowry. Letters in the Vatican revealed Henry VIII's affair with Anne Boleyn's sister Mary and Lingard described Anne and Henry marrying in secret when she was already pregnant. The suggestion that the Reformation, as Kipling put it, so 'inseparably interwoven with the British constitution', should have its origin in such base, personal and sexual motives was offensive to many people. Thomas Macaulay, whose view of the purpose of history was closer to Hume's, complained that Lingard's 'great fundamental rule of judging is that popular opinion cannot possibly be correct'.[47]

The pivotal figure for all sides in the re-examination of the Reformation was Cranmer. To Catholics he was a blood-stained persecutor, while Anglicans judged him to have been as tolerant, given the circumstances, as was possible. His place in national history as the father of the established Church, author of the beauties of the Book of Common Prayer, had been supported by generations of Anglican historians, who offered the most favourable interpretation of his *Reformatio Legum Ecclesiasticarum*. Lingard read it as a persecutor's charter, and he had no sympathy with persecution on any side. 'Fortunately for the professors of the ancient faith', he wrote, the death of Edward VI saw 'the power of the sword passed from the hand of one religious party to those of the other', thus Cranmer and his coadjutors 'perished in the flames which they had prepared to kindle for the destruction of their opponents'.[48] This gave another nasty jolt to received opinion, causing an uproar that was good for sales. It also gained Lingard many admirers, the most influential of whom was William Cobbett, who used the *History* as a basis for his popular polemic *A History of the Protestant Reformation in England and Ireland*, published in instalments from 1824 to 1826. As the campaign for Emancipation built to its final climax, Cobbett threw his considerable weight behind that vision of the Middle Ages which saw it as an age of social cohesion and the Reformation as a catastrophe.

Lingard's enemies, however, were legion and Milner was one of the most tenacious. He objected especially to the *History*'s treatment of Becket. Lingard characterized Henry II's archbishop as 'a martyr to what he deemed to be his duty', but argued that his conception of that duty, and of his own importance, had been corrupted by delusions of grandeur and 'enthusiasm' or fanaticism, until 'he identified his cause with that of God and the church'.[49] He was in the end a martyr to his own egotism. Furious, Milner began campaigning to get Lingard's *History* put on the Papal Index of forbidden books. He failed. A more effective enemy was the poet laureate, Robert Southey, a vehement opponent of Emancipation. His *The Book of the Church*, published in 1824, derided Lingard's scholarship as antiquarian pedantry and countered it with a version of events which, Southey implied, was too self-evidently correct to need footnotes:

Manifold as are the blessings for which Englishmen are beholden to the institutions of their country, there is no part of those institutions from which they derive more important advantages than from its Church Establishment . . . I offer, therefore, to those who regard with love and reverence the religion which they have received from their fathers, a brief but comprehensive record, diligently, faithfully, and conscientiously composed, which they may put to children. Herein it will be seen . . . in what manner the best interests of the country were advanced by the clergy even during the darkest ages of papal domination; the errors and crimes of the Romish church, and how when its corruptions were at the worst, the day-break of the Reformation appeared among us.[50]

After this attack, Milner found himself briefly on both sides at once; answering Southey under the thinly anagrammatic pseudonym of Merlin, he struck back sarcastically that: 'A degree of enthusiasm is requisite to constitute the character of a Poet' and thus naturally 'he raves, through the history of many centuries'.[51]

The Book of the Church was popular. It rapidly went through three editions and was reprinted as late as 1885. Still in the twentieth century John Kenyon was accusing Lingard of manipulating evidence to serve his religious position.[52] Much might and has been said of the individual points on which Lingard was right or wrong, but the evidence of his correspondence supports the more reasonable conclusion that 'Lingard made mistakes, and sometimes very big mistakes, but he did not make them because he was a Roman Catholic.'[53] Kenyon's case was that in successive editions Lingard dropped the appearance of neutrality in favour of a more openly pro-Catholic stance. Lingard took advantage of new editions of his *History* to incorporate new findings, and his approach to this kind of additional material was arguably subtly subversive, but it was sincere. In a letter to Gage about the 1832 edition he wrote:

I have extracts from the letters of Rosetti and Barbarini, but wish to see the whole of the letters so I may make no mistake . . . it is on a subject which will startle the orthodox: nothing less than a proposal for Archbishops Laud and Ussher to become catholics, if the pope would secure to them a certain provision in Rome . . . I intend to introduce the fact into the next edition of my history, without any remark, and as if it came naturally and of course in the narrative.[54]

Lingard was writing sixteen days after the passage of the Great Reform Act. Catholic Emancipation had finally been achieved, though too late for Milner who died in 1826, lamented by many friends if not universally regretted by his fellow Catholics. A month earlier Lingard had cause to congratulate Gage on his latest article for Society of Antiquaries' *Archaeologia*: 'A dissertation on St Æthelwold's Benedictional, an illuminated MS. of the 10th Century, in the Library of his Grace the Duke of Devonshire'. Gage's transcript of the Benedictional was prefaced by a long essay in which he explained its content and its historical and liturgical context. Acknowledging the safe arrival of his copy, Lingard noted: 'I admire much the research and judgement which you display in your preliminary dissertation, but still more (without disparagement to you) that extraordinary change in the public mind, which has permitted the antiquarian society to publish under its auspices so papistical a treatise. Soon I hope religious bigotry will be entirely extinguished.'[55]

Gage and Lingard covered some of the same subjects and used the same sources. Lingard described to a friend how he and Gage 'spent some hours at the Parliament Paper Office in examining the depositions respecting the Gunpowder conspiracy. We found much that appeared to us of consequence. Of all this we made minutes.'[56] The relative ease with which Gage's work found acceptance was due less, however, to growing tolerance than to differences of character and circumstance between himself and Lingard. Class had something to do with it. Gage was a gentleman, Lingard was not. Gage was also a layman, unlike Milner and Lingard. More importantly, he fitted a benign Catholic stereotype, not the 'meddling priest' but the Romantic recusant. John Henry Newman later recalled how, as an adolescent, saturated in the world of *Waverley*, he had a mental image of 'An old-fashioned house of gloomy appearance, closed in with high walls, with an iron gate and yews, and the report ... that Roman Catholics lived there.'[57] Hengrave Hall is not especially gloomy, but the ancestral home of the Gage family, the subject of Gage's most substantial work, *The History and Antiquities of Hengrave*, more or less fitted the bill, being a Tudor mansion.

Gage, who took the family name of Rokewode when he inherited the baronetcy, could trace his pedigree back through generations of recusants, including two notable Ambrose Rookwoods, the elder of whom was executed in 1605 for his part in the Gunpowder Plot, while the younger met the same fate at Tyburn in 1696 having been involved in the Barclay Conspiracy, a Jacobite attempt to assassinate William of Orange. All of this is described in the *Antiquities of Hengrave*. It was hardly surprising that Lingard, the conscientious parish priest who found himself threatened with charges of treason, should wonder at the ease with which Gage could publish accounts of his forebears' attempts to overthrow the state. But distance lends enchantment and Gage's long-dead ancestors could be absorbed into the romance of history as Lingard's awkward facts could not.

Gage was not the only Catholic antiquary to escape opprobrium. In Lincoln, Edward Willson also contrived to live a tranquil, productive life as a Catholic and an architect while working with Auguste Pugin and John Britton on the collections of *Specimens* and *Examples of Gothic Architecture*. After Emancipation he was one of the first Catholics to be made a Justice of the Peace. Yet in his Preface to the first volume of the *Examples* in 1831 he had planted the small explosive charge that had such considerable consequences.[58] It was his suggestion that, rather than 'Gothic', medieval architecture might more accurately be called 'Catholic' that opened the way for his young friend Welby Pugin to resolve the antiquary's dilemma by the deceptively simple means of cutting the Gordian knot and joining the Church of Rome.

WE ARE ALL JACOBITES NOW

In April 1815, when Catholic Emancipation still lay in the future and Napoleon, several weeks into the Hundred Days of his escape from exile, was raising troops across France, Walter Scott went to visit the Prince Regent. Long famous as a poet and newly famous in well-informed circles as the author of *Waverley*, he and the prince enjoyed what Scott later described as 'a snug little dinner'.[59] In the course of what was in fact a lavish and boisterous gathering, Scott, talking about his Jacobite novel, persuaded the prince, quite easily, that not only did he have as much Stuart blood as the Pretender, which he did, but that he was, in essence, a Highland chieftain in the great tradition. This was more questionable, but from now on Scott was set on that rearrangement of history that would turn the myth into reality. It was a truly Romantic antiquarian exercise in that it was achieved by the contextualising of particular objects, and the deployment of oral tradition and the conventions of the Picturesque.

As a first step Scott asked the prince for permission to undertake a quest, a search for the crown jewels of Scotland. As Scott's published account has it: 'In October 1817 his royal highness ... was pleased to give directions for removing the mystery which had so long hung upon the existence of the Scottish regalia.'[60] Less respectfully, Scott wrote to his friend the Classical scholar John Morritt on 13 January 1818: 'Our fat friend's curiosity ... goes to the point at once authorising and enjoining an express search for the regalia so my fingers long to be up and doing.'[61] That year he staged – there is no other word for it – what was only in the loosest sense a discovery. The regalia were found exactly where they had been left in March 1707 after the Act of Union deprived Scotland of its sovereign status. The sixteenth-century crown, sceptre and sword of state had been deposited in a chest in the Crown Room of Edinburgh Castle and the chest was still there, despite rumours that the regalia had been spirited away to England.

Scott's successive descriptions of the 'discovery' gained in solemnity and drama as time went on. By 1826, in his *Provincial Antiquities and Picturesque Scenery of Scotland*, it was practically a short story. 'The dust of a century was upon the floor; the ashes of the last fire remained still in the chimney'; after a vain search for keys a smith was sent for and at first it appeared that it was too late, for 'the chest seemed to return a hollow and empty sound to the strokes of the hammer'.[62] The whole thing was conceived as a dramatic performance; indeed, it was scripted. Writing to the Duke of Buccleuch, one of those charged along with Scott with the investigation, they agreed to do it on a mutually convenient date: 'The drama of the Iron Chest will certainly be postponed until your Grace can be one of the dramatis personae,' Scott promised.[63] It was important that the show should not flop. Scott explained to the duke:

... we have agreed to say nothing of the precise day. It is possible we may have the fate of those sapient persons who went to the vault at Clerkenwell to speak with the Cock Lane ghost, of whose expedition Churchill has recorded

> Silent, all three went in-about
> All three turn'd, silent, and came out

On these occasions the fewer spectators the better.[64]

Either Scott could not contain himself or he elaborated afterwards, for by his own account on 4 February 1818, when the chest was broken open, while there were no spectators in the room, there was no secrecy about what was going on. At the moment the regalia were found, 'the royal flag was hoisted upon the castle, and greeted by the shouts of a numerous crowd assembled on the hill, who took a deep interest in the success of the researches'.[65] Scott's *Description of the Regalia of Scotland* appeared the following year to coincide with a public exhibition of the crown jewels in the room where they had been found, now 'handsomely fitted up' for the purpose.[66] The *Description* weaves Scotland's history of noble independence seamlessly into the modern union. It begins with the crown itself which, though sixteenth-century, contained within it, Scott explained, an older diadem. 'Of its antiquity we can produce no precise evidence; but many circumstances induce us to refer it to the glorious reign of Robert the Bruce.'[67] Soon by extension he is back at the coronation of Malcolm in 1057, from where he sweeps forward again, through the depredations of Edward I, 'who took with him to England every monument of Scottish independence', to the regalia's narrow and dramatic escape from the Parliamentary forces, their long slumber in the castle and so to the present.[68] From the individual objects themselves, through the events they witnessed, Scott tells the story of Scotland until somehow, while symbolizing eight centuries of proud resistance to the forces of English oppression, the regalia also embody all that is best about the union:

The feelings with which we now view these venerable national reliques are of a nature less agitating than those of our forefathers ... We, who now reap the slow but well-ripened fruits of the painful sacrifice made at the union, can compare with calmer judgment, the certain blessings of equality of laws and rights, extended commerce, improved agriculture, individual safety, and domestic peace, with the vain though generous boast of a precarious national independence, subject to all the evils of domestic faction and delegated oppression. With such feelings we look upon the Regalia of Scotland ... blessing the wise decrees of Providence, which, after a thousand years of bloodshed, have at length indissolubly united two nations, who, speaking the same language, professing the same religion, and united by the same interest, seem formed by God and nature to compose one people.[69]

After the discovery, Scott told William Dundas that he had 'never been more pleased since the battle of Waterloo'.[70] Indeed this was, in its way, another victory for Britain. Later that year Scott was knighted.

When Scott's fat friend became George IV he decided, after much hesitation and deliberation and ultimately at short notice, that he would give full expression to his Highland chieftain side by visiting Scotland. The hesitation was due in part to the unfortunate precedents. The last reigning monarch to visit Scotland was Charles I, whose attempt to regulate the Scottish Church provoked a rebellion that was one of the crises that led to the Civil Wars. Charles II's visit during his exile was no happier an augury. When the decision was finally made it was therefore a hastily convened committee that was in charge of arrangements. Of its five members three were antiquaries, and Scott rapidly took over. The king's reception in Edinburgh was to begin with a procession, in which the recently recovered regalia were carried from Edinburgh Castle to Holyrood. This was followed by the king's landing at Leith. Another procession, along the Royal Mile, brought the king and the regalia together back to the castle. The climax was to be a Gathering of the Clans at the Assembly Rooms. The royal visit was thus steeped in historic romance by association.

None of these events had any precedent: they were all Scott's invention. He decided to augment the somewhat meagre regalia with the sword of the Great Marquess of Montrose, which he owned but which was then in London at a theatrical costumier's, where his friend the actor Daniel Terry was having a scabbard made for it. Terry was told to return it urgently so that Scott's distant cousin Alexander

Keith of Ravelston could carry it in the procession. Ravelston was, by Scott's reckoning, heir to the Knights Marischal of Scotland and he duly promoted him to that role for the ceremony. He also got Terry to organize a performance of *Rob Roy*, which is set during the Jacobite rising of 1715, in a striking instance of Hazlitt's point about Scott using the memory of treason to endorse the status quo.

The visit and its associated pageantry were a huge and widely reported success. George IV was established as a popular and proper king for the Scots, while Scotland itself was offered a Picturesque version of its history, which was accepted with enthusiasm on both sides of the border. The king was surrounded by the material relics of history and accompanied not only by the newly promoted Knight Marischal but by another, even more striking example of Scott's walking fictions, the Company of Archers. Scott was about to start work on *Quentin Durward*, the story of the Scottish archer in the French royal bodyguard, and was in correspondence with Meyrick about the construction of medieval bows, although Meyrick had to report that the only ones he knew of were at Wilton and 'nailed up too high to examine'.[71] It was his projected novel, no doubt, that lay behind Scott's decision to transform the Scottish Company of Archers, a gentlemen's sporting and dining club dating to the later seventeenth century, into a band of medieval bowmen in Lincoln green, complete with quivers and arrows. By this point there was nothing to choose between fact and fiction in what became known as the King's Jaunt.

The gathering of the clans took the form of a Highland ball. It was the single most influential event of the tour, and its legacy the most enduring. 'Highland dress', so recently illegal, was now compulsory, a condition of entry. In the 1820s the plaid was seldom if ever seen in Edinburgh. Most Lowlanders would never have thought of wearing it and would have been regarded as outlandish by the citizens of the capital if they had. As Lockhart wrote: 'With all respect and admiration for the noble and generous qualities which our countrymen of the Highland clans have so often exhibited, it was difficult to forget that they had always constituted a small, and almost always an unimportant part of the Scottish population.'[72] He might have added that they were also regarded as uncouth and troublesome. Yet now the Lowlanders suddenly realized that these were the true Scots, certainly the most 'picturesque' part, as Lockhart put it, of the national panorama. Thus 'the kilt as the national dress of all Scotsmen, should they so desire' was established.[73]

There was some initial demur in antiquarian circles, but Scott's national costume was unstoppably popular. It was also a great boost to the economy, as tartan manufacture breathed new life into the ailing Scottish textile industry.[74] Well might the *Edinburgh Observer* conclude that 'We are now all Jacobites, thorough-bred Jacobites, in acknowledging George IV.'[75] The necessary magic had been accomplished: Scott had whisked away the curtain to reveal a seamless and Romantic version of Anglo-Scottish history and everyone was mad for it. Tartan and *Waverley* were all the rage in France and by 1841, on the eve of Victoria and Albert's first visit to Scotland, the whole paraphernalia of Scottishness was in place. Catherine Sinclair, on a tour north of the border, ticked off the list: 'we have . . . old traditions, second sight, bagpipes, witchcraft, clans, tartans, whisky, heather, muir-fowl, red deer and Jacobites'.[76]

MERE DRAMATIC CHARACTERS?

It was around the time of the king's visit that there began to be signs that Scott's ingeniously constructed Scottish history might slip his grasp and take on a life of its own. That year a book of verse based on Scottish folkloric sources appeared. *The Bridal of Caölchairn; and Miscellaneous Poems. By Walter Scott* was issued by Scott's publishers, Constable in Edinburgh and John Murray in London. It was described as a fifth edition, although no earlier editions have come to light. It also appeared simultaneously from another publishing house, T. Hookham in London, over the name 'John Hay Allan'. Scott was not the author, but he himself played so many games with pseudonyms that he seems not to have minded at the time. He did not forget the impersonation, however. In 1827, in the first fiction published under his own name, *Chronicles of the Canongate*, he included copious quotations from *The Bridal of Caölchairn* with no acknowledgement of John Hay Allan. Scott had seen Allen (as the name was originally spelled) and possibly his brother Charles in Edinburgh in George IV's great procession. One of them was wearing 'the Badge of High Constable of Scotland' which, Scott remarked, 'he could have no more right to wear than the Crown'.[77] But, it might be objected, his cousin Ravelston's claim to the title of Knight Marischal was very tenuous, and the Company of Archers' right to their medieval uniform was non-existent.

The Allen brothers, who became the Sobieski Stuarts, have already made an appearance in this history, dashing briefly across the battlefield at Waterloo, unaccompanied by any credible evidence. In the intervening years they had become accepted in Edinburgh society, where they appeared in the attributes of various 'knighthoods and orders' wearing elaborate Highland dress.[78] They were young, handsome and agreeable, and against the colourful backdrop of Jacobite romance that Scott had painted they looked reasonably convincing. Gradually they transformed their names. They had begun with the slight change from the English 'Allen' to the Scottish 'Allan' and from there to Hay Allan; they eventually became John Sobieski Stuart and Charles Edward Stuart, with the additional title of Count of Albany, which they seem to have shared. They created the impression, without specifying details, that they were the legitimate grandsons of the Young Pretender, and thus heirs to the British throne in the Jacobite line, which was otherwise extinct since the death of Cardinal York (Henry IX) in 1807.

Before continuing with their story, it will be as well to establish what is now known of the facts of their lives.[79] John was born in Wales in 1795, Charles was born in about 1802; his place of birth is at present unknown. Their mother was Catherine, née Manning, the daughter of Owen Manning, an antiquarian clergyman and author of the classic *History and Antiquities of Surrey*. Their father, Thomas Allen, was a naval lieutenant, the illegitimate son of Admiral John Carter Allen, through whom he claimed a connection, never substantiated, with the Hays, the Earls of Errol, who do indeed hold the hereditary office of High Constable of Scotland. John, Charles and their sister Matilda grew up in a ramshackle household. Their mother's property was held in a trust which failed in 1818, causing their father to serve two years in debtors' prison, after which he lived a shadowy life under various names at numerous addresses. His aliases included

Thomas Gatehouse Hay Allen, Thomas MacGaradh and John Salmon. Something clearly ran in the family, albeit not the blood of the Stuarts.

John and Charles were of the generation whose imagination was formed by the *Waverley* novels. Growing up in a household where delusions of grandeur, dubious pedigrees and aliases were the stuff of everyday life, it would not have taken much to turn their minds toward Scotland. They took Gaelic lessons in London from the antiquary Donald MacPherson, becoming proficient enough to read, write and speak it. John seems to have earned a living as a heraldic painter in Covent Garden. Nobody ever denied the brothers were intelligent and artistically gifted, John apparently being the more outgoing. In about 1819, with his father in prison, he spent some months in the Highlands, writing the poems and collecting the ballads that became *The Bridal of Caölchairn*, though he later denied he had ever been in Scotland before 1823. That was the year that Charles arrived in Edinburgh with his wife. He had married Ann Beresford, a widow of means and a granddaughter of the Earl of Tyrone, some fifteen years his senior. Their first child was born in Edinburgh and christened Anna Marie Stuart Hay, daughter, according to the newspaper announcement, of 'Charles Stuart Allan Hay CBC KME'.

In these early days of their life in Scotland it was remembered that the brothers were often seen in the company of a shrunken-looking old man in spectacles. The trio were nicknamed Tom, Jerry and Logic, after the popular characters of Pierce Egan, and it is Logic who perhaps holds the key to the brothers' career. He was Robert Watson (? 1750–1838), the only person to feature in this chapter whose antiquarian activities really were an attempt to undermine the British state. Born in Elgin, Watson claimed to be a doctor; he certainly graduated MA from King's College Aberdeen in 1787. He was the one-time secretary to and later biographer of Lord George Gordon, figurehead of the anti-Catholic Gordon Riots of 1780. He was also a spy and a career revolutionary. For Watson the riots represented an uprising of Scottish Presbyterian republicanism and he was 'deeply impressed' by the young Gordon, who 'spoke gaelic, wore a kilt, played the pipes and extolled Ossianic primitivism'.[80] None of Watson's claims was entirely untrue, but all were infused with a curious blend of Celtic romance and the ideals of the Scottish Enlightenment.

Watson was only incidentally an antiquary, but he knew the usefulness of history and he invoked it to create a Radical, republican narrative that was the inverse of Scott's optimistic myth of national unity. Imprisoned in London in 1794 for sedition, Watson fled to Paris four years later with a price on his head. From France he addressed the Scots in the *Gazette nationale* in the Year VII (1798), appealing to his countrymen, 'descendants of the immortal Ossian', to rise up against England, 'the faction of St James ... Did Wallace fight for nothing? Did Buchanan and Fletcher write in vain ... Yes, the Scots will be free.'[81] Napoleon appointed Watson President of the Catholic Scots College in Paris, where his role was to act as a spy, keeping the authorities informed about Catholic opposition to the Republic. He also found himself in charge of a Jacobite shrine: the chapel in the Scots College in the rue du Cardinal Lemoine contains monuments to James II and VII, his wife, daughter and their household. The college had once possessed their papers. Since its secularization these had been taken back to Italy, where Watson set off to track them down. He wrote to the British foreign secretary, Castlereagh, saying that he had found evidence of plots by the house of Hanover against the Stuarts. This may or may not have been true. What is certain is that in 1816, in the great post-war maelstrom of displaced objects, documents and people, Watson acquired a large cache of Stuart papers, thereby causing consternation in London. The papers, or most of them, came to rest eventually in the Royal Archives at Windsor. What price Watson exacted is not clear.[82] He seems by this point to have given up hope of a Scottish revolution and become 'something (or something more) of a con-man', styling himself as a doctor and continuing to promote the Jacobite cause, in a spirit perhaps of disillusionment amounting to cynicism.[83]

Having taken up the Allen brothers, it would seem that he persuaded or coached them to assume the identity of heirs of the Young Pretender. Their story was accessorized with some possibly genuine Jacobite relics, but the centrepiece of the collection, the object which brought the Allens to national attention and became their permanent legacy, was a manuscript history of tartan, the *Vestiarium Scoticum*, which they claimed was formerly 'in the possession of . . . Mr Robert Watson', who was 'well known in the history of the Stuart papers'.[84] It was a total fake. Whether Watson was hoping to make money out of it or whether, disillusioned by the failure of his revolutionary ideals, he found some savage amusement in the creation of these two parodic figures, George Gordon's tragic history repeated as farce, is unclear. In 1838, at the age of about eighty-eight, he strangled himself in a London inn, using a poker and his cravat. The case was a newspaper sensation and Dickens used Watson's story for his novel in progress, *Barnaby Rudge*. At the time of Watson's death, the *Vestiarium* was still unpublished, though not for want of trying. Having got to know Scott's friend Sir Thomas Dick Lauder in the 1820s, the Allens told him about the manuscript, which was supposedly by 'Sir Richard Urquhart' and was known as the *Vestiarium Scoticum* or *Garderope of Scotland*. They showed him what they said was an eighteenth-century copy, the original being too sacred to the family to be exhibited. Lauder excitedly consulted Scott, who was for some time inclined to be indulgent towards these two young men for whose 'dreaming habits' he was, after all, largely responsible.[85] By June 1829, however, when Lauder talked of publishing the *Vestiarium*, Scott was becoming exercised. His reply to Lauder is worth quoting at length because it makes clear the point at which he drew the line between the Romantic evocations and extrapolations of the King's Jaunt and deliberate lies and forgery:

> I need not say I have the greatest interest in the MS. which you mention. In case it shall really prove an authentic document, there would not be the least difficulty in getting the Bannatyne Club to take, perhaps,100 copies, or obtaining support enough ... to preclude the possibility of loss to the ingenious Messrs. Hay Allan. But I think it indispensable that the original MS. should be sent for a month or so to the Register House under the charge of the Deputy Register, Mr. Thomson, that its antiquity be closely scrutinised by competent persons.
>
> The art of imitating ancient writing has got to a considerable perfection, and it has been the bane of Scottish literature, and disgrace other antiquaries [*sic*], that we have manifested an eager propensity to believe without inquiry and propagate the errors which we adopt too hastily

ourselves. The general proposition that the Lowlanders ever wore plaids is difficult to swallow. They were of twenty different races, and almost all distinctly different from the Scots Irish, who are the proper Scots, from which the Royal Family are descended. For instance, there is scarce a great family in the Lowlands of Scotland that is not to be traced to the Normans, the proudest as well as most civilised race in the eleventh and twelfth centuries. Is it natural to think that, holding the Scots in the contempt in which they did, they would have adopted their dress? . . .

It is needless to prosecute this, though I could show, I think, that there is no period in Scottish History when the manners, language, or dress of the Highlanders were adopted in the Low Country . . . where has slept this universal custom that nowhere, unless in this MS., is it even heard of? . . . I will not state other objections, though so many occur, that the authenticity of the MS. being proved, I would rather suppose the author had been some tartan-weaver zealous for his craft, who wished to extend the use of tartan over the whole kingdom . . . Now, a word to your own private ear, my dear Sir Thomas. I have understood that the Messrs. Hay Allan are young men of talent, great accomplishments, enthusiasm for Scottish manners, and an exaggerating imagination, which possibly deceives even themselves . . . Davidoff used also to amuse us with stories of knighthoods and orders which he saw them wear at Sir William Gumming Gordon's. Now this is all very well, and I conceive [these] people may . . . be very agreeable and . . . very amusing companions . . . but their authority as antiquaries must necessarily be a little apocryphal when the faith of MSS. rests upon their testimony. An old acquaintance of mine, Captain Watson of the navy, told me he knew these gentlemen's father, and had served with him; he was lieutenant, and of or about Captain Watson's age, between sixty I suppose, and seventy at present. Now what chance was there that either from age or situation he should be receiving gifts from the young Chevalier of Highland Manuscripts. All this, my dear Sir Thomas, you will make your own, but I cannot conceal from you my reasons, because I would wish you to know my real opinion. If it is an imitation, it is a very good one, but the title 'Liber Vestiarium' is false Latin I should think not likely to occur to a Scotsman of Buchanan's age. Did you look at the watermark of the MS.? If the Manuscript be of undeniable antiquity, I consider it as a great curiosity, and most worthy to be published. But I believe nothing else than ocular inspection will satisfy most cautious antiquaries . . .—Yours, my dear Sir Thomas, always.[86]

This direct challenge seems to have given Lauder and the brothers pause. No more was heard of the *Vestiarium* in Scott's lifetime, though the false Latin title of his last work, the *Reliquiae Trotcosiensis*, perhaps cast a final teasing glance at the 'ingenious' brothers. The story of the *Vestiarium*'s eventual publication and the considerable consequences belongs to a later chapter.

Meanwhile, the Allens had other means of establishing themselves. Emma Campbell, later Mrs William Russell, recorded her first impressions of them in 1827 on Islay. From the window she saw 'two young, good looking men, crossing the green in front of Islay house, dressed in elaborate fanciful highland dresses, with kilts etc, which were then rarely seen in Islay. Many of the poor people, hearing that descendants of Prince Charlie were in the Island, and in the old dress, declared that they were ready to rise for Prince Charlie.'[87]

Immediately after Scott's death in 1832 the brothers dropped the Hay and Allan soubriquets and became John Sobieski Stolberg Stuart and Charles Edward Stuart. They had indeed, as Scott suggested, long been in touch with the tartan manufacturers, notably Wilson's of Bannockburn, the principal suppliers to the ever-expanding international market. The brothers designed many patterns for them. The 'dress Stuart' was one of their first efforts. In 1845 they published *The Costume of the Clans*, a work which revealed them capable of serious, solid scholarship. With its hand-coloured plates, drawn by the authors, it was and remains a significant, if understandably neglected, contribution to the history of Scottish dress. Few subsequent historians have been as generous as H. F. McClintock, who in his *Old Irish and Highland Dress* of 1943 pays tribute to 'This huge and sumptuous book, the materials alone for which must have taken years of labour to collect', and from which, as McClintock points out, later historians borrowed shamelessly with no acknowledgement.[88]

For more than fifteen year the brothers' curious career went from strength to strength. Lord Fraser of Lovat was so impressed by them that in 1839 he took them under his protection, allowing them to choose a site on his land on which he would build them a home. By this date, as Elizabeth Grant of Rothiemurchus recalled, 'half the clans in the Highlands believed in them; for several years they actually *reigned* in the north country'.[89] The house Lovat built for them was, naturally, Gothic and its situation on Eilean Aigas, an islet in the River Beauly, was suitably Picturesque. The brothers' joint self-portrait shows them at home surrounded by oak, antlers, arms and miscellaneous curiosities, which may include Jacobite relics acquired from Watson. The effect on visitors who saw them, either in their home or at Mass, to which they sailed from their island in a boat flying the Stuart standard, generally reflected the level of faith or doubt in the eye of the beholder. The setting, the Romantic interior and Picturesque landscape, was essential. In 1842 Welby Pugin, refuting Trevor-Roper's boast that 'no Englishman seems to have taken them seriously', found them entirely convincing. His account makes no attempt to separate them from their context:[90]

> I have dined with the two princes who are the descendants of the Stewarts. the Eldest is one of the most glorious men I ever knew. he is perfect in his ideas on Christian architecture . . . they Live on a most romantic Island surrounded by waterfalls & rocks – in a vast glen between the mountains. I was quite delighed [*sic*]. I could fight for him. he has fitted up a gothic room – *& really well done*. there is a prophecy in the highlands that the stewarts are yet to be restored.[91]

Even the more sceptical Elizabeth Grant found these 'strange brothers [who] . . . one day announced that they were Stuarts . . . astonishing'.[92] In the version of the story she heard, the brothers' mother was Scottish and 'her people had been in the service of the unfortunate Stuarts in Italy and who can tell if she had not some right to call herself connected with them?'.[93] Were they perhaps, she implies, illegitimate but real descendants? Being less convinced than Pugin, she remembered their context in a more humdrum way. The house she saw as a 'villa', their garden as 'pretty' and the waterfall as 'small'.[94] She was struck, however, by the fact that Charles's wife 'played the harp like Flora McIvor' and that 'crowds went to visit them'.[95] In their own persons the brothers achieved a remarkable resemblance to their pretended ancestors. 'They always wore the Highland dress, kilt and belted plaid, and looked melancholy and spoke at times mysteriously.'[96] In about 1843 Charles sat for the Edinburgh photographers Hill and Adamson, and the result bears out Grant's description.

By now the brothers were settled into their curious life on Eilean Aigas, with an additional address in Princes Street, Edinburgh. They also earned money by journalism and enjoyed a mutually beneficial relationship with Robert Chambers, the publisher and author who was co-editor with his brother of the weekly *Edinburgh Journal* and co-author of the *Cyclopaedia of English Literature*. Chambers was also the anonymous author of one of the great publishing sensations of the nineteenth century, *Vestiges of the Natural History of Creation*, which introduced the concept of evolution to a general readership. The year after *Vestiges* was published, 1845, was the centenary of the last Jacobite rising. Victoria and Albert announced a royal costume ball to mark the occasion and John Sobieski Stuart was deeply affronted to be approached by some of the intended guests for tips on costume. He reported his annoyance to Chambers and registered his outrage at this 'Saturnalia of the victors' triumph'.[97] Chambers, it would seem, took this to heart. He decided to organize a rival centenary event at Prestonpans, site of the last Scottish victory, and asked the brothers to grace the occasion with their presence. This seems to have been a step too far. They had no interest in fomenting rebellion and they were doing much better for themselves than they could possibly have hoped. John chose to cover up untruth with apparent frankness. He told Chambers that he would not fob off such a true friend with 'any unfounded excuse'; instead he would confide the real reasons why such an appearance would be ill advised:

> We are not mere dramatic characters except in the drawing Rooms of Edinburgh. The limited and egotistical character of whose members renders them ignorant of our position elsewhere. But their Mistress & her ministers are well aware what are the feeling attached to us in France and of the professed interest & circumstances of extraordinary distinction which attend my brother in Bohemia ... Add to these (although *this is* unknown to the government) such lucid and dangerous hints given by the late duke of Gordon ... & other leaders of the

Conservative party in *the height of their despair & indignation at the measures of Wm IV in favour of the Reform bill* that we who do know it & who disregarded their views and made their party our enemies, by declining to be made the head of a faction . . . cannot commit the slightest indiscretion . . . it is for this reason that we *have* abstained, that we *will* abstain so rigidly from *any assumption* or allusion for or to the associations, events & persons of former times.'[98]

It is true, as Lingard said, that 'writers of history know nothing more respecting motives than the little which their authorities have disclosed, or the facts necessarily suggest', so we can only wonder what, by this stage, the brothers themselves believed.[99] Both were now married to women of some wealth with aristocratic connections. What did they tell them? What did they say to each other in the long winter evenings on their remote island? They said publicly that their father was dead, which was convenient for their story, but they surely knew he was not. Indeed, he lived on under various names until 1852, making no attempt either to exploit or refute his sons' claims. Scott's suspicions might have undone them, as might Chambers' credulity. Nemesis, when it came, however, was of their own making. In 1847 they published a novel, *Tales of the Century*. It took the conventional nineteenth-century form of a Preface and three volumes. Its subtitle was 'Sketches of the Romance of History between the Years 1746 and 1846', and the first sentence is a quotation from Horace Walpole: '"History", says Lord Orford, "is a Romance which is believed; Romance, a History which is not believed."'[100] It was on this delicate tightrope between fact and fiction that the authors attempted to balance.

With eye-watering brazenness the story is set in the world of antiquarian forgery, opening in the winter of 1831 at 'Puffinwell's auction-rooms', where a sale of dubious paintings is taking place. 'There is great pleasure in being cheated at an auction,' the narrator remarks, 'and I immediately turned in.'[101] As the sale goes on one painting, apparently no better than the rest, attracts considerable interest and fetches ninety guineas. It is bought by an old man, Dr Beaton, an antiquary, a Scot and a Jacobite. 'If you talk of tartan and *the prince*,' the narrator is informed, 'he will tell you as many old stories as would furnish half a dozen series of tales to the author of Waverley.'[102] Beaton's tales and the mysterious picture, floating out of Scott's fiction and Soho forgery, open the way for the main story. In Wardour Street the narrator finds the long-lost 'Black Kist of Glen-Dulochan', an heirloom of his own family for which he has long searched. When he gets it home he finds a secret compartment containing a manuscript, which yields the next stage of the narrative and so on as the supposed truth emerges from the web of fakery and lies.

Tales of the Century inverts the Scott's method in the Prefaces to *Ivanhoe* and *Quentin Durward*, where a real manuscript is described as the source of the story but is understood by the reader to be part of the fiction. *Tales of the Century* reverses this, implying that what is presented as fiction should be understood as history. 'It is credible, because it is improbable', is the concluding sentence.[103] It is impossible to know why the brothers took this risk. It may have been sheer hubris; or were they confident that they had left open an escape route down which they could retreat under a plea of its being a clearly signalled fiction? Perhaps by now they believed it themselves. In any event, this time they flew too close to the sun. *Tales of the Century*, despite the twisted paraphernalia of fact and phantasy, made their claims public and specific and thus exposed them to wider scrutiny. The *Quarterly Review*'s response was a long essay by Professor George Skene of Glasgow University.[104] It was devastating. The antiquarian relationship with history at its most fanciful met the academic at its most rigorous and did not survive the impact. The brothers were obliged to leave Scotland. They spent the next twenty years in Austria, and so they disappear again from this account, for the moment.

9

Walter Scott's 'Mighty Wizzard': Shakespeare and the antiquaries

> The Theatre will create its drama out of its history, out of the spirit of the age, manners, opinion, language, national prejudices, traditions and pastimes, even out of carnival plays and puppet plays.
>
> *Herder,* Shakespeare, *1773*

> Kemble was the first to study the antiquities of his own and other countries, to be acquainted with their architecture, their dress, their weapons, their manners.
>
> *James Boaden,* Memoirs of the Life of
> John Philip Kemble, *1825*

In the figure of Shakespeare, every current of thought and feeling that ran through Romantic antiquarianism met. The hero of the German philosophers of *Sturm und Drang*, across Europe he stood for the reaction to the Enlightenment. Everything that Voltaire decried in him, his lack of Classical form, his interest in the local and particular, his mixing of genres, spoke to Coleridge and Hazlitt, to Stendhal and Victor Hugo. Where Voltaire saw 'monstrous farce' the Romantics saw tragedy.[1] Where Voltaire found in this 'homme sans lettres' only wild sparks of natural genius illuminating 'chaos', the rising generations saw authenticity.[2] Hamlet, a character who seemed to have sprung, according to Voltaire, from the mind of an uncouth drunk, was to the critics of the late Georgian years a twin soul, a 'paralysed romantic' like themselves.[3] Voltaire's complaints were 'the last determined struggle of the classicism of the seventeenth century'.[4]

Shakespeare had never lost his popularity in Britain and there had been vociferous ripostes to Voltaire's strictures, but the eighteenth century had no qualms about 'improving' his plays any more than it did about whitewashing medieval tombs. David Garrick, when he organized the Shakespeare Jubilee in Stratford in 1769, saw no need to include any of Shakespeare's own work in the celebrations. He rewrote the *The Taming of the Shrew* as *Katharine and Petruchio*. Another actor, Colley Cibber, had earlier pieced together a successful *Richard III* out of Shakespeare's Richard, some bits of Henrys IV, V and VI and lines of his own, including the popular 'off with his head – so much for Buckingham' and 'Richard is himself again', the latter such a crowd pleaser that Laurence Olivier retained it in the film of 1955. The poet Nahum Tate's *King Lear*, in which Lear and Cordelia survive and Cordelia marries Edgar, became the established version in British theatres until 1838. But all the time that growing awareness of anachronism, the desire to see and understand the past historically, was transforming the late Georgian theatre.

The last decades of the eighteenth century were to be 'the Kemble era', in which the London theatre was a centre of cultural and intellectual life as never before or since. Sarah Siddons, the great tragedian, made her debut in 1782. 'Nothing ever was or can be like her', Byron wrote.[5] By the time her brother, John Philip Kemble, the first of the great actor-managers, gave his farewell performance in 1817 the English stage had been transformed, and not only by a generation of great actors. The Romantic theatre was an all-encompassing experience. Costumes, scenery and special effects became integral to performances: theatre design blossomed into an art form in its own right and the presentation of Shakespeare was revolutionized. Meanwhile the texts had begun to receive the same kind of attention as the medieval tombs. Accretions were brushed away, obscure terms glossed and ambiguities, where possible, resolved. It was the golden age of Shakespearean criticism, and while some of the critics, notably Hazlitt and Coleridge, argued that the text alone mattered and there was no need to see the plays on the stage, most of their contemporaries disagreed. They were delighted to have their imaginary forces enhanced by the brilliant actors and designers at the patent theatres, Covent Garden and Drury Lane.

The third aspect of the Romantics' passion for Shakespeare, in addition to the texts and the staging of the plays, was a burning desire to know the man. An age that valued personal experience, subjective response and individual character needed a biography and a portrait for the historical person who was William Shakespeare. Carlyle believed that 'in every man's writings, the character of the writer must lie recorded . . . his opinions, character, personality . . . with whatever difficulty, are and must be decipherable'.[6] Wordsworth thought the sonnets were the 'key' to Shakespeare's heart.[7] But there was an insistent demand for more tangible evidence and, as is usual in the making of history, the demand was met with a supply. Gradually, Stratford and its environs were transformed into Shakespeare country. Documents and artefacts began to appear, a number of them genuine.

Antiquaries involved themselves in every aspect of Romantic theatre. The 'theatrical antiquary' became a recognized species and antiquarianism might be combined with acting, as in Kemble's case, or playwrighting, as in the case of James Robinson Planché, or with architectural history. Much of William Capon's scenery was based on his measured drawings of the medieval Palace of Westminster. The worlds of Wardour Street and Grub Street were neither physically nor intellectually far from Covent Garden and Drury Lane, and there was considerable traffic in both directions in an age when theatrics were not confined to theatres but might extend to the royalist fancy dress of the Duchesse de Berry or the Sobieski Stuarts' performance as dramatic characters in the drawing rooms of Edinburgh. Welby Pugin embarked on his architectural career from the scenery department at Covent Garden, where he worked for the Grieve family, who dominated the profession for two generations and revolutionized it.[8] They were credited by name on play bills and were the first designers to take a curtain call. By the time of Victoria's accession the boundaries between theatre and architecture might scarcely matter. She and Albert employed Thomas Grieve to design the ballroom at Balmoral and called in Planché to advise on their Jacobite ball in 1845.

At the centre of this web of connections was Walter Scott. Author, antiquary, Shakespearian enthusiast and friend of Kemble, he was often to be found in the green room. He altered the bonnet Kemble wore as Macbeth, replacing a hefty clump of plumage with a single eagle's feather. The result, Kemble reported, was worth 'three distinct rounds of applause'.[9] Scott and Shakespeare occupied adjacent pedestals in the late-Georgian pantheon. While Shakespeare was held to be the greatest English writer of all time, Scott was indisputably the greatest living author and the one who most resembled the Bard. Parallels were seen in Scott's blending of drama with low comedy, his use of history, the mingling of kings, commoners and criminals. The direct comparison was first made in a review of his anonymously published *Tales of my Landlord*, in the *Quarterly Review*, in 1817. 'The characters of Shakespeare are not more exclusively human, not more perfectly men and women as they live and move, than those of this mysterious author', the critic wrote enthusiastically.[10] The tribute loses some of its lustre with the revelation that the reviewer was Scott himself, but many others saw the similarities. John Wilson Croker, in an essay reviewing *Waverley*, *Guy Mannering* and *The Antiquary*, singled out the author's 'curious and accurate ... delineation of human nature' as his 'peculiar merit, and no slight merit it is ... the possession of it [is] the chief merit of the greatest poet that ever lived – of Shakspeare [*sic*]'.[11] Even Hazlitt, despite his objections to Scott, noticed it, writing in *The Spirit of the Age*:

> Sir Walter has found out that there is no romance like the romance of real life, and that if we can but arrive at what men feel, do, and say in striking and singular situations, the result will be 'more lively, audible, and full of vent' than the fine-spun cobwebs of the brain ... Our author has conjured up the actual people he has to deal with ... in 'their habits as they lived' ... ransacked old chronicles ... invoked the spirits of the air ... and ... has enriched his own genius with everlasting variety, truth and freedom.[12]

Hazlitt's quotation is from *Coriolanus* and not entirely flattering in its implications, but it nevertheless embeds Shakespeare within Scott's critical reputation.

Shakespeare, as Henry Crawford says in *Mansfield Park*, is 'part of an Englishman's constitution'. His work is informed by and informative about just those national and historical customs and manners that were the antiquaries' stock in trade. Moreover, he was a kindred spirit. Shakespeare did not belong to the upper ranks of society, he was not a university man or a Classicist. On every point that Voltaire cited as a defect, the antiquaries found fellow feeling. Scott argued that it was Shakespeare's very ignorance of the Aristotelian rules that allowed his genius to develop uninhibited. Without 'access to any models of which the commanding merit might have controlled and limited his own exertions, he followed the path which a nameless crowd of obscure writers had trodden before him'.[13] Now many variously obscure antiquarian writers were happy to find themselves treading after him. Thus it was as figuratively truthful as it was historically implausible for John Faed, in his painting *Shakespeare and his Friends at the Mermaid Tavern* (1851), to place the founding father of antiquarianism, William Camden, directly opposite Shakespeare in an attitude of intense scrutiny.[14]

SEVERELY CORRECT AND BEAUTIFULLY GRACEFUL

Of Shakespeare's three faces, poet, playwright and man, the playwright was most immediately accessible. In the theatre Herder's dictum that truth is the perfection of illusion was not a metaphor but a prescription and one that Kemble took to heart, albeit not as Herder, 'who had no interest in antiquarian detail', intended.[15] In November 1790, two years after Kemble took on the management of Drury Lane, his friend the antiquarian scholar Edmond Malone published his ten-volume edition of *The Plays and Poems of William Shakespeare* and Kemble resolved that his own productions should from now on be similarly 'perfect in text and set'.[16] While the Kembles had infused the art of acting with a new Romantic intensity, stage presentation remained much as it had been for decades. Scenery was minimal, with the same flats reused for numerous plays, while costume was not considered an integral part of a production. It would be untrue to say that there were no attempts at historic dress, but there was, as Scott wrote, 'no such thing as regular costume'.[17] Companies bought clothes or had them donated. Hamlet usually wore formal evening dress, Macbeth, as a general, wore the scarlet uniform of the British army. If money was tight, and it usually was at Drury Lane, where Kemble fought a constant battle against Sheridan, the majority shareholder, and his determination to syphon off the profits for his political career, efforts would be concentrated on the principal characters, with the rest of the cast in their own clothes. Garrick had played Lear in a vaguely 'ancient' outfit, but his Cordelia wore Georgian hooped petticoats. Charles Macklin played Shylock in historic dress in the 1760s, and Richard III and Falstaff were given costumes and accoutrements that rendered them recognizable, but more in the manner of *commedia dell'arte* figures than historic characters. The overall effect was, as Planché put it, 'a melange, the absurdity of which is in our present day absolutely convulsive!'.[18]

Planché, who recreated the coronation of Charles X on the stage of Covent Garden, was the quintessential theatrical antiquary. The bilingual son of Huguenot cousins, a watchmaker Jacques and his wife Catherine, he was born in Old Burlington Street off Piccadilly and was, from an early age, an habitué of the London theatres. Author of dozens of songs, plays, melodramas and libretti, Planché made his name in 1820 with *The Vampire, or the Bride of the Isles*, at the Lyceum. The production owed much of its success to Planché's invention of the stage effect known as the 'vampire trap', by which an actor appears to walk through walls or disappear through the floor. Increasingly, however, Planché's interests became concentrated on theatrical costume and the history of dress. He had got an introduction to Meyrick, who helped him about armour and who in turn introduced him to the peppery Douce, who saw at once that Planché was serious. Douce 'most liberally placed the whole of his invaluable collection of illuminated mss' at Planché's disposal.[19] He also lent him his 'fine copy' of Strutt's *A Complete View of the Dress and Habits of the People of England*, which had been 'coloured expressly for him by its author'. Planché recalled that Douce explained: '" I will lend *you* books, sir, because you love them and will take care of them;" I think he added "and will return them;" – a more uncommon virtue to possess than the two former. At any rate, I can honestly say that I justified his confidence.'[20]

The French Revolution had been, as Planché wrote, 'productive of a revolution' in stage presentation 'on both sides of the channel'.[21] French theatre's unwavering adherence to the Aristotelean unities acquired political significance as France strove to establish itself as a republic on the model of Greece and Rome. The severely Classical taste which prevailed in art was brought to the stage by Jacques-Louis

David, who helped design a costume for his friend the actor François Joseph Talma for a production of Voltaire's *Brutus*. Talma made his entrance wearing a toga, his arms bare and his hair cut short in the Roman manner. This caused a sensation, started a trend in male hair styles and set Talma on course to become the leading French actor of his generation, painted by Delacroix and admired by Napoleon. When Kemble visited Talma in France during the Peace of Amiens he made careful notes and so it was that, as Planché explained, 'the toga and the paludamentum [the distinctive cloak fastened at one shoulder] found their way from the French stage to ours'.[22] Kemble began his costume reforms with the Roman plays, partly because of what he had seen in France, partly out of a continuing deference towards Classical subjects as intrinsically more serious and, not least, because he had very good legs which showed to advantage in a toga. *Coriolanus* and *Julius Caesar* got enthusiastic reviews, the costumes declared to be 'faultless, minutely classical, even to the long disputed *latus clavus*, severely correct, and beautifully graceful'.[23]

As usual, however, one person's accuracy was another's pedantry. Douce, who helped Kemble with the costumes, pointed out that his scenery made no distinction between the architecture of the Roman Empire and that of the Republic and urged him to 'reform it altogether'.[24] As Douce reported furiously to Planché, Kemble was appalled by the idea. 'He exclaimed ... in a tone almost of horror, "Why, if I did, sir, they would call me an antiquary." And this to me, sir! ... to *me*, who flattered myself I *was* an antiquary.'[25] Gradually, however, the movement towards historic accuracy gathered momentum. Kemble scoured 'illuminated manuscripts, ancient pictures, and other satisfactory authorities' to find as many images as he could that might be 'adopted on the theatre'.[26] He haunted the brokers' shops of Soho, building up a private collection of antiquities which he lent for productions. Scenery, however, was more complicated and expensive than props or costumes. Kemble's innovations at Drury Lane between 1796 and 1802 have been described as 'decisive' in theatre history.[27] His main coadjutor was John Carter's friend and fellow antiquary William Capon, whose life's work off stage was that 'conjectural reconstruction of the old Palace at Westminster and of the ancient sub-structure of Westminster Abbey' which is still of considerable significance for historians.[28]

In 1794 the new Drury Lane theatre, rebuilt by Henry Holland, was opened. It seated 3,600 and the stage was vast by previous standards: eighty-three feet wide and ninety-two deep. Except for church spires, Drury Lane was the tallest building in London. On the opening night, which featured a concert of 'sacred music from the works of Handel', the curtain rose to reveal a single set occupying the entire stage.[29] It was an 'actual building of a Gothic chapel, magnificent and even sublime', an early example of a 'box set', for which the wings were removed so that the entire space was filled by the flies.[30] It was the work of Capon, who went on to give Kemble Westminster Hall, St Stephen's Chapel and the Painted Chamber, all realized to scale from his own drawings. From now on the scenery began to get reviews. Not all of the designers were up to Capon's standard, and the critic of *The Gentleman's Magazine*, 'Artist and Antiquary', was often obliged to be severe. Capon himself did not always escape the censure of the pseudonymous reviewer, who he may or may not have known was his friend John Carter.[31]

In 1820 the Kemble era came to an end, or at least the first Kemble era. John Philip retired, but he was one of eleven children, six of whom went into the theatre, and he gave his shares in Covent Garden, where he had decamped after a final row with Sheridan, to his younger brother Charles. Charles, long overshadowed by Philip, now had his chance and in time built a reputation as a fine actor. As a manager, however, he took on an immense task. Covent Garden was all but bankrupt, bigger, after a rebuilding in 1809, and more expensive than ever to run and to fill. Planché, now resident playwright, conceived a plan to attract audiences by putting on Shakespeare's history plays in authentic costume. Public interest in historic dress had been boosted by Strutt's *Dress and Habits*, Smith and Meyrick's *Costume of the Original Inhabitants of the British Islands* and many cheaper publications. By now it was 'not requisite', as Planché pointed out, to be an antiquary in order to object to the same costumes being used for all the history plays and to notice 'the absurdity of the soldiers before Angiers, at the beginning of the thirteenth century, being clothed precisely the same as those fighting at Bosworth at the end of the fifteenth'.[32] Charles Kemble agreed to let Planché try out his ideas on a production of *King John* with Kemble himself in the lead, on condition that Planché did not expect to be paid – or, as he put it in his

Reminiscences, 'I undertook the necessary researches ... *gratuitously*, I beg leave to say; solely and purely for that love of the stage, which has ever induced me to sacrifice all personal considerations.'[33] Planché got to work with the help of Stothard's *The Monumental Effigies of Great Britain*, Douce's antiquarian library and Meyrick's advice on arms and armour, and carried on in the teeth of entrenched opposition from the resentful stage manager and the cast, who thought the costumes made them look ridiculous. 'Never shall I forget the dismay of some of the performers when they looked upon the flat-topped *chapeaux de fer* (*fer blanc*, I confess) of the 12th century, which they irreverently stigmatized as stewpans!' Planché later wrote:

> Nothing but the fact that the classical features of a Kemble were to be surmounted by a precisely similar abomination would, I think, have induced one of the rebellious barons to have appeared in it. They had no faith in me, and sulkily assumed their new and strange habiliments, in the full belief that they should be roared at by the audience. They *were* roared at; but in a much more agreeable way than they had contemplated. When the curtain rose, and discovered King John dressed as his effigy appears in Worcester Cathedral, surrounded by his barons sheathed in mail, with cylindrical helmets and correct armorial shields, and his courtiers in the long tunics and mantles of the thirteenth century, there was a roar of applause, so general and so hearty, that the actors were astonished, and I felt amply rewarded for all the trouble, anxiety, and annoyance I had experienced during my labours. Receipts of from 400l to 600l nightly soon reimbursed the management for the expense ... and a complete reformation of dramatic costume became from that moment inevitable upon the English stage.[34]

Planché was exaggerating. The change was neither so sudden nor so complete, but his *King John* was a landmark. It was followed by a *Henry IV Part I*, for which historic costume was augmented with six new sets. For *Henry VIII* in 1831 (a play revived almost entirely for its scenic opportunities and the trial of Catherine of Aragon) the scenery department recreated old St Paul's, London Bridge and the west front of Westminster Abbey as it stood in 1533 with its towers still unfinished: by now the anachronism of including Hawksmoor's additions would have been noticed and objected to. Meanwhile the smaller theatres tried to keep up, not always successfully. Planché was amused to spot an advertisement for a melodrama at the Coburg Theatre (now the Old Vic) of *William the Conqueror, or the Battle of Hastings*, complete with 'a long and imposing (very imposing in this instance) list of authorities . . . for the new dresses and decoration'. From the heights of Covent Garden he looked down on the little south-bank theatre and was 'curious to observe the effect of such a representation on a transpontine public'.[35] He took a box. 'The house was crammed to the ceiling; and in the very centre of the pit, a most conspicuous object amongst the dingy denizens of the New Cut and St George's Fields, who filled it to suffocation, arose the snow-white powdered head of the learned and highly respected Dr Coombe, the Keeper of the Medals at the British Museum.' The theatre had learned from the antiquaries, and now the interchange was so finely balanced that an antiquary might hope, albeit in vain in this case, to learn from the theatre.

Across the Channel matters did not proceed so evenly. The Classical drama with its unities of time, place and action was identified with the ideals of the Revolution to the point of seeming to stand for France itself. In July 1822 an English company went to Paris to perform Shakespeare, in English, at the Porte St-Martin. Their *Othello* was greeted with 'inconceivable violence'. 'The capture of Calais', as the historian and liberal politician François Guizot wrote, 'would not have excited more patriotic wrath.'[36] Amid cries of 'down with Shakespeare, a Lieutenant of Wellington', it eventually took a cavalry charge to disperse the audience.[37] Guizot's response was his essay, 'Shakespeare in France'. It was the latest of several exchanges between the Romantic and Classicist camps. Guizot's first salvo, 'Shakespeare in his Times', had appeared as a Preface to a revised translation of the plays in 1821. The Permanent Secretary of the Académie française returned fire, Stendhal retaliated with 'Racine et Shakespeare' in 1825 and in 1827 Victor Hugo joined battle in the Preface to his play *Cromwell*. The Romantics' case against the unities was that they were sclerotic vestiges of the *ancien régime* and they could not speak to post-Revolutionary France. 'We . . . have taken part in terrible events,' Guizot wrote, 'witnessed the fall and rise of empires . . . we have known conquerors, statesman, conspirators.'[38] After such knowledge, what forgiveness. The clinching argument, they all agreed, was the phenomenon of Walter Scott. Hugo had declared *Ivanhoe* the epic of the age. 'What literary work has enjoyed the greatest success in France in the last ten years', Stendhal asked rhetorically. 'What are the novels of Sir Walter Scott? Romantic tragedy.'[39] Guizot, with a tone of stating the obvious, referred to Scott as 'the most original and fertile genius' of the period.[40] In France, as in Britain, Scott and Shakespeare stood shoulder to shoulder.

By the 1840s, several decades of antiquarian advice to the theatre had perhaps been too much. Authenticity overbalanced into cumbersome literalism. The vast scale of the new theatres at Drury Lane and Covent Garden made the nuanced acting of Kemble and Siddons impossible and so productions fell back on spectacle, hugely complicated sets and pedantically accurate costumes. Whatever next, one irritated critic wondered, 'legitimate authority produced for the dressing of Puck ... authenticated wings allotted to Mustardseed'?[41] There was by now considerable pressure to remove the monopoly of the patent theatres, which had a stranglehold on productions of Shakespeare and other spoken drama. At last, in 1843 the Theatre Regulation Act was passed and, for a while at least, it seemed to represent an escape from the constraints of the overblown auditoria. Planché headed, with some relief, for the Haymarket Theatre, where he put on another groundbreaking Shakespearean production, *The Taming of the Shrew*. For twenty years while attempting to treat Shakespeare's history plays historically he had been accumulating information about the history not only of dress but also of theatrical costume. His essay of 1836, 'History of Stage Costume', was the first attempt at a narrative account of the subject and opened with a suitably dramatic flourish:

> If Stratford-upon-Avon be the Mecca of our dramatic world, Dunstable may surely be called the Medina, – the second sacred city in the estimation of the zealous play-goer ... because the little town of Bedfordshire, which is only famous in Gazetteers for the manufacture of straw hats and pillow-lace, has the honour of furnishing us with the earliest precise information concerning an English play and English theatrical wardrobe, through the medium of Matthew Paris.[42]

For his own production Planché made a simple but radical change of direction. Instead of presenting Shakespeare's history, he presented the historic Shakespeare. He used the original text, rather than Garrick's version, and put it on in contemporary, that is in Elizabethan, dress. There was no attempt to evoke 'fair Padua' and only two sets, the exterior of the inn from which Sly is ejected and the Lord's Bedchamber in which the players perform. The restoration of the framing device, the play within a play, 'this gem', gave Planché as much 'pride and satisfaction' as anything in his career and was 'eminently successful', by his account.[43] The Victorian audience shared, as nearly as possible, the experience of their sixteenth-century predecessors. This recalibration of the Romantic principle of authenticity was not much followed at the time, though it was prescient of twentieth-century ideas about Shakespearean production.

A SENSIBLE SHAKESPEARE

Throughout the second half of the eighteenth century literary opinion had been moving towards the antiquarian point of view, that Shakespeare's text should be restored rather than adapted to suit to modern taste. By the time Edmond Malone's edition appeared, inspiring Kemble's reforms, there were two generations of textual scholarship behind him. The founding father of antiquarian editors was George Steevens (1736–1800), a man who divided opinion among his contemporaries and has continued to do so since. A friend and collaborator of Dr Johnson, he made important additions to the 1765 edition of Johnson's *Shakespeare* in the form of notes and a list of twenty extant quartos. His name appeared with Johnson's on the title page of the 1773 edition, by which time he had published his own, unannotated, editions of the plays and sonnets. Beside his literary contribution there was a widespread feeling that without him Johnson would not have got his Shakespeare to the printer 'these twelve months' at least and the revisions might not have been done at all.[44] For his part Johnson appreciated Steevens' 'diligence and sagacity'. He also remarked to Boswell, however, that Steevens 'lives the life of an outlaw'.[45] Others used less romantic terms. The full story of Steevens' crimes and misdemeanours, chiefly forgery and hoaxes, does not belong here. One telling example will suffice.

In 1789, that momentous year in antiquarian history, Steevens, having fallen out with Richard Gough who had refused to lend him some books, went to the trouble of having a marble block engraved with an Anglo-Saxon inscription and placed in a broker's shop in Southwark. He told several other fellows of the Society of Antiquaries about it, saying that it was the tombstone of Hardecanute, recently dug up in Kennington. Hardecanute, who reigned in England from 1040 to 1042, was a popular subject among antiquaries. Steevens employed Schnebbelie, the draughtsman Gough sent to Salisbury Cathedral that summer, to draw it. He had the drawing published in *The Gentleman's Magazine*, where Gough was reviews editor. This prompted Samuel Pegge, author of the much-satirized paper on Dick Whittington's cat, to give another unlucky lecture, in which he expounded the meaning of the stone. The Trojan horse having been wheeled into the Society, Steevens sprang out, exposing the hoax in a second article in *The Gentleman's Magazine*. Nobody at the Society of Antiquaries thought this was funny or clever, except Sir Joseph Banks, whose feelings about the Society were at best mixed. Steevens presented him with the stone and Banks took pleasure in exhibiting it at the regular assemblies at his house in Soho Square.

Needless to say, Steevens' behaviour did nothing for the reputation of antiquaries in general and his own in particular. It obscured his contribution to scholarship, which extended beyond Shakespeare's texts to the almost untouched subject of their sources. At Steevens' instigation in 1779 John Nichols printed *Six Old Plays*, earlier versions of *Measure for Measure, The Comedy of Errors, The Taming of the Shrew, King John, Henry IV, Henry V* and *Lear*. Their publication set Shakespeare in a historical context, placing him firmly in a vernacular rather than a Classical or academic tradition. Steevens also helped Malone, who published a supplement to the Johnson *Shakespeare* in 1780 in which he acknowledged Steevens' 'numerous observations' and 'judicious hints'.[46] Malone's own *The Plays and Poems of William Shakespeare* was a complete revision with extensive notes and an essay, which was the first sustained attempt at a history of the English stage. It also contained the fullest account of the biographical evidence to date. Malone is not usually described as an antiquary, that perhaps not seeming a sufficiently dignified term for a Shakespearean scholar, especially after Steevens had brought the whole field further into disrepute; but by contemporary standards he was. He worked from primary sources and comparators, tracking down documents in Chancery, at Dulwich College, the Stamp Office, the Tower of London, the diocesan archives in Worcester, the Remembrancer's Office in the Exchequer, the Office of the Lord Chamberlain and the Bodleian and Ashmolean libraries. He ruined his eyesight in the candlelight of the corporation archives at Stratford, compared his archival discoveries with the early quartos and folios and 'more or less lived at the British Museum'.[47]

In the Romantic rediscovery of Shakespeare Malone is a transitional figure with one foot still in the Enlightenment. His work on the texts won him the admiration and gratitude of the rising generation, but his respect for literature did not extend to other antiquities. On a visit to Stratford in 1793 he decided that the expression on Shakespeare's memorial bust in the parish church was unsatisfactory for a genius, with a certain 'pertness' about it, and arranged to have it 'improved' with a thick coat of whitewash. 'In this very act', John Britton wrote, speaking for many of his contemporaries, 'our zealous annotator has passed an irrevocable sentence on his own judgment.'[48] The bust, Britton argued, should not be judged as art, but as evidence. It was originally painted 'in imitation of the countenance and dress of the Poet. The eyes were of a light hazel, and the hair and beard, auburn; the doublet, or coat, was scarlet, and covered with a loose black gown, or tabard, without sleeves; the upper part of the cushion was green, the under half crimson, and the tassels gilt'.[49] Britton did not like the colour scheme any more than Malone did. It was gaudy and 'repugnant to good taste'. That was not the point. It should have been preserved 'as illustrative of a particular age or people, and as a record of fashion and costume'.[50]

Thus Shakespeare studies, like all antiquarian endeavours, had its divisions and disagreements and, as the subject grew in popularity, it also had its temptations. The year of the bust's whitewashing brought the topographical artist and engraver Samuel Ireland and his teenage son William to Stratford. They were working on an unremarkable book of *Picturesque Views on the Upper, or Warwickshire Avon* and came to make drawings of the principal sights. The cult of the Bard was by now launched and the Irelands amplified it with the first illustration of the farmhouse at Shottery, 'where Anne Hathaway wife of William Shakespeare resided', which was soon to become 'Anne Hathaway's Cottage'. This seems to have given William an idea. Two years later the Irelands' London home at Charing Cross was opened for an exhibition of newly discovered Shakespeare papers, including 'deeds, letters, verses, drawings ... together with the entire play of K. Lear'.[51] The creation of a biography for Anne Hathaway was furthered by a lock of hair sent to her in a letter from Shakespeare. There was also a previously unknown play, *Vortigern and Rowena*. Antiquaries and others flocked, among them Joseph Ritson, the vituperative Jacobin scholar of the Robin Hood legends. Ireland Senior told Ritson that the collection had been discovered by his son 'among some old writings, in the chambers of a gentleman in the Temple, whose name he was not at liberty to mention'.[52] Ritson cast his eye rapidly over the collection, 'every article of which', he wrote to a friend afterwards, 'it would be a very easy matter to demonstrate, as well by intrinsic as by external evidence, to be a recent and palpable forgery'.[53] The only thing that interested him was the way that genuine old parchment and seals had been used, after removing the original writing.

Ritson, however, rarely ventured into print without the spur of a quarrel. He had attacked Johnson and Steevens' edition of Shakespeare, and more recently his *Cursory Criticisms* lambasted Malone. There was no such imperative to expose Ireland, who had so far only made a dupe of his father. Most antiquaries saw through the forgeries as easily as Ritson. At Drury Lane, however, Sheridan, ever on the watch for a money-making opportunity, decided to stage a production of the 'newly discovered' *Vortigern*. Kemble refused on the grounds that the play was a fake. Sheridan neither knew nor cared as long as it drew a crowd, so Kemble gave in but scheduled the production for 1 April, as a hint to the audience. Sheridan made him move it to the 2nd, but it was too late. On 31 March Malone went into print with his devastating *An Inquiry into the Authenticity of Certain Miscellaneous Papers and Legal Instruments*, which exploded the Irelands' credibility. The production was a flop and proved the final straw in Kemble's relations with Sheridan. At the end of the season he resigned.

Douce, meanwhile, was working on his own contribution to Shakespearean studies. Like Scott, he saw 'old plays' as 'the best possible record of manners' and in Shakespeare he had a subject and a source.[54] He considered both in his two-volume *Illustrations of Shakspeare [sic] and of Ancient Manners*. Douce had known Steevens, who published some of Douce's 'remarks' in the 1790s, and he followed him in the attempt to locate Shakespeare in his time, emerging from a late-medieval tradition. Malone's Enlightenment sensibilities had made his Shakespeare more genteel and better acquainted with Classical literature than Douce thought likely. Having, like Malone, 'examined the records, transcribed the documents, and weighed the evidence',[55] he found a less learned Shakespeare, one closer to folk tradition than Latin literature. It was early days for textual commentary of this sort and Douce's Preface was defensive, hoping to ward off objections to antiquarian pedantry or '*black-letter* learning'.[56] What he proposed was 'true scholarship and a laudable curiosity', justified because, as Steevens had put it, 'If Shakspeare is worth reading, he is worth explaining.'[57]

Douce had no qualms about citing the sources he found most probable, however vulgar, and in his use of Shakespeare himself as a source from which to 'augment the knowledge of our popular customs and antiquities' he expanded his notes beyond the texts with 'digressions' into social history.[58] These excursions helped to weave the plays into their contemporary context, although they also opened him up to charges of antiquarian wool-gathering. With no general summarizing comments, each of Douce's points relates to a line or a speech and is included in the order in which it occurs, obliging the reader to sift through for the important parts. To this extent Douce conformed to the worst antiquarian stereotype, listing facts with no attempt at narrative or organizing argument. Nevertheless, the accumulated information was significant. His treatment of *The Tempest* was typical in its emphasis on Shakespeare's vernacular sources. On Caliban's lines

> As wicked dew as e'er my mother brushed
> With raven's feathers from unwholesome fen
> Drop on you both! A southwest blow on ye,

he glosses the raven imagery with a reference to the Elizabethan antiquary and clergyman Stephen Batman's *Batman upon Bartholome his booke De proprietatibus rerum*, of 1582, 'in which it is said that ravens are fed on dew when they are young and that "the raven is called corvus or CORAX"'. 'Corax', Douce suggests, is the origin of 'Syco-rax'.[59] For Miranda's speech 'I am your wife, if you will marry me ...' Malone had suggested a source in 'a very apposite passage from Catul-lus'. Douce tartly opposed it with 'the pathetic old poem of *The nut-brown maid*' as a more likely inspiration.[60] Not only was his Shakespeare more familiar with traditional sources, the playwright would have found a simple ballad more apt than a Classical allusion at the moment when Miranda innocently breaks a convention she does not know by proposing marriage to Ferdinand. Dealing with Steevens' objection to the line 'This wooden slavery than to suffer', Douce argued that it was 'Shakespeare's language, and ought therefore to be restored. Mr Steevens objects on the score of defective metre: but this is not the case; the metre however rugged, is certainly perfect.'[61] The antiquaries' Shakespeare was not only more familiar with folk songs and local trad-ition than the Classics, he was 'rugged', like Johnson's antiquarian.

When Douce turned from explaining Shakespeare to using Shake-speare as a source of information, however, matters became more complicated. His essay 'On the Anachronisms and Some Other Incon-gruities of Shakspeare [*sic*]' finds Douce the antiquary at odds with Douce the admirer of the Bard. In his former character he must of course condemn all 'transgressions against the rules of chronology', from which point of view Shakespeare was highly unsatisfactory.[62] Knowing what he did about sixteenth-century drama, Douce could not condone Alexander Pope's attempts to attribute the anachronisms to the publishers of the plays. 'Nothing ... could have been less jud-icious', for Shakespeare, if not 'more culpable in this respect than most of his contemporaries', nevertheless wrote in an age when antiq-uarianism was in its infancy and history was to be bent to the tastes and purposes of posterity.[63] Douce occasionally sounds like Shake-speare's irritated schoolmaster, pointing to the absurdity of mince pies in *Troilus and Cressida* or a clock in *Julius Caesar* and, while he is prepared to overlook the Great Bed of Ware in *Twelfth Night* 'because it is referred to as in England', his paragraph on *King Lear* opens with a tetchy 'We have here a plentiful crop of blunders.'[64]

When it appeared in 1807, Douce's work was pioneering. Its imme-diate reception, however, was severely discouraging. Several favourable reviews were eclipsed by the savaging the book received in the

Edinburgh Review. The *Review*'s editor, Francis Jeffrey, commissioned a piece from the lawyer and author Barron Field (1786–1846), who praised Douce's book. Whereupon Jeffrey, possibly because of his own quarrel with the publishers, Longman's, rewrote the article, transforming what Douce was assured had been a 'skilful, honourable & gentlemanly'[65] tribute into a withering attack on 'this petty sort of antiquarianism'.[66] Jeffrey was outraged by the implication that Shakespeare belonged to a vernacular tradition. He believed that Douce and his ilk should be kept out of Shakespeare, as Gough and Schnebbelie were locked out of Salisbury Cathedral, to let their betters have the run of the place. Their 'miserable erudition', tolerable when confined to *The Gentleman's Magazine* or 'some county history', should not be allowed to acquire 'a more extended reputation'.[67] Jeffrey picked on a slip in one of Douce's quotations. This, he said, was the sort of thing to be expected of an author who engages with popular literature, for 'if a man will stuff his head full of Gammer Gurton and Gabriel Harvey, he will soon find that he has no room for Milton and Virgil'.[68] There were, he concluded patronizingly, 'many little items of information' that a reader might find useful, but he warned the antiquaries off the cultural high ground. 'We remain confirmed in our opinion that the commentators are "a feeble folk" and that they have no business to make their houses in the rocks which support the everlasting monument of Shakspeare.'[69]

An infuriated Barron Field demanded his original copy be reinstated. Jeffrey's only answer was a banker's draft for ten guineas. Douce's editors and Henry Ellis at the British Museum all told him what had happened, but his confidence was shattered. He published nothing for twenty-six years until *The Dance of Death*. Scott sent Douce an encouraging letter about his 'curious and interesting' *Illustrations of Shakspeare and of Ancient Manners* with some additional information on fools, a particular interest of Douce. These 'half-crazy and half-knavish' men had been, within living memory, Scott told him, a familiar presence in aristocratic Scottish households.[70] Scott himself sometimes thought of producing an edition of Shakespeare, a *via media* between the pedants and the improvers. It would, he told his publisher Archibald Constable, be a 'sensible Shakespeare in which the useful & readable notes should be condensed and separated from the trash'.[71] What he meant by sensible is suggested by a letter of 1822 to Heinrich Voss, on the question of annotations. Perhaps with Douce in mind, Scott wrote that the 'great fault' of many commentators was that 'They must & will have everything completely & accurately explaind [sic] without considering that Shakespeare like all other poets who write in a hurry very frequently uses a form of words the meaning of which is clear enough when the full sentence is considered although it may be very difficult to dissect the sentence grammatically and apply the special and separate meaning to each branch or word in it.'[72] To Scott, who always wrote in such a hurry that Hazlitt wondered if he ever re-read his work, Shakespeare was primarily a fellow author.

It was in 1827, two years after Hazlitt's essay in *The Spirit of the Age* that Scott formally announced his authorship of the *Waverley* novels to the Edinburgh Theatrical Fund in a speech identifying himself with two Shakespearean characters, Macbeth, 'another Scottish criminal of more consequence' and Prospero, 'it is your breath that has filled my sails'.[73] He left others to make the direct connection and they did so almost at once at a performance of James Townley's comedy, *High Life Below Stairs*. During an exchange on the subject of Lady Bab's favourite author, 'Shikspur', 'Kitty' asks 'who wrote it' and gets the answers 'Ben Jonson' and 'Finis'. One night, as Scott recorded with pleasure, the actor William Murray adlibbed to huge applause: 'It is Sir Walter Scott; he confessed it at a public meeting the other day.'[74]

A RUDE EFFIGY, A HALF-OPEN TOMB

All that was missing from the growing cult of Shakespeare was the man himself. As Chateaubriand wrote in his study of Shakespeare, 'the classic school, which did not blend the lives of authors with their works, deprived itself of a powerful medium of appreciation'.[75] However, as he also noted, the facts in this case were few, many of them uncertain and most of them discouraging. Writing in 1836, the main points he listed were the birth in Stratford, the likelihood that Shakespeare was a Catholic (a fact that English commentators were reluctant to countenance), the marriage to Anne Hathaway, the story of being caught poaching at Charlecote by Thomas Lucy, the notorious bequest of the second-best bed, the memorial bust in the parish church and the later accidental breaching of the grave by sextons. From 'a house in a hamlet' to the 'rude village effigy [and] half-open tomb . . . such is the whole life and death of this immortal bard'.[76] Chateaubriand concluded with a shrug that Shakespeare was not interested in fame, that he left the theatre as soon as he had made enough money and that his was one of those cases in which 'the man and his talents' were 'very disproportioned to each other'.[77]

Not many people then or now were willing to leave it at that. The desire for a life was irresistible, and as Samuel Schoenbaum writes in his glorious and indispensable *Shakespeare's Lives*, it was chiefly the antiquaries who provided it, making a contribution to Shakespearean biography 'more substantive as well as more prosaic' than their better-known contemporaries, Coleridge and Carlyle.[78] They added to the meagre stock of documents and, by their investigation of artefacts, of the memorial bust, the parish church and the houses more or less associated with Shakespeare, they enabled generations steeped in the Picturesque to find in the spirit of the place the spirit of the poet, until by the middle of the nineteenth century 'the bardolatry first naïvely celebrated at the Stratford Jubilee of 1769' achieved 'its imaginative apotheosis'.[79]

The first of the antiquarian accounts was by Robert Bell Wheler. Wheler was a lawyer who had lived all in his life in Stratford and his *History and Antiquities of Stratford-upon-Avon* appeared in 1806. Its promised 'Life of Shakespeare' did nothing except further what Schoenbaum calls 'the inevitable hardening of rumour into purported fact'.[80] In an appendix, however, Wheler published three previously unknown documents from 1602 and 1609, a conveyance and two writs, which proved that Shakespeare, even when he was established in London, was still involved at Stratford. Eighteen years later Wheler wrote to *The Gentleman's Magazine* with another piece of what Jeffrey regarded as 'miserable erudition', news of the discovery of Shakespeare's marriage bond, which confirmed the identity of Anne Hathaway. Meanwhile, in 1814 Wheler had published an abridged version of his book which included an account of the house in Henley Street, which was at that time divided into a butcher's shop and a pub but had certainly belonged to Shakespeare's father. It was now generally referred to as Shakespeare's birthplace and was a growing tourist attraction. As the *Monthly Magazine* observed in 1818, Stratford had no industry or trade and would be 'one of the most beggarly places in the kingdom' but for the literary pilgrims who came in their thousands.[81] Like the tartan boom, the Shakespeare trade might have a questionable basis in history, but its economic effects were real enough. The room where Shakespeare had supposedly been born was soon covered in signatures. Scott, Kemble, Byron and the Prince Regent all wrote their names on the walls. Today this would be considered vandalism, but at the time it was normal to record one's visit to a monument by signing it; indeed, it was kind of endorsement. The *Monthly* noted with satisfaction that among those 'proud of an association with Shakespeare', who had honoured his monument in the parish church with an inscription, was no less a person than 'the illustrious marquis himself', the brother of the Duke of Wellington.[82]

The quest for a face to put to Shakespeare's name was by now desperate and the memorial bust was the most obvious possibility. John Britton persuaded the antiquary and furniture maker George Bullock to take a cast of it, in the course of which Bullock became convinced of 'evident signs' that the face was either a life or a death mask and so recorded Shakespeare's own face.[83] Britton's description of the bust was an essay in Romantic antiquarian biography in which a life, deduced from material remains, moves towards an imaginative apotheosis. The monument is, he writes, 'a family record … a memorial raised by the affection and esteem of relatives'. The 'invaluable "Effigy"' was 'Attested by tradition, consecrated by time, and preserved in the inviolability of its own simplicity and sacred station. It was evidently executed immediately after the poet's decease; and probably under the superintendence of his son-in-law, Dr Hall, and of his daughter; the latter of whom, according to her epitaph, was "witty above her sexe", and therein resembled her father.'[84] As Britton glides by association from the bust to the circumstances of its creation, a narrative takes shape, a family group gathers round the tomb, with Britton himself among them.

Back in London, Bullock invited Britton to a celebratory breakfast viewing of the cast where they were joined by Scott, Benjamin West and Dr J. C. Spurzheim, a pioneer of phrenology. The bust was 'deeply scrutinized and commented on'.[85] West endorsed the view that it was taken from life, while Scott's conversation brought it to life. Spurzheim noted resemblances between its dimensions and Scott's own head. Scott bought a copy, for which Bullock made a cabinet, and it was enshrined at Abbotsford. Britton's friend John Soane also took one for his 'Shakespeare recess', a kind of shrine to the Bard, which he created just off the staircase in his home in Lincoln's Inn Fields. Edward Willson bought one and the bust appears in the background of Britton's portrait. But the cast was not the commercial success Britton had hoped. It was hard to read the mind's construction in its plump, prosaic face. Wordsworth wrote a tactful but tepid letter of thanks on receipt of a copy of the engraving of the cast, suggesting that 'the mighty genius of Shakspere [sic] would have placed any record of his physiognomy under considerable disadvantages for who could shape out to himself features and a countenance that would appear worthy of such a mind'.[86] More bluntly, the Monthly Magazine described it as 'the portrait of a well-fed alderman', and in spite of the 'ingenious reasoning of Mr Britton it is not to be believed [as having] any accurate resemblance' to the man.[87] The Monthly was also annoyed with Bullock, who, having taken the bust down for his cast, had then fixed it back in place in such a way as to prevent anyone else from doing the same.

While the quest for a reliable portrait went on, as it goes on today amid many claims, counter-claims and quarrels, other items of Shakespeariana emerged to feed the public appetite: Shakespeare's wedding ring, his 'courting chair', two pairs of his acting gloves, one for tragedy and one for comedy, his pencil case and even, according to the Monthly, some of his descendants, now in much-reduced circumstances, for whom the editor proposed to raise a subscription.[88] Meanwhile, the expanding market for popular literature such as Charles Knight's Penny Cyclopaedia, for which Britton wrote a biographical essay, furthered the hardening of contested facts. To the birthplace, the church and Anne Hathaway's cottage, literary pilgrims could now add Charlecote Park, the site of Shakespeare's supposed arrest for poaching. Thomas Willement, antiquary, herald and proprietor of the consummate antiquarian interior of Davington Priory, was at work at Charlecote on and off for fifteen years from 1829. The

Lucy family had lived there since the twelfth century but their eighteenth-century ancestors, seeing no connection between Shake-speare and the decoration of their house, had updated it in line with neo-Classical taste. They took out the panelling, put in marble fire-places and stucco cornices and commissioned Lancelot 'Capability' Brown to root up the seventeenth-century knot garden and create an expansive landscape. By 1823, when George Lucy inherited, this was seen as a disaster. Washington Irving when he came 'regretted to find that the ancient furniture of the hall had disappeared' and that the greater part of the house had been 'adapted to modern tastes'.[89] If he had he come back ten years later he would have found it looking much older.

To avoid disappointing more visitors the Lucys began 're-edifying' their house. 'Re-edifying', like 'sophisticating', was a concept that epitomized the Romantic view of truth by illusion. They wanted to make the house Shakespearean, but not to restore it in the modern sense. They built two new rooms which were decorated under Wille-ment's direction, and he designed stained glass which featured the Lucy pedigree. This pedigree was also 're-edified' when George Lucy found an extinct baronetcy from 1369 and revived it, thereby becom-ing Sir George. Furniture was ordered from Wardour Street, including the great sideboard or 'beaufet' that all medieval or Elizabethan great halls were supposed to have. This was made up out of carved oak panels of some antiquity, and for an extra charge of £2 10s the broker altered the date carved on the back to 1558, the year when the Tudor house at Charlecote, the one that Shakespeare would have known, was completed.

Attention next turned to the Church of the Holy Trinity in Strat-ford, which was also in need of 're-edification'. The chancel, where the bust was placed, had been Georgianized, with a flat roof and the east window filled with a painted transparency. Britton busied himself in the fundraising campaign of 1835, with an officiousness that caused much irritation to local antiquaries. The *Leamington Spa Courier* made 'captious criticisms' of his proposals, despite the fact that he had brought in one of the best Gothic architects of the day, Harvey Eginton.[90] Slowly, however, by way of various committees, delays and disputes work went ahead, although public opinion forced Britton to give up his scheme for having the arms of the subscribers (presumably including his own) painted on the roof. The alterations in the chancel brought Britton into the same kind of awkward situation as Douce when confronted by Shakespeare's cavalier attitude to chronology. Britton, like most antiquaries, deplored the intrusion of Jacobean monuments in medieval churches, where they were jammed into the walls regardless of architectural propriety, even, sometimes, across windows. Shakespeare's monument is a prime example of all these solecisms. Cut deep into the north wall and lower sill of a chancel window, over which it rises up to about halfway, the original glass had been removed and the lower lights blocked up to accommodate it. Britton was obliged to admit that the sacred bust was 'most taste-lessly inserted in the wall and window'.[91] But there it was. He had to be content with meeting the Bard halfway by making alterations to the chancel, which Eginton 'reformed, revolutionized' in two cam-paigns in 1836–7 and 1839–41.[92] He replaced the Georgian plaster ceiling with a new timber one true to 'the general spirit of the orig-inal'. The bust, however, had to wait until 1861 to be liberated from its whitewash. Another restoration over the years 1884–98 by the architects Bodley and Garner attracted its fair share of criticism, including a 'thunderbolt' from William Morris.[93] His Society for the Protection of Ancient Buildings regretted the decision to unblock the lower half of the window behind the bust and insert new stained glass. This, as they pointed out, makes the bust less visible by daylight, which is presumably why it was blocked up in the first place.[94]

The opening of the London–Birmingham railway in 1838 further expanded the Stratford tourist trade and in 1840 the Shakespeare Society, modelled on the antiquarian Camden and Percy Societies, was founded. Its prime movers included the antiquary Thomas Wright, Charles Knight, the popularizing publisher, and the young J. O. Halliwell, who became one of the most eminent Shakespearean authorities of the nineteenth century. Following the precedent of Steevens and Douce, the society published poetry and plays by Shake-speare's predecessors and contemporaries. Wright produced an edition of the Chester Plays. The Society's director was the journalist and antiquary John Payne Collier (1789–1883). Proposed for the Society of Antiquaries by Douce and Amyot, he was the author of *The*

History of English Dramatic Poetry to the Time of Shakespeare and Annals of the Stage to the Restoration (1831) and an eight-volume edition of Shakespeare. He was, as his biographers affirm, a gifted and industrious scholar. Alas, he was also a compulsive forger. Why he should have blighted a literary career 'already successfully advanced' remains a mystery, but the fact was that from his earliest publications he included 'whimsical fictions and slight literary impostures'.[95] Unlike young Ireland's naïve efforts or Steevens' self-detonating booby traps, Collier's faking was difficult to detect. It was only in 1852 with his 'discovery' of an annotated 'Second Folio (1632)' that suspicions were aroused. Frederic Madden asked to see the Perkins Folio, as it was known, and his colleagues at the British Museum declared in a letter to *The Times* that the supposedly seventeenth-century annotations were 'recent forgeries'. Collier's valuable research is so densely riddled with 'literally hundreds of questioned or questionable instances' that it has taken nearly a century to unravel them.[96]

In the year that the Shakespeare Society was founded, a group of local Stratford worthies drew up the Royal Shakespearean Theatre Declaration of Trust. They included a spirit merchant, a farmer, a miller, a bookseller and two innkeepers, one of whom, Edward Leyton, put up most of the money. It was nearly forty years before the Shakespeare Memorial Theatre was built at Stratford but, as the list of trustees suggests, the town's fortunes had begun to pick up. Since 1818 the abolition of the tax on brewing had helped consolidate Stratford's prominence in the trade, and when the theatre was eventually built it was on the initiative and at the expense of Charles Flowers, founder of the eponymous brewery. In September 1847, however, there was a crisis in Shakespearean tourism. The house in Henley Street was put up for sale, advertised as 'a freehold plot with a cottage and attached public house'.[97] This caused widespread alarm for, as *The Athenaeum* put it, this was 'a dwelling which has been glorified by [Shakespeare's] familiar presence'. It should never have 'found its way to the auction mart', where its significance and 'haunting memories' were to be subjected to 'the cant of the auctioneer'.[98] The Shakespeare Birthplace Committee was hastily convened to arrange its purchase. Planché, by now as much of an antiquary as a playwright, was on the committee. Britton was a member of its London branch, but, as with his efforts at the church, he seems to have made few allies. Since none of his suggestions about the purchase was taken up he felt no qualms about speaking out on the house's sketchy history. 'There is no proof that the Bard was born in this particular building', he wrote; the 'birthplace' tradition was of 'comparatively modern origin', dating back to the ownership of one Thomas Court who bought miscellaneous 'curiosities' to furnish it.[99] Britton, accordingly, 'attached no very high value' to the 'alleged Birthplace, or . . . any of the relics it contained'.[100] Even Planché, who was prominent on the committee, in his highly self-congratulatory memoirs passes swiftly over the Henley Street house as if embarrassed by it. In 1864, when it had been bought and vigorously 're-edified', the Revd J. M. Jephson, FSA, had mixed reactions: 'I was not prepared to see it look so smug and new. Many of the old timbers remain and the house is, indeed substantially the same house as it was; but new timbers have been inserted where the old were decayed, everything has been scraped and polished up, and the place looks as if it had been "restored", a word to strike terror to the heart of an antiquary, not to speak of a man of taste.'[101]

Soon, however, the powers of Romantic association began to be felt and at the sight of the 'massive' fireplace Jephson was transported: 'under its projecting jambs are cosy chimney-corners, where, doubtless, young Shakespere [sic], seated on a settle, many a time conned his lessons of a winter's evening, or read in Holinshed, or roasted crabs for the lambs'-wool, or, perhaps, dried himself after one of his raids upon a neighbouring park or warren'.[102]

By the end of the nineteenth century James Walter was speaking no more than the truth when he wrote that 'Shakespeare's biography is handed down to us through the rural scenes around Stratford'.[103] The Romantic antiquaries' Shakespeare was best understood by the criteria of the Picturesque. The landscape was Shakespeare, and Shakespeare was himself a landscape. As Scott wrote: 'Where all is elegant, nothing can be sublime . . . The touches of nature which Shakespeare has exhibited in his lower and gayer characters, like the chastened back-ground of a landscape, increase the effect of the principal group. The light and fanciful humour of Mercutio, serves, for example, to enhance and illustrate the romantic and passionate character of Romeo.'[104]

No antiquary was more devoted to Shakespeare than Britton, who recalled towards the end of his life his many pilgrimages to Stratford:

> Crowds of reflections and associations press on the mental faculties, and give exercise and pleasure at once to Memory and Imagination ... Houses shops and everyday personages are unheeded ... the whole intellect is unloosed, and expands all its perceptive and susceptive powers. It 'calls up spirits from the vasty deep' of former times ... What would we not give to be enabled to realize this vision – to grasp the hand, to hear the voice, to listen to the inspired language of the Bard ... and to stroll with him to Charlecote.[105]

We might leave Britton, near the end of his *Autobiography*, gazing on Stratford at sunset, like Caspar David Friedrich's *Wanderer Above the Sea of Fog*, when, having just come from 'the smoky worldly, hammering town of Birmingham', he was overwhelmed by a scene which 'the imagination invested with the presence of persons who were contemporary with Shakspere [*sic*], either occupied in rural labours, or in festive amusements' until he seemed to pass into it and lose himself:

> A slight shower, from a dense black cloud, had just passed over; everything was calm; Nature seemed to be reposing, after some electric conflict in the mid-regions of space; and rain-drops were hanging from every bough, branch, and leaf, catching and reflecting myriads of fairy-like prismatic rays. In front, the tall and delicate spire of Stratford Church was relieved against a dark mass of trees, which united with a heavy black cloud to the east; whilst the chimney shafts, gables, and grey, curling smoke from the houses in the town were also brightened by the setting sun. Arching over the Church were two rainbows, vividly relieved by the dark cloud and sunshine, and losing their lower limbs amid the saturated woods.[106]

In my copy of the *Autobiography* a contemporary hand has pencilled in the margin 'twaddle', so perhaps Britton did not speak for all; but he spoke for many and may certainly stand for the Romantic antiquary as a figure in the Shakespearean landscape.[107]

10

The Antiquarian Landscape:
Victorian

The age of ruins is passed.

Benjamin Disraeli, Coningsby, *1844*

Shepperton Church was a very different-looking building five-
and-twenty-years ago.

George Eliot, Scenes of Clerical Life, *1857*

By the time the long Georgian age was drawing towards its close, the
antiquarian landscape was much enlarged since the pioneering summer of 1789. From Scotland and England it extended now far into
France. On the Welsh borders, Samuel Rush Meyrick and his friend
the antiquary-architect Edward Blore were laying out the grounds of
Goodrich Court. Whewell's friend, the philosopher, engineer and historian Robert Willis, was making a tour of Gothic architecture in
Italy. Whewell himself was working on his study of medieval architecture in Germany, where, before the middle of the century, one of the
grandest and most Romantic of all antiquarian ventures would begin:
the completion of the medieval cathedral at Cologne. Despite the
coolness between France and Britain over the cross-Channel trade in
'salvage', at the personal level international relations continued to
thrive and collaborative networks proliferated. Gage made several
more trips to France, sometimes with his friend Thomas Stapleton, an
expert in 'the arcane field of the Norman Exchequer Rolls', and also
with the draughtsman and architect J. C. Buckler.[1]

Langlois continued to confide in Gage on many subjects and somehow contrived to use the diplomatic bag to convey to him various

tracings, manuscripts and books, including Thiers's *Histoire des perruques* of 1777, a volume Gage wanted for Douce, who bequeathed it to the Bodleian, where it remains. It was about this time that Langlois had the English pupil 'Catermoul', who was almost certainly Dickens's friend and illustrator George Cattermole. The antiquaries' correspondence hums with friendly activity. Gage sent copies of his own books to Langlois and Langlois's friend and fellow antiquary Deville, which delighted them, although Deville had to confess that his English was so limited that he was confined to admiring the pictures. Deville was researching the Tancerville family and wanted to know their English history, in exchange for which information he sent Gage an account of a recently excavated Roman sarcophagus, containing a female skeleton, two glass bottles and three glass goblets. A French antiquary who preferred to remain anonymous asked Deville to ask Gage if he thought that Rush Meyrick's book on arms and armour was any good, while the prickly La Rue, who had met the aristocratically laconic Lord Aberdeen with Gage in Caen, fretted that he had had no acknowledgement of the books he had sent to the earl.

Within this network, the other web of Continental connections that operated among Catholic antiquaries extended to their friends. Nicholas Wiseman, whose position at the English College in Rome enabled him to help Lingard and Gage, was also active on behalf of Meyrick, who wanted to know if there were any Welsh manuscripts in the Vatican Library, and if so what and how many. Lingard made sure that no priest of his acquaintance went abroad without some commission, although he was disappointed in the man he sent to look in the Paris archives for the papers of the Bishop of Tarbes, who had panicked when the July Revolution broke out and fled to America. In general, however, the consequences of that revolution were benign. The climate of opinion which gave rise to the Commission des monuments historiques was clement also to individual antiquaries. Caumont was actively encouraged to publish and Langlois was reluctantly drawn into the daylight. Invited to Rosny, château of the now exiled Duchesse de Berry, he met the king and although, as Langlois told Gage, it was very inconvenient to be taken away from his work like this, he made full use of the opportunity to harangue Louis Philippe over dinner on the subject of architectural conservation. The Citizen King appears to have taken the lecture on the chin, and Langlois's fortunes, in a material sense, improved slightly.

At home Gage continued to be much occupied with difficulties at the Society of Antiquaries. Mr Hunter, who had been hoping to read his paper on Queen Eleanor, was annoyed to find that Henry Ellis had double-booked, and Charles Roach Smith was now poised to speak on Roman discoveries in London. There were too many contributions for the next number of *Archaeologia* and nobody would withdraw. Lingard wanted Gage's opinion on an Anglo-Saxon coin and Meyrick was putting him right on the history of trousers in Wales: 'They were worn by the Gauls and Britons as we find from Martial, Diodorus and Strabo, and were denominated by the latter elawdyr, and continued to be worn by the Welsh down to the conclusion of the fourteenth century.'[2] Yet in the background to the ever-flowing stream of antiquarian life the national mood was darkening.

The reign of William IV from 1830 to 1837 has never acquired its own adjective, but that is not because it lacked event. The years leading up to Victoria's accession were turbulent and momentous, a period of transition, social upheaval and spiritual anxiety which saw the first outbreak of cholera in Britain, the worst civil unrest in English history and a tidal wave of millenarianism on such a scale as to make 'prophesy' an 'ordinary intellectual activity'.[3] It was, as Friedrich Engels wrote in *The Condition of the Working Class in England*, 'towards 1830' that matters began to come to a head, when 'the agricultural districts became the site of permanent, as the manufacturing districts had long been of periodic, pauperism'.[4] That year saw the so-called Swing riots, carried out in the name of the elusive folk hero Captain Swing, which began with the breaking of threshing machines in Kent. There followed attempts to control the situation with the Reform Act and the New Poor Law, both deeply divisive measures. Antiquaries felt the effects of all this to varying degrees in their lives and in their studies. 'What times we live in and who can foresee the denouement?' Lingard wrote to Gage. 'It seems to me that we cannot form any judgment from past events because we live in a state of society that never existed before.'[5]

In fact, Gage's work in progress, the editing of the *Chronicle of the Abbey of Bury St Edmunds* by the twelfth-century monk Jocelin of Brakelond, was to inspire one of the most influential attempts to judge the nineteenth century by the light of history, Carlyle's *Past and Present* of 1843. For the moment, however, antiquarianism reflected the troubled spirit of the age more obliquely. The Dance of Death, that theme in Romantic antiquarianism since Burns's 'Tam O'Shanter', loomed larger and more vivid. With its grim ironic depiction of life as a merry dance towards the grave, the *danse macabre* was a product of the later Middle Ages that had survived until the sixteenth century, when, as the medieval world view faded, it lost its moral force. By the eighteenth century, variations on the theme were usually vehicles for scenes of richly illustrated landscapes and costumes. Now it re-emerged with new resonance. For the generation that grew up with the French Revolution and the wars that followed, it was an allegory and a vehicle for social and political comment.[6] The tradition dates back to the Black Death, but the earliest surviving source for the dance is the sequence of illustrated verses inscribed in 1524 on the walls of the cemetery of Holy Innocents in Paris. In Rouen, Langlois's discovery of the vestiges of an almost exactly contemporary version in the burial ground of St-Maclou, combined with his own savagely satirical cast of mind, inspired him. His first study of the *danse macabre* appeared in 1832. The following year saw Douce's landmark study *The Dance of Death ... With a dissertation on the several representations of that subject, but more particularly on those ascribed to Macaber and Hans Holbein*, the culmination of nearly forty years of research.

Langlois and Douce compared notes from time to time via Gage. Langlois was somewhat in awe of Douce, whom he referred to always as 'Sir Francis', though Douce had no title, but he did have a large and important collection of material on the subject. Both men addressed the principal historical questions: what were the origins of the dance, who, if anyone, was Macabree for whom it was said to be named, was it ever performed liturgically, how secure was the attribution to Holbein of its most famous representation? Yet for these complicated men, both in their different ways riven with ambivalence about the age through which they had lived and its horrors, the subject held more than academic interest. As well as the material on the dance, Douce had a vast collection of other images of death and the afterlife, ranging from the thirteenth-century transcript of Revelation now in the Bodleian and known as the 'Douce Apocalypse' to drawings by

William Blake. Douce was a child of the Enlightenment. His relationship to his subject matter had an element of horrified fascination with
the 'dark ages of monkish bigotry and superstition', in which 'the
deluded people . . . appear to have derived one of their principal grat-
ifications in contemplating this necessary termination of humanity'.[7]
His stated position was that of the 'more enlightened Christian',
despite which his book dwells at length on pre-Christian sources,
which he clearly finds more congenial.[8] 'The ancients', he notes, 'often
symbolized the human soul by the figure of a butterfly, an idea that is
extremely obvious and appropriate, as well as elegant.'[9]

Langlois, too, was much possessed by death. His essay, like most of
his work, eventually appeared in book form only posthumously, having been completed by friends. He, like Douce, was torn between
Classical and Romantic views of the human condition, feeling the
same mixture of attraction and revulsion for the medieval world view
and its 'fond moral'.[10] Langlois, however, even while presenting the
plainest facts in an antiquarian study, had seen too much of the reality
of death to be objective. In a footnote he recalls walking as a child with
his father past a gibbet and seeing the corpses appear to dance in the
wind. His essay opens with a dramatic monologue in which, like the
commentator at a diorama, he promises to strike up the rebec for his
readers and lead them, to the grinding rhythm of the *danse macabre*,
through the streets of Rouen, calling out its ghosts as he takes them all
on to the cemetery at St-Maclou. It is not only a figure of speech. As
Langlois explained, there were images and inscriptions carved on the
wooden house fronts that, if properly studied, were full of information
about their former occupants. It was as Victor Hugo said: those who
know what they are looking at can find the history of a king in a door
knocker.

Death was now busy among the antiquaries themselves. Douce died
the year after his book was published. Langlois sank into a depression
in about 1834 from which he would not recover, dying, after years of
near-silence, in 1837. In 1838 his sixteen-year-old former pupil, Flaubert, composed his own *Danse des morts*, a lurid drama which, with
its opening 'Evocation', 'To the dance of death, to the dance, when
midnight strikes and all the nave shudders with the sound of lugubri-
ous melody', echoes Langlois at his most melodramatic.[11] It ends with

an encounter between History, Death and the Devil. History, which cannot die, envies Death. Satan is left alone, triumphant. Langlois would have understood it. The heroes of the battle for Salisbury Cathedral were long gone, Gough in 1809, Carter in 1817 and Milner and Nichols in 1826. In 1832 Auguste Pugin died, leaving his wayward, brilliant son Augustus Welby to finish his books of *Examples of Gothic Architecture* before embarking on his own, spectacular career. Walter Scott also died that year, although he had so thoroughly shaped the imaginative landscape of Britain and France that his physical absence at first made little difference. Those who remained of the older generation included the unquenchable John Britton, Edward Willson, John Lingard, Dawson Turner and his friend Hudson Gurney. All were still vigorous, and an energetic new generation was rising around them. Douce's intellectual heir and protégé, Planché, was beginning to transform theatrical costume on the London stage. The quest for the secrets of Gothic architecture, that holy grail of antiquarianism, had passed to Robert Willis, whose researches into the construction of vaults moved the subject far beyond any of his predecessors' efforts and laid the groundwork for architectural history as a distinct discipline. John Nichols' heirs continued the family business, industrious as ever in producing *The Gentleman's Magazine* and undertaking their own researches, while Scott's inheritors were legion.

Meanwhile, some of the great projects of the Georgian years had reached their conclusion. Ellis and Bandinel completed their edition of the *Monasticon* in 1830, the year in which Lingard published the last volume of his *History of England*, though its popularity kept him occupied revising it for new editions. Britton's *Cathedral Antiquities* came to a triumphant conclusion in 1835 with Worcester. As a figure in the public imagination the antiquary was now so familiar as to be a kind of Everyman in the portly shape of Mr Pickwick. *The Pickwick Papers* was the publishing sensation of 1836–7, but amid its jollity there are shadows like those that haunted the antiquaries. Dickens had known the Holbein *Dance of Death* since childhood and he had perhaps seen Douce's. In *Pickwick*, in 'The Stroller's Tale' Death seems to cross Dismal Jemmy's path, while in the Preface to the first cheap edition of what are, after all, the 'posthumous' papers of the Pickwick Club, Dickens's attack on the social inequality perpetrated by the authorities' 'petty boards and bodies' casts them as the skeletons who 'keep their jobbing little fiddles going for a Dance of Death'.[12] Meanwhile, in the sunnier foreground, in Part XI Mr Pickwick turns antiquary, paying an old man ten shillings for a stone with some cryptic letters carved on it. After close study he lectures to the Pickwick Club on the meaning of the inscription, presents an engraving of it to 'the Royal Antiquarian Society', causes an international controversy that divides families and leads to at least one suicide, and rises serenely above the ignorant assertions of a Mr Blotton, who suggests that the letters spell out 'BIL STUMPS HIS MARK'. The joke, well worn when John Earle made it in 1628, had rolled down two centuries to land in the lap of the common reader.

+

B I L S T

U M

P S H I

S. M.

A R K

SIGNS OF THE TIMES

The social and political disquiet of the 1830s manifested not only in machine-wrecking. At Nottingham the castle was burned down, the Bishop's Palace in Bristol was set ablaze and from Hampstead Heath it was reported that London appeared ringed with fire. On 16 October 1834 fire came to the capital itself in a way that in these feverishly millenarian days seemed to confirm that the time was out of joint. Throughout that day visitors to the House of Lords had remarked that the floor seemed unusually warm and the air in the Chamber cloudy, as if with smoke. They were reassured that this was due to the stoves in the cellar, where the old tally sticks were being burned. Tallies, 'the most ancient form of accounting used in England', were no longer needed, and in order to address the ever-urgent problem of space in the Palace of Westminster it was decided that the redundant sticks, which had accumulated in large numbers, should be disposed of.[13] The medieval palace had become the site not only of Parliament but of the Law Courts and the Exchequer and it had not been designed for any of these uses. Over the years it had been adapted, infilled and extended. Antiquaries since John Carter and William Capon had haunted the various 'improvement' works, which often revealed historic fabric and just as often went on to destroy it.

Since the Reform Act of 1832 had enlarged Parliament, the problems of accommodation had increased and the catastrophe which many had predicted now arrived. The fire, which broke out from the overloaded stoves, was impossible to contain. Crowds gathered to watch the blaze against the night sky, the last great show of Georgian London. The river was so thickly packed with boats that it was possible to walk from one side to the other. Constable and Turner drew the scene. It seemed to many people that something rotten at the heart of national life was being purged.

Antiquaries, on the whole, were not unduly dismayed. The young Welby Pugin, who happened to be in London that day and watched the conflagration, wrote to his old friend Edward Willson in Lincoln that 'there was nothing much to regret'; the fire had vindicated the antiquarian case against modern architecture.[14] It was indeed the Georgian additions, 'Soanes mixtures & Wyatts heresies', that had failed. The 'composition mullions & cement pinnacles', sash windows and brick walls went 'flying & cracking', while much of the medieval stonework survived or, as Pugin put it, 'stood triumphantly amidst this scene of ruin'.[15] The fire, like the earlier building campaigns, offered an opportunity for research. There appeared a reasonable chance that some at least of the ruins would be restored. The shell of St Stephen's still stood, while Westminster Hall, with its glorious hammer-beam roof, remained intact. Britton was on site the next day with one of his young artist draughtsmen, Robert Billings, preparing an opportune publication. The debate about what should be done with the palace began before the fire was out. It crystallized public opinion about 'jobbery' and corruption in public works. There had been too much of that in the days of George IV and John Nash. This time, as the *Morning Herald* put it, 'the British people intend to have the choosing of the architects' and the result, *The Times* insisted, must be 'a Parliamentary edifice worthy of a great nation'.[16]

Majority opinion favoured a competition, and when it was announced that entries were to be in either the Elizabethan or the Gothic style, many an antiquary reached for his pencil. A growing number of them were moving seamlessly from the study of medieval architecture to the design of new buildings in an authentic, historically based Gothic. Rickman, who had led the way, now had a substantial practice. His friend Edward Blore had been called in to finish Buckingham Palace after Nash was fired for financial irregularity and he gained a reputation for reliability and economy which endeared him to the Office of Works. It boosted his career, but perhaps also contributed to the aura of 'dull competence' that pervades his many buildings.[17] He was not helped by having a name that rhymed with 'bore'. Willson had a modest local practice, while Pugin was already calling himself an architect despite having built almost nothing. The decision about the style for the new palace had been made in part for propriety. Situated between Westminster Hall and the Abbey, a Gothic building would be more in keeping. But it was also a sign that the tide of taste had turned. The choice of Gothic for a major public work marked the point at which the medieval ceased to be a novelty style, a niche taste or an antiquarian hobby and became the national style of a great imperial power. The antiquaries had won the argument. Professional architects, as *The Gentleman's Magazine* noted with some satisfaction, would now have to take notice of the medieval, 'a class of buildings which they have hitherto regarded with contempt or apathy'.[18] Furthermore, since 'Professional men have not studied the subject while *amateurs* have devoted their time and abilities in making themselves acquainted with the merits and details of English architecture', the antiquaries were in with a chance.[19]

Brayley and Britton's *The History of the Ancient Palace and Late Houses of Parliament at Westminster* was issued promptly in 1836 and dedicated to the president of the newly founded Institute of British Architects, Earl de Grey. Architecture and antiquarianism were increasingly presented as aspects of the same discipline. Rickman, Buckler and Blore all entered the competition, from which Buckler emerged as one of the four prize winners. Pugin did not enter on his own account but worked on two of the entries, by Gillespie Graham and the eventual winner, Charles Barry. His contribution as a draughtsman, with an unrivalled repertoire of medieval details in sketchbooks filled on his travels in England, Scotland, Germany and France, was critical – all the more so since, to ensure its impartiality, the judging committee included no architects. Its members were not used to reading plans or section drawings so the attractiveness of the presentation mattered; indeed, it mattered rather too much in the opinion of *The Gentleman's Magazine*, which worried that 'the unpractised eye is too easily captivated by detail, to regard the proportions of the building on which it is so lavishly displayed'.[20]

The point in this gradual merging of architecture and antiquarianism at which the competition took place was not an entirely satisfactory one. The antiquary-architects had yet to outgrow the Gothic-by-numbers approach. Buckler was particularly proud of his stock of accumulated details which he would combine in various forms, some happier than others. He had advised the MP Charles Hanbury Tracy on the design of his manor house at Toddington in Gloucestershire; the result, though it pleased them both, was more of an anthology than an original composition and broke every law of architectural propriety. Luckily for Buckler, however, Tracy was on the panel judging the competition for the new palace and in Buckler's scheme he saw just the sort of thing he liked. Buckler won a prize. Among the younger generation who had benefited from their predecessors' efforts, a more coherent Gothic aesthetic was dawning. Anthony Salvin, who also entered the competition for the new palace, was one of the more talented. Born in 1799, he had been articled to the Edinburgh architect John Paterson and worked with him on the restoration of the medieval Brancepeth Castle. Salvin came to London with an introduction to Soane, but seems not to have taken it up. Instead, in 1824 he was elected to the Society of Antiquaries on the strength of his knowledge of Gothic structures, and in 1831 he made his first important design, Harlaxton Manor in Lincolnshire, a house in the Jacobean style and on a scale to make the visitor feel 'like Gulliver exploring Brobdingnag'.[21]

Taken together in order, Toddington, the Palace of Westminster and Harlaxton show the Gothic Revival of the last Georgian years emerging into something fully formed, an architecture of character and integrity, more than the sum of its carefully researched parts. At the same time the conceptual transformation of Gothic from, as Pugin put it, a style to a principle went on in parallel. Pugin casually put his finger on the essence of the change in 1833 when he took a trip down the most famous Picturesque tourist route, the Wye Valley, to inspect Tintern Abbey. As a ruin, he agreed, it was all very well, but 'as a building it is anything but admirable ... plan, mouldings, windows etc are very common place'.[22] This distinction between scenery and architecture, from received impression to critical expression, spoke of the dawning of a new mood, one of vigour, energy and confidence. The age of ruins was passed. Gothic became a moral as much as an aesthetic ideal in the rising generation's quest for 'reality'. 'Reality' was their watchword. It stood for clarity, sincerity, integrity both physical and ethical. In 1836 it burst out in Pugin's *Contrasts*, the first architectural manifesto, in which he compared the medieval city with the city of the present. In pairs of plates he held up the coherent, charitable, pre-Reformation world, with its monasteries, almshouses and monumental churches, against the chaotic modern city, with its cheap churches, mean houses and shoddy street fronts. If the history in *Contrasts* is naïve, the argument – that architecture has a social role and architects have moral responsibility – was original and timely. Pugin's vision of a 'real' revival, a reawakening of the spirit of the past, fell on fertile ground. It marked the effective end of Georgian architecture just as the Georgian age itself came to its conclusion.

William IV was dying. He was the relic of an age that seemed to the rising generation decadent, an era of high taste and low morals, of stucco, extravagance and adultery. When his eighteen-year-old niece was woken early on a midsummer morning in 1837 to be told that she was queen, the new reign and its lovely young monarch seemed to promise a new beginning. Britain had not had a queen regnant, a female monarch in her own right, for 123 years since Queen Anne. This added to the sense of novelty and freshness, but there was also, amid the general enthusiasm, some scratching of heads, 'a degree of uncertainty' about protocol.[23] 'The very highest authorities', Planché wrote, 'appear a little bewildered by the sudden and dazzling apparition.'[24] His *Regal Records: or a Chronicle of the Coronations of the Queens Regnant of England* was swiftly produced to help resolve any such procedural difficulties in time for Victoria's coronation.

Planché was now well on the way to being an antiquary. In 1829 he was elected to the Society of Antiquaries and in 1834 he justified Douce's confidence in him by publishing a new edition of Strutt's *Dress and Habits*. Eventually he became Somerset Herald, but in the year of Victoria's accession he was still in the thick of business at Drury Lane, where he was the resident playwright and where the notoriously reckless '*mis*-manager', Alfred Bunn, was putting on an over-elaborate and under-rehearsed production of a spectacle entitled *Caractacus*. The climax was to be a Roman triumph. 'Day after day the stage was occupied by crowds of . . . horses, goats and other animals' milling about without direction, and when the play opened it 'was deservedly roared at and hooted'.[25] *Caractacus* lasted one night. Between these unsatisfactory rehearsals, Planché continued his investigations into the history of coronations and discovered that although the leading authority on the ceremony, Arthur Taylor, asserted that there were no records available for the queens regnant, this was far from true. As well as secondary sources in Strype's *Ecclesiastical Memorials* of 1721 and others for the coronation of Mary I, there were 'in the College of Arms the original records of the entire ceremonies of her coronation etc, and in the Library of the Society of Antiquaries a ms programme drawn up immediately previous to the event'.[26] It in no way diminishes Planché's achievements to point out that, like many of his contemporaries, his discoveries lay close to the surface. The documents in his *Regal Records* relating to the coronations of Mary Tudor, Elizabeth, Mary II and Anne, 'of which the greater part is now for the first time printed', had been hiding in plain sight.[27] Where Planché, like his fellow antiquaries, was original was not so much in the answers he found but in the questions he asked.

Victoria, however, was crowned on 28 June 1838 without antiquarian ceremony, having been advised by Lord Melbourne to simplify the occasion as much as possible. This was no time for ostentatious expenditure, or to awaken recollections of the spectacular pageantry that surrounded the crowning of George IV. Accordingly, the Earl Marshal, the Queen's Champion, the throwing down of the gauntlet and the presentation of the mess of dilligrout were all dropped, as was the Coronation Banquet. Instead of a slap-up feast for the nobility, a simpler, more modern procession saw the new queen driven along a two-mile route from Buckingham Palace to Westminster Abbey past crowds a million strong, demonstrating that all her people, of whatever rank or means, could see her and share in the celebrations of the day. The Penny Coronation, as it was soon known, divided public opinion along predictable lines. Tories and Romantics were outraged. Lord Londonderry called this disregard for 'time-honoured and time-consecrated' rituals an attack on the monarchy.[28] Whigs and Utilitarians thought it entirely sensible. Among the objectors, however, the muttering grew to a grumbling, and in time there emerged a collective determination to do something to counter the cut-price Whigs in the proper spirit of the olden times. It was nineteen years since *Ivanhoe* was published, and Scott's drama of knights and maidens had been depicted in art and illustration, adapted, many times over, for the stage and shaped the imaginations of a generation of children now coming to adulthood. So it was, as Mark Girouard writes, 'inevitable' that somebody, sooner or later, would stage a full-scale medieval tournament.[29] That person was Archibald Montgomerie, 13th Earl of Eglinton.

SCOTLAND THE PICTURESQUE

The story of the Eglinton Tournament, which took place on the earl's Ayrshire estate in August 1839, has been told often and usually for comic effect. Over 100,000 people, mostly in medieval costume, managed to reach this remote spot where Salvin's former mentor, John Paterson, had built Lord Eglinton's father a Gothic castle in 1797. It strongly resembled a symmetrical bow-fronted manor house with four fat, round towers at the corners and some hefty battlements on its head, like a Georgian house in medieval fancy dress – which was, in the circumstances, appropriate. Attendees came from all over the world, from Calcutta, Copenhagen and Rio de Janeiro, and still today souvenirs of the tournament are highly prized. Despite this there is little mention of it in the antiquaries' correspondence. There are several likely reasons. Some of them would have regarded it as absurd, Lingard for one. The more scholarly may well have felt that it showed a naïve and somewhat dated approach to the Middle Ages. What the omission unquestionably demonstrates, however, is the social position of the antiquary. The active participants in the tournament were aristocratic and wealthy. Rank trumped even politics and several of the grander Whigs, including Lord and Lady Breadalbane, took part. Lord Glenlyon, who appeared as the Knight of Gael, was not untypical in spending £346 9s 6d on armour.[30] That figure comes from the bill he was sent by Samuel Pratt, an antique dealer who supplied Lord Eglinton with everything necessary for the tournament, from breastplates to marquees, out of his London premises in Lower Grosvenor Street. Pratt knew Meyrick, often acting for him as an agent in his collecting activities, and there was a copy of Meyrick's *Critical Inquiry into Antient Armour* in Lord Eglinton's library which he studied carefully while planning the tournament. Edward Jerningham, another of the knights who took part, travelled to Scotland from his Norfolk home, Costessey Hall, the imposing Gothic house designed for the Catholic Jerninghams by Buckler, with its chapel in which the glass had been arranged by Milner. This was the antiquary's position in relation to the upper classes, filling a variety of supporting roles, sometimes directly employed, never quite a social equal, like Scott's Oldbuck: 'the country gentlemen were generally above him in fortune', even if they were not always 'beneath him in intellect'.[31]

At last, after months of preparation, a dress rehearsal was organized in front of a hand-picked gathering of 2,690 guests. All was ready for the great day when, as on many days in Ayrshire, it rained torrentially. Knights and maidens, the Queen of Beauty, the Marshal of the Lists and all the spectators squelched home, soggy and disappointed. Yet the tournament was not a complete flop. It lives on in myth and history and it had an immediate influence on art, on architecture and, before long, on Queen Victoria herself. Among those who returned from the tournament muddy but unbowed was the 2nd Marquis of Breadalbane. His own castle, Taymouth in Perthshire, was at its core ancient, but the original tower house had been expanded and modernized until it did not look nearly old enough. A year before, the Breadalbanes had called in Gillespie Graham, now the default architect to the Scottish landowning classes, and he in turn brought in his young friend Pugin. Between them, over the next five years, they gave the Breadalbanes a home that presented a more up-to-date version of history. Pugin used his own sketches and a quantity of historic carvings to design glamorously dark oak interiors, highlighted here and there with gilding. There was a grand Banner Hall for entertaining and a more gently Romantic and contemplative library. Work went on at an increasingly frenetic pace until, by 1842, all was ready. As Asa Briggs wrote in *The Age of Improvement*, 'there was no gloomier year in the whole nineteenth century'. Britain was in a state of unrest and 'distress', strikes and riots, and agitation to repeal the Corn Laws and rise up against the 'bread-taxing oligarchy' of landowners was rife.[32] It was at this moment that the queen and Prince Albert decided to make their first tour to Scotland.

The queen was insistent that this was to be a private visit, just a 'little trip' with Albert, 'without pomp or parade'.[33] That was never going to be possible. The extent to which it became a political and social event of epic proportions is conveyed by Thomas Dick Lauder, who followed the royal party at every step and wrote a monumental and cloyingly sycophantic account of it, which is nevertheless rich in useful detail. In the background to his grand panorama were the politics. Victoria and Albert were accompanied by the prime minister, Robert Peel, who was hoping to improve the Tories' personal relations with the queen while snubbing the Radical councillors of Edinburgh, who booed his carriage, and flattering the Tories of Perth. Press coverage of the tour was mixed. *The Times* reported with indignation on the hostility displayed by Edinburgh Council and was unimpressed by the attitude of the Church of Scotland. It noted that, despite the union, the Scots were still full of 'bigotry'.[34] This was the Scotland of Radicalism, Knox and the Kirk. It was also the Scotland of the Lowlands. That other Scotland, so carefully nurtured by Scott among his vast reading public, was to be found among the Highlanders, who, *The Times* noted, were 'loyal and faithful representatives of the old Scottish cavaliers'.[35] The current Scottish cavaliers were happy to fulfil expectations, and as the royal couple progressed through Perthshire from one aristocratic house to another 'a vision of tartan feudalism unfolded' which reached its climax in their reception at Taymouth.[36]

Victoria and Albert's carriage approached the castle towards dusk, and as it came in sight a band of pipers struck up the Highland salute. Amid the 'huge forms and swarthy features of the Lochaber-axemen who surrounded her', Lady Breadalbane cut an 'elegant and sylph-like figure' as she came out to greet the queen and present her with sprigs of Highland myrtle, 'the badge of the clan Campbell'. As the royal party entered the house, 'two Admiralty bargemen stood ready' to lower the Breadalbane flag and raise the Royal Standard amid wild cheers from the large crowd on the lawn. Meanwhile from the Fort, a folly 'high up among the towering woods', a royal salute was 'blazing away ... and two batteries in the valley below were answering it, producing one continued roar of thunder all around the hills'.[37] It was Scotland the Picturesque at full throttle. The Highlanders' arms glinted 'in the sober light of evening, which was already embrowning the wooded hills in front of the castle, from whose face successive flashes of the red artillery were pouring, – whilst their summits were half veiled by the curling smoke dispersing itself over them!'.[38] It was 'the finest thing' the queen had seen in Scotland and she fully grasped the historic references. As she wrote in her journal: 'It seemed as if a great chieftain in old and feudal times was receiving his sovereign.'[39] She admired the 'newly and exquisitely furnished' parts of the house, choosing to make Pugin's library her private sitting room during her stay.[40] The highlight of the visit was a ball in the magnificent new Banner Hall, where Victoria showed herself a spritely dancer, sporting a sash in Royal Stuart tartan.[41]

Tartan had by now been a fashion for years, amounting, as the French press had remarked, to an international craze. The Scottish manufacturers did good business. Tartan had not, however, been a subject of much historical study until this moment. It was in 1842, by no coincidence at all, that the Sobieski Stuarts decided to publish their dubious 'manuscript' as a lavishly illustrated volume. The *Vestiarium Scoticum* was presented as an antiquarian work containing previously unpublished material on the history of Scottish dress. The Breadalbanes, naturally, bought a copy to put in their Gothic library. The Preface is cast in familiar antiquarian terms. The work aspires to fill 'that vacancy in Scottish Archaeologia' where the Scots could boast of nothing comparable to the accounts of French and English costume in the works of Montfaucon and Strutt.[42] The editorial method is explained: one manuscript has been 'collated with the transcript of another in the library of the Monastery of St Augustine in Cadiz'.[43] The material (vellum), the size and script ('small black-letter quarto') and the provenance (from the 'historian and faithful adherent of Queen Mary, John Lesly bishop of Ross' who signed this copy) are all laid out.[44] Variants are noted, dating is attempted by 'the use of several words ... which were obsolete a considerable period before the reign of queen Mary' and garments such as the 'Craccow' or 'English hood' which were not common in Scotland before 1470.[45] Readers are referred to Camden and supporting documents cited, including those 'in the possession of the late Mr Robert Watson, well known in the history of the Stuart papers'.[46] The absence of any previous such detailed account of Highland costume is attributed to the lack of interest in 'manners and customs' among earlier antiquaries. The original manuscript, by Sir Richard Urquhart, would have been regarded in its time, Sobieski Stuart suggests, much as 'Lingard ... might have valued the pattern-book of a Manchester traveller'.[47] There is perhaps, in that glancing blow at one of the most rigorous and sceptical of living historians, a hint that all is not quite as it seems, but overall it would be difficult for the common reader of 1842 to recognize in this magnificent volume anything very different from Planché's study of unpublished material on historic coronations.

Ten years after Scott's death had liberated them from close scrutiny, John and Charles Sobieski Stuart, as they now were, had established a reputation as antiquaries such that by 1842 they were felt to have been 'long and honourably distinguished for their devotion to the Antiquities of the Gael'.[48] Indeed, they contributed notes to the posthumous Abbotsford edition of the *Waverley* novels. It was not until 1980 that the *Vestiarium Scoticum* was conclusively proved to be a total fake, and its long success reflects its appeal to the essence of Romantic antiquarian sensibility, the combination of the historic with the personal. It wove the individual into the wider fabric of history, all but literally, by promoting two false ideas: firstly that families had distinct tartan patterns associated with their names, and secondly that tartan had been worn throughout Scotland, not only in the Highlands. The *Vestiarium* claimed indeed that tartan had once been the dress of most of northern Europe, surviving last among the Highlanders, who, 'aboriginal and unmixed, isolated in their society, and tenacious in their manners ... retained it unchanged when it was lost among others'.[49] Tartan, was, by this account, ancient, Romantic, and at the same time available to everyone in personal family forms. It also represented a system, it was codified as well as individualistic, and this combination, as the last Georgians became the Victorians, was attractive. The quest for 'reality' meant a preference for facts, which, however Romantic, should also be organized and systematic. The myth of the clan tartans was perfectly calculated to appeal to the spirit of the new age.

The queen was delighted with the *Vestiarium Scoticum*. The fact that the author and his brother went about claiming the right to her throne and were in the habit of flying the Royal Standard from their rowing boat seems not to have given her pause. She ordered her own copy at once, thereby delighting the Scottish press, who congratulated John Sobieski Stuart on producing 'a work ... worthy of a place in the royal library'.[50] So began the royal family's love affair with all things Scottish, an enthusiasm which continues to this day. Victoria became an important patron of the tartan manufacturers and her family and household were soon kitted out with 'Victoria' and 'Albert' tartans. The royal visit was thus part of that 'resurgence of aristocratic paternalism' in Scotland which played its part in the latest, post-*Waverley* version of the Scottish sense of national identity.[51] It was consummated soon afterwards with Victoria and Albert's purchase of the Balmoral estate, on which the royal couple duly built their own Romantic castle and the age of Balmorality was born.

WE HIS SERVANTS WILL ARISE
AND BUILD

Minds do not change with the monarch, and if much of what we now mean by 'Victorian' – the attitudes of mind, the aesthetics, ethics and politics – were detectable in William IV's reign, it was only after the 1830s that they developed to the point where they might be said to represent the ethos of the age. It was in about 1841 that, as Carlyle put it, the times began to 'crystallise themselves'.[52] Pevsner, considering that year from the point of view of architectural history, called it the 'annus mirabilis in the story of the Gothic Revival in England'.[53] Pugin published his *The True Principles of Pointed or Christian Architecture*, which set out a doctrine of truth to materials and functional design. He also completed the Church of Our Lady and St Wilfred at Warwick Bridge in Cumbria, commissioned by the Catholic antiquary Henry Howard of Naworth. This was the building which for Pevsner marked the peak of that gradual progress whereby a coherent Gothic architecture emerged: 'It is here and more or less precisely in 1841', he wrote, 'that archaeological accuracy begins in English church design.'[54] Truth, integrity, reality, the moral virtues Pugin had proclaimed in *Contrasts* in 1836, were now manifesting as architecture and, significantly, church architecture. As the country house had been the great Georgian building type, so the Victorians' pre-eminent achievement was to be the parish church. There had been many new churches since the establishment of the Church Building Commission in 1818. They varied in style and even more in quality. 'Commissioners Gothic' was by now a pejorative term among the architecturally well informed. If new churches were to address what Carlyle called the 'condition of England' question, to bring a sense of permanence and solidity to the sprawling cities, they had to have gravitas, the weight of history, that 'archaeological accuracy' that antiquary-architects in general, and Pugin more than any other, possessed.

It was also in 1841 that Robert Willis, now Jacksonian Professor of Natural and Experimental Philosophy at Cambridge University, completed his series of lectures to the university's Philosophical Society on the construction of medieval vaults. Willis, arguably the first and 'probably the greatest' architectural historian England produced, brought a breadth of reference and depth of knowledge to the subject that revolutionized it.[55] As his nephew later wrote, Willis 'treated a building as he treated a machine: he took it to pieces; he pointed out what was structural and what was decorative, what was imitated and what was original; and how the most complex forms of mediaeval invention might be reduced to simple elements'.[56] Willis, with his mechanical approach to construction, was an antiquary for the Steam Age, harbinger of a new world of academic specialization and professionalism. To Willis's engineering Pugin added the emotional and moral imperative. That year he published a second edition of *Contrasts* in which he greatly expanded (and partly contradicted) the argument of the first. He also included two new plates, destined to rank among the most famous images of Victorian Britain. In the first he compared the 'Catholic town of 1440', with its spires and towers, its open road, wide bridge and comfortable houses, with 'The same town in 1840'. Here the spires are broken. Around them furnaces smoke, a panopticon prison squats on the riverbank and a toll booth controls the bridge. In the other new plate, 'Contrasted Residences of the Poor', a medieval monastic hospital, based on St Cross in Winchester, embodies dignity and charity, while the modern workhouse, another panopticon, punishes and degrades the poor in life and, after death, sends them off in wooden boxes 'for dissection'. The argument was not merely rhetorical. The Utilitarian panopticon and the Catholic monastery were each the built expressions of the world view of their creators. This argument – that buildings speak not only of the style of the age that created them, they also embody its spirit – marked another step in the theory of historical consciousness.

By 1841 it was plain to antiquaries and non-antiquaries alike that the British landscape had been radically transformed since the days when the Georgians went sightseeing down the Wye Valley. Now, as Carlyle wrote, 'The picturesque Tourist, in a sunny autumn day' travelling through 'the bounteous realm of England, descries the union Workhouse in his path ... all Lancashire and Yorkshire, and how many other shires and counties, with their machineries and industries ... [are] flaming with steam fires and useful labour ... towards the stars'.[57] In Gage's newly published *Chronica Jocelini de Brakelonda* Carlyle found the ideal text to give his argument narrative and rhetorical force. Like Pugin, he invoked comparison with medieval society as a corrective to the present, borrowing Willson's image: 'out of old Books, new Writings'.[58] Carlyle was one of those who liked to have his antiquarianism both ways, sneering at 'Dryasdust' Dugdale and 'Giant Pedantry' while using the antiquaries' material. Nevertheless, he acknowledged Gage, praising his attention to details such as his inclusion of the mistakes in Jocelin's 'Monk-Latin' and the provision of an index and not too many footnotes.[59] The *Chronica* describes the community at Bury St Edmunds without sentiment. It tells of arguments, inefficiency and financial irregularities, all that makes up the essential antiquarian subject, 'manners and customs'. It gave Carlyle the sense that twelfth-century England was 'a green solid place' inhabited by real people, where 'we look into a pair of eyes deep as

our own'.[60] The monastery was a community rich in 'true social vital-
ity' based on 'Nature and Fact not Redtape ... and cash payment'.[61]
It had 'reality', the wisdom of an era which had 'no telescopes but
[had] better eyes' than the nineteenth century, for all its 'hustings ...
and enlightened free press'.[62]

Thus, as the Victorian age took shape, the streams of antiquarian
thought and practice that had run down from the Reformation began
to flow into the broader current of national life. In 1839 the Cambridge Camden Society, named for William Camden, was founded by
a group of undergraduates. Prominent among them was John Mason
Neale (1818–66), whose great passion was for medieval churches. He
began to see how their form could be interpreted, as he had been
taught to interpret scripture, in terms of symbolism and typology.
This led to another signal development of 1841, the launch of the
society's magazine, *The Ecclesiologist*. 'Ecclesiology' is defined by the
OED firstly as 'the study of churches, especially church building and
decoration', and secondly 'Theology as applied to the nature and
structure of the Christian Church'. Though derived from the Greek
ekklesia, 'ecclesiology' was a neologism coined by Neale and his
friends and it was an attempt to resolve the antiquaries' old dilemma:
how to reconcile a love of Gothic architecture with loyalty to the
post-Reformation dispensation. There was of course nothing new
about the study of churches as buildings, or the use of their records
and monuments as source material, or an interest in the history of the
Church as an institution. These had all had been antiquarian subjects
for centuries and, since 1789 at least, antiquaries had expressed strong
views about the treatment of historic fabric. The Cambridge Camden
Society did all of this but, in addition, it promoted in the 'science' of
ecclesiology – there was much emphasis placed on its being a science – a
set of principles and rules based on medieval precedent, for the correct ordering of churches and applicable equally to new and old
buildings.

The font, Neale explained, should be by the door, to symbolize the
beginning of the Christian life. From here the arrangement of the
church as a whole should lead the eye and the mind towards the altar.
From the nave, which represents this life, the transition to the sacred
space of the chancel is marked by the rood, symbolizing Christ's death

and resurrection. 'Thus beautifully does the plan of a church hang together.'[63] A church on this model was certainly true to medieval precedent, and this had theological implications. In Georgian churches the dominating feature was usually the pulpit. By shifting the focus towards the sanctuary and the altar, the ecclesiologists were implying a shift from the Gospel of the Word, on which Protestantism was based, towards a more sacramental form of worship centred on the mystery of the eucharist. In just what that mystery consists, whether it is a symbolic ritual or an actual transubstantiation of bread and wine into the body and blood of Christ, was one of the central points of dispute at the Reformation and it remains a doctrinal difference between Protestant and Catholic theologies. So the charge of 'popery', levelled against antiquaries since Raleigh's day, was soon brought against the Cambridge Camden Society by those who saw it as a Trojan horse full of propaganda for High Church or even Roman Catholic doctrine. Willis, one the society's founding vice-presidents, resigned in protest against the tendency 'in some quarters ... to convert the Society into an engine of polemical theology, instead of an instrument for promoting the study and the practice of Ecclesiastical Architecture'.[64]

Many more people, however, responded to what was an essentially Romantic conception. The ecclesiologists were, like Pugin and Milner before him, combining the physical and the metaphysical. What a church looked like was also what it meant. It was Coleridge's theory of the living symbol made Christian. Ecclesiology appealed because it was both spiritual and factual. Like tartan it combined romance with a checkable system and was thus ideally suited to the Victorian cast of mind. Membership of the Cambridge Camden Society rose from eighty to 180 within a year, and by 1841 the original group of undergraduates had been joined by sixteen bishops and thirty-one peers and MPs. Their influence was felt on a national scale as the society began to address the often parlous state of historic parish churches. Between ignorance, negligence and the Georgians' confident belief in improvement, medieval churches had suffered many indignities. Some were little better cared for than in the days when Stothard applied his nail-brush to the whitewashed tombs in Kent. Old churches were often damp, and parishioners who could afford it had private box pews in which they sat round four sides facing one another through the immensely long sermons of those days. Curtains were not infrequently raised above the pew to keep out draughts, stoves were installed and rent was paid to ensure exclusive use for the proprietors. Much less consideration was shown to the building. Three-decker pulpits obscured altars. The dreaded draughts were dealt with in some cases by bricking up the chancel arch and in others by stovepipes running along an aisle and pushed out through the nearest exterior point, even if that was the medieval west window. A drawing of the Duke of Wellington at the Norman Church of St Mary in Walmer, Kent, which he attended in his capacity as Warden of the Cinq Ports, shows him seated, in splendid isolation, on a dining-room chair in the aisle. A vast pulpit looms over him and behind the preacher, in the south wall, a wide sash window has been inserted, complete with curtains and a pelmet.

If the ecclesiologists dwelled on such atrocities – and they undoubtedly exaggerated their scale and number for their own campaigning purposes – the problems were real. Neale addressed them in two pamphlets of 1841 under the title *A Few Words to Church Wardens on Churches and Church Ornaments*. These offered practical advice about curing damp by preventing earth from piling up around the exterior and tips on how to remove whitewash from medieval wall paintings. Neale made aesthetic suggestions as to the inadvisability of attempting to make gas pipes 'showy and gay' by having them 'in the shape of snakes' twirling down the nave or of cheering up a dark church by painting the pillars yellow or touching up the monuments with lamp black.[65] Where more complicated repairs to medieval tracery were needed, he urged, with an audible intake of breath, never to trust a country mason but 'to send an account of the window' with a drawing if possible 'to the Camden Society at Cambridge'.[66] 'In a church,' he explained, 'every thing should be real and good.'[67] The second instalment of *A Few Words to Church Wardens* lists the patrons of the society, beginning with the Archbishop of Canterbury and running down through the Duke of Northumberland, the Lord Chancellor of England and the Regius Professor of Divinity. By 1842 the first *Few Words* had gone through eleven editions and the balance of power had completely reversed from the days when Gough took on Bishop Barrington. The Church, the State and, increasingly, the architects were with the antiquaries. Pugin had already built St Chad's

Birmingham, the first new English cathedral since St Paul's. Soon his contemporary George Gilbert Scott was startled out of his drab practice building Union workhouses by the 'thunder' of Pugin's writings, 'like a person awakened from a long feverish dream, which had rendered him unconscious of what was going on about him'.[68] Scott became the great Victorian church architect. His St Giles Camberwell opened in 1844, to be followed by hundreds of other Gothic churches, by him and others. 'Few changes in our history can have been more sudden, more rapid, and more complete', Thomas Mozley, John Henry Newman's brother-in-law reflected later, 'than that from the Greek and Roman styles in church building to ... the mediaeval.'[69]

The belief that in a Gothic church, of any date, the spiritual meaning of Christianity was embodied sank deep into the national psyche. The building was to be respected and any minister who wished to be on good terms with his congregation was now almost bound to start repairing the roof, introducing red baize, open pews and free seats. There were those, like George Eliot, who regretted the 'dear, old, brown, crumbling, picturesque inefficiency', the box pews and the three-decker pulpits.[70] If they regretted the damp, the damage or the insanitary burial vaults, they mentioned it less. But the ecclesiologists had other, more determined enemies. Those who thought they smelt a whiff of incense about the Cambridge Camden Society were in no way reassured by events at Oxford, where the Tractarian Movement was leading a national debate on the status of the English Church since the Reformation. 'The effect of the Tractarian agitation' began, as George Eliot recalled, to be felt even in 'backward provincial regions'.[71] Thus the somewhat flustered country parson felt the need not only to unblock his chancel arch and repair his windows, but to brush up his theology. The Oxford Movement, as it was also known, provided 'ample friction of the clerical mind'.[72]

RELIGION, FATHERLAND AND ART

The age that began to crystallize in the early 1840s reached its High Victorian apogee a decade later in the Crystal Palace. The intervening years saw the antiquaries' cause gain ground on some fronts while stalling on others. New organizations and new ways of organizing people and ideas were emerging. The Institute of British Architects received its royal charter in the year of Victoria's accession. In 1841 the Wiltshire Topographical Society and the Shakespeare Society and in 1844 the British Archaeological Association were among the new bodies which took some of the central subjects of antiquarian enquiry in new directions. In the case of the BAA, the substitution of 'archaeological' for 'antiquarian' was significant. By the 1840s it was the more attractive term. In addition to the general opprobrium antiquarianism had always attracted, the Society of Antiquaries was felt by many to have slipped so far from the centre of the debate as to be, as John Britton wrote in 1850, in the grip of 'a long and morbid fit of apathy and uselessness ... constitutionally unfitted to administer to the reasonable demands of the majority of its fellows'.[73] Gage's sudden death in 1842 considerably undermined its intellectual and social standing. Moreover, an Archaeological Association suited better the ethos of the new reign, it sounded more serious and systematic, marking another step towards specialization, professionalization and gentility. That this was not to be an entirely smooth transition was indicated by the rapid and bitter split in the BAA which resulted in the creation of a new body, the Archaeological Institute, of which Britton was not a member. His was not the only case in which veterans of the somewhat improvisational Georgian days found there was no room for them in the more efficient world of the Victorians. Others seized the opportunities it offered. In 1837 Frederic Madden became keeper of manuscripts at the British Museum and the following year Dawson Turner's son-in-law and some-time collaborator, Francis Palgrave, became Deputy Keeper of the Public Records. The spirit of the changing age was bringing recognition to the antiquaries, taking up some of their central areas of interest and, in the process, absorbing and transforming them. Antiquaries were becoming archaeologists, architects, civil servants.

Conservation campaigns of the modern kind became more common and overall they were more successful, although the ecclesiologists failed to stop Charles Barry destroying the remains of St Stephen's Chapel at the Palace of Westminster. It had in substantial part survived the fire, but it was in the way of Barry's own design and he had it demolished with ruthless speed. It was a pyrrhic victory, earning Barry the enmity of the rising generation and marking him out as yesterday's man. [74] At York, where the choir of the Minster had been badly damaged in 1829 in an arson attack, a twelve-year restoration programme was carried out under the auspices of Robert Smirke and, after 1840, by his son Sydney. It generated huge public interest and the succession of pamphlets, official minutes and open letters thrown up by the inevitable controversies demonstrate how complete was the reverse since Wyatt's day. Respectful restoration and care for historic fabric were coming to be the expected standard, although in exactly what that might consist was often a matter of debate, then as now. The work at York cost £90,000, probably the most expensive restoration project to date. In the course of it Robert Smirke uncovered the twelfth-century crypt. This and Pevsner's praise in *The Buildings of England* for Sydney Smirke's 'skilful' restoration of the Chapter House are among the cases that should be borne in mind when 'the Victorians' are unthinkingly accused of ruining buildings which would, in truth, have been lost without them. [75]

Yet while these individual campaigns were increasingly successful, the idea of state protection for historic monuments remained anathema to the British. Parliament continued to resist successive attempts by antiquaries to interfere, as MPs saw it, with the rights of private property. Matters were very different on the Continent. Britton, writing in 1840, argued that

> France ... has set us an example which our ambition, or our shame, will, at no distant time, induce us to imitate. The Monarch has commanded the Minister of the Interior to appoint an 'Historical Committee on the Arts and Monuments'; one object of which is to obtain good accounts, with drawings, of all the public edifices of the country; and appropriate funds are granted to preserve or renovate the best of them. This is true patriotism, worthy an enlightened country. [76]

Enlightenment did not dawn on Britton's side of the Channel, however, for another half-century.

In other ways too, the international scene had rearranged itself since the 1830s. Railways, the electric telegraph and the rotary printing press all speeded up communications. Antiquaries in Britain and

France could keep one another regularly up to date. The French counterpart of *The Ecclesiologist* was Adolphe-Napoleon Didron's magazine the *Annales archéologiques*, which began publication in 1844. Didron, a journalist, stained-glass artist, dealer in antiquities and Secretary to the Commission des monuments historiques, offered a platform to architects, most notably Viollet-le-Duc, to oppose the view of the still all-powerful Académie française, that while the study of historic architecture was valuable, imitation of the medieval was unnecessary and wrong in principle. Viollet did not argue for Gothic as uniquely Christian. That case could never be made in a country that had remained Catholic throughout the seventeenth and eighteenth centuries and had seen the style of its church buildings develop in step with the rest of its architecture. Instead he argued for it as originally French, and therefore correct and patriotic.

Yet while the British, who now accepted that they had not invented the pointed arch, embraced the Gothic as a national style, the French, despite the arguments of Viollet, the invocations of Chateaubriand and Hugo and the popularity of Walter Scott, did not. There were few new buildings in the medieval style and none of significance. In France the Gothic was celebrated chiefly for its technical ingenuity. Restorations under the auspices of the Commission were carried out, often by Viollet, on the Rationalist principles set out by the Jesuit antiquaries and the encyclopaedists Jean-Louis de Cordemoy and Marc-Antoine Laugier. They proposed a theoretical basis for 'correct' Gothic. French restorations accordingly sought to even out those qualities the British most admired, the higgledy-piggledy Picturesque. Victor Hugo, in his eulogy of Notre-Dame, praises its technical precision rather than its engaging asymmetry: 'What we say here about the façade may be said of the whole church and what we say of the cathedral church of Paris may be said of all the churches of Christendom in the Middle Ages. Everything has its place in this self-generated art, logical and well proportioned. To measure the big toe, is to measure the giant.'[77] Thus in France the ravages of time, war, revolution and neglect were not only restored, they were 'corrected' to conform to logical principles of construction. Despite such differences of approach the lively and largely respectful exchange of ideas between Britain and France continued. Didron knew and liked Pugin. Visiting him in England, he so far forgot himself at Lincoln Cathedral as to prefer the sculpture to that of Rheims.

France and Britain were still at the forefront of the antiquarian quest for the Gothic, but they were no longer alone. Among Gage's papers is a flyer from the Royal Society of Northern Antiquaries, based in Copenhagen. Its president was August William Schlegel (1767–1845), now an old man, but in his youth one of the protagonists of German Romanticism, the brother of Friedrich, friend of Herder and of Schiller, and author of what are still often regarded as the best German translations of Shakespeare. Thus in the 1840s Romantic antiquarianism began in a sense to return to its source with the originators of *Sturm und Drang*. The German Gothic Revival of the early nineteenth century was a poetic, scholarly affair and, with the group of painters around Johann Friedrich Overbeck (1789–1869) who called themselves the Nazarenes, an artistic one. The 'slow ebb and flow of stylistic change in the royal academies', lack of private patronage and the long-established preference for the Classical all militated against any revival of medieval architecture.[78] In 1840, however, with the accession of Frederick William IV, Prussia at last had 'a romantic on the throne' and in the annus mirabilis of 1841 a group of artists and antiquaries in Cologne formed the Zentral-Dombau-Verein, a union committed to the most ambitious antiquarian project of all: the completion of the city's unfinished Gothic cathedral.[79] Soon *The Ecclesiologist* and the *Annales archéologiques* acquired a German counterpart in the *Kölner Domblatt*.

Work on the cathedral had stopped in 1528, when the Reformation knocked the bottom out of the lucrative pilgrimage trade that began when Archbishop Rainald von Dassel brought the relics of the Magi to Cologne in 1164, drawing thousands of the faithful to the city. The new building had been begun in 1264. Over the intervening years there had been many calls to complete it. Friedrich von Schlegel had hailed it as a national monument. Yet in the 1840s it stood as it had for more than three centuries, complete in some parts, temporarily roofed in others, with a builder's crane still in place over one of the west towers. It was a local antiquary, Sulpiz Boisserée, who took the first practical steps. In 1808 he began on his life's work, a series of measured drawings of the cathedral as it stood, accomplished with the help of the draughtsman and antiquary Georg Möller. Boisserée found a number of medieval plans which he believed reflected the intentions of the first architect of the cathedral, Meister Gerhard, as well as a later elevation drawing of the west front.[80] By dint of comparison with Strasbourg and other records in Cologne he produced a plan for completion. In 1813 he submitted his study and proposals to the then Crown Prince Friedrich Wilhelm, who was so moved and excited by them he couldn't sleep for three nights. But the country was at war. After 1815 Boisserée pressed on, persuading Goethe to support his campaign. The great Prussian architect Karl Schinkel came to examine the cathedral and in the 1820s under Schinkel's auspices work to restore the medieval fabric began. Meanwhile Boisserée travelled around France trying to raise funds to publish his *magnum opus*, the *Domwerk*, a study showing the cathedral as it would look, according to his researches, if it were finished. Finally, with Friedrich's accession, Boisserée's persistence was rewarded. On 4 September 1842 the king laid the first stone. From then on work continued until October 1880 when, 652 years and two months after it was begun, Cologne's Gothic cathedral was complete.

It was a project to inspire and excite any antiquary. Progress was keenly watched by the British, whose example in turn encouraged the Germans. In 1845 the editor of the *Domblatt*, the Catholic lawyer August Reichensperger, published *Die Christlich-germanische Baukunst and ihr Verhältniss zur Gegenwart*. Much influenced by Pugin, it was an appeal to German architects to build in the Gothic style, but first to undertake a thorough study of the Middle Ages, its architecture and its social structures. Germany had to make up for lost time. In 1846 Reichensperger set off for England, sailing directly to Ramsgate, where Pugin lived. The visit, the first of four, made a great impression on Reichensperger, and through him on Germany. In the 'fresh and energetic essence' of England he found something 'fundamentally Germanic' – in fact, he added, he felt more thoroughly German in England than he did in Cologne, where academic orthodoxy stifled the true national character.[81] This was to be the mid-century ethos of Gothic. The British, French and Germans all felt it was in some way their own, a national style which at the same time represented an ideal that transcended nationalism. So the horizon of the antiquarian landscape expanded to meet the new age.

A Change of Dynasty in the Historic Realm

History begins in novel and ends in essay.
Thomas Babington Macaulay, 1828

It will not do, Macaulay does not write history.
Lingard on Macaulay's The History of England
from the Accession of James the Second, *1848*

By the later 1840s the shadows were lengthening. The Romantic view of history as a lived relationship with the past had had its day, or nearly so. That imaginative flexibility which made possible 'the tolerable deception' of Scott's well at Abbotsford or Meyrick's Edwardian castle seemed unsatisfactory to the age that crystallized around 1841. Ambiguity, a positive pleasure for many of the Georgians, made the Victorians uneasy. Theirs would not be an age noted for irony. They wanted clarity, reality and scientific organization. History was on the move again.

Walter Scott had seen the early signs. In 1830 he suffered a stroke. Sensing that his own life was entering its final phase, he wrote what became in effect an elegy for the age of Romantic antiquarianism. *Reliquiae Trotcosienses* was left unfinished when he died, after a series of further strokes, two years later and remained unpublished until 2004.[1] *Reliquiae Trotcosienses: Or, the Gabions of the Late Jonathan Oldbuck Esq. of Monkbarns*, to give its full title, is a *jeu d'esprit*, a short text saturated with Scott's delight in ironizing antiquarian habits. The title, which means, 'of the relics of Trotcosey', refers back to Oldbuck's home in *The Antiquary*, built on land that had belonged to the Abbey of Trotcosey, a Scottish term for a hooded cape in which the wearer can trot, cosily, like a monk in a habit. The convoluted title was perhaps a tease to Thomas Dick Lauder, whom Scott had warned off the Sobieski Stuarts on the grounds of their 'false Latin', while the idea of antiquities as 'gabions' was borrowed from Henry Adamson's elegy of 1638, *The Muses Threnodie*.

Beyond the curious title the short text is arranged in three volumes, like a miniature novel, and Scott amuses himself with mock-scholarly attempts to define his gabions before concluding that they are 'curiosities' of little or no intrinsic value. The prevailing mood is one of melancholy. The curiosities belonged to 'the late' Oldbuck. Scott's fictional alter ego is dead. Before he died Oldbuck asked a friend to write about his collection, but the friend refused, as Scott had earlier refused to write about Abbotsford, on the grounds that it would be ridiculous: 'Remember the fate of Woodward who brought every wit in London upon his head by his antiquarian essays.'[2] What we are presented with instead is the account Oldbuck himself left of his collection, yet the narrator explicitly distinguishes himself from Oldbuck. Who is this, then, who has transferred the gabions to his own home and now takes the reader on a tour of it? The person and the persona are breaking down, fragmenting with Scott's own mind. Oldbuck survives through his antiquities but they depend on his explanation to speak to posterity, their meaning resides in association, 'in the name of the persons to whom they have belonged, or the account of the deeds in which they have been employed'.[3] On the tour of the gabions the reader follows the speaker through the memory theatre of Scott's home, pausing at significant points. Gradually the fiction falls away. The characters who emerge are Scott's own friends and acquaintances, the donors or makers of his collection and his own antiquarian feats: 'Before I quit the hall I ought to say that the end which terminates it upon the west or left side of the entrance is garnished with spoils from the immortal field of Waterloo, when I collected them in person very shortly after the immortal action.'[4] The repetition of 'immortal' is one moment when the reader is aware of Scott's failing concentration. In a final irony, after his death in 1832, Scott's son-in-law and executor John Lockhart decided that *Reliquiae* did indeed show its author in a poor light and declined to publish it.

Abbotsford was not entirely broken up – it survives today – but it was, as Scott predicted, much diminished by his absence. Without

43. Fools, from Douce's *Illustrations of Shakespeare*, 1807. Douce's attempts to set Shakespeare in a local medieval tradition attracted hostile reviews from Classicists.

44. 'Shakespeare's birthplace', the house in Henley Street, Stratford-upon-Avon, in 1858 before 're-edification'.

45. *Shakespeare and his Friends at the Mermaid Tavern*, 1850. An historically unlikely but Romantically apt gathering that places William Camden directly opposite the Bard.

46. *The Melée at the Eglinton Tournament*, 1839. The event itself was a washout, but it lived on in myth and history and contributed to the vision of Gothic Scotland.

47. Dancing by torchlight at Taymouth Castle, Perthshire, during Queen Victoria and Prince Albert's Scottish tour of 1842, which led to the purchase of Balmoral.

48. Victoria and Albert dressed as Queen Philippa and Edward III for their *bal costumé* of 12 May 1842.

49. Marie-Caroline, Duchesse de Berry, sailing to exile in Scotland after the July Revolution of 1830, depicted as Mary Queen of Scots.

50. 'Charles Edward Stuart', né Charles Allen, *c.*1802–80. Photographed *c.*1843–7.

51. *Le Cabinet d'Alexandre du Sommerard*. Du Sommerard's collection became the foundation of the Musée de Cluny, Paris.

52. 'Nell's New Home', 1840, by George Cattermole, an illustration for his friend Charles Dickens's *Old Curiosity Shop*. Cattermole, an antiquary himself, shows a realistically detailed medieval ruin, crudely adapted for domestic use.

53. *L'Abside de Notre-Dame de Paris*, 1854. The mutilated and neglected state of the cathedral was the spur for Victor Hugo's novel.

54 & 55. Victor Hugo (1802–85) with his son François-Victor. Hugo led the Romantics' campaign to restore France's Gothic architecture. In his apartment in Paris, and later in exile from 1855 to 1870 at Hauteville House on Guernsey (*right*), he took the concept of the romantic interior to operatic heights.

Scene on the Norwich and Cambridge Railway. 1836

56. John Gage (later Rokewode) (1786–1842) imagined by an unknown correspondent taking advantage of the Eastern Counties Railway. Incorporated in 1836 to build a line from London to Ipswich, in Gage's lifetime the railway got no further than Colchester.

57. Thomas Willement (1786–1871), 1845, herald, stained-glass designer and creator of the quintessential antiquarian interior at Davington Priory, Kent.

58. Stained glass at Davington showing Willement's arms and motto. In true Romantic fashion, he built his own history into the fabric of his home.

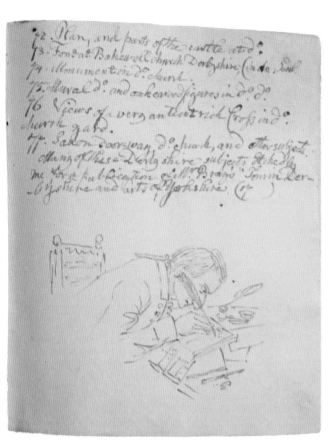

60. John Milner (1752–1826),
Catholic bishop, antiquary
and controversialist.

9. John Carter (1748–1817), self-portrait from a journal.
Draughtsman, journalist and collaborator with Milner,
Carter saved the Galilee Porch at Durham Cathedral from
emolition. It is now a World Heritage Site.

61. Samuel Rush Meyrick
(1783–1848), expert on
historic armour and
weaponry.

. Goodrich Court, Herefordshire, designed by Edward Blore in 1828 for his friend
eyrick. It housed at one time the most important collection of medieval and Renaissance
bjects in Britain.

63. Laying the cornerstone at Cologne Cathedral, 4 September 1842. The completion of the medieval cathedral 652 years after it was begun was the grandest of all Romantic antiquarian projects. The crane over the west tower had been *in situ* since building stopped in 1528.

64. The former chapel at the Hôtel de Cluny, badly vandalized in the Revolutionary years. Cluny was bought by the French state in 1842 and became a museum.

65. A. W. N. Pugin's Mediaeval Court at the Great Exhibition, 1851, embodied the Romantic reinvention of the past at the heart of the new Victorian ideal of 'reality'.

their magus the gabions were unstrung beads, and in the bright light of the new reign Scott's Romantic interior looked tired and trumpery. In 1838 one of his most devoted admirers, the nineteen-year-old John Ruskin, made a pilgrimage to Abbotsford with a view to writing an account of it. He was bitterly disappointed. The exterior was 'a jumble of jagged and flanky towers, ending in chimneys, and full of black slits with plaster mouldings, copied from Melrose, stuck all over it'.[5] The richly panelled library with its carved ceiling bosses was in reality plaster painted to look like wood, and the discrepancy between the scale of the house and its pretensions struck Ruskin as bathetic. 'We enter through a painted glass door into a hall about the size of merchantman's cabin, fitted up as if it were as large as the Louvre.'[6] Scott, he concluded, 'notwithstanding all his nonsense about moonlight at Melrose, had not the slightest feeling of the real beauty and application of Gothic architecture'.[7]

A more sympathetic evocation of the fading of Scott's vision was left by a French visitor old enough to remember the spirit of the departing age. In 1843 the Vicomte Walsh was accompanying the Comte de Chambord, *soi-disant* Henri V of France, on a tour of Britain. Born in 1820 after his father's death, Henri d'Artois, the son of the Duchesse de Berry, had been 'l'enfant du miracle'. He had 'reigned' in name at least for seven days during the July Revolution, which saw his mother flee to Scotland in the footsteps of Mary Queen of Scots. The adult Henri was a prosaic contrast to his romantic past, but when the royal party visited Abbotsford Walsh, watching the last Bourbon king wandering through the empty rooms, seemed to see a ghost surrounded by other ghosts, the fictional and the historic indiscriminately mingled:

> It was terrible weather, the snow and rain falling relentlessly, when Monseigneur arrived at Abbotsford; not a ray of sun on the home of the poet and novelist, the wind blowing through the evergreens that surround the house and shaking the long branches of the willows that weep on the waves of the lake . . . Walter Scott often described the sadness of abandoned houses, that of Abbotsford was worthy to be described by him . . .
>
> Monseigneur looked at everything with interest and emotion . . . genius having been there something remained . . . instead of the master

of the house, the young descendant of Robert the Strong could call up, beneath the vaults of the deserted rooms, Richard the Lionheart, Rebecca, Philippe-Auguste, Louis XI, Elizabeth, Amy Robsart, Mary Stuart ... Peveril of the Peak, Miss Vernon, the fair maid of Perth ... and many other figures which haunt Abbotsford like spirits.[8]

Despite his disappointment with Scott's house, Ruskin continued to read the *Waverley* novels, and Scott's literary reputation held up for the rest of the century and into the next. There were signs, however, that it too was beginning its steep decline. Carlyle, writing in the year of Ruskin's visit, put his finger deftly on the secret of Scott's success and the reason for its inevitable passing. His fictions were the product of their times, of 'an age at once destitute of faith and terrified at scepticism', an age easily beguiled by romance.[9] This was how the first Victorians saw their parents. As the rising generation looked forward, revived in faith and full of vigorous optimism, the world of *Waverley* began to look decadent, escapist, a 'fat beatific Lubberland where one can enjoy and do nothing'.[10] The historic scenes, once so convincing, started to look stagey, the characters just Georgian actors in doublets and farthingales. Carlyle understood this latest step in that fitful dawning of the sense of anachronism. All creations bear the stamp of their age and it will become plainer with the passage of time. This is a limitation only if the intention is to escape history, to impersonate another time. Shakespeare's 'mistakes', his indifference to period detail, allowed his work to become timeless, while Scott's plethora of historic accoutrements, the attempt to ventriloquize the past, weighed his fiction down and eventually made it seem not merely old, but dated. 'The phraseology, fashion of arms, of dress and life, belonging to one age is brought suddenly with singular vividness before the eyes of another', Carlyle acknowledged. 'A great effect this; yet by the very nature of it, an altogether temporary one', for that age too would pass.[11]

'TIS SIXTY YEARS SINCE

In 1849 the Archaeological Institute held its annual congress in Salisbury. Sixty years after the antiquaries had taken on James Wyatt,

Bishop Barrington and George III in an attempt to save the cathedral's medieval fabric, the meeting marked 'a memorable epoch', as John Britton noted.[12] But the anniversary was an end as well as a beginning, not least for Britton, now ageing and in declining health. The Archaeological Institute, soon to become the Royal Archaeological Institute, had come into being as a result of a split within the British Archaeological Association, of which Britton was a founder member and John Lingard a vice-president. At its first meeting Robert Willis read a paper on Canterbury Cathedral, but there was a dispute over its publication which some members thought should not be undertaken for profit. This led to the secession of Willis and others and the formation of the rival institute. It was remembered by one of the witnesses to the row that 'there was a small clique of ignorant persons who set up poor old John Britton as a rival to Willis' and that 'Willis's friends and pupils could not stand such nonsense'.[13] Willis himself seems to have prevented Britton from speaking at the meeting.

The schism was as much about class as money. Britton had to publish for a living. Willis was, in the old sense, a gentleman amateur as well as a professional in the new sense, being a university professor. The two men represented incompatible attitudes and approaches and Willis's was the way of the future. Introducing his study of Winchester Cathedral, he set out his intentions:

> To bring together all the recorded evidence that belongs to the building, excluding historical matter that relates only to the see or district; to examine the building itself for the purpose of investigating the mode of its construction, and the successive changes and additions that have been made to it; and lastly, to compare the recorded evidence with the structural evidence as much as possible. A complete delineation and description of the building must not be expected, any more than a complete history of the see. The first have been most admirably supplied in the plates and text of Mr Britton's well known volume, and the able and copious work of Milner contains every particular that can be required for the second.[14]

Milner, Britton and their kind were damned with faint praise and given their congé. The cathedral could be 'disentangled with advantage from the mass of local information in which it is enveloped'.[15] This was the beginning of architectural history as an academic discipline, distinct from topography, divorced, indeed, from almost all historical context. Willis's focus on structure was combined with great aplomb as a lecturer, and his novel method of conducting a tour of the building he was discussing ensured both scholarly and popular success. His *Architectural History of Canterbury Cathedral* was 'the first book ever to be defined by its author as an "architectural history"'.[16] It would take more than Willis's logic, however, to exorcize the spirit of place. Among the events of 1849 was the publication of E. A. Freeman's *A History of Architecture*. Freeman was critical of Willis and of his friend Whewell, who had given 'archaeology' its modern meaning: 'Though of equal merit in their own line, I cannot consider that line quite such a high one; at all events it is not the same, nor so directly connected with my own view. Their writings treat as much of building as of architecture; their aim is to exhibit the mechanical rather than the artistic view.'[17]

The shifting attitudes of the early and High Victorian years were just that, rearrangements and changes of emphasis rather than the complete breaks with the past that they appeared, both to contemporaries and sometimes to later historians. While they were intolerant of ambiguity, what the Victorians meant by 'reality' was not what Willis meant by 'evidence'. The sensibility of the new age found expression in Ruskin's *The Seven Lamps of Architecture*, which was also published in 1849 and could truly be said to be epoch-making. One of the foundation texts of the nineteenth century, it put forward an aesthetic theory that was essentially a reinvention of the Picturesque. However, where Knight and Price had dealt with perception as a partially subjective experience, Ruskin proposed a Christian aesthetics, its principles absolute and eternal. The revolutions that spread across the Continent in 1848, the year that *Seven Lamps* was written, lent his Introduction an apocalyptic tone: 'The aspect of the years that approach us is as solemn as it is full of mystery; and the weight of evil against which we have to contend is increasing like the letting out of water.'[18] This was, he concluded, 'no time for the idleness of metaphysics'. [19] He declined to 'enter into any enquiry' on the definition of Beauty because its perception is 'universal and instinctive'.[20] The chapters, or 'Lamps', in reference to the sanctuary lamps that hang in front of the altar are, in order, Sacrifice, Truth, Power, Beauty, Life, Memory and Obedience. The Georgians' 'pleasing variety' was reconfigured more energetically as 'The Lamp of Life'. The power of association became the 'Lamp of Memory': 'It is well to have, not only what men have thought and felt, but what their hands have handled, and their strength wrought, and their eyes beheld.'[21] Where Knight and Price found the ideal Picturesque landscape in the semi-tones and shadows of Claude, Ruskin found the 'Lamp of Truth' in a scene, encountered 'some years ago', that might have been painted by Caspar David Friedrich:

> . . . near time of sunset, among the broken masses of pine forest which skirt the course of the Ain . . . a spot . . . where there is a sense of a great power beginning to be manifested in the earth, and of a deep and majestic concord . . . the far reaching ridges of pastoral mountain succeed each other, like the long and sighing swell which moves over quiet waters from some far off stormy sea. And there is a deep tenderness pervading that vast monotony.[22]

God is immanent in the landscape. His presence must be reflected in all the works of humanity. 'The snow, the vapour, and the stormy wind fulfil His word. Are our acts and thoughts lighter and wilder than these that we should forget it?'[23] Ruskin cast his essay as a 'statement of principles illustrated each by one or two examples'.[24] Architecture should be Gothic, but with only such decoration as could be built into the fabric. This part of his prescription was immediately influential. The use of contrasting brick, stone and inset minerals came to be known as 'structural polychromy', and this was the watchword of the rising architectural generation. Surface decoration was superficial, physical integrity was moral integrity. This was what 'reality' meant. Soon Ruskin's vision was being realized across the country in robust churches, their fonts and pulpits embedded with gob-stoppers of semi-precious stone, and in sturdy town halls and generously proportioned municipal art galleries and museums that expressed the civic pride of Victorian Britain.

Another, less sombre response to the political upheavals of 1848 which also became a landmark of nineteenth-century literature was Macaulay's *History of England from the Accession of James the*

Second. It was in some ways a throw-back, the last of 'the great classical and neo-classical' histories in the manner of Hume.[25] If its third chapter, the most often cited today, made a pioneering excursion into social history, its sweeping narrative made overall scant use of primary sources and dealt chiefly with political events and public figures. It illustrated Macaulay's belief, first floated in his essay of 1828, in the 'progress of civil society', which was best achieved by 'noiseless revolutions'.[26] His argument, that the English had avoided a violent revolution in 1789 because they had a peaceful one in 1688, was reassuring in a year described by *The Times*, as one of 'alarm and excitement indescribable'.[27] It was Macaulay's style, however, that brought his *History* such success. He was of the generation that grew up reading Scott and he believed that fiction had had all the best tunes for too long. The history that began in the *Waverley* novels and ended in Macaulay's *History* was intended, as he famously hoped, to 'supersede the last fashionable novel on the tables of young ladies'.[28] It did. Sales were phenomenal. Macaulay was 'an unsurpassed impresario of history as dramatic action'.[29] Like Scott he made use of the 'lighter literature' of the past, the ballads and popular songs that had long been the province of the antiquary, to give colour and immediacy. Macaulay did not invent his history any more than Scott did, but like him he made up a lot of the details. The arrival of William of Orange in Exeter is a set piece that would have been at home in a *Waverley* novel:

> Surrounded by a goodly company of gentlemen and pages, was borne aloft the Prince's banner. On its broad folds the crowd which covered the roofs and filled the windows read with delight that memorable inscription, 'The Protestant religion and the liberties of England.' But the acclamations redoubled when, attended by forty running footmen, the Prince himself appeared, armed on back and breast, wearing a white plume and mounted on a white charger. With how martial an air he curbed his horse, how thoughtful and commanding was the expression of his ample forehead and falcon eye, may still be seen on the canvas of Kneller. Once those grave features relaxed into a smile. It was when an ancient woman, perhaps one of the zealous Puritans who, through twenty-eight years of persecution, had waited with firm faith

for the consolation of Israel, perhaps the mother of some rebel who had perished in the carnage of Sedgemoor, or in the more fearful carnage of the Bloody Circuit, broke from the crowd, rushed through the drawn swords and curvetting horses, touched the hand of the deliverer, and cried out that now she was happy.[30]

Between Scott's fiction and Macaulay's *History*, as between Knight and Price's Picturesque and Ruskin's, there was once again more of a shift in emphasis than an absolute distinction. John Lingard was outraged. Given Macaulay's vehement anti-Catholicism, this was to be expected, but it was not Lingard's principal objection. He considered the passages denouncing 'popish idolatry and superstition, popish cruelty and intolerance, etc etc' merely glib.[31] What he minded was the sloppiness. While Macaulay objected to Lingard's *History* for its scepticism and debunking of popular traditions, Lingard despised Macaulay's over-reliance on them. 'One half of the quotations from him are of no authority', he complained to a friend.[32] But Macaulay gave his readers what they wanted: all the pleasures of *Waverley* with the reassurance that this was no Georgian Lubberland fantasy, but solid English history, made of facts, its all-pervading Romanticism so deeply absorbed as to pass unremarked. The following year Macaulay was offered the Regius Professorship of History at Cambridge. He declined, but he did advise on subjects for the murals in the new Palace of Westminster, intended to make the interior a monumental history of Britain, from King Arthur to Waterloo.

In 1851, when the new order unequivocally came of age with the Great Exhibition of the Works of Industry of All Nations in the Crystal Palace in Hyde Park, Macaulay thought it 'a most gorgeous sight; vast, graceful, beyond the dreams of the Arabian romances'.[33] Prince Albert was the moving spirit behind it, and he intended that it should be a display of the totality of human knowledge throughout the world. Objects were to be arranged according to materials and by nationality. This was the modern, rational way. Yet, at the heart of this international celebration of order, industry and scientific progress, was a Romantic vision, Pugin's much-praised 'Mediaeval Court', for which Henry Cole, who masterminded the whole affair, bent the rules. Pugin and his collaborators laid out the prospect of a Victorian

Britain endued with all that was best in the pre-Reformation past, in its art and its morality. Churches dignified with stained glass and altar plate in the medieval style, respectable homes wallpapered and carpeted and furnished, down to the cups and saucers, with designs that conformed to Pugin's 'true principles' of truth to materials and Christian Gothic ideals. The undoubted change that came over the use and understanding of history in the middle of the nineteenth century, often described in terms of a move towards professionalization and the development of rigorous historical method, was not so simple.

There were certain fundamental changes, many of them the direct results of the antiquaries' campaigning efforts. Some of the new professionals were, as we have seen, the old antiquaries with new jobs. Frederic Madden at the British Museum and Francis Palgrave at the Public Record Office were among those whose lives spanned the changing times and whose abilities enabled them to thrive. The transition was not always smooth. At the British Museum, where Madden was the bristliest of new brooms, the atmosphere was stormy as he 'abruptly ended' the museum's 'amiably torpid eighteenth-century ways'.[34] 'Abrupt' barely does justice to the state of permanent war, revealed in Madden's furious journal entries, that existed between him and the librarian, Anthony Panizzi, and the *ancien régime* in the person of Gage's old friend Henry Ellis, co-editor of the revised and expanded *Monasticon Anglicanum*. Ellis's scholarship could be slapdash, and Madden had no gift for tact or compromise, describing Ellis on one occasion as 'a reptile beneath contempt'.[35]

As the British Museum expanded and was restructured 'to support the specialisation of scholarship and the new professions', it was finally decided in 1850, on the recommendation of a Royal Commission, that it should establish a collection of British antiquities.[36] Sir Augustus Wollaston Franks (1826–97), a moving force in the Archaeological Institute, was appointed to oversee it. Madden, when not infuriated, was entertained by the quaint old ways he had dispatched and in 1851 he made notes about the successive catalogues 'so as to exhibit the entire progress of the Museum'.[37] He looked back with smiling condescension to the days when 'The whole of the Collections were divided into three Departments, namely 1. Mss medals & coins, deposited in six rooms; 2 Natural and artificial productions, in six other rooms; 3. Printed Books, maps Globes, Drawings, etc in twelve rooms. The account of the contents of the various rooms is very amusing, and presents a striking contrast with the present state of the collections.'[38] If he lacked tact, Madden had energy and intelligence. He deserves much of the credit for bringing the museum to that 'standing in the world of scholarship which it has maintained ever since'.[39]

While the younger generation of antiquaries were moving into museums as curators, the older might be said to be entering them posthumously. The collections of Meyrick, Gough and others were bequeathed to or bought by public institutions. Francis Douce had endured a brief, unhappy spell as Keeper of Manuscripts in the British Museum from 1807 to 1811, resigning in fury with a list of complaints about everything from the lack of staff to the smell of the drains. At his death in 1834 he left his collection instead to the Bodleian, a bequest 'of such richness that it must rank as one of the most valuable gifts which the Library has ever received'.[40] The great private collections of the antiquaries had served their purpose. They had preserved and documented what the eighteenth century thought beneath its notice; their faith was vindicated and their gabions were safe, up to a point.

The casualties of the new order were not exclusively human. Some objects, like some people, did not fit into the new taxonomies. The occasionally queasy process whereby institutions changed or emerged is illustrated in the convoluted history of the Royal Architectural Museum. In 1847 the antiquarian architect Lewis Cottingham, Willement's friend, who had worked for Lord Brougham in Westmorland, died. A preservationist in the heroic mould of John Carter, he had campaigned successfully, with Pugin and others, to save the Lady Chapel of St Saviour, Southwark (now Southwark Cathedral) and most of the fifteenth-century Crosby Hall in Bishopsgate. What could not be saved *in situ*, such as the timber roof of the Crosby Hall Council Chamber, he rescued and preserved, along with drawings and casts of other details in his private museum in the Waterloo Bridge Road.[41] By the time of his death this contained 31,000 items. Arranged in chronological order like Lenoir's Musée des monumens historiques, Cottingham's was the first museum of its kind in Britain. A movement was launched to buy the collection for the nation. But despite the support of George Gilbert Scott, Ruskin, Willement, Henry Shaw, Anthony Salvin and many more, it failed. William Butterfield refused to support it, as did Pugin, whose opposition was decisive. He thought the £7,000 that Cottingham's son was asking was too much when 'any fellow could get the casts himself for £500 ... my own belief is when they pull it down it will be all muck and broken plaster only fit for the Rubbish Cart'.[42] Pugin was quite wrong. But the museum was, to him, too redolent of the previous generation, of the copy-and-paste Georgian Gothic Revival. Architecture, as Pugin and Butterfield understood it, had moved beyond the study of the past to create new buildings informed by the spirit, but not dependent on the detail, of medieval precedents.

The attempt to preserve the collection as a museum foundered, only partly for lack of money.[43] The fact was, as Pugin's reaction demonstrated, that architecture and antiquarianism were diverging. The museum sat uneasily amid the emerging categories. Was it a teaching aide, a collection of *objets d'art* or of testaments to Christian art? At one stage it was all but taken over by the Ecclesiological Society, then in 1862 Henry Cole, now Director of the South Kensington Museum (later the Victoria and Albert), invited the collection in with gently smiling jaws. 'Never', George Gilbert Scott recalled with some bitterness in his memoirs, '[was] hook better baited for hungry fish.'[44] At South Kensington it was neglected and rendered 'comparatively useless'.[45] Scott and others took it back, re-siting it in Westminster in 1869. Yet more rearrangements, by chronology, by material, by type, followed over the decades. None was satisfactory. In 1914 it was in the hands of the Architectural Association which offloaded it yet again to the V&A, where it was divided once more into Sculpture, Woodwork, Metalwork and so forth.[46] Inevitably, over the years, much was lost, notably Cottingham's invaluable model and drawings of the interior of St Stephen's Chapel before the fire of 1834.

Even if an object did not itself fall between taxonomic stools, its significance might. As the winds of efficiency swept through Oxford in 1860, the books and manuscripts were removed from the Ashmolean Museum and transferred to the Bodleian. A logical reorganization that brought objects of the same type together, it could not accommodate the unclassifiable John Aubrey. His notes were tidied up and 'any loose papers, or paper fragments pinned into the manuscripts, were firmly bound into place', thus erasing those traces of his working methods and half-formed thoughts that the present editor of his *Brief Lives* would have liked to understand, while the coins and other objects from Aubrey's collection were absorbed into the university's own holding and so, like Adamson's gabions, they lost their associative meaning.[47]

International relations were, yet again, reconfigured by revolutions and 1848, like 1789, brought exiles to England, albeit in smaller numbers. On 24 February *The Times*'s Paris correspondent reported that the disorder of recent days had culminated in the abdication of Louis Philippe. The Tuileries had been sacked and at the moment of writing the royal throne was being carried through the streets, soon to be smashed to pieces. This was, very nearly, the end of the July Monarchy and it marked the end of the political career of the historian, Anglophile and former ambassador to London, François Guizot. Guizot, who coined the phrase *entente cordiale*, had been Minister of Foreign Affairs and de facto head of Louis Philippe's administration. He decided it would be prudent to come to London, arriving on 3 March. On the 22nd he was at the British Museum under the hostile scrutiny of Madden, who was alarmed to see him in the King's Library with Guglielmo Libri. Libri, Count Guglielmo Bruto Icilio Timoleone Libri-Carrucci dalla Sommaia (1802–69), was a bibliophile who had left his native Italy, become a French citizen and been appointed, as part of the continuing project to organize the post-Revolutionary archives, to help compile the *Catalogue général des manuscrits des départements*. Libri duly toured the provincial libraries and the Bibliothèques royale and Mazarine, stealing lavishly from them as he went. In 1845 he decided to cash in his hoard and tried to sell it to the British Museum. Attitudes had changed since 1815. The acquisition of displaced objects of dubious provenance was not to be countenanced by a national institution. Madden was outraged that Libri's friendships with Prosper Mérimée, now Inspector of Monuments, and Guizot had enabled him to escape justice, and even more furious to see him strolling through the museum. He resolved to keep a close eye on the pair of them.

The July Revolution had been propitious for French antiquaries and historians and this latest change of regime, despite the alarm it caused, did not reverse the advances of the last eighteen years. Guizot's political life was at an end, but he returned to France and continued his historical studies. Nor was he the last important French historian to be involved in national government. Adolphe Thiers, author of the first major history of the Revolution, the *Waverley*-inspired *Histoire de la Révolution française* (1823–7), became President of the Third Republic, while the author of the pre-eminent nineteenth-century history of France was Jules Michelet, one of those who as children experienced Lenoir's Museé des monumens français as a kind of epiphany. Michelet was not a politician, but his lectures when he took over Guizot's post at the Collège de France were political enough for his former mentor to suspend them. In Britain there were politicians who wrote history, but in France history and politics continued, as they had been since 1789, synonymous. The significance of the Revolution was all-pervading. The analysis that began with Thiers has, as John Burrow remarks, simply 'never ceased'.[48]

It was in Germany that the events of 1848 had the greatest consequences for history as an academic discipline and a philosophical idea. After the failure in that year of an attempted pan-German parliament, the unification of Germany into a nation state became an ideal, to be achieved by any necessary means. The term for this, coined in 1851, was *Realpolitik*. But, like the British 'reality', it was as much a metaphysical as a pragmatic theory. The State, as a concept, 'was gathered into the thought world of Romanticism' by the historians of the so-called Prussian School.[49] They developed a teleological theory of national history, based on a term derived from Herder, the idea of the state as an 'Individuality', an 'embodiment of ethical life, a spiritual agent'.[50] This quasi-religious vision was combined with rigorous critical interrogation of primary sources. German scholarship was admired across Europe and in the United States, and the most admired of its exponents, the doyen of the German profession, was Leopold von Ranke (1795–1886). His enormous oeuvre was mostly devoted to political history. His famous dictum, that he wished to write history so as to recover 'wie es eigentlich gewesen war', or 'how it really was', was both romantic in the general sense of setting up an unachievable ambition and Romantic in the philosophic sense. Ranke believed that objectivity was possible because all time was immediate to divine providence. States as Individualities were 'thoughts in the mind of God'.[51]

In Britain meanwhile, the acceptance of history as an academic subject moved slowly. The Regius Professorships at Oxford and Cambridge were established in 1724, but 'for political rather than academic reasons'.[52] It was still not possible to take a complete degree in 'modern', as distinct from Classical, history. From 1848 the Cambridge Moral Sciences Tripos included modern history, but in 1862, the year he was elected to the Chichele Professorship of Modern History at Oxford, Montagu Burrows (1819–1905) questioned the viability of an independent degree because of the shortage of reliable texts. 'Gibbon with all his avowed infidelity and the ribaldry of his notes' was not palatable to the Victorians; 'Hume had been exploded'; 'No-one but Lingard appeared as a competitor', yet 'it was far from desirable that English History should be taught . . . by a Roman Catholic'.[53] Not until 1871 did Modern History become a degree course at Oxford and it was two years later, in 1873, that a separate Cambridge History Tripos was created.

Lingard, however, was still not considered a suitable authority. It was to Ranke that Lord Acton referred in 1895 in his inaugural lecture as Regius Professor of Modern History at Cambridge as he surveyed what had amounted to 'a change of dynasty in the historic realm'.[54] This new era, he said, marked 'the accession of the critic in place of the indefatigable compiler'.[55] The idea of consulting all the primary sources and making critical comparisons was not exactly revolutionary; it was the method set out by Aubrey, and it had been the practice of antiquaries for three centuries.[56] Ranke, with his combination of scholarship with mystical theology, was closer to Milner and Pugin than to Lingard. The 'new dynasty', however, felt itself to be distinct. It was unwilling, perhaps unable to acknowledge its debts. History as an academic discipline was to be essentially, sometimes narrowly, political history. The university historians distanced themselves not only from antiquarianism, social history, art or architectural history, archaeology, the history of the applied arts, the history of science and of religion, but also from popular histories, many of which were written with a female audience in mind. 'Muscular' was another High Victorian term of praise along with 'reality', applicable to Christianity or to architecture, and there was now a distinct gendering of the divide between History and antiquarianism. The latter became, in the popular phrase, the handmaiden of History. The emergent profession was, John Burrow writes, 'masculine in its ethos and largely in its composition', adding that 'the smell of pipe smoke still clung to it in the 1950s'.[57]

So it came about that the antiquaries, who were despised at the beginning of the period by the gentleman amateurs for their involvement in professional authorship, came to be despised all over again at the end by academics, who thought them not professional enough.

CODA

The mid-century marked the physical as well as the intellectual passing of a generation. John Lingard died in 1851 at the age of eighty. He was much missed in Hornby, where his commitment to the non-sectarian pursuit of knowledge is honoured with an affectionate memorial plaque in the Anglican parish church. Lingard used the profits from his *History of England* to build a Catholic church next to his house which, since it was largely funded by the volumes covering the Reformation, he liked to call Henry VIII's Chapel. It is a plain, Classical building with a pair of neo-Classical busts at the entrance representing the Emperor Constantine and St Oswin. An architectural riposte to Milner and Pugin, it is as much the built expression of Lingard's understanding of his faith as the former's St Peter's, Winchester or the latter's chapel at Ushaw. Edward Willson died in 1854, having outlived his young friend Pugin by two years. He was buried, as he had wished, at St Mary's Hainton, near the old stones in which he believed that the old faith endured. Some of his papers found their way to the Society of Antiquaries. John Britton lived long enough to write many of his friends' obituaries, in which his own importance sometimes threatened to eclipse that of his subjects. He died in 1857, aged eighty-six. His grave in Norwood cemetery is marked by a megalith. Britton had hoped that his unbuilt design for a memorial to Chatterton could be used for his own monument, but it proved too expensive. The single standing stone is a poignant tribute to a man whose intellectual reach so often exceeded his financial grasp. Among those who lived on into the 1870s were Robert Willis, James Robinson Planché and the brothers Sobieski Stuart, whose legacy proved remarkably resistant to the age of reality on which it casts a sharp and slanting light.

After twenty years on the Continent, spent mostly in Prague and Pressburg (now Bratislava), the brothers returned to England with their families and took rooms in Pimlico at 52 Stanley Street (now Alderney Street), which was not at that time a smart address. Despite the debacle of 1848 and their reduced circumstances, they made no attempt at discretion. The 1871 census lists both brothers as the Count d'Albanie. They went, almost daily, to work in the Reading Room of the British Museum where they sat at a table reserved for them, with silver ink wells bearing the Stuart crest, and where the noise of their boots and spurs annoyed other readers. In due course they encountered a revenant from their earlier life, the antiquary John Francis Campbell, 'Campbell of Islay' (1821–85), whose papers are now in the National Library of Scotland. These chart the slow and agonizing process whereby he came to realize the truth, not only about the brothers but about their effect on history, the latter as real as the former was fantastic. In his notes we see the new age struggling to come to terms with the old as personal loyalty, pragmatism and scholarship presented mutually incompatible demands.

Campbell first met the brothers as a child on Islay, where they spent most of the winter of 1825. A three-year-old, wearing a kilt for the first time, he was charmed by them. They amused him by making 'pen guns . . . fired in the little drawing room for [my] gratification'.[58] Now in middle age, Campbell had a range of antiquarian interests. His *Popular Tales of the West Highlands Orally Collected with a Translation* appeared in four volumes in 1860–62, comprising English translations, mostly by Campbell, from the Gaelic. It is a scrupulous work. The original teller, their occupation and the place where the story had been told are all duly recorded. In the same methodical spirit Campbell turned to his next subject, the history of tartan. 'In putting together all that I have found out about Tartans', he wrote in the front of his collected notes, 'I shall begin at the present time and work back as far as I can go, to endeavour to shew [sic] the origin of the luxuriant crop of tartans which now pervades all the world. I take the Campbell Tartan as my text because I have taken some trouble to find out what *is* Campbell Tartan.'[59] His principal source – indeed, as he noted, his only source – was 'Sir Richard Urquhart's manuscript', the basis of the *Vestiarium Scoticum*. He made the same point as Walter Scott: 'Previous to the publication of 1842 nobody knew anything certainly about clan tartans least of all the heads of the clans, and the clans and the painters who painted them the weavers who wove them & the men & women who wore tartans. But in 1571 Sir R Urquhart knew about it though Buchanan did not.'[60] He decided to ask his old friends. On 19 March 1871 'Count Charles Edward' dined with Campbell at his London home in Campden Hill, Kensington, and lent him a copy of the *Vestiarium*. A correspondence ensued. Being an honest and perhaps somewhat unimaginative person, Campbell seems at first to have missed the implications of John's letter to him in response to direct questions. This stated that the *Vestiarium* was 'perfectly authentic in *principle*, and ... like Sir W Scott's identification of the *"Abbotts ford"* if it wasn't it might have been ... I piously believe that the author of the *Vestiarium* was a genius exactly similar to the heralds and genealogists who found armorial coats for Joshua, Judas Maccabeus, Hector & Julius Caesar and deduced the lineage of Ed: I of England, & Sr Richd. Urquhart in a right line from *Adam* and some of the grandees of Spain from *Noah*'.[61] Only on rereading the letter some years later did it strike Campbell that 'it seems almost to give up the case and acknowledge the invention ... of clan tartans about the days of George IV ... The only reliable authority is Sir R Urquhart and Sir R is disposed of as an old inventor.'[62]

It was as close as the brothers could come to telling the truth. In February 1872 John died. His brother answered Campbell's letter of condolence in what by then must have been his permanent tone, a mixture of real emotion and invented circumstances. 'Like the bard my thoughts are all with the days that are gone', Charles wrote, and with 'the shades of the departed ... I have no communion here, excepting with the rare hearts like yours – now so few and lonely.'[63] His brother had asked to be buried 'In the land of his Fathers, and under the rustling oaks and weeping birches of St Marie's in Eskdale'.[64] He was. On Christmas Day 1880 Charles died and was buried with him. They lie under an impressive Celtic cross inscribed with inaccurate dates.

By now Campbell was sure that the *Vestiarium* was a fake and that the 'highly interesting relics of Prince Charles Edward Stuart' sold under the terms of Charles's will would turn out to be like the box the brothers gave his aunt as a relic of the prince: 'new, the leather is fresh … I might have bought tons of like work in Prague.'[65] Caught between loyalties to his friends, historic truth and the effect on the Scottish economy, which relied greatly on the popularity of tartan, in 1872 Campbell now came down on the side of scholarship. He wrote an article on Highland dress and sent it to the Editor of *Macmillan's Magazine*. It was rejected. 'Obviously,' Campbell reflected, 'anything which throws doubt on the authenticity of clan tartans would be unpopular with manufacturers and wearers of these popular Scotch fabrics.'[66] As a historian he was angry. 'Clan tartans nowadays are shams, and most of the people who wear kilts wear fancy dresses.'[67] As a man he was ambivalent. In January 1874 he reconsidered his essay: 'Looked through this & decided that it would be foolish to print it. It is good for trade to believe in Clan Tartans. Why should I take any step to disturb Scotch manufacturers.' Nor could he quite give up his old friends, these 'two agreeable accomplished men whom I have known for 44 years, & who were friends of my people before I was born'.[68]

He left a final instruction, of which I have ignored the letter but, I hope, observed the spirit in endeavouring to portray the brothers as something more than imposters:

The Authors

Note. Anything here noticed about these gentlemen personally I wish not to be published. They are old friends, and I really have no *proof* that they are not grandsons of Prince Charles. They have never said to me that they are. It is vaguely understood that they are supposed to claim to be the rightful heirs to the throne, and people argue about their authenticity, and write about it. In looking to the authenticity of Campbell tartan, I was led first to the book, then to the author, and to the question of his descent. I have noted all that I heard but I wished only to get at the genuine Campbell Tartan. Therefore if anybody ever takes to printing this I beg the editor to avoid any injury to the authors of the Vestiarium, or to their memory.

I Campbell June 1873

Campbell need not have feared for the tartan industry. When in 1980 the truth was irrefutably established by Stewart and Thompson's *Scotland's Forged Tartans*, it made no difference.[69] By the time the brothers died their curious blend of fact and fiction had hardened into history. The Victorians were, in certain ways, less realistic than their parents and grandparents and much more literal-minded. If they left a rose on the tomb of Abélard and Héloïse, or wore the family tartan, they did so in the belief that the material reality was linked to an objective historical truth. So the past became fixed and was carried into the new, professional institutions whose doors closed against the antiquaries. By the time George Eliot published *Middlemarch* in 1872, as the High Victorians looked back to the late Georgians, the image of the antiquary had been transformed. Bonington's abstracted alchemist, Scott's engaging curmudgeon and Hazlitt's noble, dreaming Quixote, had all vanished, and in their place was only the unlovely figure of Edward Casaubon.

Acknowledgements

The antiquaries of the Romantic period operated through a system of collaboration, mutual support and (mostly) constructive criticism. I have been lucky to be part of a similar network over the years that I have been working on this book. As the architectural antiquary John Carter wrote in his memoirs, 'Few I believe know how smoothly the moments fly that pass over the head of an antiquary, lost to the common occurrences of life, he immerses himself into the stream of remote ages and every object dating its origin from such sources, gives a charm that never fades.'

Among those few kindred spirits who have been my constant intellectual companions Michael Hall is my oldest friend, a source of support, advice and information since the days when we were students together. From the beginning of my research on antiquaries Roey Sweet, the foremost scholar in the field, has been generous with suggestions, information and profitable conversation. It was she who introduced me to Julian Pooley, whose chance discovery in 1982 in a Hampstead bookshop of the unidentified pocket diaries of Mary Anne Iliffe Nichols was the start of the Nichols Archive Project, a rescue operation in the heroic spirit of the Georgians which has uncovered the personal and business records of the family who ran *The Gentleman's Magazine* and made it possible to trace intellectual networks across Europe through three generations.

From my first arrival at All Souls College, Oxford, Colin Kidd and Keith Thomas have provided invaluable encouragement and advice on all antiquarian matters. Colin gave me a copy of *The Hobby-Horsical Antiquary*, kept an eye on my accounts of Scott and the Union and he and his wife Lucy were kind and indulgent hosts during my visits to Scottish archives. Colin also agreed to read 'Tam O'Shanter' at one of my seminars, a performance which brought the house down and proved impossible to follow. Keith directed me to sources in the Historical Manuscripts Commission, corrected mistakes and asked usefully difficult questions. They both read and commented on the text as it neared completion, as did Michael Hall, Roey Sweet and Julian Pooley. The remaining errors are of course my own.

The seminar series I held in All Souls in 2010–11 allowed me to work out my ideas and these were further enriched by those who attended, especially James Adams, John Drury, Caroline Elam, Noel Malcolm and the late Michael Sheridan, with whom I talked at length about Chateaubriand, the French experience of history and the Revolution.

In Paris, Stephane Jettot invited me to talk to his students at the Sorbonne and at the École des Beaux-Arts Emmanuel Schwartz guided me through the remains of Lenoir's museum and the Jardin Élysée and showed me where Victor Hugo's childhood home stood.

Steven Robb and Craig Buchanan have been immensely generous in sharing the fruit of their researches into the elusive facts of the Sobieski Stuarts' story.

Others to thank are: Megan Aldrich for her insights into the life and work of Thomas Rickman; the late Christopher Barker for showing me material about his ancestor Dawson Turner; Kate Bennett, John Aubrey's greatest editor and champion, for help and comradeship; Alexandrina Buchanan for information about Robert Willis; Hugh Cheape for advice about tartan and its history; Stephen Clarke for sharing his research on the Noviomagians, their festivities and their homes; Tim Clayton for suggesting that Steevens involved Gillray in his outrageous hoaxing; Anthony Geraghty for taking me and my husband, on our honeymoon, to the Druids' Temple at Swinton; the late Christopher Gibbs for introducing me to Bob Geldof, who generously gave me the run of Davington Priory; Simon Gurney, who provided the picture of his ancestor Anna Gurney; Elizabeth Hallam-Smith shared her unique knowledge of the Palace of Westminster and took me with her on explorations of its oldest surviving fabric; the late Christian Hesketh first introduced me to the Sobieski Stuarts, of whom she took a benign view; Jeremy Warren shared his expert knowledge of medieval armour in the Wallace Collection and elsewhere; Michael Whiteway taught me many years ago how to look critically at historic furniture and gave me a copy of Shaw's *Specimens*; Stephen Wyatt shared information on theatre history and gave me Planché's *Recollections*.

Like anyone who works on antiquarianism I owe a great debt to the late Clive Wainwright, assistant keeper in the furniture department of the Victoria and Albert Museum, whose *The Romantic Interior* of 1989 was a landmark and opened up the subject. His sudden death ten years later was a tremendous loss. I am grateful to his widow Jane for making his archives available to me and helping to track down references in his work. Clive was a true antiquary who believed in handling objects and undertaking site visits. However much the place had changed one should always, he said, 'go and psych it out on the ground'. I knew him for twenty years and have spent another twenty working through the implications of our conversations and excursions, firstly in my biography of A. W. N. Pugin and now in *Time's Witness*.

As my editor at the *London Review of Books*, Mary-Kay Wilmers was indulgent of my antiquarian hobby horse, providing many relevant books for me on the understanding that I would not write about them in her paper and encouraging me to venture into other areas. Hers is the editorial voice in my head whether I am writing for her or not.

The staff of the London Library, always tirelessly helpful, excelled themselves through the latter stages of work on the book when the Library itself was inaccessible, answering questions and ensuring that even a volume so unwieldy as H. P. Danloux's folio *Journal durant l'émigration* reached me safely.

For institutional support I am grateful to Queen Mary, University of London for a studentship which enabled me to begin my research in the form of a doctoral thesis and to Annie Janowitz who supervised it; to the Warden and Fellows of All Souls College, Oxford, for two fellowships which allowed me to develop my work and to the Paul Mellon Centre for a Senior Fellowship which enabled me to carry it towards completion.

At Allen Lane Stuart Proffitt, ably assisted by Alice Skinner, piloted the book safely and skilfully through a publishing process made all the more complicated by the varying constraints of a pandemic. Cecilia Mackay brought her own wide-ranging historical knowledge to the picture research and has greatly enriched the book. Mark Bannister kindly took the author photograph.

Time's Witness is dedicated to the memory of my husband Gavin Stamp, an antiquary and historian in the Romantic tradition. He was a fellow of the Society of Antiquaries who achieved his most important work as a freelance author and journalist. As Piloti, the heir to John Carter's 'An Architect', he was a fearless irritant in the pages of *Private Eye* to those who would spoil or destroy what is best in the remains of the past. This book was researched in trips we made together, augmented by his vast library, informed by his encyclopaedic knowledge of the buildings of Britain and France, carried forward by his enthusiasm and sustained by his encouragement. My debt to him is beyond words.

Notes

PREFACE

1. Thomas Carlyle, 'Sir Walter Scott', *London and Westminster Review*, 12 (1838), p. 337.
2. Ibid.
3. *The Rambler*, 2(60), 13 October 1750, p. 53.
4. Hugh Trevor-Roper, *The Romantic Movement and the Study of History* (London, 1969), p. 1.
5. Quoted ibid., p. 7.
6. Samuel Johnson and James Boswell, *To the Hebrides: Samuel Johnson's Journey to the Western Islands of Scotland and James Boswell's Journal of a Tour to the Hebrides* (1775, 1785; Edinburgh, 2007), p. 16.
7. Quoted in 'Nineteenth Century Romantic Aesthetics', in the online *Stanford Encyclopedia of Philosophy* (2016).
8. Isaiah Berlin, *The Roots of Romanticism* (1999; London, 2000), p. 20.
9. Samuel Taylor Coleridge, *Biographia Literaria* (1817; London, 1960, Everyman's Library), p. 48.
10. Wilhelm von Humboldt, 'On the historian's task' (1821), *History and Theory*, 6(1) (1967), p. 59.
11. Ibid.
12. Stephen Bann, *The Inventions of History: Essays on the Representation of the Past* (Manchester, 1990), p. 102.
13. See Nigel Leask, 'Sir Walter Scott's *The Antiquary* and the *Ossian* controversy', *The Yearbook of English Studies, Walter Scott: New Interpretations*, 47 (2017). This was not to say that Ossian had lost its popularity; Leask cites twenty-seven new editions between 1801 and 1830.
14. *Archaeologia* (1770), p. ii.
15. K. D. Reynolds, 'Stuart, John Sobieski Stolberg', *Oxford Dictionary of National Biography* online. *The Invention of Tradition*, ed. Eric Hobsbawm and Terence Ranger (Cambridge, 1992); Hugh Trevor-Roper, *The*

Invention of Scotland: Myth and History (London and New Haven, 2008).

16. Margaret Macmillan, *Women of the Raj* (1988; London, 2018), p. 7.
17. Jean Wilson, 'The Queen's Feasts', *Times Literary Supplement*, 20 September 2019, p. 32.
18. Humboldt, 'On the historian's task', p. 58.

I. A LANTERNE UNTO LATE SUCCEEDING AGE

1. Edmund Spenser, 'The Ruines of Time', ll. 168–9, *https://www.bartleby.com/people/Spenser.html*. Spenser is referring to Camden.
2. *The Life, Diary and Correspondence of Sir William Dugdale*, ed. William Hamper (London, 1827).
3. Rosemary Sweet, *Antiquaries: The Discovery of the Past in Eighteenth-century Britain* (London and New York, 2004), p. 1.
4. Keith Thomas, *Religion and the Decline of Magic* (London, 1971), p. 509.
5. Margaret Aston, 'English ruins and English history: The Dissolution and the sense of the past', *Journal of the Warburg and Courtauld Institutes*, 36 (1973), p. 255.
6. Joan Evans, *A History of the Society of Antiquaries* (Oxford, 1956), p. 2 and Aston, p. 232.
7. Quoted in Aston, p. 234.
8. See in particular Alexandra Walsham, *The Reformation of the Landscape: Religion, Identity and Memory in Early Modern Britain and Ireland* (Oxford, 2011) and Eamon Duffy, *The Stripping of the Altars: Traditional Religion in England c.1400–c.1580* (London and New Haven, 1992).
9. Thomas Hay Marshall, *The History of Perth from the Earliest Period to the Present Time: with a supplement, containing the 'Inventory of the Gabions' and the 'Muses Threnodie' by Henry Adamson* (Perth, 1849), p. vi.
10. William Drummond of Hawthornden, 1637, quoted in ibid., p. ix.
11. Marshall, p. vii.
12. 'Memoir of Henry Adamson', in ibid., pp. 489–95. A gabion is a wicker or wire basket filled with stones or earth and used to make an embankment or fortification. Perhaps in deploying it here Ruthven was appropriating the caricature of the antiquary as a collector of miscellaneous rubbish.
13. Henry Adamson, *The Muses' Threnodie, or Mirthful Mournings on the Death of Mr Gall . . . compiled from authentic records by James Cant* (Perth, 1774), p. 13.
14. See in particular Graham Parry, *The Trophies of Time* (Oxford, 1995); David C. Douglas, *English Scholars, 1660–1730* (London, 1951); and

Stuart Piggott, *Ruins in a Landscape: Antiquarian Thought in the Six-teenth and Seventeenth Centuries* (Edinburgh, 1976).

15. James P. Carley, 'John Leland', *Oxford Dictionary of National Biography*.
16. Ibid.
17. John Leland, *The Itinerary of John Leland the Antiquary, in Nine Volumes*, ed. Thomas Hearne (2nd edn, Oxford, 1742–45), Preface, p. vi.
18. Ibid., vol. 1, p. vii.
19. Ibid.
20. Quoted in Aston, p. 245.
21. Quoted in Piggott, p. 12.
22. Quoted in Parry, *The Trophies of Time*, p. 28.
23. Ibid., p. 37.
24. From Edmund Gibson's translation of the *Britannia*, 1695, Preface, quoted in Wyman H. Herendeen, 'William Camden', *Oxford Dictionary of National Biography*.
25. Walsham, p. 471.
26. The *Oxford English Dictionary* gives the first instance of 'middle age' to J. Foxe in *Actes & Monumentes* (rev. edn) I.iii. 204/1 of 1570, with Camden using it in *Remaines of Greater Worke* of 1605. The first use of 'Middle Ages' seems to be Spelman in his *De non Temerandis Ecclesiis* (new edn, 1616).
27. Joan Evans, p.11.
28. Ibid.
29. Quoted in ibid., p.14.
30. Walter Raleigh, *The Historie of the World, in five bookes* (London, 1614), Preface. Ultimately it cost Raleigh not only his teeth, but his head.
31. *Archaeologia* (1770), pp. xiv–xv.
32. Walsham, p.14
33. Hamper, p. vi.
34. Ibid.
35. John Aubrey, *Brief Lives*, ed. Kate Bennett (2 vols, Oxford, 2015), vol. 1, p. 283.
36. Quoted in Parry, *The Trophies of Time*, p. 220.
37. Margery Corbett, 'The title-page and illustrations to the *Monasticon Anglicanum* 1655–1673', *The Antiquaries Journal*, 67(1) (1987), p. 102.
38. Quoted in Parry, *The Trophies of Time*, p. 221.
39. William Dugdale, *Monasticon Anglicanum or the History of the antient Abbies, and other Monasteries . . . in England and Wales, now epitomised in English*, trans. James Wright (London, 1693), p. 1.
40. Ibid., p. 2.
41. Parry, *The Trophies of Time*, p. 231.

42. Ibid.
43. Adam Fox, 'John Aubrey', *Oxford Dictionary of National Biography*.
44. John Britton, *Memoir of John Aubrey FRS* (London, 1845), p. 13.
45. Ibid.
46. Ibid., p. 15.
47. Ibid., p. 14.
48. Ibid., p. 28.
49. Ibid., p. 16.
50. Quoted in Parry, *The Trophies of Time*, p. 295.
51. Revd Francis Kilvert quoted in Aubrey, *Brief Lives*, vol. 1, General Introduction, p. lx.
52. John Aubrey, *The Natural History of Wiltshire*, ed. John Britton (London, 1847), p. 5.
53. John Aubrey, *Monumenta Britannica*, ed. Rodney Legg and John Fowles (3 vols, Sherborne, 1908–82), vol. 1, p. 23.
54. Ibid., p. 23.
55. Ibid., p. 32.
56. Ibid., p. 129.
57. Quoted in Aubrey, *Brief Lives*, vol. 1, Textual Introduction, p. cxxxvi.
58. Joan Evans, p. 1.
59. Douglas, p. 14.
60. Dai Morgan Evans, 'The Society of Antiquaries, 1707–18: Meeting places and origin stories', *The Antiquaries Journal*, 89 (2009), pp. 323–35.
61. Ibid., p. 342.
62. Ibid., p. 332.
63. Douglas, p. 13.
64. Minutes of a meeting held on Friday, 12 December 1707, quoted in Joan Evans, p. 36.
65. Ibid., p. 93.
66. Quoted in Douglas, p. 278.
67. Edward Gibbon, *Memoirs of My Life*, ed. Betty Radice (1796; London, 1984), Introduction, p. 18 .
68. Ibid., p. 76.
69. Quoted in 'Pierre Bayle' in the online *Stanford Encyclopedia of Philosophy* (2013).
70. Douglas, p. 274.
71. Gibbon, Introduction, p. 25.
72. Ibid.
73. See 'Gibbon's Last Project' in Hugh Trevor-Roper, *History and the Enlightenment* (London and New Haven, 2010).

74. Robert D. Thornton, 'The influence of the Enlightenment upon eighteenth-century British antiquaries, 1750–1800', *Studies on Voltaire and the Eighteenth Century*, 27 (1963), p. 1599.

75. Camden, *Remaines*, p. 350.

76. Hugh Trevor-Roper, *The Romantic Movement and the Study of History* (London,1969), p. 13.

77. Joan Evans, p. 79.

78. Leland, vol. 1, Preface, p. xv.

79. William Poole, 'Skeletons, crocodiles, human skin', *Times Literary Supplement*, 9 June 2017, p. 14.

80. Douglas, p. 245.

81. Douglas, p. 180.

82. *The Dunciad*, book 3, ll.189–190, *The Poems of Alexander Pope*, ed. James Sutherland (London, 1965), p. 758.

83. Piggott, p. 116.

84. Quoted in Joan Evans, p. 130.

85. Ibid.

86. John Earle, *The Autograph Manuscript of Microcosmographie* (c.1628; Leeds, 1966), pp 26–7.

87. Ibid., p. 28.

88. Antiquaries were popular subjects of satire in late-Georgian pantomime, featuring for example in the Harlequinade in *Gog Magog* at Drury Lane in 1822.

89. Samuel Foote, *The Nabob*, in *Plays by Samuel Foote and Arthur Murphy*, ed. George Taylor (Cambridge, 1984), p. 104.

90. Ibid.

91. Ibid., p. 105.

92. Johnson, *Dictionary* (1755) has 'Cat, n, s, a sort of ship'.

93. Quoted in Joan Evans, p. 168.

94. See for example Thornton, p. 1612 and Douglas, p. 275.

95. See Rosemary Hill, 'A Gothic Vatican! Horace Walpole and Strawberry Hill', *Times Literary Supplement*, 21 May 2010, pp. 3–4.

96. Quoted in Iain Gordon Brown, *The Hobby-Horsical Antiquary: A Scottish Character 1640–1830* (Edinburgh, 1980), p. 11, and see pp. 15–17 for a survey of parodies from Earle to Pope. See also Sweet, *Antiquaries*, p. xiii.

2. THE ROMANTIC ANTIQUARY

1. John H. Farrant, 'Francis Grose', *Oxford Dictionary of National Biography*.

2. Francis Grose, *The Olio: being a collection of essays . . . by the late Francis Grose* (London, 1792), p. 16.

3. Ibid., p. 57.

4. Quoted in Iain Gordon Brown, *The Hobby-Horsical Antiquary: A Scottish Character 1640–1830* (Edinburgh 1980), p. 43.

5. Grose, pp. 133–5.

6. Johnson, *Dictionary* (1755).

7. James Boswell, *Boswell's Life of Johnson* (1791; Oxford, 1953), p. 937.

8. Grose, p. 2.

9. *The Letters of Robert Burns*, ed. G. Ross Roy (2 vols, Oxford, 1985), vol. 1, p. 423.

10. *The Complete Poems and Songs of Robert Burns* (New Lanark, 2000), pp. 260–62.

11. William Wordsworth and Samuel Taylor Coleridge, *Lyrical Ballads*, ed. R. L. and A. R. James Brett (1800; Cambridge, 1965), p. 244.

12. William Wordsworth, 'The Solitary Reaper', *The Poems*, ed. John O. Hayden (2 vols, London, 1981), vol. 1, pp 659–60.

13. Walter Scott, *The Antiquary*, ed. David Hewitt (1816; The Edinburgh Edition of the Waverley Novels, Edinburgh and Columbia, 1995), p. 28.

14. Ibid., p. 15.

15. Ibid.

16. Gordon Brown, p. 42.

17. Scott, *The Antiquary*, p. 23.

18. Quoted in Patrick Noon, *Richard Parkes Bonington: The Complete Paintings* (London and New Haven, 2008), p. 428.

19. Quoted in *E.-H. Langlois*, Bibliothèque Municipale de Rouen (Rouen, 1977), p. 86.

20. Gordon Brown, p. 9.

21. Quoted in ibid., p. 6.

22. Ibid., pp. 44–5.

23. Scott to Anna Seward, 1806, *The Letters of Sir Walter Scott*, ed. Herbert Grierson (12 vols, London, 1932–7), vol. 1, p. 322. See Johnson, *To the Hebrides*, p. 210 for the original remark.

24. Quoted in Gordon Brown, p. 46.

25. Hengrave Hall MSS, 21/9/90, Cambridge University Library.

26. Ibid.

27. There was some limited provision for Catholics to study at Cambridge, but they could not take a degree.

28. John Nichols, *Literary Anecdotes of the Eighteenth Century* (9 vols, London, 1812–15), vol. 8, p. 387.

29. T A. Birrell, 'The Circle of John Gage (1786–1842), Director of the Society of Antiquaries, and the Bibliography of Medievalism', in *Antiquaries, Book Collectors and the Circles of Learning*, ed. Robin Myers and Michael Harris (Winchester and New Castle, Del., 1996).

30. Journals of Frederic Madden, 140, f.96, Bodleian Library.

31. M. A. Caygill, 'Frederic Madden', *Oxford Dictionary of National Biography*.

32. See Anna Catalani and Susan Pearce, '"Particular thanks and obligations": The communications made by women to the Society of Antiquaries between 1776 and 1837, and their significance', *The Antiquaries Journal* 86 (2006), pp. 254–78.

33. See Birrell, 'The Circle of John Gage'.

34. Helen Brookman, 'Anna Gurney', *Oxford Dictionary of National Biography*.

35. Ibid.

36. William Donaldson, 'Anna Gordon', *Oxford Dictionary of National Biography*.

37. Ibid.

38. Quoted in Julian Pooley, 'The papers of the Nichols family and business: New discoveries and the work of the Nichols Archive Project', *Transactions of the Bibliographical Society*, seventh series, 2(1) (2001), p. 35.

39. John Nichols to Anne Susannah Nichols, 22 October 1822, Nichols Archive, PC24/1/1 NAD15516.

40. Kenneth Clark, *The Gothic Revival: An Essay in the History of Taste* (London, 1928), p. 72.

41. Francis Jeffrey, 'Douce's illustrations of Shakespeare', *Edinburgh Review*, 12 (1808), p. 449.

42. Scott, *The Antiquary*, p. 106.

43. Nichols, *Literary Anecdotes*, vol. 8, p. 664.

44. Ibid.

45. Douce papers, e.32 Cogit. Miscell. f10, Bodleian Library.

46. Dai Morgan Evans, '"Banks is the Villain!"? Sir Joseph Banks and the governance of the Society of Antiquaries', *The Antiquaries Journal*, 89 (2009), p. 355.

47. Ellis to Gage, 7 March 1841, Hengrave Hall MSS, 21/13/23, Cambridge University Library.

48. Meyrick to Gage, 28 April 1839, Hengrave Hall MSS, 21/11/56, Cambridge University Library.

49. Joan Evans, *A History of the Society of Antiquaries* (Oxford, 1956), p. 239.

50. Website of the Athenaeum.
51. Journals of Frederic Madden, Bodelian Library, 149, ff20–24v.
52. Ibid., 162, f350.
53. M. L. Caygill, 'Frederic Madden', *Oxford Dictionary of National Biography*.
54. Journals of Frederic Madden, 162, f350, Bodleian Library.
55. Stephanie L. Barczewski, 'Joseph Ritson', *Oxford Dictionary of National Biography*.
56. *The Autobiography of John Britton, FSA, honorary member of numerous English and foreign societies ... in three parts ... copiously Illustrated, London, printed for the author as presents to subscribers to 'The Britton Testimonial'* (3 vols, London, 1850), vol. 2, p. 131n.
57. Mackenzie copied the wrapper and sent it to James Elmes (1782–1862), who forwarded it to Britton, BL Add. MSS 42864 f46.
58. G. H. Martin, 'Craven Ord', *Oxford Dictionary of National Biography*.
59. Quoted in Julian Pooley, 'Owen Manning, William Bray and the writing of Surrey's county history, 1760–1832', *Surrey Archaeological Collections*, 92 (2005), p.103.
60. John Britton, *Chronological History and Graphic Illustrations of Christian Architecture in England* (London, 1818–26), pp. i–ii.
61. J. D. Parry, *An historical and descriptive account of the coasts of Sussex, Brighton, Eastbourn[sic], Hastings, St. Leonard's, Rye ... Chichester ... and Tonbridge Wells, forming also a guide to all the watering places, etc.* (Brighton, 1833), pp. iii–v.
62. Ibid., p. iv.
63. John Britton, *The Rights of Literature; or an inquiry into the policy and justice of the claims of certain public libraries on all the publishers and authors of the United Kingdom, for eleven copies, on the best paper, of every new publication* (London, 1814), p. v.
64. Lingard to Gage, 14 January 1833, Hengrave Hall MSS, 21/5/5, Cambridge University Library.
65. Faraday to Gage, 11 February 1832, Hengrave Hall MSS, 21/4/64, Cambridge University Library.
66. Ibid.
67. Scott, *The Antiquary*, David Daiches, Foreword.
68. Martin, 'Craven Ord', *Oxford Dictionary of National Biography*.
69. J. C. Buckler to Gage, 30 December 1836, Hengrave Hall MSS, 21/8/185, Cambridge University Library.
70. Ibid.

71. Lingard to Gage, 16 May 1835, Hengrave Hall MSS, 21/7/114, Cambridge University Library.
72. Journals of Frederic Madden, 162 f177, Bodleian Library.
73. Phillipps to Gage, c.411, fol.138v, Bodleian Library.
74. Meyrick to Gage, 28 April 1839, Hengrave Hall MSS, 21/11/56, Cambridge University Library.
75. Hengrave Hall MSS, 21/6/182, Cambridge University Library.
76. Quoted in Bernard Nurse, with a contribution by J. Mordaunt Crook, 'John Carter, FSA (1748–1817): "The Ingenious, and Very Accurate Draughtsman"', *The Antiquaries Journal*, 91 (2011), p. 235.
77. Ibid., p. 235.
78. Wiseman to Gage, 14 April 1837, Hengrave Hall MSS, 21/10/70, Cambridge University Library.
79. Lingard to Gage, n.d. [August–December 1830], Hengrave Hall MSS, 21/4/80, Cambridge University Library.

3. THE ANTIQUARIAN LANDSCAPE: GEORGIAN

1. Schnebbelie Correspondence, Society of Antiquaries (1789), MS 267/84.
2. Ibid., MS 267/84.
3. Ibid., MS267/89.
4. *The Gentleman's Magazine*, 59 (1789), p. 1064.
5. Schnebbelie Correspondence, MS267/85.
6. *The Gentleman's Magazine*, 59 (1789), p. 873.
7. Ibid., 58 (1788), pp. 689–91, p. 690.
8. Ibid., pp. 689–91, p. 689.
9. Ibid.
10. E. A. Varley, 'Shute Barrington', *Oxford Dictionary of National Biography*.
11. Robert D. Thornton, 'The influence of the Enlightenment upon eighteenth-century British antiquaries, 1750–1800', *Studies on Voltaire and the Eighteenth Century*, 27 (1963), p. 1595.
12. *The Gentleman's Magazine*, 58 (1788), pp. 689–91, p. 689.
13. Mrs Charles Stothard, *Memoirs, including original journals, letters, papers, and antiquarian tracts, of the late Charles Alfred Stothard* (London, 1823), p. 23.
14. *Hydriotaphia, Urn-Burial, or, a Discourse of the Sepulchral Urns Lately Found in Norfolk*, 1658.
15. Stothard, *Memoirs*, p. 45.

16. English Heritage website, 'Richborough'.

17. Stothard, *Memoirs*, pp. 46–7.

18. Ibid., p. 47.

19. Ibid., p. 43.

20. *The Gentleman's Magazine*, 59 (1789), p. 60.

21. Richard Payne Knight, *The Landscape, a didactic poem in three books* (2nd edn, London, 1795) book 2, line 191.

22. Uvedale Price, *An Essay on the Picturesque* (London, 1794–8), p. 280.

23. Stephen Croad, 'Sham Castles', *The Oxford Art Journal*, 5(2) (1983), p. 68.

24. Nikolaus Pevsner, 'Richard Payne Knight', *The Art Bulletin*, 31(4) (1949), p. 297.

25. Price, p. 19.

26. Richard Payne Knight, *An Analytical Inquiry into the Principles of Taste* (London, 1805), p. 16.

27. 'The rich hues of the ripened fruit and of the changing foliage are rendered still more so by the warm haze which often, on a fine day ... spreads the last varnish over every part of the picture.' Price, *An Essay on the Picturesque*, p. 158. This recalls the 'last oozings' of the cider press and the 'rosy hue' on the stubble plain in 'To Autumn'. In the month he composed the poem Keats wrote in a letter that 'somehow a stubble plain looks warm – in the same way that some pictures look warm.'

28. John Britton, *The Autobiography of John Britton, FSA, honorary member of numerous English and foreign societies ... in three parts ... copiously Illustrated, London, printed for the author as presents to subscribers to 'The Britton Testimonial'* (3 vols, London, 1850), vol. 1, p. 73.

29. Ibid., p. 135.

30. Ibid., p. 136.

31. Ibid., p. 137.

32. John Britton to William Cunningham, Letters addressed to to Mr Cunningham FSA, 3 March 1804, Devizes Museum.

33. *The Beauties of England and Wales* (25 vols, London, 1801–16), vol. 1, p. xxxvi.

34. Ibid., p.xxxv.

35. William Gilpin, *Observations on the River Wye and several parts of South Wales etc ... in the summer of the year 1770* (2nd edn, London, 1789), p. 47.

36. Price, p. 174.

37. Ibid., pp. 159–64.

38. John Britton, *Memoir of John Aubrey FRS* (London, 1845), p. 3.

39. *The Gentleman's Magazine*, 71 (1801), pp. 413–14.

40. T. Warton et al., *Essays on Gothic Architecture* (2nd edn, London, 1802), p. 128.

41. Ibid., p. 127.

42. It has come to be accepted in recent decades. See Peter Draper, 'Islam and the West: The early use of the pointed arch revisited', *Architectural History*, 48 (2005), and most recently Diana Darke, *Stealing from the Saracens: How Islamic Architecture Shaped Europe* (London, 2020).

43. See Rosemary Hill, '"Proceeding like Guy Faux": The antiquarian investigation of St Stephen's Chapel, Westminster', *Architectural History*, 59 (2016).

44. 'Minutes', Society of Antiquaries, 29 June 1797.

45. Ibid.

46. John Milner, *A Dissertation on the Modern Style of Altering Antient Cathedrals, as Exemplified in the Cathedral of Salisbury* (London, 1798), p. ix.

47. Charles L. Eastlake, *A History of the Gothic Revival* (London, 1872), p. 120.

48. *The Gentleman's Magazine*, 69 (1799), p. 190.

49. George Whittington, *An historical survey of the ecclesiastical antiquities of France: with a view to illustrate the rise and progress of Gothic architecture in Europe* (London, 1809), p. xiv.

50. *The Gentleman's Magazine*, 79 (1809), pp. 929–31.

51. See Simon Bradley, 'The Englishness of Gothic: Theories and interpretations from William Gilpin to J. H. Parker', *Architectural History*, 45 (2002), pp. 325–46.

52. John Milner, *A Treatise on the Ecclesiastical Architecture of England During the Middle Ages* (London, 1811), p. 22.

53. John Carter, *Specimens of the Ancient Sculpture and Painting, now remaining in the Kingdom* (London, 1780–94).

54. Milner, *A Dissertation on the Modern Style of Altering Antient Cathedrals*, p. 48.

55. Kenneth Clark, *The Gothic Revival: An Essay in the History of Taste* (London, 1928), p. 102.

56. John Milner, *The History, Civil and Ecclesiastical, and Survey of the Antiquities of Winchester* (2 vols, Winchester, 1798, 1801), vol. 2, p. 340.

57. Ibid., p. 242.

58. Quoted in Alex Kerr, 'Thomas Rickman in France', in *A Quaker Miscellany for Edward H Milligan*, ed. Jeremy Greenwood and Alex Kerr David Blamires (Manchester, 1985), p. 120.

59. Thomas Rickman, *An Attempt to Discriminate the Styles of Architecture in England* (4th edn, London, 1835), p. 37.

60. Rickman to Edward Blore, 16 September 1817, Rickman–Blore letters, British Library.

61. Ibid., 21 October 1817.

62. Ibid., 4 January 1818.

63. *The Gentleman's Magazine*, 69 (1799), p. 190.

64. Rickman to Edward Blore, 31 October 1818, Rickman–Blore letters.

65. Ibid., 20 August 1822.

66. See Christopher Webster, 'The 1818 Church Building Act: A bicentenary retrospective', *Ecclesiology Today*, 55–6 (2017), pp. 47–74.

67. *Arnold's Library of the Fine Arts* (London, 1833), p. 321.

68. A. C. Pugin and Edward Willson, *Specimens of Gothic Architecture* (2 vols, London, 1821–3), vol. 1, p. xx.

69. 20 December 1819, Rickman–Blore letters.

70. 'Bartlett' to Britton, 2 August 1827, Correspondence of John Britton, Edinburgh University Library, LaII 426/34.

71. John Britton, *The Cathedral Antiquities of England* (5 vols, London 1814–35), vol. 2, p. 67.

72. Ibid., p. vi.

73. 'The Topographer for the year 1789', in *A Variety of Original Articles Illustrative of the Local History and Antiquities of England* (London, 1789), p. 3.

74. Joseph Strutt, *A Complete View of the Dress and Habits of the People of England* (2 vols, London, 1796, 1799), p. iv.

75. Ibid.

76. Ibid.

77. Ibid.

78. *Glig-Gamena Angel Deod or the Sports and Pastimes of the People of England* (London, 1801), p. 202.

79. Ibid., p.i.

80. Ibid.

81. Joseph Ritson, *The Letters of Joseph Ritson* (2 vols, London, 1833), vol. 1, p. 203.

82. *Robin Hood* (2 vols, London, 1795), vol. 1, pp. xi–xii.

83. Ibid., p.i

84. Annette B. Hopkins, 'Ritson's Life of King Arthur', *PMLA*, 43(1) (1928), p. 252.

85. Sharon Turner, *The History of the Anglo-Saxons from the Earliest Period to the Norman Conquest* (3 vols, 1799–1805; 6th edn, London, 1842), Preface to the 3rd edn, p. iii.

86. Ritson, *The Letters of Joseph Ritson*, vol. 1, p. xx.

87. Joseph Strutt, 'Emma Darcy, or, the Manners of Old Times' (1801–2), f1, Abbotsford Collection, National Library of Scotland.

88. Quoted in William B. and Ann Bowden Todd, *Sir Walter Scott: A Bibliographical History 1796–1832* (New Castle, Del., 1998), p. 19.

89. Ritson, *The Letters of Joseph Ritson*, vol. 2, p. 222.

90. *The Letters of Sir Walter Scott*, ed. Herbert Grierson (12 vols, London, 1932–7), vol. 1, p. 123.

91. Ibid., p. 355.

92. Ibid., p. 355.

93. Ibid., p. 356.

94. Ibid.

95. Quoted in William B. and Ann Bowden Todd, p. 39.

96. *The Letters of Sir Walter Scott*, vol. 1, p. 356.

97. Quoted in William B. and Ann Bowden Todd, p. 19.

98. Quoted in ibid., p. 135.

99. Quoted in Rosalind Lowe, *Sir Samuel Meyrick and Goodrich Court* (Little Logaston, Herefordshire, 2003), p. 65.

100. Ibid., p. 70.

101. Quoted in ibid., pp. 60–61.

102. Quoted in ibid., p. 61.

103. Samuel Meyrick and Charles Hamilton Smith, *The Costume of the Original Inhabitants of the British Islands* (1815), p. 30.

104. Quoted in William B. and Ann Bowden Todd, p. 135.

105. Quoted in ibid., p. 502.

106. Walter Scott, *Ivanhoe*, ed. Graham Tulloch (1819; The Edinburgh Edition of the Waverley Novels, Edinburgh, 1998), p. 9.

107. Quoted in Todd, *Sir Walter Scott: A Bibliographical History*, p. 503.

108. *The Letters of John Keats*, ed. Hyder Edward Rollins (2 vols, Cambridge, 1958), vol. 1, p. 301.

109. Ibid., p. 317.

110. John Keats, *Poetical Works*, ed. H. W. Garrod (1956; Oxford, 1970), pp. 385–6.

111. Mark Girouard, *The Return to Camelot: Chivalry and the English Gentleman* (London and New Haven, 1981), p. 49.

112. Eastlake, p. 111.

113. 'Britton's Cathedral Antiquities', *Quarterly Review*, 34 (1826), p. 306. The article is unsigned but Britton attributes it to Southey in his *Autobiography* (1850), and there is no reason to doubt him. Southey was a principal contributor to the *Quarterly* at the time.

114. Carter to Richard Gough, 15 August 1800, Nichols Archive, PC1/9626 NAD8839.
115. *Quarterly Review*, 34 (1826), p. 348.
116. Ibid., p. 307.
117. William Cobbett, *Rural Rides* (London, 1830), p. 397.

4. REVOLUTION, WAR AND PEACE

1. Francis Haskell, *History and its Images* (London and New Haven, 1993), p. 512. 'Comprennent' means 'comprise' but also implies 'reflect', a suggestion that the monuments in some sense also embody history.
2. Quoted in Françoise Choay, *The Invention of the Historic Monument*, trans. Lauren M. O'Connell (Cambridge, 2001), p. 46.
3. Quoted in ibid.
4. Ibid., p. 50.
5. Pierre Jean Baptiste Le Grand d'Aussy, *Histoire de la vie privée des Français* (Paris, 1782), p. 3
6. Aubin-Louis Millin, *Antiquités nationales ou receuil de monumens* (Paris, 1790–99), unnumbered first page.
7. Dominique Poulot, *Une Histoire des musées de France XVIII–XX siècle* (Paris, 2008), p. 56.
8. Ibid., p. 59.
9. For Moysant's story see Georges Mancel, *Notice sur la bibliothèque de Caen* (Caen, 1840).
10. Louis Courajod, *Alexandre Lenoir: son journal et le musée des monuments français* (2 vols, Paris, 1878, 1886), vol. 2, p. 2.
11. Louis Réau, Michel Fleury and Guy-Michel Leproux, *Histoire du vandalisme: les monuments detruits de l'art français* (Paris, 1994), p. 512.
12. E.-H. Langlois, Charles Richard and A. Deville, *Stalles de la Cathédrale de Rouen* (Rouen, 1838), pp. 200–204.
13. Réau, Fleury and Leproux, p. 288.
14. James Stourton and Charles Sebag Montefiore, *The British as Art Collectors from the Tudors to the Present* (London, 2012), p. 165.
15. Quoted in Clive Wainwright, 'In Lucifer's Metropolis', *Country Life*, 1 October 1992, p. 83.
16. Ibid.
17. Réau, Fleury and Leproux, p. 359.
18. Quoted in Carola Hicks, *The Bayeux Tapestry: The Life Story of a Masterpiece* (London, 2006), p. 76.

19. Réau, Fleury and Leproux, p. 9.

20. Quoted in Poulot, p. 71.

21. Tom Stammers, 'Down with weathercocks', *London Review of Books*, 39 (23) (2017), p. 34.

22. Joseph Ritson, *The Letters of Joseph Ritson* (2 vols, London, 1833), vol. 2, p. 39.

23. Ibid., p. 128.

24. Douce papers, MS Douce e.32 Cogit. Miscell, f.10, Bodleian Library.

25. Ritson, *The Letters of Joseph Ritson*, vol. 1, p. 142.

26. It has been said, in the *Oxford Dictionary of National Biography* and 'The Douce Legacy', that Douce was unhappily married. That no birth date is given in his wife's burial record has been taken to imply he didn't attend the funeral. In justice it should be pointed out that La Rue's letters, which invariably mention Douce's wife with gratitude and affection, draw a very different picture, as does Douce's own correspondence after he was widowed. I suggest that if he did not attend her funeral, this was due to his very particular ideas about death.

27. Douce papers, Douce–de La Rue letters, MSS Douce c. 7 f.19, Bodleian Library.

28. Ibid., f.12v.

29. Ibid., ff.4 and 1.

30. Ibid., f.4,

31. Ibid., f.6.

32. John Milner, *A Dissertation on the Modern Style of Altering Antient Cathedrals, as Exemplified in the Cathedral of Salisbury* (London, 1798), p. 32.

33. John Carter, 'Occurrences in the life, and memorandums relating to the professional persuits [*sic*] of J C F.A.S. Architect', in Papers of Philip Hammersly Leathes, King's College, London (Leathes Collection, n.d.), vol. 2. See also Matthew M. Reeve and Peter N. Lindfield, '"A Child of Strawberry": Thomas Barrett and Lee Priory, Kent', *The Burlington Magazine*, CLVII (December 2015), p. 840.

34. Desmond Fitz-Gibbon, *Marketable Values: Inventing the Property Market in Modern Britain* (Chicago, 2018), p. 54. See also *London and the Emergence of a European Art Market 1780–1820*, ed. Susanna Avery-Quash and Christian Huemer (Los Angeles, 2019); Vanessa I. Schmid and Julia I. Armstrong-Totten, *The Orléans Collection* (New Orleans, 2018).

35. William Hazlitt, *The Complete Works of William Hazlitt*, ed. P. P. Howe (21 vols, London and Toronto, 1930–34), vol. 17, pp. 196–7.

36. Ritson, *The Letters of Joseph Ritson*, vol. 2, p. 236.

37. H. C. G. Matthew, *Times Literary Supplement*, 10 November 1978, p. 1300.

38. Muriel E. Chamberlain, 'George Hamilton-Gordon', *Oxford Dictionary of National Biography*.

39. Hudson Gurney, 'Journal of a tour through France to Rome and Naples by Hudson Gurney Esq MP FRS etc in company with the Earl of Aberdeen and Rev G D Whittington', Society of Antiquaries (1802–3), f.2.

40. Ibid., f.4.

41. Ibid., f.7.

42. Ibid., f.12.

43. Ibid., f.7.

44. Ibid., f.90.

45. George Whittington, *An historical survey of the ecclesiastical antiquities of France: with a view to illustrate the rise and progress of Gothic architecture in Europe* (London, 1809), pp. 165–7.

46. Béatrice de Chancel-Bardelot, 'Les salles du musée des monuments français', in *Un Musée révolutionaire*, ed. Geneviève Bresc-Bautier and Béatrice de Chancel-Bardelot (Paris, 2016), gives a vivid account of the experience of the visitor.

47. Whittington, p. 169.

48. Gurney, 'Journal of a tour through France', f.29.

49. Ibid., f.102.

50. Ibid.

51. Ibid., f.99.

52. Douce papers, Douce–de La Rue letters, MSS Douce c.7 f.23, Bodleian Library.

53. *The Gentleman's Magazine*, 73(2), December 1803, pp. 1136–8.

54. 'Observations on the Bayeux Tapestry', *Archaeologia*, 18 (1817), p. 359.

55. Ibid.

56. Ibid.

57. Dawson Turner, 'Journal of a Tour to France 1814', Shirehall, Castle Museum, Norwich.

58. Ibid., f.107.

59. Grimaldi sang: 'London now is out of town / Who in England tarries? / Who can bear to linger there / When all the world's in Paris'.

60. Turner, 'Journal of a Tour to France 1814', f.190.

61. Ibid., f.149.

62. Gurney, 'Journal of a tour through France', f.99.

63. Turner, 'Journal of a Tour to France 1814', f.188.

64. Ibid., f.149.
65. Cecilia Hurley, 'Écrire la visite au musée: Lenoir et le catalogue du musée des monuments français', in *Un musée révolutionnaire* makes this point.
66. Turner, 'Journal of a Tour to France 1814', f.174.
67. Ibid., f.175.
68. Alexandre Lenoir, *Musée impérial des monumens français, histoire des arts en France, et description chronologique* (Paris, 1810), p. 185.
69. Turner, 'Journal of a Tour to France 1814', f.175.
70. Ibid., f.176.
71. Ibid.
72. Ibid., f.237.
73. Quoted in Wainwright, 'In Lucifer's Metropolis', p. 84.
74. Douce papers, Douce–de La Rue letters, MSS Douce c.7. f.46, Bodleian Library.
75. Ibid., MSS Douce c.7. f.68

5. THE FIELD OF WATERLOO

1. Quoted in Stuart Semmel, 'Reading the tangible past: British tourism, collecting, and memory after Waterloo', *Representations*, 69 (2000), p. 17.
2. Richard Altick, *The Shows of London* (Cambridge, Mass. and London, 1978), p. 239.
3. Semmel, p. 11.
4. Quoted in ibid., p. 22.
5. Walter Scott, *Paul's Letters to his Kinsfolk* (2nd edn, Edinburgh, 1816), p. 197. John Scott, *Paris Revisited, in 1815, by way of Brussels* (2nd edn, London, 1816), p. 210.
6. Semmel, p. 22.
7. William Thackeray, *Vanity Fair* (London, 1848; Penguin Classics, London, 1968), p. 313.
8. Hengrave Hall MSS, MS 126, unnumbered pages, Cambridge University Library.
9. Ibid.
10. Ibid.
11. Ibid.
12. Ibid.
13. Ibid.
14. Ibid.
15. Ibid.

16. Ibid.

17. Ibid.

18. Ibid.

19. Ibid.

20. Mrs Charles Stothard, *Memoirs, including original journals, letters, papers, and antiquarian tracts, of the late Charles Alfred Stothard* (London, 1823), p. 420.

21. Ibid., p. 419.

22. Douce papers, MS e.91 f.8v, Bodleian Library.

23. Scott, *Paul's Letters to his Kinsfolk*, pp. 196–7.

24. Ibid., p. 209.

25. Ibid., p. 213.

26. Ibid., p. 211.

27. *Complete Poetical and Dramatic Works* (London, 1887), p. 534.

28. Ibid.

29. Quoted in Beth Segal Wright, 'Scott's Historical Novels and French Historical Painting 1815–1855', *The Art Bulletin*, 63(2) (1981), p. 287.

30. Scott, *Paul's Letters to his Kinsfolk*, p. 319.

31. *The Letters of Sir Walter Scott*, ed. Herbert Grierson (12 vols, London, 1932–7), vol. 4, pp. 99–100.

32. Ibid.

33. 'The Antiquary, by the Author of Waverley and Guy Mannering', *Quarterly Review*, 15(29), pp. 125–39.

34. Walter Scott, *Ivanhoe*, ed. Graham Tulloch (1819; The Edinburgh Edition of the Waverley Novels, Edinburgh, 1998), p. 7.

35. Quoted in Sir Charles Petrie, *The Jacobite Movement: The Last Phase 1716–1807* (London, 1956), p. 190.

36. Dawson Turner, 'Journal of a Three-Weeks Tour ... in the Autumn of 1815', f.1, Trinity College, Cambridge.

37. Ibid., f.3.

38. Ibid., f.10.

39. Ibid., f.10.

40. Ibid., f.11.

41. Ibid., f.32.

42. Ibid., f.43.

43. Ibid., f.34.

44. Ibid., f.45.

45. Ibid., f.34.

46. Ibid., f.46.

47. Ibid., f.21.

48. Ibid., f.42.
49. Ibid., f.33.
50. Ibid., f.33.
51. Ibid., f.48.
52. Ibid., f.53.
53. Ibid., f.55.
54. Ibid., f.92.
55. Ibid., f.92.
56. Ibid., f.94.
57. Ibid., f.62.

6. ANGLO-NORMAN ATTITUDES

1. Jean Laspougeas, 'La Normandie au temps d'Arcisse de Caumont', in *Arcisse de Caumont: érudit normand et fondateur de l'archéologie française*, ed. Société des Antiquaires de Normandie (Caen, 2004), p. 11.
2. Francis Palgrave, 'Normandy-Architecture of the Middle Ages', *Quarterly Review*, 25(49), p. 113. Palgrave refers to Sir Edward Coke's *The Fourth Part of the Institution of the Laws of England Concerning the Jurisdiction of Courts* (1648).
3. Michael Hall points out that 'To be pedantic, part of Normandy still does belong to Britain, the Channel Islands, which are the possession of the monarch as Duke of Normandy.'
4. Palgrave, p. 113.
5. Quoted in Nikolaus Pevsner, *Some Architectural Writers of the Nineteenth Century* (Oxford, 1972), p. 22.
6. André Pottier, in N. X .Willemin, *Monuments français inédits pour servir à l'histoire des arts* (Paris, 1839), p. ii.
7. Quoted in Pevsner, *Some Architectural Writers*, p. 91.
8. Dawson Turner, *Account of a Tour in Normandy; undertaken chiefly for the purpose of investigating the Architectural Antiquities of the Duchy with observations on its history, on the country, and on its inhabitants illustrated with numerous engravings* (2 vols, London, 1820), vol. 2, p. 242.
9. La Rue to Douce, Douce papers, f.94, 29 November 1816, Bodleian Library.
10. Ibid., f111, 20 January 1818.
11. Thomas Amyot, 'Observations on an Historical Fact supposed to be established by the Bayeux Tapestry by Thomas Amyot esq. F.S.A. in a letter addressed to Henry Ellis esq. FRS Secretary, dated February 24, 1818', *Archaeologia*, 19 (1821).

12. Ibid., p. 88.

13. Charles Stothard, 'Some Observations on the Bayeux Tapestry by Mr Charles Stothard, in a Letter addressed to Samuel Lysons Esq. V.P. FRS', ibid., p. 186.

14. Ibid., p. 191.

15. See inter alia Andrew Bridgeford, 1066: The Hidden History in the Bayeux Tapestry (New York, 2005).

16. Stothard, 'Some Observations on the Bayeux Tapestry', p. 185.

17. Thomas Frognall Dibdin, A Bibliographical Antiquarian and Picturesque Tour in France and Germany (2 vols, London, 1821), vol. 1, p. 143.

18. John Lingard, The History of England (London, 1819), vol. 1, p. 335.

19. See Wolfgang Grape, The Bayeux Tapestry: Monument to a Norman Triumph (New York, 1994), p. 24.

20. Amyot, 'Observations on an Historical Fact', p. 93.

21. Mrs Charles Stothard, Letters Written during a Tour through Normandy, Britanny [sic] and other Parts of France in 1818 (London, 1820), p.131.

22. Stothard, 'Some Observations on the Bayeux Tapestry'.

23. 'Antiquariolus', 'Tapestry of William the Conqueror's Queen', The Gentleman's Magazine, 73–4 (1803–4), 74, p. 19.

24. E. A. Freeman, The Norman Conquest of England: Its Causes and Results (1870–76; 2nd edn, Oxford, 1875), p. 498.

25. Ibid.

26. Stothard, Letters Written during a Tour, p. 2, p. 1.

27. Dibdin, A Bibliographical, Antiquarian and Picturesque Tour, vol. 1, p. 13.

28. Stothard, Letters Written during a Tour, p. 21. Dibdin, A Bibliographical Antiquarian and Picturesque Tour, vol. 1, p. 83.

29. Dibdin, A Bibliographical Antiquarian and Picturesque Tour, vol. 1, p. 49.

30. Turner, Account of a Tour in Normandy, vol. 2, p. 122.

31. Ibid.

32. Stothard, Letters Written during a Tour, p. 4.

33. Turner, Account of a Tour in Normandy, vol. 2, p. 164.

34. Stothard, Letters Written during a Tour, p. 104.

35. Ibid., p. 104.

36. Ibid., p.13.

37. Dibdin, A Bibliographical Antiquarian and Picturesque Tour, vol. 1, p. 72.

38. Ibid., p. 103.

39. Ibid.

40. Ibid., p. 95.

41. Stothard, *Letters Written during a Tour*, p. 21.

42. Turner, *Account of a Tour in Normandy*, vol. 1, p. 90. Douce papers, f112, 8 March 1818, Bodleian Library.

43. Turner, *Account of a Tour in Normandy*, vol. 1, p. 137.

44. Stothard, *Letters Written during a Tour*, p. 23.

45. Turner, *Account of a Tour in Normandy*, vol. 1, pp. 120–21.

46. Andrew W. Moore, 'John Sell Cotman', *Oxford Dictionary of National Biography*.

47. Douce papers, f108, 25 July 1817, Bodleian Library.

48. Quoted in François Guillot, *L'Invention de la Normandie* (Caen, 2011), p. 44. Douce papers, f77, 25 March 1816, Bodleian Library.

49. Douce papers, 17 f174, 22 September 1825, Bodleian Library.

50. E.-H. *Langlois*, Bibliothèque Municipale de Rouen (Rouen, 1977), p. 86.

51. E.-H. Langlois, *Les Énervés de Jumièges* (Rouen, 1838), p. 23.

52. E.-H. Langlois, Charles Richard and A. Deville, *Stalles de la Cathédrale de Rouen* (Rouen, 1838), pp. 23–4.

53. Benjamin Ferrey, *Recollections of A. N. Welby Pugin and his father Augustus Pugin*, reprinted with an introduction by Clive Wainwright and an index by Jane Wainwright (1861; London, 1978), p. 18.

54. Ibid.

55. Ibid., p. 19.

56. Ibid.

57. Langlois, Richard and Deville, *Stalles de la Cathédrale de Rouen*, p. 8.

58. Hengrave Hall MSS, 21/10/28, Cambridge University Library.

59. Louis Réau, Michel Fleury and Guy-Michel Leproux, *Histoire du Vandalisme, les Monuments detruits de l'art Français* (Paris, 1994), p. 672.

60. Ibid., p. 628.

61. Stothard, *Letters Written during a Tour*, p. 78.

62. Quoted in Réau, Fleury and Leproux, *Histoire du Vandalisme*, p. 630.

63. Nicole Savy, 'Victor Hugo et le Musée des Monuments français: les effets d'une enfance au musée', *Revue d'histoire littéraire de la France*, 95(1) (1995), p. 18.

64. Dibdin, *A Bibliographical Antiquarian and Picturesque Tour*, vol. 2, pp. 491–2.

65. Stothard, *Letters Written during a Tour*, p. 104.

66. Hengrave Hall MSS, 21/4/152, Cambridge University Library.

67. Ibid. 21/5/47

68. Langlois thus inscribed a book, now in a private collection, which he sent to Gage.

69. Turner, *Account of a Tour in Normandy*, vol. 1, p. 40.

70. Ibid., p. 15.

71. Stothard, *Letters Written during a Tour*, p. 5.

72. Douce papers, c.7/168, 22 September 1825, Bodleian Library.

73. Guillot, *L'Invention de la Normandie*, p. 82.

74. Quoted in Alex Kerr, 'Thomas Rickman in France', in *A Quaker Miscellany for Edward H. Milligan*, ed. Jeremy Greenwood, Alex Kerr and David Blamires (Manchester, 1985), p. 115.

75. William Whewell, *Architectural notes on German Churches; with remarks on the origin of Gothic Architecture* (Cambridge, 1830).

76. Thomas Rickman, *An Attempt to Discriminate the Styles of Architecture in England* (4th edn, London, 1835), p. 166.

77. Ibid.

78. Ibid., p. 177.

79. Elizabeth Lewis, 'Les Rapports avec les antiquaires anglais', in *Arcisse de Caumont, érudit normand et fondateur de l'archéologie français* (Caen, 2004), p. 273.

80. Quoted in Kerr, 'Thomas Rickman in France', p. 120.

81. Guillot, *L'Invention de la Normandie*, p. 94.

82. Quoted in Ethel Jones, *Les Voyageurs français en Angleterre de 1815 à 1830* (Paris, 1930), p. 83.

83. Quoted in Stephen Bann, *The Inventions of History: Essays on the Representation of the Past* (Manchester, 1990), p. 59.

84. Guillot, *L'Invention de la Normandie*, p. 15.

85. Quoted in ibid., p. 15.

86. Ibid., p. 77.

87. Georges Huard, '"Notre-Dame de Paris" et les antiquaires de Normandie', *Revue d'histoire littéraire de la France*, 53(3) (1953), p. 325.

88. Ibid.

89. Jones, *Les Voyageurs français*, p. 83.

90. Quoted in E. Preston Dargan, 'Scott and the French Romantics', *Publications of the Modern Languages Association of America*, 49(2) (1934), p. 605.

91. Hélène Denis, 'L'imaginaire du gout: motifs "ecossais" dans le paysage parisien au debut du XIXe siècle', *French Historical Studies*, 22(4) (1999), p. 547.

92. Honoré de Balzac, *Lost Illusions*, trans. Herbert J. Hunt (1837–43; Penguin Classics, London, 1971), p. 441.

93. See Beth Segal Wright, 'Scott's Historical Novels and French Historical Painting 1815–1855', *The Art Bulletin*, 63(2) (1981).

94. See Stephen Duffy, 'French artists and the Meyrick armoury', *The Burlington Magazine*, CLI, May 2009.

95. Quoted in ibid., p. 285

96. Auguste-Jean-Baptiste Defauconpret, *Quinze jours à Londres* (Paris, 1816), p. 105.

97. Jacques G. A. Bereaud, 'La Traduction en France à l'époque romantique', *Comparative Literature Studies*, 8(3) (1971), p. 236.

98. James Robinson Planché, *The Recollections and Reflections of J. R. Planché (Somerset Herald)* (2 vols, London, 1872), vol. 1, p. 65.

99. Jacqueline du Pasquier, 'La duchesse de Berry, arbitre de la mode et reine du style troubadour', in Hildegard Kremers et al., *Marie-Caroline de Berry* (Paris, 2002), p. 135.

100. Keith Randell, *France: Monarchy, Republic and Empire, 1814–70* (London, 1986), p. 39.

101. Dargan, 'Scott and the French Romantics', p. 609.

102. Meyrick to Douce, 21 October 1833, Douce papers, 39204, d.28 f168, Bodleian Library.

103. Victor Hugo, *Notre-Dame de Paris*, trans. John Sturrock, Introduction (1831; Penguin Classics, London, 2004), p. 16.

104. Hugo, *Notre-Dame de Paris*, ed. Benedikte Andersson with a Preface by Adrien Goetz (Paris, 2009), p. 229.

105. See Hugo, *Notre-Dame de Paris*, Sturrock Introduction, p. 14.

106. Honoré de Balzac, *La Peau de chagrin* (1831; *Oeuvres Complètes*, Paris, 1960), vol. 18, p. 95.

107. Ibid., p. 91.

108. E.-H. Langlois, *Essai historique et descriptif sur l'Abbaye de Fontanelle ou Saint-Wandrille* (Rouen, 1832), p. 244.

109. E.-H. Langlois, *Essai historique et descriptif sur la peinture sur verre ancienne et moderne* (Rouen, 1832), pp. 100–101.

110. Turner, *Account of a Tour in Normandy*, vol. 2, p. 102.

111. Langlois, *Les Énervés de Jumièges*, p.14.

112. Ferrey, *Recollections*, p. 20.

113. Pugin, 'Autobiographical Notes', in Alexandra Wedgwood, *A. W. N. Pugin and the Pugin Family: Catalogue of Architectural Drawings in the Victoria and Albert Museum* (London, 1985), p. 24.

114. Charles Nodier and Isidore Taylor, *Voyages pittoresques et romantiques dans l'ancienne France* (24 vols, Paris, 1820–78), vol. 1, Picardy, f35.

7. THE ROMANTIC INTERIOR

1. See Rosemary Hill, 'A Gothic Vatican! Horace Walpole and Strawberry Hill', *Times Literary Supplement*, 21 May 2010 for a discussion of Strawberry Hill and changing attitudes towards it; also Gordon Campbell, *The Hermit in the Garden: From Imperial Rome to Ornamental Gnome* (Oxford, 2013) and John F. H. Smith, 'William Stukeley in Stamford: His houses, gardens and a project for a Palladian triumphal arch over Barn Hill', *The Antiquaries Journal*, 93 (2013).

2. Clive Wainwright, *The Romantic Interior: The British Collector at Home, 1750–1850* (London and New Haven, 1989), p. 25.

3. Scott to Matthew Weld Hartstonge, *The Letters of Sir Walter Scott*, ed. Herbert Grierson (12 vols, London, 1932–7), vol. 3, p. 185.

4. Walter Scott, *The Antiquary*, ed. David Hewitt (1816; The Edinburgh Edition of the Waverley Novels, Edinburgh and Columbia, 1995), p. 22.

5. Hampton and Sons, *A catalogue of the whole of the very interesting and historical contents of Hengrave Hall* (London, 1897).

6. 'A Catalogue of the . . . Collection . . . of the late Edward James Willson' (Lincoln, 1854), pp 24–5.

7. Pugin to Willson, 6 November 1834, in *The Collected Letters of A. W. N. Pugin*, ed. Margaret Belcher (5 vols, Oxford, 2000–2015), vol. 1, p. 43.

8. Cooke's diary, quoted in Wainwright, *The Romantic Interior*, p. 40.

9. Thomas Frognall Dibdin, *Bibliophobia* (London, 1832), p. 45.

10. Quoted in 'The Douce Legacy: An exhibition to commemorate the 150th anniversary of the bequest of Francis Douce', Bodleian Library (Oxford, 1984), p. 20

11. Ibid., p. 36.

12. See Douglas Brine, '"An unrivalled brass Lectorium": the Cloisters lectern and the Gothic Revival in England', *Sculpture Journal*, 29(1) (2020), p. 49.

13. Quoted in Simon Jervis, 'The Pryor's Bank, Fulham', *Furniture History*, 10 (1974), p. 89. See also Charles Tracy, *Continental Church Furniture in England: A Traffic in Piety* (Woodbridge, 2001).

14. Quoted in Wainwright, *The Romantic Interior*, p. 49.

15. Letters of Samuel Rush Meyrick to Sir Walter Scott, f.85, 9 April 1821, National Library of Scotland.

16. Scott, *The Antiquary*, p. 38.

17. Ex inf. the late Clive Wainwright.

18. J. C. Loudon, *An Encyclopaedia of Cottage Farm and Villa Architecture and Furniture* (1839), p. 1102, quoted in Clive Wainwright, 'Specimens of ancient furniture', *The Connoisseur*, October 1973, p. 107.

19. Henry Shaw, *Specimens of Ancient Furniture drawn from existing authorities* (London, 1836), pp. 25–6.
20. Rosalind Lowe, *Sir Samuel Meyrick and Goodrich Court* (Little Logaston, Herefordshire, 2003), p. 216.
21. Ibid., p. xii.
22. Obituary, *The Gentleman's Magazine*, 2nd series, 30 (1848), pp 92–5.
23. Meyrick to Scott, 30 December 1824, Meyrick–Scott Letters, 3899, f263.
24. Quoted in Lowe, *Sir Samuel Meyrick and Goodrich Court*, p. 2.
25. Meyrick to Scott, 30 December 1824, Meyrick–Scott Letters, 3899, f263.
26. Ibid.
27. Quoted in Wainwright, *The Romantic Interior*, pp. 246–7.
28. Letter to Scott quoted in ibid., p. 244.
29. Quoted in ibid., p. 247.
30. Quoted in ibid.
31. See John Harris, *Moving Rooms: The Trade in Architectural Salvage* (London and New Haven, 2007) and Lowe, *Sir Samuel Meyrick and Goodrich Court*, p. 216.
32. Lowe, *Sir Samuel Meyrick and Goodrich Court*, p. 157.
33. Wainwright, *The Romantic Interior*, p. 253.
34. Quoted in Sydney Smith, 'Dr Meyrick on Ancient Armour', *Edinburgh Review*, 39(78) (1824), p. 361.
35. Ibid., p. 358.
36. Paolo Venturoli, *Dal Disegno Alla Fotografia: L'aremeria reale illustrata, 1837–1898* (Turin, 2004).
37. Quoted in Wainwright, *The Romantic Interior*, p. 252.
38. Ibid., p. 261.
39. Craven Ord to Douce, 25 July 1780, Douce papers, 39196 f10, Bodleian Library.
40. Thomas Willement, *Historical Sketch of the Parish of Davington . . . and of the Priory There Dedicated to S Mary Magdalene* (London, 1862), p. 39.
41. Ibid.
42. Ibid., pp. 37–8.
43. John Britton, *The Autobiography of John Britton, FSA, honorary member of numerous English and foreign societies . . . in three parts . . . copiously Illustrated, London, printed for the author as presents to subscribers to 'The Britton Testimonial'* (3 vols, London, 1850), vol. 3, p. 155
44. Pugin, Diaries in Alexandra Wedgwood, *A. W. N. Pugin and the Pugin Family: Catalogue of Architectural Drawings in the Victoria and Albert Museum* (London, 1985) p. 51.

45. Quoted in Stephen Clarke, 'Rosamond's Bower, The Pryor's Bank, and the long shadow of Strawberry Hill', *Journal of the History of Collections*, 26(2) (2014).

46. Ibid., p. 294.

47. Quoted in ibid., p. 300.

48. Quoted in ibid., p. 288.

49. Ibid., p. 291.

50. Quoted in ibid., p. 296.

51. Ibid., pp. 298–9.

52. William Makepeace Thackeray, *The History of Pendennis* (1850; Penguin Classics, London, 1986), p. 398.

53. Charles Dickens, *Great Expectations* (London, 1861), p. 503.

54. Charles Richard, 'Notice sur E.-H. Langlois', in E.-H. Langlois, *Stalles de la Cathédrale de Rouen* (Rouen, 1838), pp. 8–10.

55. Ibid., p. 10.

56. Honoré de Balzac, *Lost Illusions*, trans. Herbert J. Hunt (Paris, 1837–43; Penguin Classics, London, 1971), p. 28.

57. Elizabeth Wilson, *Bohemians: The Glamorous Outcasts* (London and New York, 2000), p. 25.

58. See Laurence Flavigny, *Musée départemental des antiquités, 1831–1981* (Rouen, 1981).

59. Ibid., p. 15.

60. In E.-H. Langlois, *Essai historique, philosophique et pittoresque sur les danses des morts* (2 vols, Rouen, 1852), p. 98; there is reference to a 'M Cathermoul a young Englishman who was a pupil in [Langlois's] studio'. I have taken this to be George Cattermole.

61. Della Clayson Sperling, 'George Cattermole', *Oxford Dictionary of National Biography*.

62. Dickens to the Countess of Blessington, 27 January 1847, *The Letters of Charles Dickens*, ed. Graham Storey and K. J. Fielding, vol. 5 (Oxford, 1981), p. 15.

63. Balzac, *Lost Illusions*, p. 213.

64. Alexandre du Sommerard, *Les Arts du Moyen Age*, vol. 1 (Paris, 1838), p. iv.

65. Balzac, *Lost Illusions*, p. 190.

66. Quoted in Wainwright, *The Romantic Interior*, p. 12.

67. Ibid.

68. Quoted in Alain Erlande-Brandenburg, 'Évolution du Musée de Cluny', *Monuments Historiques* 104 (1979), p. 22.

69. Ibid., p. 23.

70. Edmond du Sommerard, *Musée des Thermes et de l'Hôtel de Cluny: catalogue et description des objets d'art* (Paris, 1864), *table et classifications*.

71. Correspondence of John Lingard, Lingard to the Revd Robert Tate, 27 September 1843, Ushaw College, County Durham.

72. Quoted in Mary B. Shepherd, '"Our Fine Gothic Magnificence": The nineteenth-century chapel at Costessey Hall, Norfolk and its medieval glazing', *Journal of the Society of Architectural Historians*, 54(2) (1995), p. 190.

73. Ibid., p. 186 n.11.

74. Ibid., p. 3.

75. Ibid., p. 186 n.1.

76. Ibid., p. 187 n.16.

77. Perry Butler, 'John Keble', *Oxford Dictionary of National Biography*.

78. Quoted in ibid.

79. Charlotte M. Yonge, *John Keble's Parishes: A History of Hursley and Otterbourne* (London, 1898), p. 83.

80. Ibid., p. 92.

81. Butler, 'John Keble'.

82. Quoted in Robert Dudley Middleton, *Magdalen Studies* (London, 1936), pp. 51–2.

83. Nikolaus Pevsner, *Bedfordshire, Huntingdon and Peterborough* (The Buildings of England Series, Harmondsworth, 1968), pp. 130–31.

84. Robert Needham Cust, *Some Account of the Church of Cockayne Hatley, Bedfordshire* (1851, privately printed), p. 8.

85. Ibid.

86. Ibid.

8. TARTAN, TREASON AND PLOT

1. Asa Briggs, *The Age of Improvement: 1783–1867* (1959; London, 1960), p. 195.

2. Thomas Mozley, 'New Churches', *British Critic and Quarterly Theological Review*, 1840, p. 514.

3. Hugh Cheape, *Tartan: The Highland Habit* (Edinburgh, 2006), p. 39.

4. John Prebble, *The King's Jaunt: George IV in Scotland, August 1822* (London, 1988), p. 6.

5. Hugh Trevor-Roper, 'The Invention of Tradition: The Highland Tradition of Scotland', in *The Invention of Tradition*, ed. Eric Hobsbawm and Terence Ranger (Cambridge, 1992), p. 30.

6. Colin Kidd, *Subverting Scotland's Past* (Cambridge, 1993), p. 259.

7. Scott justified the subtitle by claiming that he started work on the novel in 1805.

8. Quoted in Introduction, p. viii, Walter Scott, *Waverley; or, 'Tis Sixty Years Since*, ed. Claire Lamont (1814; Oxford World's Classics, Oxford, 1998).

9. Samuel Johnson and James Boswell, *To the Hebrides: Samuel Johnson's Journey to the Western Islands of Scotland and James Boswell's Journal of a Tour to the Hebrides*, ed. Ronald Black (1775, 1785; Edinburgh, 2007), p. 228.

10. *Parliamentary History of England from the Earliest Period to the Year 1803*, vol. 35, 1800–1801 (London, 1819), p. 340.

11. Ibid., p. 343.

12. Ibid., p. 366.

13. Lady Anne Elizabeth Brydges, 1779–1836, daughter of the 3rd Duke of Chandos, in 1796 married the 1st Duke of Buckingham and Chandos, Richard Temple-Nugent-Brydges-Chandos-Grenville.

14. *Parliamentary History of England*, p. 2.

15. *Letters to a Prebendary* (London, 1800), p. 218.

16. John Milner, *The History, Civil and Ecclesiastical, and Survey of the Antiquities of Winchester* (2 vols, Winchester, 1798, 1801, vol. 2, p. 33.

17. *The Gentleman's Magazine*, 70 (June 1800), p. 239.

18. Quoted in Milner, *Winchester*, vol. 2, p. 285; *Monthly Review*, April 1800, quoted in *Lingard Remembered: Essays to Mark the Sesquicentenary of John Lingard's Death*, ed. Peter Phillips (London, 2004), pp. 84–5.

19. *Quarterly Review*, 3 (1800), p. 361.

20. Ibid., 6(11), pp. 63–4.

21. Walter Scott, *The Antiquary*, ed. David Hewitt (1816; The Edinburgh Edition of the Waverley Novels, Edinburgh and Columbia, 1995), p. 131.

22. Ibid., p. 132.

23. *The Gentleman's Magazine* 70(1) (January 1800), p. 239.

24. Ibid., 69(2), (August 1799), p. 653.

25. Ibid.

26. John Carter, *Specimens of the Ancient Sculpture and Painting, now remaining in the Kingdom* (London, 1780–94), p. ii.

27. Letter to John Walker, October 1842, in *Life and Letters of John Lingard, 1771–1851*, ed. Martin Haile and Edwin Bonney (St Louis, Mo., and London, 1911), p. 73.

28. John Lingard, *The Antiquities of the Anglo-Saxon Church* (1806; Newcastle, 1810), p. iv.

29. Ibid., p. iv.
30. Sharon Turner, *The History of the Anglo-Saxons from the Earliest Period to the Norman Conquest* (3 vols, 1799–1805; 6th edn, London, 1842), Preface to the 3rd edn, p. iv.
31. Ibid., p. 231.
32. Lingard, *The Antiquities of the Anglo-Saxon Church*, p. 180.
33. *Quarterly Review*, 7(13), p. 92.
34. Ibid., p. 93.
35. Ibid., p. 92.
36. See Leo Gooch, 'Lingard v Barrington, et al: ecclesiastical politics in Durham, 1805–29', in *Lingard Remembered*, ed. Phillips, pp. 35–64.
37. Ibid., p. 35.
38. Quoted in ibid., p. 44.
39. Quoted in ibid., Introduction, p. 5.
40. M. N. L. Couve de Murville, *John Milner, 1752–1826* (Birmingham, 1986), p. 26.
41. Hengrave Hall MSS, 21/1/83–4ed, Cambridge University Library.
42. Ibid., 21/1/93.
43. Quoted in John E. Drabble, 'Mary's Protestant martyrs and Elizabeth's Catholic traitors in the age of Catholic Emancipation', *Church History*, 51(2) (1982), p. 181.
44. John Lingard, in Shepherd Collection, f25, Harris Manchester College, Oxford. Lingard sent the letter with the explanation to a young friend for her autograph collection on 22 July 1842
45. John Allen, *Edinburgh Review*, 1826, 44, p. 125.
46. Edwin Jones, 'John Lingard and the Simancas Archives', *The Historical Journal*, 10(1) (1967), p. 67.
47. Quoted in Edwin Jones, *John Lingard and the Pursuit of Historical Truth* (Brighton, 2001), p. 11.
48. John Lingard, *The History of England from the first invasion of the Romans to the revolution in 1688* (8 vols, London, 1819–1830), vol. 5, p. 81.
49. Ibid., vol. 1, pp. 89 and 78.
50. Robert Southey, *The Book of the Church* (2 vols, London, 1824), vol. 1, Introduction.
51. John Milner, *Strictures on the Poet Laureate's 'Book of the Church' by John Merlin* (London, 1824), pp. 3–4.
52. Quoted in John Vidmar, 'John Lingard's History of the English Reformation: History or apologetics?', *The Catholic Historical Review* 85(3) (1999), p. 383.

53. Ibid., p. 384.

54. Hengrave Hall MSS, 21/4/167.

55. Ibid., c7/4/129.

56. John Lingard, in Shepherd Collection, f43, 13 December 1823, Harris Manchester College, Oxford.

57. John Henry Newman, 'The Second Spring', in *Sermons Preached on Various Occasions* (Birmingham Oratory Millennium Edition of the Works of John Henry Newman, Hereford and Notre-Dame, Ind., 2009), p. 172.

58. A. C. Pugin, A. W. N. Pugin and Edward J. Willson, *Examples of Gothic Architecture* (3 vols, London, 1831–6), vol. 1, p. xiv.

59. Prebble, *The King's Jaunt*, p. 73.

60. Walter Scott, *Description of the Regalia of Scotland* (Edinburgh, 1819), p. 29.

61. *The Letters of Sir Walter Scott*, ed. Herbert Grierson (12 vols, London, 1932–7), vol. 5, p. 50.

62. *Provincial Antiquities and Picturesque Scenery of Scotland with descriptive illustrations* (London and Edinburgh, 1826), p. xxxviii.

63. Scott, *Letters*, vol. 5, p. 59, 16 January 1818. *The Iron Chest* was a popular play based on the novel *Caleb Williams* by William Godwin.

64. Ibid., p. 60. The supposed haunting in Cock Lane, Smithfield was a national sensation in 1762, attracting huge crowds. A commission of inquiry concluded it was a fraud for which a parish clerk, Richard Parsons, was sent to prison.

65. Scott, *Description of the Regalia of Scotland*, p. 30.

66. Ibid., p. 30.

67. Ibid., p. 5.

68. Ibid., p. 6.

69. Ibid., p. 34.

70. Scott, *Letters*, vol. 5, p. 82, 14 February 1818.

71. Samuel Rush Meyrick, Letters of Samuel Rush Meyrick to Sir Walter Scott, 3894 f1, c.5 January 1822, National Library of Scotland.

72. J. G. Lockhart, *The Life of Sir Walter Scott* (New Popular Edition, London, 1896), p. 481.

73. Prebble, *The King's Jaunt*, p. 103.

74. See Cheape, *Tartan*, pp 63–9.

75. Quoted in Prebble, *The King's Jaunt*, p. 123.

76. Catherine Sinclair, *Scotland and the Scotch, or the Western Circuit* (Edinburgh, 1841), p. vi.

77. Scott, *Letters*, vol. 5, p. 207.

78. Ibid., vol. 11, p. 207.

79. Ex inf. Craig Buchanan and Steven Robb.

80. Iain Mccalman, 'Controlling the riots: Dickens, *Barnaby Rudge* and Romantic revolution', *History*, 84(275) (1999), p. 465.

81. Quoted in ibid., p. 464.

82. See ibid., p. 464 n.22 for sources relating to Watson's 'long and complex involvement' with the Stuart papers; and Henrietta Taylor, *The Stuart Papers at Windsor, being selections from hitherto unprinted royal archives, with introduction and notes by Alistair and Henrietta Taylor* (London, 1938).

83. Mccalman, 'Controlling the riots', p. 469.

84. John Sobieski Stuart, *Vestiarium Scoticum* (Edinburgh, 1842), p. xi.

85. Scott, *Letters*, vol. 11, pp. 201–2.

86. Ibid., pp. 205–8.

87. Recorded in Ian Campbell, 'Campbell Tartan', f.19 (National Library of Scotland, 1871).

88. H. F. McClintock, *Old Highland Dress and Tartans* (Dundalk, 1943), pp. 51–5.

89. Elizabeth Grant, *Memoirs of a Highland Lady: The autobiography of Elizabeth Grant of Rothiemurchus afterwards Mrs Smith of Baltiboys 1797–1830*, ed. Lady Strachey (London, 1898), p. 388.

90. Hugh Trevor-Roper, *The Invention of Scotland: Myth and History* (London and New Haven, 2008), p. 232.

91. A. W. N. Pugin, *The Collected Letters of A. W. N. Pugin*, ed. Margaret Belcher (5 vols, Oxford, 2000–2015), vol. 1, p. 373, 6 August 1842, letter to the Earl of Shrewsbury.

92. Grant, *Memoirs of a Highland Lady*, p. 388.

93. Ibid.

94. Ibid.

95. Ibid.

96. Ibid.

97. John Sobieski Stuart, correspondence of Robert Chambers, Dep. 341 94 51–53, National Library of Scotland.

98. Ibid.

99. Introduction to the 1842 edition of Lingard's *History of England*, p. xxv.

100. John Sobieski Stuart, Charles Edward Stuart, *Tales of the Century or Sketches from the Romance of History* (Edinburgh, 1847), p. v.

101. Ibid., p. 1.

102. Ibid., p. 10.

103. Ibid., p. xii

104. George Skene, 'The heirs of the Stuarts', *Quarterly Review* (81) (1847).

9. WALTER SCOTT'S 'MIGHTY WIZZARD':
SHAKESPEARE AND THE ANTIQUARIES

1. Letter to the Académie française, 1776: artfl-project.uchicago.edu/tout-voltaire.
2. Ibid., 'Essai sur les moeurs', 1756, Chapitre des arts.
3. Jonathan Bate, *The Romantics on Shakespeare* (1992; Penguin Classics, London, 1997), p. 2.
4. J. G. Robertson, *Shakespeare on the Continent, 1660–1700*, vol. 12 (*Cambridge History of English and American Literature*, Cambridge, 1910).
5. See Linda Kelly, *The Kemble Era: John Philip Kemble, Sarah Siddons and the London Stage* (London, 1980).
6. Quoted in Samuel Schoenbaum, *Shakespeare's Lives* (Oxford, 1970), p. 252.
7. Ibid.
8. See Sybil Rosenfeld, *Georgian Scene Painters and Scene Painting* (Cambridge, 1981).
9. Walter Scott, 'Life of John Philip Kemble', *Quarterly Review*, 34 (1826), p. 226.
10. Quoted in Lidia Garbin, '"Not fit to tie his brogues": Shakespeare and Scott', in *Shakespeare and Scotland*, ed. Willy Maley and Andrew Murphy (Manchester, 2004), p. 142.
11. 'The Antiquary, by the Author of Waverley and Guy Mannering', *Quarterly Review*, 15(29), pp. 125–39.
12. William Hazlitt, *The Spirit of the Age* (4th edn, London, 1825), p. 107.
13. Walter Scott, 'An Essay on the Drama, first published in the supplement to the Encyclopedia Britannica', in *Miscellaneous Prose Works*, vol. 6 (Edinburgh, 1834), p. 197.
14. John Faed, Scottish artist (1819–1902).
15. Johann Gottfried Herder, *Shakespeare* (1773), ed. and trans. Gregory Moore (Princeton, 2008), Introduction, p. xxxvi.
16. Quoted in Diana de Marly, *Costume on Stage 1600–1949* (Totowa, N.J., 1982), p. 59.
17. Scott, 'Life of John Philip Kemble', p. 225.
18. James Robinson Planché, 'History of Theatrical Costume', in *The Book of Table-Talk*, ed. Charles Knight, vol. 1 (London, 1836), p. 164.
19. *The Recollections and Reflections of J. R. Planché (Somerset Herald)* (2 vols, London, 1872), vol. 1, p. 37.
20. Ibid., p. 37.

21. Planché, 'History of Theatrical Costume', p. 172.
22. Ibid.
23. John Cole, quoted in de Marly, *Costume on Stage 1600–1949*, p. 63.
24. Planché, *Recollections and* Reflections, vol. 1, p. 54.
25. Ibid.
26. Scott, 'Life of John Philip Kemble', p. 225.
27. Ralph B. Allen, 'Kemble and Capon at Drury Lane', *Educational Theatre Journal*, 23(1) (1971), p. 35.
28. Ibid., p. 24. See also Rosemary Hill, '"Proceeding like Guy Faux": The antiquarian investigation of St Stephen's Chapel, Westminster', *Architectural History*, 59 (2016).
29. Ralph Allen, p. 25.
30. Ibid., pp. 25–6.
31. I am grateful for Julian Pooley for helping me to establish that Carter was 'Artist and Antiquary'.
32. Planché, *Recollections and* Reflections, vol. 1, p. 52.
33. Ibid.
34. Ibid., p. 57.
35. Ibid., p. 60.
36. François Guizot, *Shakespeare and His Times* (New York, 1855), p. 230.
37. Bate, *The Romantics on Shakespeare*, p. 26.
38. Guizot, *Shakespeare and His Times*, p. 252.
39. Stendhal, *Racine and Shakespeare* (1822), trans. Guy Daniels with a Foreword by André Maurois (New York, 1962), p. 15.
40. Guizot, *Shakespeare and His Times*, p. 250.
41. Quoted in Sybil Rosenfeld, 'The Grieves Shakespearean Scene Designs', *Shakespeare Survey* 20 (Cambridge, 1967), p. 109; from an unsigned theatre notice in the Enthoven Collection at the Victoria and Albert Museum.
42. Planché, 'History of Theatrical Costume', p. 143.
43. Planché, *Recollections and Reflections*, vol. 2, pp. 85–6.
44. Quoted in Arthur Sherbo, 'George Steevens', *Oxford Dictionary of National Biography*. He may also have involved Gillray in the hoax described below (ex inf. Tim Clayton).
45. Ibid.
46. Ibid.
47. Peter Martin, 'Edmond Malone', *Oxford Dictionary of National Biography*.
48. John Britton, 'Essays on the Merits and Characteristics of William Shakspere [sic] also remarks on his birth and burial-place, his monument,

portraits, and associations', in Appendix (London, 1849), p. 14. In *Auto-biography* (1850).

49. Ibid.
50. Ibid.
51. Joseph Ritson, *The Letters of Joseph Ritson* (2 vols, London, 1833), vol. 2, p. 92.
52. Ibid.
53. Ibid., p. 93.
54. Walter Scott, *The Letters of Sir Walter Scott*, ed. Herbert Grierson (12 vols, London, 1932–7), vol. 1, p. 267.
55. Schoenbaum, *Shakespeare's Lives*, p. 178.
56. Francis Douce, *Illustrations of Shakspeare [sic] and of Ancient Manners: with dissertations on the clowns and fools of Shakspeare; on the collecting of popular tales entitled gest romanorum; and on the English morris dance* (2 vols, London, 1807), vol. 1, p. x.
57. Ibid., p. vi.
58. Ibid.
59. Ibid., p. 8.
60. Ibid., p. 19.
61. Ibid., p. 18.
62. Ibid., vol. 2, p. 281.
63. Ibid., p. 284.
64. Ibid., p. 295.
65. The story is told in William Christie, *The Edinburgh Literary Review in the Literary Culture of Romantic Britain* (London, 2009), p. 41.
66. Francis Jeffrey, 'Douce's illustrations of Shakespeare', *Edinburgh Review*, 12 (1808), p. 449.
67. Ibid.
68. Ibid., p. 459.
69. Ibid., p. 468.
70. *The Letters of Sir Walter Scott*, ed. Grierson, vol. 2, p. 16.
71. Ibid., vol. 7, p. 79.
72. Ibid., vol. 12, p. 450.
73. Quoted in Garbin, '"Not fit to tie his brogues"', p. 141.
74. Walter Scott, *The Journal of Sir Walter Scott*, ed. W. E. K. Anderson (Edinburgh, 1998), p. 323.
75. François-René Chateaubriand, *Sketches of English Literature* (2 vols, London, 1836), vol. 1, p. 236.
76. Ibid., p. 310.
77. Ibid., p. 309.

78. Schoenbaum, *Shakespeare's Lives*, p. 262.

79. Ibid.

80. Ibid., p. 263.

81. *Monthly Magazine or British Register*, February 1818, p. 4.

82. Ibid., p. 8.

83. Britton, 'Essays on . . . Shakspere', p. 6.

84. Ibid., p. 12.

85. Ibid., p. 7.

86. Ibid., p. 17.

87. *Monthly Magazine*, February 1818, p. 4.

88. For the dubious status of the latest 'portrait' see Katherine Duncan-Jones, 'Shakespeare unfound(ed)? The real identity for the new "Shakespeare" portrait', *Times Literary Supplement*, 18 March 2009.

89. Quoted in Clive Wainwright, *The Romantic Interior: The British Collector at Home, 1750–1850* (London and New Haven, 1989), p. 213.

90. Britton, 'Essays on . . . Shakspere', p. 29.

91. Ibid., p. 26.

92. Ibid., p. 29.

93. Michael Hall, *George Frederick Bodley and the Later Gothic Revival in Britain and America* (London and New Haven, 2014), p. 332.

94. For details of the work and reactions to it see ibid., pp. 330–33.

95. Arthur Freeman and Janet Ing Freeman, 'John Payne Collier', *Oxford Dictionary of National Biography*.

96. Ibid. The Freemans have been the most energetic labourers in this vast and muddy field. See Arthur Freeman and Janet Ing Freeman, *John Payne Collier: Scholarship and Forgery in the Nineteenth Century* (2 vols, London and New Haven, 2004).

97. Desmond Fitz-Gibbon, *Marketable Values: Inventing the Property Market in Modern Britain* (Chicago, 2018), p. 35.

98. Quoted in ibid. p. 35.

99. Britton, 'Essays on . . . Shakspere', p. 33.

100. Ibid., p. 34.

101. The Revd J. M. Jephson, *Shakespere: his birthplace, home, and grave. A Pilgimage to Stratford-on-Avon in the autumn of 1863* (London, 1864), p. 36.

102. Ibid., p. 37

103. Quoted in Katherine West Scheil, *Imagining Shakespeare's Wife: The Afterlife of Anne Hathaway* (Cambridge, 2018), p. 49.

104. Scott, 'Essay on the Drama', pp 186–7.

105. Britton, 'Essays on ... Shakspere', p. 40.

106. Ibid., p. 39.

107. This copy was presented by Britton to Thomas Estcourt, Conservative MP for Oxford University until 1847, as one of the subscribers to the Britton Testimonial. It was perhaps not so greatly appreciated as Britton hoped.

10. THE ANTIQUARIAN LANDSCAPE: VICTORIAN

1. T. A. Birrell, 'The Circle of John Gage (1786–1842), Director of the Society of Antiquaries, and the Bibliography of Medievalism', in *Antiquaries, Book Collectors and the Circles of Learning*, ed. Robin Myers and Michael Harris (Winchester and New Castle, Del., 1996), p. 78.

2. Hengrave Hall MSS, 21/14/12, Cambridge University Library.

3. W. Oliver, *Prophets and Millenialists* (Oxford, 1978), p.11.

4. Friedrich Engels, *The Condition of the Working Class in England* (1845; Penguin Classics, London, 1987), p. 264.

5. Hengrave Hall MSS, 21/2/176, Cambridge University Library.

6. See Marcia Collins, *The Dance of Death in Book Illustration* (Columbia, Mo., 1978), p. 8.

7. Francis Douce, *The Dance of Death* (London, 1833), p. 5.

8. Ibid.

9. Ibid., p. 2.

10. E.-H. Langlois, *Essai historique, philosophique et pittoresque sur les danses des morts* (2 vols, Rouen, 1852), p. 1.

11. Gustave Flaubert, *Oeuvres complètes* (Paris, 2001), p. 403.

12. See Lauriat Lane, 'Mr Pickwick and the Dance of Death', *Nineteenth-Century Fiction*, 14(2), (1959).

13. Caroline Shenton, *The Day Parliament Burned Down* (Oxford, 2012), p. 50.

14. A. W. N. Pugin, *The Collected Letters of A. W. N. Pugin*, ed. Margaret Belcher (5 vols, Oxford, 2000–2015), vol. 1, p. 42.

15. Ibid., p. 42.

16. Quoted in Michael Port, *The Houses of Parliament* (London, 1976), p. 23.

17. Howard Colvin, *A Biographical Dictionary of British Architects 1600–1840* (3rd edn, London and New Haven, 1995), p. 130.

18. *The Gentleman's Magazine*, ns, (5) (1836), p. 523. These articles were by the antiquary and topographical artist Edward John Carlos.

19. Ibid., p. 524.

20. Ibid., p. 635.

21. John Goodall, 'An American evolution, Harlaxton Manor, Lincolnshire', *Country Life*, 16 May 2018, p. 122.

22. Pugin, *Collected Letters*, vol. 1, pp. 17–18.

23. James Robinson Planché, *Regal Records: or a Chronicle of the Coronations of the Queens Regnant of England* (London, 1838), p. vii.

24. Ibid., pp. vii–viii.

25. *The Recollections and Reflections of J. R. Planché (Somerset Herald)* (2 vols, London, 1872), p. 196.

26. Planché, *Regal Records*, p. ix.

27. Ibid., p. xi.

28. Quoted in Mark Girouard, *The Return to Camelot: Chivalry and the English Gentleman* (London and New Haven, 1981), p. 92.

29. Ibid., p. 90.

30. Quoted in ibid., p. 93.

31. Walter Scott, *The Antiquary*, ed. David Hewitt (1816; The Edinburgh Edition of the Waverley Novels, Edinburgh and Columbia, 1995), p. 15.

32. Asa Briggs, *The Age of Improvement: 1783–1867* (1959; London, 1960), p. 295.

33. Thomas Dick Lauder, *Memorial of the Royal Progress in Scotland* (Edinburgh 1843), p. 3.

34. Quoted in Alex Tyrrell, 'The Queen's "Little Trip": The Royal Visit to Scotland in 1842', *The Scottish Historical Review*, 82 (213), part 1 (2003), p. 62.

35. Ibid.

36. Ibid., p. 63.

37. Lauder, *Memorial of the Royal Progress*, pp. 300–303.

38. Ibid., p. 303.

39. Quoted in Alistair Rowan, 'Taymouth Castle, Perthshire, II', *Country Life*, 15 October 1964.

40. Ibid.

41. Lauder, *Memorial of the Royal Progress*, p. 303.

42. John Sobieski Stuart, *Vestiarium Scoticum* (Edinburgh, 1842), p. xiii.

43. Ibid., p. 38.

44. Ibid., p. iii.

45. Ibid., p. x.

46. Ibid., p. xi.

47. Ibid., p. xii.

48. Walter Scott, *Abbotsford Edition of the Waverley Novels* (6 vols, Edinburgh and London, 1842), vol. 1, p. 4.

49. Stuart, *Vestiarium Scoticum*, p. 29.

50. Quoted in Tyrrell, 'The Queen's "Little Trip"', p. 66.

51. Ibid., p. 49.

52. Thomas Carlyle, *Past and Present* (Shilling Edition of Carlyle's Works, London, 1843), p. 115.

53. Nikolaus Pevsner, *Some Architectural Writers of the Nineteenth Century* (Oxford, 1972), p. 54.

54. Nikolaus Pevsner, *Cumberland and Westmorland* (1967; The Buildings of England Series, Harmondsworth, 1977), p. 198.

55. David Watkin, *The Rise of Architectural History* (London, 1980), p. 65.

56. Robert Willis, *The Architectural History of Winchester Cathedral* (1846; London, 1992), p. ii.

57. Carlyle, *Past and Present*, p. 115.

58. Ibid., p. 99.

59. Ibid., p. 104.

60. Ibid., p. 109.

61. Ibid., pp 136, 122.

62. Ibid., p. 137.

63. John Mason Neale, *A Few Words to Churchwardens on Churches and Church Ornaments Suited to Town and Manufacturing Parishes* (4th edn, Cambridge, 1842), p. 7.

64. *The Ecclesiologist* (Cambridge, 1842), vol. 1, p. 25.

65. Neale, *A Few Words to Churchwardens ... Town and Manufacturing Parishes*, p. 11.

66. John Mason Neale, *A Few Words to Churchwardens on Churches and Church Ornaments Suited to Country Parishes* (4th edn, Cambridge, 1841), p. 8.

67. Neale, *A Few Words to Churchwardens ... Town and Manufacturing Parishes*, p. 16.

68. Sir George Gilbert Scott, *Personal and Professional Recollections*, ed. Gavin Stamp (1879; Stamford, 1995), p. 88.

69. Thomas Mozley, *Reminiscences Chiefly of Oriel College and the Oxford Movement* (2 vols, London, 1882), vol. 2, p. 150.

70. George Eliot, *Scenes of Clerical Life* (1857), p. 4.

71. Ibid., p. 46.

72. Ibid.

73. John Britton, *The Autobiography of John Britton, FSA, honorary member of numerous English and foreign societies ... in three parts ... copiously Illustrated, London, printed for the author as presents to subscribers to 'The Britton Testimonial'* (3 vols, London, 1850), vol. 2, Appendix, p. 103.

74. See Rosemary Hill, '"The Single Blot upon the Fair Shield of Sir Charles Barry": Antiquaries, Architects and the Palace of Westminster', in *St Stephen's Chapel and the Palace of Westminster*, ed. John Cooper (London and New Haven, forthcoming).

75. Nikolaus Pevsner and David Neave, *Yorkshire: York and the East Riding* (The Buildings of England Series, London, 1995), p. 135.

76. John Britton, *Graphic Illustrations with Historical and Descriptive Accounts of Toddington, Gloucestershire* (London, 1840), p. xvi.

77. Victor Hugo, *Notre-Dame de Paris*, trans. John Sturrock (1831; Penguin Classics, London, 2004), p. 194.

78. Michael J. Lewis, *The Politics of the German Gothic Revival* (Cambridge, Mass., 1993), p. 88.

79. Georg Germann, *Gothic Revival in Europe and Britain: Sources, Influences and Ideas* (London, 1972), p. 94.

80. Ibid.

81. Quoted in Lewis, *German Gothic Revival*, p. 90.

11. A CHANGE OF DYNASTY IN THE HISTORIC REALM

1. Parts of the text were published by Scott's great-granddaughter, Mary Monica Maxwell Scott, between 1893 and 1905 but the 'often muddled' manuscript was edited and published in full by Gerrard Carruthers and Alison Lumsden in 2004.

2. Walter Scott, *Reliquiae Trotcosienses or the Gabions of the Late Jonathan Oldbuck Esq of Monkbarns*, ed. Gerrard Carruthers and Alison Lumsden (Edinburgh, 2004), p. 21. John Woodward (1665/8–1728) an antiquary whose 'contentious nature and personal ambition' rendered him the butt of satire which outlived his 'real contributions to modern scientific and historical method'. J. M. Levine, *Oxford Dictionary of National Biography*.

3. Scott, *Reliquiae Trotcosienses*, p. 25.

4. Ibid., p. 34.

5. Letter to J. C. Loudon, September 1838, John Ruskin, *The Complete Works of John Ruskin*, ed. E. T. Cook and Alexander Wedderburn (39 vols, London, 1903–12), vol. 36, pp. 15–17.

6. Scott, *Reliquia Trotcosienses*, p. 34.

7. Ibid.

8. M. le Vicomte Walsh, *Relation du voyage de Henri de France en Écosse et en Angleterre* (Paris, 1844), pp. 80–81.

9. Thomas Carlyle, 'Sir Walter Scott', *London and Westminster Review*, 12 (1838), p. 315.

10. Ibid., p. 315.

11. Ibid., p. 336.

12. John Britton, *An address from John Britton, FSA, to the nobility, gentry, and clergy of the county, generally; and particularly to those assembled at the congress of the Archaeological Institute at Salisbury in July 1849* (Wiltshire, 1849), p. 2.

13. Quoted in Alexandrina Buchanan, 'Robert Willis and the Rise of Architectural History' (University College London PhD thesis, 1994), p. 104.

14. Robert Willis, *The Architectural History of Winchester Cathedral* (1846; London, 1992), p. 1.

15. Ibid.

16. Alexandrina Buchanan, *Robert Willis (1800–1875) and the Foundation of Architectural History* (vol. 8, *The History of the University of Cambridge*, Woodbridge, 2013), p. 163.

17. E. A. Freeman, *A History of Architecture* (London, 1849), p. xiii.

18. John Ruskin, *The Seven Lamps of Architecture* (London, 1849), p. 6.

19. Ibid.

20. Ibid., p. 94.

21. Ibid., p. 164.

22. Ibid., p. 162.

23. Ibid., p. 5.

24. Ibid., p. vii.

25. Thomas Babington Macaulay, *Lord Macaulay's History of England, Introduced and Selected by John Burrow* (New York, 2009), p. 2.

26. Quoted in ibid., p. 8.

27. *The Times*, Saturday, 26 February 1848.

28. Thomas Babington Macaulay, *The Letters of Thomas Babington Macaulay*, ed. Thomas Pinney, vol. 4 (Cambridge, 1977), p. 15.

29. *Lord Macaulay's History of England*, Introduction, p. 10.

30. Ibid., pp. 95–6.

31. *Life and Letters of John Lingard, 1771–1851*, ed. Martin Haile and Edwin Bonney (St Louis, Mo., and London, 1911), p. 344.

32. Ibid., p. 345.

33. Quoted in *Lord Macaulay's History of England*, Introduction, p. 10.

34. Michael Borrie, 'Sir Frederic Madden', *Oxford Dictionary of National Biography*.

35. Journals of Frederic Madden, 9 September 1850, Bodleian Library.

36. James Delbourgo, *Collecting the World: The Life and Curiosity of Hans Sloane* (London, 2017), p. 336.

37. Journals of Frederic Madden, 4 January 1851.

38. Ibid., 4 January 1851.

39. Borrie, 'Sir Frederic Madden'.

40. 'The Douce Legacy: An exhibition to commemorate the 150th anniversary of the bequest of Francis Douce', Bodleian Library (Oxford 1984), p. v.

41. For the contents of Cottingham's Museum and his career see Janet Myles, *L. N. Cottingham 1787–1847: Architect of the Gothic Revival* (London, 1996).

42. A. W. N. Pugin, *The Collected Letters of A. W. N. Pugin*, ed. Margaret Belcher (5 vols, Oxford, 2000–2015), vol. 5, p. 88.

43. Edward Bottoms, 'The Royal Architectural Museum in the light of new documentary evidence', *Journal of the History of Collections*, 19(1) (2007), p. 120.

44. Quoted in ibid., p. 121.

45. Quoted in ibid., p. 124.

46. Quoted in ibid., p. 130.

47. John Aubrey, *Brief Lives*, ed. Kate Bennett (2 vols, Oxford, 2015), vol. 1, p. lxxiv.

48. John Burrow, *A History of Histories* (London, 2007), p. 388.

49. Ibid., p. 459.

50. Ibid.

51. Ibid., p. 460.

52. Philippa Levine, *The Amateur and the Professional: Antiquaries, Historians and Archaeologists in Victorian England 1838–1886* (Cambridge, 1986), p. 155.

53. Quoted in ibid., p. 138.

54. Burrow, *A History of Histories*, p. 462.

55. Quoted in ibid.

56. Ibid., p. 462.

57. Ibid., p. 465.

58. Ian Campbell, 'Campbell Tartan' (National Library of Scotland, 1871).

59. Ibid. inside front cover.

60. Ibid., f.32v.

61. Ibid., f.31.

62. Ibid., 9, f.71v.

63. Ibid., 10, ff.81–2.

64. Ibid., ff.86–7.

65. Ibid., f.129.
66. Ibid., 9, f.3.
67. Ibid., f.128.
68. Ibid., 10, f.3v.
69. Donald C. Stewart and J. Charles Thompson, *Scotland's Forged Tartans: An Analytical Study of the 'Vestiarium Scoticum'*, ed. James Scarlett (Edinburgh, 1980).

Bibliography

ARCHIVAL SOURCES

John Britton, Correspondence of John Britton, Edinburgh University Library.
——— Letters addressed to Mr Cunningham FSA, Devizes Museum, Wiltshire.
Ian Campbell, 'Campbell Tartan', National Library of Scotland.
John Carter, 'Occurrences in the life, and memorandums relating to the professional persuits [sic] of J C F.A.S. Architect', papers of Philip Hammersly Leathes, Leathes Collection, King's College, London.
Francis Douce papers, Bodleian Library, Oxford.
John Gage, literary correspondence, Hengrave Hall MSS (1815–42), Cambridge University Library.
——— Letters to and from John Gage, Bodleian Library, Oxford.
Hudson Gurney, 'Journal of a tour through France to Rome and Naples by Hudson Gurney Esq MP FRS etc in company with the Earl of Aberdeen and Rev G D Whittington', Society of Antiquaries, London.
John Lingard, correspondence, Shepherd Collection, Harris Manchester College, Oxford.
——— Correspondence, Ushaw College, County Durham.
Frederic Madden, Journals of Frederic Madden, Bodleian Library, Oxford.
Samuel Rush Meyrick, letters of Samuel Rush Meyrick to Sir Walter Scott, 1821–6, National Library of Scotland.
Nichols Archive (private collection). The archive can be consulted by appointment with Dr Julian Pooley via the Surrey History Centre, Woking.
Thomas Rickman–Edward Blore letters, 1813–19, British Library.
Jacob Schnebbelie correspondence, Society of Antiquaries.
The Walter Scott Digital Archive, University of Edinburgh.
Minutes, Society of Antiquaries, London.
Joseph Strutt, 'Emma Darcy, or, the Manners of Old Times' (1801–2), Abbotsford Collection, National Library of Scotland.

John Sobieski Stuart, correspondence of Robert Chambers, National Library of Scotland.

Dawson Turner, 'Journal of a Tour to France 1814', Shirehall, Castle Museum, Norwich.

—— 'Journal of a Three-Weeks Tour ... in the Autumn of 1815', Trinity College, Cambridge.

PRINTED SOURCES

A catalogue of the whole of the very interesting and historical contents of Hengrave Hall (London, 1897).

Adamson, Henry, The Muses' Threnodie, or Mirthful Mournings on the Death of Mr Gall ... compiled from authentic records by James Cant (Perth, 1774).

Allen, John, Edinburgh Review, 37 (1826), pp. 94–155.

Allen, Ralph B., 'Kemble and Capon at Drury Lane', Educational Theatre Journal, 23(1) (1971), pp. 22–35.

Altick, Richard, The Shows of London (Cambridge, Mass. and London, 1978).

Amyot, Thomas, 'A Defence of the Early Antiquity of the Bayeux Tapestry', Archaeologia (19) (1821), pp. 192–208.

—— 'Observations on an Historical Fact supposed to be established by the Bayeux Tapestry by Thomas Amyot esq. F.S.A. in a letter addressed to Henry Ellis esq. FRS Secretary, dated February 24, 1818', Archaeologia, 19 (1821), p. 88.

'Antiquariolus', 'Tapestry of William the Conqueror's Queen', The Gentleman's Magazine, 73–4 (1803–4), 74, pp. 18–19.

Arnold's Library of the Fine Arts (London, 1833).

Aston, Margaret, 'English ruins and English history: The Dissolution and the sense of the past', Journal of the Warburg and Courtauld Institutes, 36 (1973), pp. 231–55.

Aubrey, John, The Natural History of Wiltshire, ed. John Britton (London, 1847).

—— Monumenta Britannica, ed. Rodney Legg and John Fowles (3 vols, Sherborne, 1980–82).

—— Brief Lives, ed. Kate Bennett (2 vols, Oxford, 2015).

Balzac, Honoré de, La Peau de chagrin (1831), Oeuvres Complètes, vol. 18 (1831; Paris, 1960).

—— Lost Illusions (Illusions perdues) (1837–43), trans. Herbert J. Hunt (Penguin Classics, London, 1971).

Bann, Stephen, *The Inventions of History: Essays on the Representation of the Past* (Manchester, 1990).

Bate, Jonathan, *The Romantics on Shakespeare* (1992; Penguin Classics, London, 1997).

The Bayeux Tapestry: New Interpretations, ed. Martin K. Foys, Karen Eileen Overbey and Dan Terkla (Woodbridge, 2009).

Bereaud, Jacques G. A., 'La Traduction en France à l'époque romantique', *Comparative Literature Studies*, 8(3) (1971), pp. 224–44.

Berlin, Isaiah, *The Roots of Romanticism* (1999; London, 2000).

Biddle, Martin et al., *King Arthur's Round Table: An Archaeological Investigation* (Winchester, 2000).

Birrell, T. A. 'The Circle of John Gage (1786–1842), Director of the Society of Antiquaries, and the Bibliography of Medievalism', in *Antiquaries, Book Collectors and the Circles of Learning*, ed. Robin Myers and Michael Harris (Winchester and New Castle, Del., 1996)

—— 'The Society of Antiquaries and the taste for Old English', *Neophilologus*, 50 (1966), pp. 107–17.

Boswell, James, *Boswell's Life of Johnson* (1791; Oxford, 1953).

Bottoms, Edward, 'The Royal Architectural Museum in the light of new documentary evidence', *Journal of the History of Collections*, 19(1) (2007), pp. 115–39.

Bradley, Simon, 'The Englishness of Gothic: Theories and interpretations from William Gilpin to J. H. Parker', *Architectural History*, 45 (2002), pp. 325–46.

Bray, Anna (Eliza Stothard) (see also Stothard, Mrs Charles), *Traditions, Legends, Superstitions and Sketches of Devonshire* (3 vols, London, 1838).

Bresc-Bautier, Geneviève and Béatrice de Chancel-Bardelot (eds), *Un Musée révolutionnaire: Le musée des monuments français d'Alexandre Lenoir*, (Paris, 2016).

Bridgeford, Andrew, *1066: The Hidden History in the Bayeux Tapestry* (New York, 2005).

Briggs, Asa, *The Age of Improvement: 1783–1867* (1959; London, 1960).

Brine, Douglas, '"An unrivalled brass Lectorium": The Cloisters lectern and the Gothic Revival in England', *Sculpture Journal*, 29(1) 2020, pp. 45–63.

Britton, John, *The Beauties of England and Wales* (25 vols, London, 1801–16).

—— *The Cathedral Antiquities of England* (5 vols, London, 1814–35).

—— *The Rights of Literature; or an inquiry into the policy and justice of the claims of certain public libraries on all the publishers and authors of the United Kingdom, for eleven copies, on the best paper, of every new publication* (London, 1814).

—— *Chronological History and Graphic Illustrations of Christian Architecture in England* (London, 1818–26).

—— *Graphic Illustrations with Historical and Descriptive Accounts of Toddington, Gloucestershire* (London, 1840).

—— *Memoir of John Aubrey FRS* (London, 1845).

—— *An address from John Britton, FSA, to the nobility, gentry, and clergy of the county, generally; and particularly to those assembled at the congress of the Archaeological Institute at Salisbury in July 1849* (Wiltshire, 1849).

—— 'Essays on the Merits and Characteristics of William Shakspere [*sic*] also remarks on his birth and burial-place, his monument, portraits, and associations' (London, 1849). In *Autobiography* (1850).

—— *The Autobiography of John Britton, FSA, honorary member of numerous English and foreign societies … in three parts … copiously Illustrated, London, printed for the author as presents to subscribers to 'The Britton Testimonial'* (3 vols, London, 1850).

Brown, Iain Gordon, *The Hobby-Horsical Antiquary: A Scottish Character 1640–1830* (Edinburgh, 1980).

Brown, Shirley Ann, *The Bayeux Tapestry: History and Bibliography* (Woodbridge, 1988).

Buchanan, Alexandrina, 'Robert Willis and the rise of Architectural History' (University College London PhD thesis, 1994).

—— '"Wyatt the Destroyer": A vandal at Salisbury Cathedral?', in *Iconoclasm: Contested Objects, Contested Terms*, ed. Stacy Boldrick and Richard Clay (Aldershot, 2007).

—— *Robert Willis (1800–1875) and the Foundation of Architectural History* (vol. 8, *The History of the University of Cambridge*, Woodbridge, 2013).

Burd, Henry A., 'Joseph Ritson and Some Editors of Shakespeare', in *Shakespeare Studies by Members of the Department of English of the University of Wisconsin to Commemorate the Three-Hundredth Anniversary of the Death of William Shakespeare* (Madison, Wis., 1916), pp. 253–75.

Burns, Robert, *The Letters of Robert Burns*, ed. G. Ross Roy (2 vols, Oxford, 1985).

—— *The Complete Poems and Songs* (New Lanark, 2000).

—— *The Oxford Edition of the Works of Robert Burns*, ed. Nigel Leask, vol. 1 (Oxford, 2014).

Burrow, John, *A Liberal Descent: Victorian Historians and the English Past* (Cambridge, 1981).

—— *A History of Histories* (2007; London, 2009).

Camden, William, *Remaines concerning Britaine, but especially England, and the Inhabitants thereof* ... (London, 1614).

Campbell, Gordon, *The Hermit in the Garden: From Imperial Rome to Ornamental Gnome* (Oxford, 2013).

Capwell, Tobias, 'The greatest of the giants on whose shoulders we stand', *Apollo*, February 2016, p. 21.

Carlyle, Thomas, 'Sir Walter Scott', *London and Westminster Review*, 12 (1838).

—— *Past and Present* (Shilling Edition of Carlyle's Works, London, 1843).

Carter, John, *Specimens of the Ancient Sculpture and Painting, now remaining in the Kingdom* (London, 1780–94).

Cash, Arthur H., *John Wilkes: The Scandalous Father of Civil Liberty* (London and New Haven, 2006).

Catalani, Anna and Susan Pearce, '"Particular thanks and obligations": The communications made by women to the Society of Antiquaries between 1776 and 1837, and their significance', *The Antiquaries Journal*, 86 (2006), pp. 254–78.

Chateaubriand, François-René, *Sketches of English Literature* (2 vols, London, 1836).

Cheape, Hugh, *Tartan: The Highland Habit* (Edinburgh, 2006).

Chippindale, Christopher, 'John Britton's "Celtic Cabinet" in Devizes Museum and its context', *Antiquaries Journal*, 65(1) (1985), pp. 121–38.

Choay, Françoise, *The Invention of the Historic Monument*, trans. Lauren M. O'Connell (Cambridge, 2001).

Christie, William, *The Edinburgh Literary Review in the Literary Culture of Romantic Britain* (London, 2009).

Clark, Kenneth, *The Gothic Revival: An Essay in the History of Taste* (London, 1928).

Clarke, Stephen, 'Rosamond's Bower, The Pryor's Bank, and the long shadow of Strawberry Hill', *Journal of the History of Collections*, 26(2) (2014), pp. 287–306.

Cobbett, William, *Rural Rides* (London, 1830).

Coleridge, Samuel Taylor, *Biographia Literaria* (1817. Everyman's Library, London, 1960).

Collins, Marcia, *The Dance of Death in Book Illustration* (Columbia, Mo., 1978).

Colvin, Howard, *A Biographical Dictionary of British Architects 1600–1840* (3rd edn, London and New Haven, 1995).

Corbett, Margery, 'The title-page and illustrations to the *Monasticon Anglicanum* 1655–1673', *The Antiquaries Journal*, 67(1) (1987), pp. 102–10.

Courajod, Louis, *Alexandre Lenoir: son journal et le musée des monuments français* (2 vols, Paris, 1878, 1886).

Coutil, Léon, *Eustache-Hyacinthe Langlois de Pont-de-l'Arche* (Rouen, 1925).

Couve de Murville, M. N. L., *John Milner, 1752–1826* (Birmingham, 1986).

Croad, Stephen, 'Sham Castles', *The Oxford Art Journal*, 5(2) (1983), pp. 68–9.

Crook, J. Mordaunt, 'John Britton and the Genesis of the Gothic Revival', in *Concerning Architecture: Essays on Architectural Writers and Writing Presented to Nikolaus Pevsner*, ed. John Summerson (London, 1968).

―――― and M. H. Port, *The History of the King's Works Volume VI, 1782–1851*, ed. H. M. Colvin (London, 1973).

Cust, Robert Needham, *Some Account of the Church of Cockayne Hatley, Bedfordshire* (1851, privately printed).

d'Aussy, Pierre Jean Baptiste Le Grand, *Histoire de la vie privée des Français* (Paris, 1782).

Danloux, Henri Pierre, *Henry [sic] Pierre Danloux, peintre de portraits, et son journal durant l'émigration . . .*, ed. Roger Portalis (Paris, 1910).

Dargan, E. Preston, 'Scott and the French Romantics', *Publications of the Modern Languages Association of America*, 49(2) (1934), pp. 599–629.

Darke, Diana, *Stealing from the Saracens: How Islamic Architecture Shaped Europe* (London, 2020).

de Chancel-Bardelot, Béatrice, 'Les salles du musée des monuments français', in *Un Musée révolutionnaire: Le musée des monuments français d'Alexandre Lenoir*, ed. Geneviève Bresc-Bautier and Béatrice de Chancel-Bardelot (Paris, 2016), pp. 120–37.

de Marly, Diana, *Costume on Stage 1600–1949* (Totowa, N.J., 1982).

Defauconpret, Auguste-Jean-Baptiste, *Quinze jours à Londres* (Paris, 1816).

Delbourgo, James, *Collecting the World: The Life and Curiosity of Hans Sloane* (London, 2017).

Denis, Hélène, 'L'imaginaire du gout: motifs "ecossais" dans le paysage parisien au debut du XIXe siècle', *French Historical Studies*, 22(4) (1999), pp. 535–56.

Dibdin, Thomas Frognall, *A Bibliographical, Antiquarian and Picturesque Tour in France and Germany* (2 vols, London, 1821).

―――― *Bibliophobia* (London, 1832).

Dickens, Charles, *The Posthumous Papers of the Pickwick Club* (London, 1836–7).

―――― *Great Expectations* (London, 1861).

―――― *The Letters of Charles Dickens*, ed. Graham Storey and K. J. Fielding, vol. 5 (Oxford, 1981).

Douce, Francis, *Illustrations of Shakspeare* [sic] *and of Ancient Manners: with dissertations on the clowns and fools of Shakspeare; on the collecting of popular tales entitled gest romanorum; and on the English morris dance* (2 vols, London, 1807).

———— *The Dance of Death, exhibited in elegant engravings on wood. With a dissertation on the several representations of that subject, but more particularly on those ascribed to Macaber and Hans Holbein* (London, 1833).

'The Douce Legacy: An exhibition to commemorate the 150th anniversary of the bequest of Francis Douce', Bodleian Library (Oxford, 1984).

Douglas, David C., *English Scholars, 1660–1730* (London, 1951).

Drabble, John E., 'Mary's Protestant martyrs and Elizabeth's Catholic traitors in the age of Catholic Emancipation', *Church History* 51(2) (1982), pp. 172–85.

Draper, Peter, 'Islam and the West: The early use of the pointed arch revisited', *Architectural History*, 48 (2005), pp. 1–20.

du Pasquier, Jacqueline, 'La Duchesse de Berry, arbitre de la mode et reine du style troubadour', in Hildegard Kremers et al., *Marie-Caroline de Berry* (Paris, 2002), pp. 124–37.

du Sommerard, Alexandre, *Les Arts du Moyen Age*, vol. 1 (Paris, 1838).

du Sommerard, Edmond, *Musée des Thermes et de l'Hôtel de Cluny: catalogue et description des objets d'art* (Paris, 1864).

Duffy, Eamon, *The Stripping of the Altars: Traditional Religion in England c.1400–c.1580* (London and New Haven, 1992).

Duffy, Stephen, 'French artists and the Meyrick armoury', *The Burlington Magazine*, CLI, May 2009, pp. 284–92.

Dugdale, William, *Monasticon Anglicanum or the History of the antient Abbies, and other Monasteries . . . in England and Wales, now epitomised in English*, trans. James Wright (London, 1693).

Duncan-Jones, Katherine, 'Shakespeare unfound(ed)? The real identity for the new "Shakespeare" portrait', *Times Literary Supplement*, 20 March 2009.

Earle, John, *The Autograph Manuscript of Microcosmographie* (c.1628; Leeds, 1966).

Eastlake, Charles L., *A History of the Gothic Revival* (London, 1872).

Eliot, George, *Scenes of Clerical Life* (London, 1857).

Ellis, Henry, *A General Introduction to the Domesday Book* (London, 1833).

Engels, Friedrich, *The Condition of the Working Class in England* (1845; London, Penguin Classics, 1987).

English County Histories: A Guide, ed. C. R. J. Currie and C. P. Lewis (Stroud, 1994).

Entre cour et jardin: Marie-Caroline, Duchesse de Berry, Musée de l'Île de France (Sceaux, 2007).

Erlande-Brandenburg, Alain, 'Évolution du Musée de Cluny', *Monuments Historiques*, 104 (1979), pp. 21–6.

Evans, Dai Morgan, '"Banks is the Villain!"? Sir Joseph Banks and the governance of the Society of Antiquaries', *The Antiquaries Journal*, 89 (2009), pp. 337–63.

—— 'The Society of Antiquaries, 1707–18: Meeting places and origin stories', *The Antiquaries Journal*, 89 (2009), pp. 323–35.

Evans, Joan, *A History of the Society of Antiquaries* (Oxford, 1956).

Ferrey, Benjamin, *Recollections of A. N. Welby Pugin and his father Augustus Pugin*, reprinted with an introduction by Clive Wainwright and an index by Jane Wainwright (1861; London, 1978).

Fitz-Gibbon, Desmond, *Marketable Values: Inventing the Property Market in Modern Britain* (Chicago, 2018).

Flaubert, Gustave, *Oeuvres complètes* (Paris, 2001).

Flavigny, Laurence, *Musée départemental des antiquités, 1831–1981* (Rouen, 1981).

Foote, Samuel, *The Nabob* (1772), in *Plays by Samuel Foote and Arthur Murphy*, ed. George Taylor (Cambridge, 1984).

Freeman, Arthur and Janet Ing Freeman, *John Payne Collier: Scholarship and Forgery in the Nineteenth Century* (2 vols, London and New Haven, 2004).

Freeman, E. A., *A History of Architecture* (London, 1849).

—— *The Norman Conquest of England: Its Causes and Results* (1870–76; 2nd edn, Oxford, 1875).

Frew, John M., 'Richard Gough, James Wyatt, and Late 18th-Century Preservation', *Journal of the Society of Architectural Historians*, 38(4) 1979, pp. 366–74.

—— 'Gothic is English: John Carter and the revival of the Gothic as England's national style', *The Art Bulletin*, 64(2) (1982), pp. 315–19.

Garbin, Lidia, '"Not fit to tie his brogues": Shakespeare and Scott', in *Shakespeare and Scotland*, ed. Willy Maley and Andrew Murphy (Manchester, 2004), pp. 141–56.

Garside, P. D., 'Scott, the Romantic past and the nineteenth century', *The Review of English Studies*, new series, 23(90) (1972), pp. 147–61.

Germann, Georg, *Gothic Revival in Europe and Britain: Sources, Influences and Ideas* (London, 1972)

Gibbon, Edward, *Memoirs of My Life*, ed. Betty Radice (1796; London, 1984).

Gibbs, Christopher, *Davington Priory* (privately published, n.d.).

Gilpin, William, *Observations on the River Wye and several parts of South Wales etc ... in the summer of the year 1770* (1782; 2nd edn, London, 1789).

Girouard, Mark, *The Return to Camelot: Chivalry and the English Gentleman* (London and New Haven, 1981).

Goodall, John, 'An American evolution, Harlaxton Manor, Lincolnshire', *Country Life*, 16 May 2018, pp. 120–28.

Goodman, Nigel (ed.), *Dawson Turner: A Norfolk Antiquary and his Remarkable Family* (Chichester, 2007).

Grant, Elizabeth, *Memoirs of a Highland Lady: The autobiography of Elizabeth Grant of Rothiemurchus afterwards Mrs Smith of Baltiboys 1797–1830*, ed. Lady Strachey (London, 1898).

Grape, Wolfgang, *The Bayeux Tapestry: Monument to a Norman Triumph* (New York, 1994).

Grose, Francis, *The Olio: being a collection of essays ... by the late Francis Grose* (London, 1792).

Guillot, François, *L'Invention de la Normandie* (Caen, 2011).

Guizot, François, *Shakespeare and His Times* (1821; New York, 1855).

Gurney, Hudson, 'Observations on the Bayeux Tapestry', *Archaeologia*, 18 (1817), pp. 359–70.

Haile, Martin and Edwin Bonney (eds), *Life and Letters of John Lingard, 1771–1851* (St Louis, Mo., and London, 1911).

Hall, Michael, *George Frederick Bodley and the later Gothic Revival in Britain and America* (London and New Haven, 2014).

Hamper, William (ed.), *The Life, Diary and Correspondence of Sir William Dugdale* (London, 1827).

Harmsen, Theodor, *Antiquarianism in the Augustan Age: Thomas Hearne 1678–1735* (Oxford, 2000).

Harris, John, *Moving Rooms: The Trade in Architectural Salvage* (London and New Haven, 2007).

Haskell, Francis, *History and its Images* (London and New Haven, 1993).

Hazlitt, William, *The Spirit of the Age* (4th edn, London, 1825).

—— *The Complete Works of William Hazlitt*, ed. P. P. Howe (21 vols, London and Toronto, 1930–34).

Herder, Johann Gottfried, *Shakespeare*, ed. and trans. Gregory Moore (1773; Princeton, 2008).

Hicks, Carola, *The Bayeux Tapestry: The Life Story of a Masterpiece* (London, 2006).

Hill, Rosemary, 'A Gothic Vatican! Horace Walpole and Strawberry Hill', *Times Literary Supplement*, 21 May 2010, pp. 3–4.

—— '"Proceeding like Guy Faux": The antiquarian investigation of St Stephen's Chapel, Westminster', *Architectural History*, 59 (2016), pp. 253–79.

Hobsbawm, Eric and Terence Ranger (eds), *The Invention of Tradition* (Cambridge, 1992).

Hopkins, Annette B., 'Ritson's Life of King Arthur', *PMLA*, 43(1) (1928), pp. 251–87.

Huard, Georges, '"Notre-Dame de Paris" et les antiquaires de Normandie', *Revue d'histoire littéraire de la France*, 53(3) (1953), pp. 319–44.

Hugo, Victor, *Notre-Dame de Paris*, ed. Benedikte Andersson, Preface by Adrien Goetz (1831; Paris, 2009).

—— *Notre-Dame de Paris*, trans. John Sturrock (Penguin Classics, London, 2004).

Hulme, T. E., 'Romanticism and Classicism', in *Art, Humanism and the Philosophy of Art*, ed. Herbert Read (London, 1936), pp. 113–40.

Humboldt, Wilhelm von, 'On the historian's task' (1821), *History and Theory*, 6(1) (1967), pp. 57–71.

Hurley, Cecilia, 'Écrire la visite au musée: Lenoir et le catalogue du musée des monuments français', in *Un musée révolutionaire* (Paris, 2016), pp. 228–40.

Jay, Elisabeth, 'Charlotte Mary Yonge', *Oxford Dictionary of National Biography*.

Jeffrey, Francis, 'Douce's illustrations of Shakespeare', *Edinburgh Review*, 12 (1808), pp. 449–68.

Jephson, the Revd J. M., *Shakespere: his birthplace, home, and grave. A Pilgimage to Stratford-on-Avon in the autumn of 1863* (London, 1864).

Jervis, Simon, 'The Pryor's Bank, Fulham', *Furniture History*, 10 (1974), pp. 87–98.

Johnson, Samuel and James Boswell, *To the Hebrides: Samuel Johnson's Journey to the Western Islands of Scotland and James Boswell's Journal of a Tour to the Hebrides*, ed. Ronald Black (1775, 1785; Edinburgh, 2007).

Jones, Edwin, 'John Lingard and the Simancas Archives', *The Historical Journal*, 10(1) (1967), pp. 57–76.

—— *John Lingard and the Pursuit of Historical Truth* (Brighton, 2001).

Jones, Ethel, *Les Voyageurs français en Angleterre de 1815 à 1830* (Paris, 1930).

Keats, *Poetical Works*, ed. H. W. Garrod (1956; Oxford, 1970).

Kelly, Linda, *The Kemble Era: John Philip Kemble, Sarah Siddons and the London Stage* (London, 1980).

Kerr, Alex, 'Thomas Rickman in France', in *A Quaker Miscellany for Edward H. Milligan*, ed. Jeremy Greenwood, Alex Kerr and David Blamires (Manchester, 1985), pp. 111–20.

Kidd, Colin, *Subverting Scotland's Past* (Cambridge, 1993).

Knight, Richard Payne, *The Landscape, a didactic poem in three books* (2nd edn, London, 1795).

―――― *An Analytical Inquiry into the Principles of Taste* (London, 1805).

Kremer, Hildegard et al., *Marie Caroline de Berry, Naples, Paris, Graz: itinéraire d'une princesse romantique* (Paris, 2002).

Lacroix, Sophie, *Ce que nous disent les Ruines* (Paris, 2007).

Lane, Lauriat, 'Mr Pickwick and the Dance of Death', *Nineteenth-Century Fiction*, 14(2) (1959), pp. 171–2.

Lang, S., 'Richard Payne Knight and the Idea of Modernity', in *Concerning Architecture: Essays on Architectural Writers and Writing Presented to Nikolaus Pevsner*, ed. John Summerson (London, 1968).

Langlois, E.-H., *Essai historique et descriptif sur l'Abbaye de Fontanelle ou Saint-Wandrille* (Rouen, 1832).

―――― *Essai historique et descriptif sur la peinture sur verre ancienne et moderne* (Rouen, 1832).

―――― *Hymne à la cloche* (Rouen, 1832).

―――― *Les Énervés de Jumièges* (Rouen, 1838).

―――― *Essai historique, philosophique et pittoresque sur les danses des morts* (2 vols, Rouen, 1852).

―――― and Charles Richard and A. Deville, *Stalles de la Cathédrale de Rouen* (Rouen, 1838).

E.-H. Langlois, Bibliothèque Municipale de Rouen (Rouen, 1977).

Laspougeas, Jean, 'La Normandie au temps d'Arcisse de Caumont', in *Arcisse de Caumont: érudit normand et fondateur de l'archéologie française*, ed. Société des Antiquaires de Normandie (Caen, 2004), pp. 11–23.

Lauder, Thomas Dick, *Memorial of the Royal Progress in Scotland* (Edinburgh, 1843).

Le Pogam, Pierre-Yves and Florian Meunier, 'Le tombeau d'Héloïse et d'Abélard: la mise en scène d'une histoire ... d'amour?', in *Un Musée révolutionnaire: Le musée des monuments français d'Alexandre Lenoir*, ed. Geneviève Bresc-Bautier and Béatrice de Chancel-Bardelot (Paris, 2016), pp. 138–53.

Leask, Nigel, 'Sir Walter Scott's *The Antiquary* and the *Ossian* controversy', *The Yearbook of English Studies, Walter Scott: New Interpretations*, 47 (2017), pp. 189–202.

Leland, John, *The Itinerary of John Leland the Antiquary, in Nine Volumes*, ed. Thomas Hearne (1710–12; 2nd edn, Oxford, 1742–5).

Lenoir, Alexandre, *Musée impérial des monumens français, histoire des arts en France, et description chronologique* (Paris, 1810).

Levine, Philippa, *The Amateur and the Professional: Antiquaries, Historians and Archaeologists in Victorian England 1838–1886* (Cambridge, 1986).

Lew, Laurie Kane, 'William Hazlitt and the poetics of memory', *Studies in Romanticism*, 36(3) (1997), pp. 349–89.

Lewis, Elizabeth, 'Les Rapports avec les antiquaires anglais', in *Arcisse de Caumont, érudit normand et fondateur de l'archéologie français* (Caen, 2004).

Lewis, Michael J., *The Politics of the German Gothic Revival* (Cambridge, Mass., 1993).

Lingard, John, *The Antiquities of the Anglo-Saxon Church* (1806; 2nd edn, Newcastle, 1810)

—— *The History of England from the first invasion of the Romans to the revolution in 1688* (8 vols, London, 1819–30).

—— *A Vindication of Certain Passages in the fourth and fifth volumes of the History of England* (2nd edn, London, 1826).

Lockhart, J. G., *The Life of Sir Walter Scott* (1837–8; New Popular Edition, London, 1896).

Lolla, Maria Grazia, 'Monuments and texts: Antiquarianism and the beauty of antiquity', *Art History*, 25(4) (2002), pp. 431–49.

London and the Emergence of a European Art Market 1780–1820, ed. Susanna Avery-Quash and Christian Huemer (Los Angeles, 2019).

Lovejoy, Arthur O., *Essays in the History of Ideas* (Baltimore, 1948).

Lowe, Rosalind, *Sir Samuel Meyrick and Goodrich Court* (Little Logaston, Herefordshire, 2003).

Lutz, Alfred, 'The politics of reception: The case of Goldsmith's "The Deserted Village"', *Studies in Philology*, 95(2) (1998), pp. 174–96.

Macaulay, Thomas Babington, *Critical and Historical Essays Contributed to the Edinburgh Review by Lord Macaulay* (2 vols, London, 1869).

—— *The Letters of Thomas Babington Macaulay*, ed. Thomas Pinney, vol. 4 (Cambridge, 1977).

—— *Lord Macaulay's History of England, Introduced and Selected by John Burrow* (New York, 2009).

Maclean, H. N., 'Mr Pickwick and the Seven Deadly Sins', *Nineteenth-Century Fiction*, 8(3) (1953), pp. 198–212.

Macmillan, Margaret, *Women of the Raj* (1988; rev. edn, London, 2018).

Mancel, Georges, *Notice sur la bibliothèque de Caen* (Caen, 1840).

Mandler, Peter, '"Against 'Englishness": English culture and the limits to rural nostalgia, 1850–1940', *Transactions of the Royal Historical Society*, sixth series, 7 (1997), pp. 155–75.

Marshall, Thomas Hay, *The History of Perth from the Earliest Period to the Present Time: with a supplement, containing the 'Inventory of the Gabions' and the 'Muses Threnodie' by Henry Adamson* (Perth, 1849).

Mccalman, Iain, 'Controlling the riots: Dickens, *Barnaby Rudge* and Romantic revolution', *History*, 84(275) (1999), pp. 458–76.

McClintock, H. F., *Old Highland Dress and Tartans* (Dundalk, 1943).

Meyrick, Samuel and Charles Hamilton Smith, *The Costume of the Original Inhabitants of the British Islands, and Adjacent Coasts of the Baltic . . . from the Earliest Periods to the Sixth Century* (1815).

Middleton, Robert Dudley, *Magdalen Studies* (London, 1936).

Millin, Aubin-Louis, *Antiquités nationales ou receuil de monumens* (Paris, 1790–99).

Milner, John, *A Dissertation on the Modern Style of Altering Antient Cathedrals, as Exemplified in the Cathedral of Salisbury* (London, 1798).

———— *The History, Civil and Ecclesiastical, and Survey of the Antiquities of Winchester* (2 vols, Winchester, 1798, 1801).

———— *Letters to a Prebendary* (London, 1800).

———— *A Treatise on the Ecclesiastical Architecture of England During the Middle Ages* (London, 1811).

———— *Strictures on the Poet Laureate's 'Book of the Church' by John Merlin* (London, 1824).

Mitchell, Rosemary, *Picturing the Past: English History in Text and Image 1830–1870* (Oxford, 2000).

Momigliano, Arnaldo, with a Foreword by Riccardo Di Donato, *The Classical Foundations of Modern Historiography* (Oxford, 1990).

Monthly Magazine or British Register, 1818.

Moore, Andrew W., 'John Sell Cotman', *Oxford Dictionary of National Biography*.

Mozley, Thomas, 'New churches', *British Critic and Quarterly Theological Review*, 1840, pp. 471–521.

———— *Reminiscences Chiefly of Oriel College and the Oxford Movement* (2 vols, London, 1882).

Myles, Janet, *L. N. Cottingham 1787–1847: Architect of the Gothic Revival* (London, 1996).

Myrone, Martin and Lucy Peltz (eds), *Producing the Past: Aspects of Antiquarian Culture and Practice 1700–1850* (Aldershot, 1999).

Neale, John Mason, *A Few Words to Churchwardens on Churches and Church Ornaments Suited to Country Parishes* (4th edn, Cambridge, 1841).

———— *A Few Words to Churchwardens on Churches and Church Ornaments Suited to Town and Manufacturing Parishes* (4th edn, Cambridge, 1842).

Newman, John Henry, 'The Second Spring', in *Sermons Preached on Various Occasions* (Birmingham Oratory Millennium Edition of the Works of John Henry Newman, Hereford and Notre Dame, Ind., 2009).

Nichols, John, *Literary Anecdotes of the Eighteenth Century* (9 vols, London, 1812–15).

Nodier, Charles and Isidore Taylor, *Voyages pittoresques et romantiques dans l'ancienne France* (24 vols, Paris, 1820–78).

Noon, Patrick, *Richard Parkes Bonington: The Complete Paintings* (London and New Haven, 2008).

Nurse, Bernard with a contribution by J. Mordaunt Crook, 'John Carter, FSA (1748–1817): "The Ingenious, and Very Accurate Draughtsman"', *The Antiquaries Journal*, 91 (2011), pp. 211–52.

Oliver, W., *Prophets and Millenialists* (Oxford, 1978).

Oxford Dictionary of National Biography Online.

Palgrave, Francis, 'Normandy-Architecture of the Middle Ages', *Quarterly Review*, 25(49), pp. 112–47.

Parliamentary History of England from the Earliest Period to the Year 1803, vol. 35, 1800–1801 (London, 1819).

Parry, Graham, *The Trophies of Time* (Oxford, 1995).

Parry, J. D., *An Historical and Descriptive Account of the Coasts of Sussex, Brighton, Eastbourn,[sic] Hastings, St. Leonard's, Rye . . . Chichester . . . and Tonbridge Wells, Forming Also a Guide to All the Watering Places, etc.* (Brighton, 1833).

Patten, Bridget, *Catholicism and the Gothic Revival: John Milner and St Peter's Chapel Winchester* (Winchester, 2001)

Petrie, Sir Charles, *The Jacobite Movement: The Last Phase 1716–1807* (London, 1956).

Pevsner, Nikolaus, 'Richard Payne Knight', *The Art Bulletin*, 31(4) (1949), pp. 293–320.

—— *Cumberland and Westmorland* (1967; The Buildings of England Series, Harmondsworth, 1977).

—— *Bedfordshire, Huntingdon and Peterborough* (The Buildings of England Series, Harmondsworth, 1968).

—— *Some Architectural Writers of the Nineteenth Century* (Oxford, 1972).

—— and David Neave, *Yorkshire: York and the East Riding* (The Buildings of England Series, London, 1995).

Phillips, Peter (ed.), *Lingard Remembered: Essays to Mark the Sesquicentenary of John Lingard's Death* (London, 2004).

Piggott, Stuart, *Ruins in a Landscape: Antiquarian Thought in the Sixteenth and Seventeenth Centuries* (Edinburgh, 1976).

Planché, James Robinson, 'History of Theatrical Costume', in *The Book of Table-Talk*, ed. Charles Knight (London, 1836), pp. 143–75.

—— *Regal Records: or a Chronicle of the Coronations of the Queens Regnant of England* (London, 1838).

—— *The Recollections and Reflections of J. R. Planché (Somerset Herald)* (2 vols, London, 1872).

Pooley, Julian, 'The papers of the Nichols family and business: New discoveries and the work of the Nichols Archive Project', *Transactions of the Bibliographical Society*, seventh series, 2(1) (2001), pp. 10–52.

—— '"And now a fig for Mr Nichols!" Samuel Johnson, John Nichols and their circle', *The New Rambler: Journal of the Johnson Society of London*, VII (2003), pp. 30–45.

—— 'Owen Manning, William Bray and the writing of Surrey's county history, 1760–1832', *Surrey Archaeological Collections*, 92 (2005), pp. 91–123.

Pope, Alexander, *The Poems of Alexander Pope*, ed. John Butt (London, 1965).

Port, Michael, *The Houses of Parliament* (London, 1976).

Poulot, Dominique, *Une Histoire des musées de France XVIII–XX siècle* (Paris, 2008).

Prebble, John, *The King's Jaunt: George IV in Scotland, August 1822* (London, 1988).

Price, Uvedale, *An Essay on the Picturesque* (London, 1794–8).

Producing the Past: Aspects of Antiquarian Culture and Practice 1700–1850, ed. Martin Myrone and Lucy Peltz (Aldershot, 1999).

Pugin, A. W. N., *The Collected Letters of A. W. N. Pugin*, ed. Margaret Belcher (5 vols, Oxford, 2000–2015).

—— and A. C. Pugin and Edward J. Willson, *Examples of Gothic Architecture* (3 vols, London, 1831–6).

Raleigh, Walter, *The Historie of the World, in five bookes* (London, 1614).

Randell, Keith, *France: Monarchy, Republic and Empire, 1814–70* (London, 1986).

Réau, Louis, Michel Fleury and Guy-Michel Leproux, *Histoire du vandalisme, les monuments detruits de l'art français* (Paris, 1994).

Reeve, Matthew M. and Peter N. Lindfield, '"A Child of Strawberry": Thomas Barrett and Lee Priory, Kent', *The Burlington Magazine*, CLVII (December 2015), pp. 836–42.

Richard, Charles, 'Notice sur E.-H. Langlois', in E.-H. Langlois, Charles Richard and A. Deville, *Stalles de la Cathédrale de Rouen* (Rouen, 1838), pp. 1–89.

Rickman, Thomas, 'Four letters on the ecclesiastical architecture of France', *Archaeologia*, 25 (1834), pp. 159–87.

––––– *An Attempt to Discriminate the Styles of Architecture in England, from the Conquest to the Reformation* (4th edn, London, 1835).

Ritson, Joseph, *Robin Hood* (2 vols, London, 1795).

––––– *The Letters of Joseph Ritson* (2 vols, London, 1833).

Rosenfeld, Sybil, 'The Grieves Shakespearian Scene Designs', *Shakespeare Survey*, 20 (1967).

––––– *Georgian Scene Painters and Scene Painting* (Cambridge, 1981).

Rowan, Alistair, 'Taymouth Castle, Perthshire, II', *Country Life*, 15 October 1964, pp. 978–81.

Ruskin, John, *The Seven Lamps of Architecture* (London, 1849).

––––– *The Complete Works of John Ruskin*, ed. E. T. Cook and Alexander Wedderburn (39 vols, London, 1903–12).

Russell, Francis, *Portraits of Sir Walter Scott: A Study of Romantic Portraiture* (London, 1987).

Savy, Nicole, 'Victor Hugo et le Musée des monuments français: les effets d'une enfance au musée', *Revue d'histoire littéraire de la France*, 95(1) (1995), pp. 13–26.

Scheil, Katherine West, *Imagining Shakespeare's Wife: The Afterlife of Anne Hathaway* (Cambridge, 2018).

Schmid, Vanessa I. and Julia I. Armstrong-Totten, *The Orléans Collection* (New Orleans, 2018).

Schoenbaum, Samuel, *Shakespeare's Lives* (Oxford, 1970).

Scott, John, *Paris Revisited, in 1815, by way of Brussels* (1815; 2nd edn, London, 1816).

Scott, Sir George Gilbert, *Personal and Professional Recollections*, ed. Gavin Stamp (1879; Stamford 1995).

Scott, Walter, *Waverley; or, 'Tis Sixty Years Since*, ed. Claire Lamont (1814; Oxford World's Classics, Oxford, 1998).

––––– *Paul's Letters to his Kinsfolk* (2nd edn, Edinburgh, 1816).

––––– *The Antiquary*, ed. David Hewitt with a Preface by David Daiches (1816; The Edinburgh Edition of the Waverley Novels, Edinburgh and Columbia, 1995).

––––– *The Antiquary*, ed. and with an Introduction by W. M. Parker (1816; Everyman's Library, 1954).

––––– *Description of the Regalia of Scotland* (Edinburgh, 1819).

––––– *Ivanhoe*, ed. Graham Tulloch (1819; The Edinburgh Edition of the Waverley Novels, Edinburgh, 1998).

—— *Ivanhoe*, ed. David Hewitt and Claire Lamont (1819; London, 2000).

—— 'Life of John Philip Kemble', *Quarterly Review*, 34 (1826), p. 226.

—— *Provincial Antiquities and Picturesque Scenery of Scotland with descriptive illustrations* (London and Edinburgh, 1826).

—— 'An Essay on the Drama, first published in the supplement to the Encyclopedia Britannica', in *Miscellaneous Prose Works* (Edinburgh, 1834).

—— *Abbotsford Edition of the Waverley Novels* (6 vols, Edinburgh and London, 1842).

—— *The Poetical Works of Sir Walter Scott* (London, 1852).

—— *Complete Poetical and Dramatic Works* (London, 1887).

—— *The Letters of Sir Walter Scott*, ed. Herbert Grierson (12 vols, London, 1932–7).

—— *The Journal of Sir Walter Scott*, ed. W. E. K. Anderson (Edinburgh, 1998).

—— *Reliquiae Trotcosienses or the Gabions of the Late Jonathan Oldbuck Esq of Monkbarns*, ed. Gerard Carruthers and Alison Lumsden (Edinburgh, 2004).

Semmel, Stuart, 'Reading the tangible past: British tourism, collecting, and memory after Waterloo', *Representations*, 69 (2000), pp. 9–37.

Shaw, Henry, *Specimens of Ancient Furniture drawn from existing authorities* (London, 1836).

Shenton, Caroline, *The Day Parliament Burned Down* (Oxford, 2012).

Shepherd, Mary B., '"Our Fine Gothic Magnificence": The nineteenth-century chapel at Costessey Hall, Norfolk and its medieval glazing', *Journal of the Society of Architectural Historians*, 54(2) (1995), pp. 186–207.

Sinclair, Catherine, *Scotland and the Scotch, or the Western Circuit* (Edinburgh, 1841).

Skene, George, 'The heirs of the Stuarts', *Quarterly Review*, 81 (1847), pp. 57–85.

Smiles, Sam, *The Image of Antiquity* (London and New Haven, 1994).

Smith, John F. H., 'William Stukeley in Stamford: His houses, gardens and a project for a Palladian triumphal arch over Barn Hill', *The Antiquaries Journal*, 93 (2013), pp. 353–400.

Smith, Sydney, 'Dr Meyrick on Ancient Armour', *Edinburgh Review*, 39(78) (1824), pp. 346–63.

Southey, Robert, *The Book of the Church* (2 vols, London, 1824).

—— 'Britton's Cathedral Antiquities', *Quarterly Review*, 34 (1826), pp. 305–49.

Stammers, Tom, 'Down with weathercocks', *London Review of Books*, 39(23) (2017), pp. 33–4.

Stanford Encyclopedia of Philosophy online: https://plato.stanford.edu.

Stendhal, *Racine and Shakespeare*, trans. Guy Daniels with a Foreword by André Maurois (1822; New York, 1962).

Stewart, Donald C., and J. Charles Thompson, *Scotland's Forged Tartans: An Analytical Study of the 'Vestiarium Scoticum'*, ed. James Scarlett (Edinburgh, 1980).

Stothard, Charles, 'Some Observations on the Bayeux Tapestry by Mr Charles Stothard, in a Letter addressed to Samuel Lysons Esq. V.P. F.R.S.', *Archaeologia* 19 (1821), pp. 184–91.

Stothard, Mrs Charles, *Letters Written during a Tour through Normandy, Britanny [sic] and other Parts of France in 1818* (London, 1820).

—— *Memoirs, including original journals, letters, papers, and antiquarian tracts, of the late Charles Alfred Stothard* (London, 1823).

Stourton, James and Charles Sebag Montefiore, *The British as Art Collectors from the Tudors to the Present* (London, 2012).

Strutt, Joseph, *Horda-Angel-Cynnan: Or a Compleat View of the Manners and Customs, Arms, Habits etc. of the Inhabitants of England* (3 vols, London, 1775–6).

—— *A Complete View of the Dress and Habits of the People of England* (2 vols, London, 1796, 1799).

—— *Glig-Gamena Angel Deod or the Sports and Pastimes of the People of England* (London, 1801).

—— *A Complete View of the Dress and Habits of the People of England*, ed. James Robinson Planché (rev. edn, 2 vols, London, 1842).

Stuart, John Sobieski, *Vestiarium Scoticum* (Edinburgh, 1842).

—— and Charles Edward Stuart, *Tales of the Century or Sketches from the Romance of History* (Edinburgh, 1847).

Sweet, Rosemary, 'Antiquaries and antiquities in eighteenth-century England', *Eighteenth-Century Studies*, 34 (2001), pp. 181–206.

—— *Antiquaries: The Discovery of the Past in Eighteenth-century Britain* (London and New York, 2004).

—— 'The preservation of Crosby Hall, 1830–50', *Historical Journal*, 60(3) (2017), pp. 687–719.

Taylor, Henrietta, *The Stuart Papers at Windsor, being selections from hitherto unprinted royal archives, with introduction and notes by Alistair and Henrietta Taylor* (London, 1938).

Temple, Nigel, *John Nash and the Village Picturesque* (London, 1979).

Thackeray, William Makepeace, *Vanity Fair* (1848; Penguin Classics, London, 1968).

—— *The History of Pendennis* (1850; Penguin Classics, London, 1986).

'The Topographer for the year 1789', in *A Variety of Original Articles Illustrative of the Local History and Antiquities of England* (London, 1789).

Thomas, Keith, *Religion and the Decline of Magic* (London, 1971).

Thornton, Robert D., 'The influence of the Enlightenment upon eighteenth-century British antiquaries, 1750–1800', *Studies on Voltaire and the Eighteenth Century*, 27 (1963), pp. 1593–618.

Todd, Henry John, *A Vindication of the Most Reverend Thomas Cranmer . . . against some of the allegations which have recently been made by the Reverend Dr Lingard, the Rev. Dr Milner and Charles Butler Esq* (London, 1826).

Todd, William B. and Ann Bowden, *Sir Walter Scott: A Bibliographical History 1796–1832* (New Castle, Del., 1998).

Tracy, Charles, *Continental Church Furniture in England: A Traffic in Piety* (Woodbridge, 2001).

Trevor-Roper, Hugh, *The Romantic Movement and the Study of History* (London, 1969).

—— *The Invention of Scotland: Myth and History* (London and New Haven, 2008).

—— *History and the Enlightenment* (London and New Haven, 2010).

Turner, Dawson, *Account of a Tour in Normandy; undertaken chiefly for the purpose of investigating the Architectural Antiquities of the Duchy with observations on its history, on the country, and on its inhabitants illustrated with numerous engravings* (2 vols, London, 1820).

Turner, Sharon, *The History of the Anglo-Saxons from the Earliest Period to the Norman Conquest* (1799–1805; 6th edn, 3 vols, London, 1842).

Two Huguenot Brothers: Letters of Andrew and James Coltée Ducarel 1732–1773, ed. Gerard de Lisle and Robin Myers (Leicester, 2019).

Tyrrell, Alex, 'The Queen's "Little Trip": The Royal Visit to Scotland in 1842', *The Scottish Historical Review*, 82(213), part 1 (2003), pp. 47–73.

Venturoli, Paolo, *Dal Disegno Alla Fotografia: L'aremeria reale illustrata, 1837–1898* (Turin, 2004).

Vidmar, John, 'John Lingard's History of the English Reformation: History or apologetics?', *The Catholic Historical Review*, 85(3) (1999), pp. 383–419.

Voltaire, artfl-project.uchicago.edu/tout-voltaire.

Wainwright, Clive, 'Specimens of ancient furniture', *The Connoisseur*, October 1973, pp. 105–13.

—— *The Romantic Interior: The British Collector at Home, 1750–1850* (London and New Haven, 1989).

—— 'In Lucifer's Metropolis', *Country Life*, 1 October 1992, pp. 82–4.

Walsh, M. le Vicomte, *Relation du voyage de Henri de France en Écosse et en Angleterre* (Paris, 1844).

Walsham, Alexandra, *The Reformation of the Landscape: Religion, Identity and Memory in Early Modern Britain and Ireland* (Oxford, 2011).

Warton, T. et al., *Essays on Gothic Architecture* (2nd edn, London, 1802).

Watkin, David, *The Rise of Architectural History* (London, 1980).

Webster, Christopher, 'The 1818 Church Building Act: A bicentenary retrospective', *Ecclesiology Today*, 55–6 (2017), pp. 47–74.

Wedgwood, Alexandra, *A. W. N. Pugin and the Pugin Family: Catalogue of Architectural Drawings in the Victoria and Albert Museum* (London, 1985).

Whewell, William, *Architectural notes on German Churches; with remarks on the origin of Gothic Architecture* (Cambridge, 1830).

Whittington, George, *An Historical Survey of the Ecclesiastical Antiquities of France: With a View to Illustrate the Rise and Progress of Gothic Architecture in Europe* (London, 1809).

Willement, Thomas, *Historical Sketch of the Parish of Davington ... and of the Priory There Dedicated to S Mary Magdalene* (London, 1862).

Willemin, N. X., *Monuments français inédits pour servir à l'histoire des arts* (Paris, 1839).

Willis, Robert, *The Architectural History of Winchester Cathedral* (1846; London, 1992).

'A Catalogue of the ... Collection ... of the late Edward James Willson' (Lincoln, 1854).

Wilson, Elizabeth, *Bohemians: The Glamorous Outcasts* (London and New York, 2000).

Wood, Anthony A., *Athenae Oxoniensis* (Oxford, 1692).

Wordsworth, William, *The Poems*, ed. John O. Hayden (2 vols, London, 1981).

—— and Samuel Taylor Coleridge, *Lyrical Ballads*, ed. R. L. and A. R. James Brett (1800; Cambridge, 1965).

Wright, Beth Segal, 'Scott's historical novels and French historical painting 1815–1855', *The Art Bulletin*, 63(2) (1981), pp. 268–87.

Yanni, Carla, 'On nature and nomenclature: William Whewell and the production of architectural knowledge in early Victorian Britain', *Architectural History*, 40 (1997), pp. 204–21.

Yonge, Charlotte M., *Hopes and Fears, or scenes from the life of a Spinster* (2 vols, London, 1860).

—— *John Keble's Parishes: A History of Hursley and Otterbourne* (London, 1898).

Index